NEW AMERICANISTS

A Series Edited by Donald E. Pease

CONTAINMENT

CULTURE

American Narratives, Postmodernism,

and the Atomic Age

Alan Nadel

Duke University Press Durham and London 1995

© 1995 Duke University Press

Printed in the United States of America

on acid-free paper ∞

Designed by Cherie H. Westmoreland

Typeset in Palatino with Frutiger display

type by Tseng Information Systems, Inc.

Library of Congress Cataloging-in-Publication

Data appear on the last printed page of

this book.

TO VIRGIL LOKKE

CONTENTS

CODA DEMOCRACY   273

PREFACE

I n the mid-1950s—I was eight or nine years old—my parents ran into Abe Brothman, an old friend of my father's. In 1950, he had been convicted of impeding a federal grand jury investigation of Soviet espionage, pertaining in part to blueprints he may have sold to Soviet agents, although the government never claimed that the blueprints were secret. Brothman was sentenced to two years in prison, and my parents lost touch with him.

Delighted by the chance meeting, Brothman invited us to visit his home so that he and I could celebrate our joint birthdays together. He had always wanted a son but had only daughters, while my father, who married late and was childless until age fifty-one, had me, born—ironically, Brothman thought—on his birthday. So, in the absence of superhighways, my parents and I took a long drive that August, from Brooklyn to Port Jervis, New York, for what was to me—a child alone with four adults in their forties and fifties—a very boring weekend. Years later, however, my mother told me that it was more than boring, for Brothman's wife, who had not been told about the invitation, was very displeased by our visit, a point she underscored by refusing to feed us. The people in the movement, she felt, should have taken better care of her while Brothman was in prison. "But how could we," my mother said to me, "the FBI was watching everyone!"

At the time of this discussion, although I was already in college, I did not think to ask what "movement" or exactly why the FBI was watching them, even though by then I knew a fair amount about the Red scare that had permeated the country throughout my childhood. I remember watching the "duck and cover" public service spots on the television set that entered my house when I was four. To upbeat music, in rather optimistic tones, "duck and cover" told children how to survive a surprise nuclear attack, one that could come, it warned us, at any second. Although my parents did not discuss politics much—in any case, not in front of me—I at least knew they admired Adlai Stevenson and hated Joseph McCarthy, and I remember with unusual vividness the flurry of excitement and anxiety that the televised Army–McCarthy hearings provoked in my home. Piecing together the past, it now seems probable to me, moreover, that my parents knew Ethel and Julius Rosenberg. If so, I have no idea how well.

Even a passing acquaintance would help explain the mild paranoia—a fear of being examined, pinned down, or judged, an anxiety about my schools' "permanent records"—with which I associate my mother. Whether McCarthyism created or merely focused her surveillance-state mentality, I cannot guess, but certainly knowing people who were executed—*Jews* who were executed—less than a decade after the revelation of Nazi atrocities would have contributed profoundly to the uncomfortable caution with which she regarded so many things. It may have been part of the decision, for example, to store—they never said "hide"—certain books in the cellar, rather than expose the titles on our bookshelves.

Thus the books on my shelves, the advice I received about school, my antagonism toward authority, even the thought I harbored for many of my elementary school years that we should ask the landlady to let us build a bomb shelter in a corner of the tiny back yard were all products of what I now call "containment culture," as was the process I shared with my friends of growing into gender roles that fit like hair suits and were equally becoming.

Repeatedly we absorbed nuggets of advice—from movies, television, song lyrics, and last, but also least, our parents—about how to be "normal" Americans. More even than wealth I envied a normality in all things that I absolutely believed existed, although I could find no observable examples in my home or anyplace else. Although I was officially born in the United States to U.S. citizens, that faith in normality provided me my unofficial citizenship, allowing me to celebrate national holidays that long antedated and in no way echoed my ancestors' association with this nation; it was the glue for a narrative of "America" that bound me to millions of "normal" Americans whose ability to solve problems expeditiously fed the plots of television shows. I doubt I even suspected, until I was an adolescent, that it was the other way around—that TV was the projection booth, not the reflecting pool, of America's faith in normality.

The proliferation of that normality—its stories and accoutrement, its mandates and repressions—may have been, I now think, a pervasive symptom of the trauma caused by witnessing a Great Depression, a Second World War, an ascent to atomic power, and a fantasy-like economic boom in less than one generation. Although the question of how national trauma effects personal narratives is beyond the scope of this book, in some ways it informs virtually every page, just as it does in Salman Rushdie's *Midnight's Children*. The nation of India, like the novel's protagonist, Saleem, was born at exactly midnight, August 15, 1947. Thus in some sense, Saleem's life and India's are one, and teasing out that uncanny, absurd connection between the history of a nation and the histories of the people who comprise it is the task of Rushdie's novel. As one critic put it, "Saleem has been handcuffed to history."

Like India and the character Saleem, I was born on August 15, 1947. (That birth date, after all, brought me to the home of a minor historical figure of the Atomic Age, Abe Brothman, for a celebration that never quite took place.) And *Containment Culture* in some ways is my *Midnight's Children*, that is, my attempt to articulate with anecdotal clarity some of the narratives that handcuffed me to the nation I have spent the last quarter century studying in one way or another. Those narratives, filled with repressed duality, attempted to reconcile the cult of domesticity with the demand for domestic security. Setting up a mythic nuclear family as the universal container of democratic values, the cultural narratives of my childhood made personal behavior part of a global strategy at the same time as they personalized the international struggle with communism. The Soviet Union was a Godless place, television constantly reminded us, while in America "the family that prays together stays together" (although Mommy and Daddy do so in separate beds). And although America was the "leader of the Free World," we had to be ready at any second to duck and cover. Behind containment culture and in front of it lay nuclear power, with all its heft and threat.

Like the narratives it authorized and the nuclear family it valorized, containment culture was thus a product of large, unstable elements—nuclei radiating their detritus. Accumulating to critical mass by the mid-1960s, the narratives of containment eventually split one another asunder, contaminating the slogans of the cold war and the cliches of the modernist academy. The aftermath, its fractured frames of reference, its infinite regression of half-lives, its proliferation of contaminated sites, its bounty of waste, can be called American postmodernism. At least that is the tentative conclusion to which my education as a baby-boomer has brought me.

Of course, I had help—from my mother and father, dead twenty-six and fifteen years respectively; from people with whom I talked through the cold war as its later stages unfolded: my cousins Suzanne and Sheila; my friends from college and graduate school, Dan Turner, Pete Rotolo, Marshall Levine, Sheri Bretan, Sam Weiss, David and Sandy Eisenberg, Fred Isquith, Holly Beth King, Stephanie Pinson; from colleagues who helped me wrestle with "postmodernism," Tim Brennan, Vince Leitch, Len Neufeldt, Dick Thompson, and Virgil Lokke; from professors with whom I team-taught courses based on some of the material in this book, Mickey Abrash, Brian Ladd, and Ray Stokes.

For important editorial advice, thanks to Reynolds Smith, editor at Duke University Press, and to the press's anonymous readers who astutely highlighted places where my argument was unclear, incomplete, or just wrong. Gratitude goes also to the readers and editors at various journals which published and thus helped shape and refine portions of some of the chapters: Chapter 3 draws in large part on an essay that appeared in *Centennial Review;* the portion of chapter 8 on the work of John A. Williams was published in *Obsidian II;* and a significant part of the discussion of Alice Walker's *Meridian,* contained in chapter 9, first appeared in *Modern Fiction Studies,* where it won the Margaret Church *MFS* Memorial Prize.

Tania Modleski, on the Advisory Board of *PMLA,* made invaluable suggestions for the essay "God's Law and the Wide Screen: *The Ten Commandments* as Cold War 'Epic,' " which subsequently won the Modern Language Association's William Riley Parker Prize. It is reprinted here (by permission of the Modern Language Association, which holds the copyright) as a substantial part of chapter 4. Chapter 10 is based on an essay that originally ran in a special issue of *boundary 2,* edited by Donald Pease, who is also the editor of the New Americanists series, in which this book appears. Don's stimulating intellect as a scholar and professional colleague, as well as an editor, have in countless intangible ways deeply nuanced the shape of my thought.

My wife, Amy Perkins, has viewed with me more times than can possibly be wise the videos of *The Ten Commandments, Lady and the Tramp,* and *Pillow Talk* and has also engaged at the highest intellectual level the numerous gaps, gaffs, and flaws in my attempts to describe aspects of containment culture. She has done so with patience, wisdom, and love for which I am far more grateful than this acknowledgment can possibly express.

CONTAINMENT CULTURE

In Cecil B. deMille's *The Ten Commandments,* the black actor Woody Strode appears in the credits as the Ethiopian king. The king's presence as a guest in the Egyptian court attests early in the film to an alliance Moses has made, bringing Ethiopia into the Egyptian realm of influence. Much later in the film, on the night that the Angel of Death stalks the first-born of Egypt, Moses' adoptive mother seeks shelter in the home of his Hebrew family, where Moses and his relatives have gathered for a proto-Passover seder. She also asks shelter for her four black bearers, the first of whom, prominently shown on the big VistaVision screen, is also played by Woody Strode in an uncredited appearance. Strode, in an interview years later, said that deMille gave him the second role because deMille liked him, but he also cautioned Strode not to tell anyone "that I gave you two roles." Clearly, deMille believed that the dual roles would go unnoticed. For deMille, in other words, Strode's visibility as a performer was subordinate to his invisibility as a black.

Another anecdote about *The Ten Commandments* provides a contrast to this one. During the production, when star Charlton Heston's wife became pregnant, deMille decided that if the child was a boy, it could play the role of the infant Moses. When Heston's wife did deliver a boy, deMille sent her a telegram that said, "Congratulations. He's got the part." For deMille, in other words, the gender of the swaddled infant was far more visible than the face of the adult black actor. This hierarchy of visibility could be written off as one of deMille's eccentricities, were it not true that deMille was a master at gauging American taste, and that *The Ten Commandments* was his coup de grace. In this light, these anecdotes suggest some informing narratives through which deMille and significant portions of his American audience read performances in the public, private, social, and political arenas, during the 1950s.

By the 1960s, many readers and writers had begun to interpret the social text in terms of new narratives, narratives they received from fictions like *Catch-22* and, equally, narratives that made possible an audience able to read *Catch-22*. Consider Michael Miller's description of the state of mind of the Berkeley student in 1964:

> To many students, there is something ineffectual and a little slippery about the new liberal-bureaucrat with his tools of mediation and compromise. He reminds them too closely of Peter Sellers playing the U.S. President in *Dr. Strangelove*, who tries unsuccessfully to juggle forces in a society gone mad; or of Major Major Major, the squadron commander in *Catch-22*, who signs his daily allotment of papers but leaps out of his office window whenever anyone shows up with a problem.
>
> Furthermore, the more militant students regard modern liberalism as a whole with something less than pleasure. They feel it is somehow implicated, if only by default, in the heritage of nightmares that compose recent history: Auschwitz, Hiroshima, the Cold War, McCarthy. They consider liberalism far too cumbersome an instrument for altering evils like the nuclear stalemate, U.S. support for tyrannical rule in foreign lands, the exclusion of the Negro from his fair share of society's rewards. (60)

Miller's summary identifies a cultural topography of the atomic age—virtually an aerial photograph of containment culture—as sites in two fictional narratives, *Dr. Strangelove* and *Catch-22*. A. H. Raskin, writing for the *New York Times Magazine*, described his interview with the leaders of the Free Speech Movement as "a somewhat formless encounter, a blend of a graduate seminar in political science and *Catch-22*. . . . It was an engaging group— lucid in exposition, quick in rebuttal, manifesting no unease at differences in interpretation or emphasis within their own circle" (79).

It is not surprising that Miller and Raskin, in describing aspects of discourse in the mid-1960s, elevate fictions such as *Catch-22* and *Dr. Strangelove* to paradigmatic status, for both Miller and Raskin are marking a breakdown in containment culture. Containment was the name of a privileged American narrative during the cold war. Although technically referring to U.S. foreign policy from 1948 until at least the mid-1960s, it also describes American life in numerous venues and under sundry rubrics during that

period: to the extent that corporate production and biological reproduction, military deployment and industrial technology, televised hearings and
filmed teleplays, the cult of domesticity and the fetishizing of domestic security, the arms race and atoms for peace all contributed to the containment
of communism, the disparate acts performed in the name of these practices
joined the legible agenda of American history as aspects of containment
culture.

The story of containment had derived its logic from the rigid major
premise that the world was divided into two monolithic camps, one dedicated to promoting the inextricable combination of capitalism, democracy,
and (Judeo-Christian) religion, and one seeking to destroy that ideological amalgamation by any means. By the mid-1960s, the problems with the
logic of containment—its blindness, its contradictions, and its duplicities—
had started to be manifest in a public discourse displaying many traits
that would later be associated with "postmodernism." Those traits included
not only the assertion that history depended on fictional representation
but also that frames and roles were arbitrary, and that centered meaning
and authority was a myth. The discourse was also characterized by a self-
referential awareness of historicity and artificiality and a cognizance of the
fissure between "history" and "event."

In personal experience, as it is in culture, the fissure between event and
history is broached by narrative. Individuals construct a "self," according
to psychologist Jerome Bruner, out of disparate activity valorized by narratives that turn that activity into what he calls "acts of meaning." A life
devoid of such acts, I think, can be best exemplified by the very advanced
Alzheimer sufferer. Without narratives of the role actions perform in time,
advanced Alzheimer sufferers lack knowledge of the roles they perform in
their own lives. Alzheimer sufferers who cannot retain the actions of their
immediate or derivative environment cannot organize the sequences or perceive the patterns that permit events to become recognizable qua events.
This is the uneventful life taken to its logical limits, "writing degree zero"
or escape from the "myth of presence."

There are a few points that I want to emphasize from this example. The
first is that narratives are not the opposite of facts, but rather their source
and their condition of possibility. The second is that personal narration is required for any form of historical narrative and also, necessarily, disrupts it.
While the more pervasive, cultural narratives are echoed and reiterated—in

the forms of national narratives, religious dogma, class signifiers, courtship rituals—with a contagion that resembles viral epidemics, personal narration oscillates, situationally, between identification with and alienation from a historical order.

In this regard the American cold war is a particularly useful example of the power of large cultural narratives to unify, codify, and contain— perhaps *intimidate* is the best word—the personal narratives of its population. Supported as it was by the technological mandate (often treated as a theological one) ascribed first to nuclear monopoly and subsequently to nuclear supremacy, cold war America asserted the claim to global authority in a narrative that permeated most aspects of American culture. Because of the United States' unprecedented capacity in the decades following World War II to deploy arms and images, to construct alliances and markets, to dominate global entertainment, capitalize global production, and epitomize global power, containment was perhaps one of the most powerfully deployed national narratives in recorded history.

What differentiates peak cold war America (1946–1964) from contemporary America, in this light, was the general acceptance during the cold war of a relatively small set of narratives by a relatively large portion of the population. It was a period, as many prominent studies indicated, when "conformity" became a positive value in and of itself. The virtue of conformity—to some idea of religion, to "middle-class" values, to distinct gender roles and rigid courtship rituals—became a form of public knowledge through the pervasive performances of and allusions to containment narratives. In the contemporary world, however, Lyotard has shown, the power to produce knowledge exceeds the power to comprehend it. Political power thus resides in containing the resulting surplus, and the name that Lyotard gives to the strategies of containment is *metanarratives.* However, because the scientific status of knowledge in the contemporary world makes impossible the representation of a totality, he argues that metanarratives have lost their authority and hence their strategic efficacy. Denuded in this way, metanarratives become particularly legible as discourses that function to separate "substance" from "waste," to select events that will be represented as history, and to effect the repetition of privileged narratives.

One of my goals, therefore, will be to describe the selection process of containment culture. My analysis of this process places great importance on the duality—concealed by containment—that is located in attitudes toward the atomic bomb and the United States' ascent and assent to atomic power. Of particular interest, therefore, is John Hersey's *Hiroshima*. Written less than a year after the dropping of the bomb, the book calls into question not only the ethics and efficacy of the bombing but also the rhetoric of history itself, the relationship of "fact" to verification, and the role of time and space as the creators both of "fact" and of "uncertainty." In the third section of his book, for example, Hersey uses the rhetoric of documentary realism— the indifferent voice of anonymous authority—to recount events retold in the fourth section as part of a letter steeped in the rhetoric of "biased" nationalism. The problem of historical discourse arises when we realize that Hersey's source for the "accurate" reportage in the third section, Mr. Tanimoto, also wrote the "biased" letter in the fourth. Why does Hersey sound more credible than the eyewitness whose account he reports? Why does Hersey include the letter? Whose authority is he discrediting? Tanimoto's? His own? Both?

In the first section of this book, I take a detailed look at the ways in which *Hiroshima*'s attempts at containment—manifest in its genre and rhetoric— appropriate the victims' experience as a special, nonfiction form of fiction. This nonfiction novel makes the bombing of Hiroshima knowable through a narrative that validates Christian humanism by privileging the bourgeois sensibility of what has been called the classical style of Hollywood cinema. In so doing, I think, *Hiroshima* raises formal and epistemological questions about the relationship between writing and experience foregrounded in postmodern aesthetics, as it attempts to construct a narrative of atomic warfare legible within the codes of containment culture.

My discussion of *Hiroshima* is framed by a more general examination of the relation between fiction and history manifest in the rhetoric of George Kennan's "containment" essay, which embeds the cold war in a sexual narrative of courtship and rivalry: the Other and the Same, the virile and the impotent, the satisfied and the frustrated. The unspoken source of potency in this narrative, I argue, is atomic power, which is also the source of its incoherence, an incoherence closeted by containment in the same way that sexual and political roles were. In attempts to keep the narrative straight, containment equated containment of communism with containment of atomic secrets, of sexual license, of gender roles, of nuclear energy, and of artistic expression. Read through the fracture between "history" and "event," and in light of the early figurings of the cold war and the Soviets on the one hand and the conventions of postmodernism on the other hand, *Hiroshima*, in its failure to contain the implications of its topic, anticipates postmodernism, I believe, by metonymically suggesting characteristics that will be broadly manifest in many aspects of American culture a quarter of a century later. What makes *Hiroshima* so interesting, therefore, is that its attempts to comprehend the bombing in a way that will not substantially undermine the ideological assumptions of the book's American audience requires Hersey to adopt fictional rhetoric. In so doing, he makes the book, on the one hand, an early symptom of problems in the strategies of containment and on the other a subtle but uncanny anticipation of postmodern writing.

From the initial period of America's nuclear supremacy—what Paul Boyer calls "the bomb's early light"—I move to discussions of high cold war culture. Focused primarily on the 1950s and early 1960s, I delineate containment narratives as manifest in such works as *The Catcher in the Rye, The Ten Commandments, Lady and the Tramp, Playboy* magazine, *What's New, Pussycat?, What's Up, Tiger Lily?,* and the early James Bond movies. These works repeat or modify the narrative that unifies the sexual, political, and economic aspects of containment, lodging the cold war in a gendered courtship narrative that is constantly trying to make impossible distinctions between Other and Same, partner and rival, for the purpose of acquiring or excluding, proliferating or containing proliferation.

Against the background of these examples, the third section of the book focuses on the emergence of postmodernism in the early 1960s, when the failures of containment become publicly visible as forms of duplicity. The first of its two chapters deals with JFK's affection for James Bond, who combined sexual and political double agency, and JFK's initial affection for the CIA. The Bay of Pigs fiasco not only ended that romance but laid bare its impossible premises, because—like *Catch-22* and *The Man Who Shot Liberty Valance*—the fiasco manifested a national narrative whose singular authority depended on uncontrollable doubling, a gendered narrative whose couplings depended on unstable distinctions, a historical narrative that functioned independently of events, a form of writing that undermined the authority of its referents. The second chapter of the section examines how the Free Speech movement at Berkeley, similarly, laid bare the impossibility of distinguishing free speech from political speech, in the same way that Derrida demonstrated the impossibility of speech act theory's containing the implications of speech. Finally, by considering the fluid remapping of territoriality manifest in the fictional, political, and philosophical works in this section, I think we can see ways in which they mark the narratives that would reread the Vietnam era in a postnational context.

Moving from the centered discourse of containment to a discussion of marginalized discourse, in the fourth section of the book I focus on the work of two African American writers, John A. Williams and Alice Walker, in such a way as to distinguish it from the mainstream of American postmodern fiction. At stake in this section of the book is, among other things, the importance of avoiding the tacit suggestion that American culture during the cold war—as is sometimes suggested by a 1950s revival mentality— was, for all *significant* purposes, white. Equally to be avoided, I think, is the assumption, tacit or active, that black Americans shared in the burdens and assumptions about power of those who controlled the nation's financial, military, and political discourse. Despite the levels of experimentation, therefore, it is hard to classify specific African American texts as "postmodernist," because writing from a marginalized position makes it more difficult, *and less desirable*—both epistemologically and politically—to deny the status of hierarchies.

As a coda, I discuss Joan Didion's *Democracy*, a metafictional novel written in 1984 that examines the relationship between literary form and national narrative by constructing an elegy for both, effected by the failure of containment. The novel challenges the work of all narratives—by indicating that they purchase survival at a political price. "We live entirely," Didion states in *White Album*, "especially if we are writers, by the imposition of a narrative line upon disparate images, by the 'ideas' with which we have learned to freeze the shifting phantasmagoria which is our actual experience" (11). In *Democracy*, the narrator explains that "first looks are widely believed instructive . . . meant to be remembered later, recalled not only by novelists but by survivors of accidents and by witnesses to murders; recalled in fact by anyone at all forced to resort to the narrative method" (31). The authority invested in narrative breaks down the distinctions between fiction and nonfiction, a point emphasized by *Democracy*'s equation between a novel's necessarily hegemonic use of narrative and American use of the story of "democracy" to extend global hegemony. From the first atomic bomb tests to Vietnam, "democracy" has named stories produced under the rubric of containment.

Throughout this book, I trace themes in narratives that have been performed in an array of cultural venues. Against the background of the political and economic history of the twentieth century, I have undertaken to examine some of the ways in which large, multifarious, national policies become part of the cultural agenda of a citizenry. To rephrase that problem, I am suggesting some of the ways tropes performed the ideological task of constructing narratives that allowed a significant portion of the population to link its sense of self—the story of its life—to national history. We know such a process occurred, and I believe that its means was the rampant performance of narratives, in such a variety of sites and forms as to create the illusion that national narratives were knowable and unquestionable realities. In some ways this book could be seen as contributing to a tropology of the American cold war that identifies disparate activities within a common and apparently reciprocal network. If so, then it is important to underscore my belief that a *trope* should not be mistaken for a *cause*. The repetition of tropes, however, facilitates narratives that by virtue of their repetition seem "natural," like clichés, and, like "common sense," refer to what everyone "knows" is true.

There is no way, therefore, to escape the anecdotal quality of this book. Of the thousands of films and novels produced between 1945 and 1965, I discuss only a handful. For every privileged political event or trend examined in detail, I ignore countless more: the Bay of Pigs invasion, but not the Cuban missile crisis; the Hollywood HUAC hearings, but not the Kefauver Senate hearings on organized crime; Alger Hiss briefly, but Sherman Adams not at all; Philadelphia, Mississippi, but not Little Rock, Arkansas. Nothing about the integration of professional baseball, Frances Gary Powers, the 1956 Hungarian Revolution; television shows only in passing reference. November 22, 1963, in this book, is a day just like any other day.

These omissions were not simply caused by space constraints, although given my topic I certainly could never escape those. More significantly, from the perspective that situates this book, even infinite space would not provide enough space. History is a cipher for omission, and the process of representation is never one of proportionality but of narrativity. We all offer narratives in the hope that they will be repeated in ways that make some activity recognizable. One could counter, of course, that a narrative identifying CIA-trained mass murderers in Nicaragua as "freedom fighters" made their performance *un*recognizable. I would reply that that example of misrecognition is the reason for analyzing cultural narratives, however partial and suggestive the resulting analysis must necessarily be.

PART I

The Straight Story and the Dual Nature

1. APPEARANCE, CONTAINMENT,

AND ATOMIC POWER

lthough some date the beginnings of the cold war to Churchill's iron curtain speech,[1] and others to U.S.-Soviet relations that antedate even World War II,[2] the crucial factor, I would argue, that gives the cold war its unique qualities is the atomic bomb. Whether Gar Alperovitz is correct in asserting that the desire to intimidate Moscow rather than to defeat Japan motivated the bombing of Hiroshima and Nagasaki, it is harder to deny that that act gave the cold war unique characteristics. In assuming (both actively and tacitly) the use of atomic weaponry, the United States created an adversarial relationship that, like atomic energy itself, differed in kind as well as in scope from previous power relationships in any part of the globe.

"The atomic age was opened with a prayer," Paul Boyer writes in *By the Bomb's Early Light,* his history of America's cultural ascent to its role as the world's first nuclear power (211). Although specifically referring to the chaplain blessing the crew of the *Enola Gay* as it embarked on the mission that would terminate in the sky over Hiroshima, Boyer is alluding more generally to the narrative that has in Western discourse mandated the fusing of divine power with secular: warfare, particularly as situated in the assumption that God always sides with the winners.

That tautological premise informs much cold war rhetoric and practice, a point I will be developing at length in my discussion of *The Ten Commandments.* The unprecedented image of atomic energy coupled unnatural and universal destruction with the most natural source of universal power. As early as President Truman's first public statement after the bombing of Hiroshima, nuclear attacks were mutated into divine purification: "If [the Japanese leaders] do not now accept our terms, they may expect a rain of ruin from the air, the like of which has never been seen on this earth"

(U.S. Dept. of State, *International*, 8). Atomic power was totalizing and miniscule, secreted and omnipresent, capable of binding or of rendering asunder. It could, in other words, be figured within the same tropic scheme as the Christian Almighty, whose gifts and demands had, even prior to the nation's formal declaration of independence, constructed an important narrative of Euro-American culture. The "American Adam" in this latest covenant thus took possession of the American atom bomb, invoking in the process holy blessings. "Such benedictions," as Boyer notes, "were undoubtedly intended to enfold atomic weapons within America's religious and moral traditions, and, in truth, for some it posed no ethical difficulties: God had given America the secret, and its further development would reflect the divine plan" (211).

Boyer's book, which deals almost exclusively with the impact of the atomic bomb in the first five years after Hiroshima, documents a whole language of awe and terror, apocalypse and utopia, internationalism and xenophobia emerging specifically around atomic weaponry and generally about atomic power. Very shortly after the bomb initially exploded upon American consciousness, however, a national narrative developed to control the fear and responsibility endemic to possessing atomic power. The central motif of that narrative was "containment," in which insecurity was absorbed by internal security, internationalism by global strategy, apocalypse and utopia by a Christian theological mandate, and xenophobia — the fear of the Other — by courtship, the activity in which Otherness is the necessary supplement to seduction, whether that seduction is formal or illicit, voluntary or coerced, hetero- or homosexual, the product of romantic alliance, business transaction, or date rape.

If containment thus names a foreign and domestic policy, it also names the rhetorical strategy that functioned to foreclose dissent, preempt dialogue, and preclude contradiction. The United States, empowered by the binding energy of the universe, was to become the universal container. As the peaceful applications of atomic energy would expand, vie with, and ultimately reinforce its complementary martial uses, huge containment domes would identify atomic energy plants on the American landscape at the same time that sundry military and economic initiatives would identify global strategies of containment. As Donald Pease has noted, American cold war foreign policy is marked by a complex narrative of Other and Same.

Friday
21
June

Long-haired cats must be combed and brushed daily. If not, their fur can become so tangled and matted that the cat must finally be shaved under anesthesia by a vet.

CAGNEY

OWNER: ANGELA KWAN

KENNAN, COURTSHIP, AND MAKING THE RUSSIANS HORNY

Started under President Truman as a form of financial aid to stabilize non-Soviet-bloc countries in the economically shaky period of recovery from the destruction caused by World War II, the ideas behind containment were first publicly introduced in Truman's address to a joint session of Congress, March 12, 1947, that requested financial aid for Greece, aid deemed "imperative if Greece is to survive as a free nation," (3) and for Turkey because the "future of Turkey is clearly no less important to the freedom-loving peoples of the world than the future of Greece" (5). Truman also requested authority to dispense American personnel to supervise the use of the appropriated money and to train "selected Greek and Turkish personnel" (8). The principle behind this program was the explicit belief that "it must be the policy of the United States to support free peoples who are resisting subjugation by armed minorities or outside pressures" (8).

If, in Truman's speech, "democracy" was an important aspect of narrative governing American foreign aid, it was a questionable description of the exemplary cases. Turkey especially, many believed, was hardly a fit example then—any more than it is now—of a "democracy." One of the skeptics, in fact, was George Kennan, director of Secretary of State George Marshall's policy planning staff. Kennan's 1947 essay, "The Sources of Soviet Conduct," published anonymously in *Foreign Affairs,* introduced the word *containment* and articulated the philosophical underpinnings of American foreign policy for nearly half a century to follow. Whether this essay crucially influenced American policy or whether it merely articulated an already extant consensus in the Truman administration,[3] it nevertheless focuses most sharply America's understanding of its cold war role.

It does so by juxtaposing two kinds of narrative. The first assembles background material in order to construct a profile of the Soviet mentality, and the second projects scenarios of American response to that mentality. Kennan's narrative of "democracy" is thus steeped in the conventions of psychological realism. Implicitly equating the body politic with the human body, Kennan undertakes to delineate the "political personality" of that body—a difficult task of "psychological analysis"—so that Soviet conduct could "be understood and effectively countered" (566). This unquestioned need to counter the Soviets motivates Kennan's analysis, one that shows this political analysand to be full of contradictions: flexible and intransigent, impetuous but patient; monomaniacal and monolithic but filled with enough hidden rivalries and disagreements to doom it; committed to ideology above pragmatics but also using ideology as a mere excuse for practical actions; part of the long-term political landscape but also likely to collapse with the first transition of power.

Kennan's subject, in other words, is not only hostile but also so clearly schizoid that Kennan's metaphor—the "political personality of Soviet power" (571)—cannot control its disparate properties. For Kennan the power therefore changes from a "personality" to a "fluid": "Basically the [Soviet] antagonism remains. It is postulated. And from it *flow* many of the phenomena which we find disturbing in the Kremlin's conduct of foreign policy: the secretiveness, the lack of frankness, the duplicity, the wary suspiciousness, and the basic unfriendliness of purpose" (572; emphasis added). These paranoic characteristics run with fluidity from their schizoid source and, "like the postulate from which they flow, are basic to the internal nature of Soviet power" (572). The "internal nature" becomes in Kennan's rhetoric a source of essential fluids and Soviet aggression a form of incontinence: "Its political action is a fluid stream which moves constantly, wherever it is permitted to move, toward a given goal. Its main concern is to make sure it has filled every nook and cranny available to it in the basin of world power. But if it finds unassailable barriers in its path, it accepts these philosophically and accommodates itself to them" (575).

With incontinence the implicit problem, Kennan recommends we not try to change the essential nature of the fluid, but rather to limit its flow with "a long-term, patient but firm and vigilant *containment* of Russian expansive tendencies" (575; emphasis added). Linking this prolonged policy to a projection of Soviet economic impotence (578), Kennan's rhetoric suggests that the fluid's fearful nature is its seminal quality and that containing the flow long enough will make Soviet impotence apparent or cause a mutation. In the eventual ascent of new leaders, Kennan suggests, "strange consequences could flow for the Communist Party" (579).

But the United States must do more than prevent Soviet flow by "entering with reasonable confidence upon a policy of firm containment designed to confront the Russians with unalterable counterforce at every point where they show signs of encroaching upon the interests of a peaceful and stable world" (Kennan, 581); it must also make the source of that flow "appear sterile and quixotic" (581), not by counterforce, but by counterexample. The impression of American potency—decisiveness, power, spiritual vitality—a matter of internal as well as external affairs, will further the interests of containment by making the Soviets look less potent and attractive, and thus by depriving them of partners, of receptors for their seminal flow, with the goal being "to increase enormously the strains under which Soviet policy must operate . . . and in this way to promote tendencies which must eventually find their outlet in either the break-up or gradual mellowing of Soviet power. [For the Kremlin cannot] face frustration indefinitely without eventually adjusting itself in one way or another . . ." (582).

These increased strains, attempts to frustrate by containing the flow, suggest less the tactics of a twentieth-century statesman than those of Aristophanes' Lysistrata. They do not constitute the foundations of a foreign policy so much as they do the motivations for a national narrative, a point implicit in Kennan's closing paragraphs:

> Thus the decision will really fall in large measure in this country itself. The issue of Soviet-American relations is in essence a test of the over-all worth of the United States as a nation among nations. To avoid destruction the United States need only measure up to its own best traditions and prove itself worthy of preservation as a great nation.
>
> Surely, there was never a fairer test of national quality than this. In the light of these circumstances, the thoughtful observer of Russian-American relations will find no cause for complaint in the Kremlin's challenge to American society. He will rather experience a certain gratitude to a Providence which, by providing the American people with its implacable challenge, has made their entire security as a nation dependent on their pulling themselves together and accepting the responsibilities of moral and political leadership that history plainly intended them to bear. (582)

Although this national narrative rather consistently informs cold war thinking—even, arguably, through the 1980s—the specific actions impelled by this narrative were from the outset subject to debate. As John Lewis Gaddis points out, "there has developed a kind of cottage industry among Cold War scholars devoted to elucidating 'what Kennan really meant to say' " (26).[4] Gaddis himself, noting consistent distinctions between policy and implementation, delineates in *Strategies of Containment* the ways successive administrations acted in accordance with their understandings of the policy. These included the expansion of economic support, a series of military treaties, a global rather than a merely European perspective, a network of covert actions, and active military interventions that either supported or suppressed sundry insurgencies.

Although I cannot here summarize Gaddis's superb work, one aspect of his approach is important to note. Rather than presume that the national narrative of containment required or caused specific acts, Gaddis examines the actions of an administration so as to reconstruct that administration's interpretation of the national narrative. In so doing, he demonstrates that under the common name of containment we have generated numerous, often contradictory or mutually exclusive, stories, each grounding its authority in the claim that it is part of the same story. Without that story, none of the narratives would have the authority to generate the actions committed in its name; at the same time the claim to a common narrative renders the narrative itself incoherent.

Although it is neither Gaddis's thesis nor goal, one could argue that the evidence and analysis in *Strategies of Containment* demonstrate that the "strategic," as Michel de Certeau says on the scale of contemporary history in general, is "transformed, as if defeated by its own success," so that "what was represented as a matrix-form of history [becomes] a mobile infinity of tactics" (de Certeau, *Practice,* 41). *Strategies of Containment* thus constitutes the narrative of a narrative, a narrative that neither generates events nor results from their sum; rather it is a narrative completely divorced from its constituent events, a free-floating signifier designating an infinity of possible referents.

CONTAINING THE DUAL NATURE

We can see the varied and conflicting interpretations of the United States' responsibility to contain nuclear power even in the earliest post-Hiroshima discussions of the problem. In an essay for *Collier's,* written almost immediately after the bombing of Hiroshima, Philip Wylie begins by noting the confusions—not only ethical and emotional but also temporal and historical—that the explosion impelled:

> All of us who have given real thought and careful imagination to an "Atomic Age" have made one common blunder: We have assumed that it would be

the hope and horror of future persons; we never dreamed that we, ourselves, would be asked by the newspapers and magazines for which we work to sit down and write, "Here it is. We must now do thus and so." And in that all-too-real circumstance, I feel a sense of shock that mingles with elation over having lived, myself, to see the day. It is a great day. (18)

This opening paragraph, intended to situate Wylie and his readers in the atomic age, is full of dual, even contradictory, suggestions. "Real thought and careful imagination" have yielded a "common blunder": they have misplaced the thinkers and imaginers historically in relation to the object of their thought and imagination. But that historical misplacement has evidently obscured another vagueness—that the atomic age was thought of and continues to be thought of as both hope and horror. The explosion that brings the thinkers into the "now" of the atomic age does nothing to clarify the event of their arrival, an event that remains mediated by contradictory emotions, experienced by an imaginary group of people.

The paragraph attempts, as well, to unify the contradictions by classifying them as responses to a single experience. *All* who had given thought and imagination participated in a *common* blunder, just as the future persons all implicitly share in both the hope and the horror. If that is so, then these imaginary future people differ greatly from Wylie's contemporaries. As its military use—the only use that enables Wylie to assert that the atomic age has arrived—makes absolutely clear, for some persons, the initiation (or detonation) of the atomic age was a meaningful hope, while for others it was, no doubt, significantly horrific. Those who died in the explosion, of course, were not the people Wylie had in mind, as they could be neither future nor present persons, but rather past persons, and thus exempt from the common blunder of assessing the immediate impact of the atomic age.

In this context, Wylie's "sense of shock that mingles with elation over having lived, myself, to see the day" identifies him not only with those universally living in the historical present but also more specifically with the people who were the bomb's deliverers, and not its targets. Certainly news of Hiroshima to a nation at war would have to bring its population some shock at the possibility that the atomic bomb might have been developed by the enemy and dropped on them. And certainly the news should produce some elation that the opposite was true. Situated in the present, this shock and elation must carry elements of gloat and guilt, triumph and mass murder, so Wylie situates them in the future, which the present has now become. Hiroshima is part of the past, and now: "It is [in present tense] a great day." The greatness derives from the axiomatic assertion that "Atomic energy is *only incidentally* a military weapon. As a source of power it will be more important to human beings than all the wars recorded" (18).

Without lingering excessively on Wylie's piece, it is important to note two things. The first is that his attempt to contain rhetorically the contradictory implications of the atomic age typifies much of the response to Hiroshima, whether in popular, specialized, official, or private discourse. These contradictions, more importantly, reveal repeatedly the need for and the inability to stabilize the distinctions between Other and Same. In Wylie's essay, this is most apparent in his call that "science be internationalized" (79) and that "atomic energy *must stay nationalized*" (79). Both of these arguments are meant to benefit the United States in its competition with socialist nations such as Russia and, according to Wylie, possibly Britain, and thereby preserve capitalism, which would not otherwise be able to compete with socialistic nations: "At the same time, it will keep the rest of the capitalistic system the way it has been. We thrive on capitalistic competition. And I believe, myself, that socialism is tyranny" (79). And yet it is exactly the weakness of capitalistic competition, its profit incentive, upon which Wylie develops his argument: "If atomic energy is not nationalized, it will instead become corporate property. Corporations will use it for profit. They will be more interested in making profit than in new experiment, replacement of still usable equipment and so on. They will fall behind the science of socialistic nations" (79). Even in his jingoistic endorsements of capitalism, Wylie must make exceptions for the uses of atomic energy, exceptions based specifically on the common critiques of capitalism. Similarly, he must endorse the internationalization of nuclear science and reconcile it with the national interests of the United States, located again in the rhetoric of the American Adam: "For we, who have gone so far in two centuries, now own infinity and eternity. We have become the people physically most powerful on earth. . . . [Many] of us have been unable to discern in the future a proper heritage for Americans—a thing of sufficient challenge and possibility to give us endless incentive and the dignity that belongs to a *race* which pays its respects alike to Thomas Jefferson and Paul Bunyan" (80; emphasis added). Now "we" refers specifically to the "race" that dropped the bomb and won the war. "For this opportunity," Wylie points out, "the globe is everywhere marked with the white crosses of our young dead" (80). International interests are subsumed under the universal power of the American atom, power earned not by the world that thought and imagined but by the globe of American Christian soldiers. This appeal based on white, Western, theological authority thus reconciles the conflict between the national and international, the eternal and the historically specific, the ethical and the pragmatic, the Other and the Same.

The American government also sought to develop policies for dealing with similar problems. In the six months after bombing Hiroshima, Undersecretary of State Dean Acheson oversaw a committee to investigate the problem of atomic energy. Acknowledging that development of peaceful uses for atomic power, which were looked upon positively, could not be completely separated at any stage from the development of atomic weaponry, which was to be prevented or at least discouraged and inhibited, the committee's consultants call for a system of safeguards:

> The proposal contemplates an international agency with exclusive jurisdiction to conduct all intrinsically dangerous operations in the field. . . . The large field of non-dangerous and relatively non-dangerous activities would be left to national hands. . . . National controls in these fields would be subject to moderate controls by the international agency. . . . The international agency would also maintain inspection facilities to assure that illicit operations were not occurring, primarily in the exploitation of raw materials. It would further be a function of the Atomic Development Authority continually to reexamine *the boundary between dangerous and non-dangerous activities. For it must be recognized that although the field is subject to reasonable division, the dividing line is not sharp and may shift from time to time in either direction.* (U.S. Dept. of State, *International,* 44; emphasis added)

Repeatedly these recommendations attempt to stabilize exactly the distinctions that atomic power destabilizes: the distinction between national interests and international, between dangerous and nondangerous activities, and, most important, between the legitimate and illegitimate authorities for making these distinctions. If international interests are served by diminishing the spread of nuclear weaponry, then those interests become an extension of U.S. national interest in maintaining a nuclear arms monopoly. Implicit in this aspect of the recommendations is the subordination of international to U.S. national interests. Yet the national oversight of "dangerous" activities, such as making weapons, is not recommended. That task falls to a proposed international committee, although, as the consultants note, the task could not be performed under international jurisdiction so long as the United States maintained its nuclear monopoly; the committee further suggests that adoption of the international plan would accelerate the end of the U.S. monopoly:

> Under Secretary Acheson summed up briefly the utility of the report in a radio discussion . . . :
>
> "In plain words, the *Report* sets up a plan under which no nation would make atomic bombs or materials for them. All dangerous activities would be carried on—not merely inspected—by a live, functioning international Authority with a real purpose in the world and capable of attracting competent personnel. This monopoly of the dangerous activities would still leave a large and tremendously productive field of *safe* activities open to individual nations, their industries and universities.
>
> ". . . the extremely favored position with regard to atomic devices which the United States enjoys at present, is *only temporary. It will not last.* We must use that advantage now to promote international security and to carry out our policy of building a lasting peace through international agreement. (U.S. Dept. of State, *International*, 47)

In order to facilitate this end to the U.S. monopoly, the report identified four stages, the last being international control of nuclear explosives, but emphasized that the plan did *not* "call for the United States to cease making bombs." In the implied order of events, the authority to produce nuclear weapons would transfer away from individual nations only after the United States had lost its monopoly. In other words, only after an increase in the type of dangerous activity that the recommendations attempted to diminish could those recommendations take effect. In its initial stages, the U.S. monopoly is the benign version of national control, the version of national control that will lead, unlike its bad Other, to the end of national control. Because national control will increase, according to Acheson, "we must use that advantage now to promote international security and to carry out our policy of building a lasting peace through international agreement." The safeguard against U.S. participation in dangerous activities is the international control toward which the United States is working; the safeguard against other nations' participation in dangerous activities is the United States' continued national control of atomic bomb production.

At the same time, of course, the report admits problems in distinguishing dangerous from nondangerous activities. Prior to fixing the definitions, for example, the report makes redefinition a structural necessity of its plan. Such a structure necessarily makes definition impossible, for the marginal case—the dangerous activity that appears to be safe—is exactly the case that the definitions intend to prevent but also upon which they depend. As long as we admit that we can't tell safe from dangerous, how can we devise safe divisions of authority? By the same token, if we opt for rigid boundaries, instead of allowing flexibility, then how can we be sure that the boundaries won't end up sanctioning exactly the kind of activity they were intended to prevent? The principle thus becomes: If something appears safe, we should treat it as safe until it isn't. When we see that we have allowed a dangerous activity to take place, we may change the law so as to make the formerly safe activity dangerous.

Although a subsequent State Department report would assert that "Nuclear fuel has a dual nature," the real problem, as that report's explanation makes clear, is not the nature's duality but rather its invisibility: "Nuclear fuel has a dual nature. The processes for the production of atomic weapons and for development of atomic energy for peaceful purposes are, through most of their courses, identical and inseparable. Under a control plan which left individual nations free to do as they pleased with the atom, inspectors would have to look not only into the operations of the plant but also into the motives of the operators" (U.S. Dept. of State, *Policy,* v). The truth is that nuclear fuel has no nature at all; it is no more natural than it is naturally dual. For the energy in the atom to become fuel, "unnatural" acts must be performed; nature must be violated and its power spent in some exterior way. The duality comes not from the fuel but from those who tap and spend its energies. There too, however, the duality is not visible, providing dual courses of action that are for the most part, nevertheless, "identical and inseparable." Surveillance is necessary, but it is also inadequate, because global safety requires scrutiny not only of actions but also of motives.

That invisible common denominator, something akin to the "soul" of the Other, thus intrudes, making observable actions the inadequate clues to secret orientations. The only possible solution is the implicitly monotheistic system of universal control, instead of "a control plan which left individual nations free to do as they pleased with the atom." Autonomy, constructed here as the failure to submit to universal rule, allows the possibility of acts with inappropriate, dangerous motives, while universal control contains that possibility. That universal control, however, would also need the assistance of active observation, but the goal under a system of universal control would be to prevent all acts that admitted to ambiguous motives.

THE NUCLEAR GAZE

To put it another way, the atomic age mandated a gaze—a nuclear gaze— that defined the difference between dangerous and nondangerous activity, universal and specific jurisdiction, containment and proliferation. At the same time, this gaze was also the product of the universal jurisdiction that it was supposed to create, because that jurisdiction was the only possible condition under which the nuclear gaze could perform its most important task: to prohibit actions with ambiguous motives.

The role of surveillance in the 1950s, as made legible by Alfred Hitchcock's films of that period, has been elaborately detailed by Robert Corber. Showing the connection between McCarthyism, appeals to internal security, and the pervasive modes of scrutiny, Corber demonstrates that "one of the ways that Cold War liberals tried to contain the increasing heterogeneity of American society was by linking questions of gender and social identity directly to questions of national security" (8).

In his discussion of *Rear Window,* for example, he argues that Jeff (James Stewart), a photojournalist confined to his apartment because of a broken leg, develops a voyeuristic interest in his backyard neighbors that is correlated in the film with the McCarthy witch-hunts. The correlation, according to Corber, "indicates the extent to which progressive liberal intellectuals had succeeded in establishing hegemonic control over the postwar subject" (106).

While Corber is correct in arguing that "rather than representing the voyeuristic economy of the filmic text as necessarily corrupt and corrupting, [the] film tries to show that under the scopic regime of the national security state, voyeurism had become a surveillance practice" (100), one could further point out that the film in every aspect is about deviance. Jeff has had to deviate from his normal, very "masculine" role as travel photographer, shooting in an array of Hemingwayesque locales and situations, because of the broken leg. Forced out of his normal outdoor surroundings, he is confined by the small interior space of his Manhattan apartment. In search of some supplementary adventure, he adopts a deviant activity: peeping on his neighbors. The spread of windows across his backyard avails him of a selection of stories, each apparently clichéd: the flirtatious woman entertaining sundry suitors, the newlywed couple, the lonely woman, the blocked composer, the middle-aged man caring for his invalid wife. These clichéd characters, easily classified by Jeff with generic names (e.g., "Miss Torso," "Miss Lonelyhearts"), vie for Jeff's interest, but that interest is captured only when one of the stories appears to deviate from the cliché: the middle-aged man may have murdered and mutilated his invalid wife.

Most important, this deviant behavior is *un*observed. Jeff must construct its narrative, therefore, based in part on the ways he has seen the suspected murderer, Thorwald (Raymond Burr), deviate from his normal activities and in equal part from the normal acts he has *not* seen Thorwald perform. These deviations, seen and unseen, allow Jeff's reconstruction of a larger, more deviant perversion that remains forever out of sight. Further deviations thus become necessary to uncover the gross deviation. Jeff's girlfriend, Lisa (Grace Kelly), must deviate from her very feminine role as Manhattan socialite to become the dangerous prowler in the suspected murderer's apartment. Jeff balks at her offer to perform this deviant act: it's not appropriate for a woman like her; it's a man's role. Although he can allow her to make aggressive sexual overtures to him or to spend the night with him, there are some acts he feels he cannot allow her to perform. When she persists, he has to follow her actions by putting the telephoto lens of his camera to a deviant use as a telescope. And when Jeff and Lisa's deviations become visible to Thorwald, Jeff becomes the object of Thorwald's deviant gaze.

Although Corber is correct that, like Thorwald, Jeff and Lisa have deviated from social and legal norms, in the end the more dangerous deviant is put away, but the act of uncovering has also effected changes in the life of Jeff and Lisa. She has now convinced him that she is a suitable mate, capable of facing danger with him on his jobs around the world, as signified in the final shot by her wearing dungarees, a sports shirt, and penny loafers instead of her usual high-fashion outfits. This certainly demonstrates, as Corber notes, a concession to nuclear family values, wherein compromise is achieved by the woman's willingness to relinquish her career in order to marry. But it is also an act of cross-dressing, signifying her openness to a deviant gender role, as much or more than her willingness to follow Jeff. Jeff after all is going nowhere because all his deviant activity has replaced one broken leg with two. And Lisa's concluding glimpse at *Harper's Bazaar* only further confounds the gender distinctions by suggesting an aspect of the feminine beneath her masculine attire that has escaped the surveillance of the sleeping Jeff. The film thus concludes by doubly emphasizing the limits of visual representation.

At the same time, however, it universalizes the pervasive possibility of deviance—in gender roles, in en-gendered violence, in sexual promiscuity, in hiding and spying—and hence the need for commensurate and reciprocal surveillance. The multiple symmetries in the film consistently create parallels, reciprocities, and identifications that break down the binary oppositions of good and bad, viewer and spectacle, male and female, aggressor and victim. As Tania Modleski astutely points out, important parallels exist "between Lisa and Thorwald, on the one hand, and Jeff and the wife, on the other" that critics have generally overlooked, "preferring instead to stress a symmetry along sexual lines" (76–77). Modleski also notes Lisa's identification with the various women across the backyard who, as she does, vie for the attention of Jeff's gaze. Yet when Lisa enters that visual field, she does so in the "masculine" role of aggressor, which mirrors the role she has played in her relationship with Jeff and with the camera. "In our very first view of her," Modleski points out, "Lisa is experienced [by Jeff and the viewer] as an overwhelmingly powerful presence," first as a shadow ominously falling across the face of the sleeping Jeff and then in close-up, as "a vision of loveliness, bending down toward him and us" (76). In similar fashion, Jeff's passive and debilitated state beneath Lisa's shadow at the outset is replicated in more frenetic fashion before the ominous shadow of Thorwald in the doorway at the end.

If the semiotics of the scene identify Thorwald with Lisa—each the threatening trespasser—and Jeff with Mrs. Thorwald, Thorwald's other invalid victim, the script disrupts this orientation by emphasizing Thorwald's role as victim of Jeff's illegal conspiracy. "What do you want from me?" Thorwald begs to know, sounding more pathetic than maniacal. Jeff has indeed been tormenting him, and Thorwald, who confesses that he has no money, fears that he is being blackmailed, probably by a sadist. In these brief instances we see that Thorwald, who wants to kill Jeff, in making Jeff his victim is simply working out his own sense of desperate victimization. He is merely doing to Jeff what Jeff has been doing to him: violating his space, threatening his life. These reciprocal acts, moreover, were both motivated by a sense of entrapment, just as the reciprocal acts performed by Thorwald and Lisa were each motivated by a sense of desperation in a sexual relationship. The parallels, however skewed or disruptive, are further complicated by an important bifurcation that differentiates rather than connects the two couples: the attempted separation of the verbal plane from the visual. The complex of apartment windows, regardless of their assistance from overheard speech or diegetic music, form a visual tableau—almost a *tableau vivant*—for the idle spectator, just as the verbal commentary of the spectators provides a narrative matrix for the spectacle. The movie exemplifies the way cultural narratives work to redeem visual information through formulaic structures. In this context, the disappearance of Mrs. Thorwald has two effects: On the visual level makes the gendered symmetries impossible, and on the verbal it undermines the spectator's narratives. Without the gendered symmetry Thorwald's identification becomes undecidable. Like atomic power and, as we shall see, like the Soviets, he has a "dual nature." He can be identified with the man, Jeff, on the basis of Jeff's masculine qualities as victimizer or Jeff's feminine qualities as victim, or with the woman, Lisa, on the basis of Lisa's feminine qualities as assistant to her mate or Lisa's masculine qualities as aggressor. The failure of these gendered symmetries, as signified by the absence of Mrs. Thorwald, incapacitates Jeff and Lisa's narrative by depriving it of its performative power. The law, in the form of Jeff's policeman friend, Tom Doyle (Wendell Corey), cannot adequately solve the problem, for legal distinctions, just like gender roles, complicate equally the lives of the observer and the observed. Because his indefinite orientation threatens the tenets of cultural containment, the only solution is the removal of Thorwald, a point underscored by the fact that his removal is marked by restoration of symmetrical gendered couplings throughout the entire community under observation in the film. But our close view of the primary relationship reveals the price of this restoration: Jeff is more injured and dependent than at the outset; Lisa's rivalry with the spectacle outside his rear window has been overcome, not because he now focuses on her but because he closes his eyes to everything, especially the fluidity of her, or anyone's, gender identification.

The film is thus not just about the powers of surveillance to contain gender roles; it is also about the inadequacy of observation to identify deviant behavior or distinguish it from normative. The conflating of public and private spheres, as Corber implies, does not extend the power of the state to normalize engendered behavior, rather it problematizes the tenets upon which normality relies. The dual nature of the observed, always potentially normal and deviant, makes the act of observing similarly dual. Like Jeff, the deviant act of observation itself needs supplementary deviance, a deviant intervention to ascertain the motive for that which is not readily apparent.

But appearances were crucial not only for the plot of this cold war production but also for the narrative that produced the cold war. As Gaddis points out, in discussing the 1950 National Security Council document (N S C-68) that comprehensively defined containment,

> World order, and with it American security, had come to depend as much on *perceptions* of the balance of power as on what that balance actually was. And the perceptions involved were not just those of statesmen customarily charged with making policy; they reflected as well mass opinion, foreign as well as domestic, informed as well as uninformed, rational as well as irrational. Before such an audience even the appearance of a shift in power relationships could have unnerving consequences; judgments based on such traditional criteria as geography, economic capacity, or military potential now had to be balanced against considerations of image, prestige, and credibility. The effect was vastly to increase the number and variety of interests deemed relevant to the national security, and to blur the distinctions between them. (92)

The broadened gaze marked by blurry distinctions, with which Gaddis characterizes containment's effect, also characterizes the domestic security interests — marriage, safe neighbors — in *Rear Window*. But in that film, just as in the discourses surrounding the Soviets or atomic power itself, an invisible duality betrays appearances and confounds the powers of observation, upon which nevertheless rely the cold war's necessary bifurcations.

What is remarkable about these relationships between dangerous and safe, different and same, visibility and epistemology is how much they identify the tenents of what Eve Kosofsky Sedgwick calls the epistemology of the closet. In Sedgwick's construction, the "gay closet" does not describe merely the "identity" that homosexuals (male or female) hide from the (primarily) nonhomosexual population. As she insists, "the gay closet is not a feature only of the lives of gay people" (68). Rather it describes the fulcrum upon which the cultural codes that construct that identity leverage one another. It focuses on the process by which that leveraging creates the (ever-shifting, always conflicted) conditions that engender specific acts, distribute them within a matrix of gendered motives, and thus define sexuality according to a weighted set of social norms.

It disciplines the conditions that circumscribe all activities in which competing narratives inform human interaction. These competing narratives are often complementary—people who work together can become friends and/or sexual partners—and often adversarial, reflecting wholly incompatible personal, social, or political agendas. What is important, however, is that the initial secretiveness of these narratives constructs the closeted conditions that the historic specificity of post-Enlightenment Western discourse (according to Foucault) has made most legible in terms of "homosexuality," just as late twentieth-century American (or Euro-American) culture makes it possible to historicize that legibility.

My point, however, is not in developing the myriad applications of Sedgwick's insights but rather in noting more narrowly the similarity between the narrative of the closet and the narrative of containment. In distributing the potentials for domination and submission, allegiance and disaffection, proliferation and self-containment, loyalty and subversion—all of which require clear, legible boundaries between Other and Same—the narrative of the American cold war takes the same form as the narratives that contain gender roles.

GAZING AT THE RUSSIANS' DUAL NATURE

Much of Kennan's rhetoric, in fact, conflates these narratives. In his *Memoirs 1925–1950*, he describes atomic scientists whom he addressed in 1946 as "politically . . . as innocent as six-year-old maidens" (301), and the narrative that the government report used to assert the dual nature of nuclear fuel is mirrored by one that Kennan used to describe the dual nature of the Soviets:

> I began by emphasizing the duality of the political personality that had confronted us in Moscow. There was one side of this personality with which

we could sympathize and which we could to some extent admire; there was another of which this could not be said. One saw in the positive side "a great devotion to principle: a sort of Spartan-puritan strictness of thought, combined with a real eagerness to know about the West, to learn about us, to share with us thoughts and ideas." This was mixed, to be sure, with oversensitivity, with pride, with a shame for Russia's backwardness; but these were understandable things. (302)

These were the peaceful uses of Soviet power, figured by Kennan as a suitability for courtship. The Soviets were like us in that they combined the best of Mediterranean and New England traditions, "a sort of Spartan-puritan strictness of thought." They were also willing, open, and eager. More problematic were the ways in which Russia was proud, oversensitive, ashamed of its backwardness, but these problems Kennan found "understandable." What appears to make them understandable, however, is that they confirm a narrative that defines the Soviets in a mutually acknowledged subordinate role, "backward" in comparison to the United States. The oversensitivity, pride, and shame all function to confirm the United States as the role model for the Soviet Union.

The other side of the dual nature, however, represents the Soviets not as puritan but as Deceiver, the Satanic evil that true Puritans were ever vigilant to resist:

The other side of the personality was so full of ill will that it was "hard to believe that it was sincere." One had to assume that it was inspired by some ulterior purpose. What was clear was that we had to have a policy which took account of, and was addressed to, both of these personalities: a policy "devised in such a way as not to antagonize the one, while discouraging the other."

The tough side could only be confronted by superior military and political force. (302)

The warning here is that we must not be seduced by the Evil Empire (as Ronald Reagan four decades later would name the Soviets, reaffirming Kennan's narrative by appropriately conflating the lexicons of cold war politics and science fiction film). In an odd twist, however, that makes clear the problematically unstable quality of that dual nature, Kennan couples his distrust with a plan to groom the Soviets. Although the United States should not be seduced, he implies, it should be seductive.

Kennan thus outlines a scenario wherein the United States seduces the Soviet Union through a slow process of courtship that situates the United States in the superior role, having the power to create obstacles or bestow favors, contingent on the cooperativeness of the proud, oversensitive, backward object of its desire: "[Changing the behavior of Soviet leaders could occur only through] a long-term set of circumstances which makes it evident that non-collaborative purposes on their part will not pay—will rebound to Russia's disadvantage, whereas a more kindly policy toward us would win them advantages. If we can keep them maneuvered into a position where it is always hard and unprofitable for them to take action contrary . . . to our policies and where there is always an open door to collaboration . . ." (*Memoirs*, 303). Anticipating aspects of Baca's seduction of the slave girl in *The Ten Commandments*, which I discuss in chapter 4, and the Doris Day/Rock Hudson movie, *Pillow Talk*, which I discuss at length in chapter 5, Kennan recommends that American foreign policy imitate the proverbial boss trying to exact sexual favors from his proverbial secretary by exploiting the advantages that accrue to his physical, financial, and educational superiority, in order to thwart or reward her material desires. The danger in this scenario is the boss's libidinal drive that will test his patience, or the prolonged courtship period that will soften his firmness. To combat these dangers Kennan, recommending Hemingwayesque masculinity, prescribes a strong dose of grace under pressure: "if we can maintain that situation, keeping cool nerves, and maintaining it consistently, not in a provocative way but in a polite way, a calm way, persevering at all times with our own strength and our firmness, but never blustering or threatening, always keeping the door open for them when they finally decide to come in—I personally am quite convinced that they will not be able to withstand . . . that sooner or later the logic of it will penetrate their government . . ." (*Memoirs*, 303). This penetration may take a very long time to consummate, Kennan cautions, because the iron curtain was suspended "from the basic backwardness of Russia; from the differentness of Russia; from its close proximity to the Orient; from its love-hate complex with respect to the West; from its fear that the West will be superior and will put something over on it; and at the same time from its basic faith that they in Russia have something way down there, behind all the . . . poverty and misery, that they could teach us, too; and they don't want to lose it" (*Memoirs*, 303). The difficulty in courting Russia, as Kennan concludes, is that "they don't want to lose it," and the iron curtain is their chastity belt. The curtain signifies and protects their Otherness. That Otherness, marked by different class values, a fear of domination, and a faith in "something way down there," also reveals exotic associations with the Orient that help facilitate a "love-hate" relationship with the Occident. As the Orient, they are the West's Other, potentially a part of the Oriental harem.

The proximity of the Orient also evokes the other side of that dual nature, the side not motivated by an innocence they don't want to lose but by a perversity they cannot contain: the inscrutable Oriental, insincere, "full of ill will." If not contained, Russia, approximating the Orient, may seduce not with its preserved virtue but with its exposed vice. As with nuclear power, the problem of differentiating the evil nature from the good, the dangerous activity from the nondangerous, is complicated by the possibility that they may look equally attractive, that, as in *Rear Window*, surveillance may prove inadequate. The question, after all, is not appearance but motive.

That question redoubles in the strategies for dealing with the dual Other. We want to penetrate the iron curtain—the barrier suspended because they "don't want to lose it"—at the same time that we want to contain Russia because we're afraid they'll give it away, if we figure Russia as the perverse seductress. But Russia can also occupy the role of rival suitor, in which case it is not sexually Other but sexually Same. This construction germinates the "make the Russians horny" version of containment, discussed earlier, that informed Kennan's famous essay. Kennan, however, explicitly connects the two versions, indicating in the earlier speech that our policies might enable us "to contain them . . . for a long time" (*Memoirs*, 304), and pointing out in his *Memoirs* that "it is for obvious reasons that I have underlined here the word 'contain.' The reader will wish to note that this use of it occurred months before I was called to any policy-making position in government . . ." (304). To reconcile the roles of Russia as backward maiden, evil seductress, and rival suitor requires, of course, scrambling a set of gender distinctions, such that the proximity to the Orient raises questions about Russia's orientation. It is exactly Russia's closeted motives that Kennan seeks to explain when he later delves the sources of Soviet conduct. Only after understanding the motive can we narrate the story in which Russia is attractive *and* attracted to us, can we pursue our relationship, can we orient ourselves and them in relation to third parties in the world at large.

KEEPING THE NARRATIVES STRAIGHT

Sedgwick identifies two important contradictions involved in homo/heterosexual definition:

> The first is the contradiction between seeing homo/heterosexual definition on the one hand as an issue of active importance primarily for a small, distinct, relatively fixed homosexual minority (what I refer to as the minoritizing view), and seeing it on the other hand as an issue of continuing, determinative importance in the lives of people across the spectrum of sexualities (what I refer to as a universalizing view). The second is the contradiction between seeing same-sex object choice on the one hand as a matter of liminality or transitivity between genders, and seeing it on the other hand as reflecting an impulse of separatism—though by no means necessarily political separatism—within each gender. (1–2)

Not adjudicating between "the poles of . . . these contradictions," Sedgwick argues instead for "the centrality of this nominally marginal, conceptually intractable set of definitional issues to the important knowledges and understandings of twentieth-century Western culture as a whole" (2).

We have seen the ways in which minoritizing and universalizing views have conflicted over the discourse surrounding the natural power of the atom and the political or scientific interventions that release or contain it. These conflicts produce its dual nature. The dual nature of the Soviets distributes along a spectrum of similarity and difference that hopelessly taints the courtship paradigm under which its "love-hate complex with the West" is constructed. The question is not simply whether the Soviet desire to be like us is sincere or deceptive but, in addition, whether that desire is a natural affinity or a form of perversion. If attraction to or emulation of the West represents a perverted socialism, does that perversion create greater or less affinity with the West? Or is it the differences between the Soviets and the West that comprise the perversion? Is communism a perverted form of Western democracy? of capitalism? Is the world balance of power threatened more by sincere difference or perverted similarity? In the triangulated rivalry for partners in global politics, does success come from changing the orientation of the third party or from affirming it? Is orientation, in any case, the determining factor or merely one—perhaps trivial—element in the array of pleasures, pains, benefits, and drawbacks involved in making any choice to couple?

And how privileged should these gendered metaphors be? Perhaps they are only valuable for sketching a rhetorical pattern that helps us recognize cold war discourse. That narrative structure relies on a number of motifs recurring both in the cold war narratives that attempt to contain them and, I will argue, in the postmodern narratives that make legible the failure of containment:

1. The atom, atomic power, rival nations, rival systems, the national body politic, the international body, the gendered body, the corporal body, the spiritual body are all made visible through a matrix of binary oppositions.
2. These binary oppositions are represented as contained by the object they define, *naturally* contained by that object.
3. This form of containment is called the object's dual nature.
4. Because of the dual nature, observation is often inadequate to definition.
5. The inadequacy of observation mandates heightened vigilance, greater surveillance, more universalized authority.
6. This authority must be external to the powers of scrutiny; in other words, it must be theological.
7. Internal security thus becomes synonymous with external, universal scrutiny.

If the closet is a vehicle of containment, the policy of containment requires straight narratives. But although the closet may be the product of straight narratives, the closet also makes it impossible to keep the narratives straight. At issue is the myth of the dual nature, whose construction can be figured by a vast array of narratives, but never eradicated. Whether the duality names distinctions called masculine/feminine, homosexual/heterosexual, dominant/submissive, natural/perverted, righteous/sinful, good/evil, hard/ soft, sensitive/callous, backward/advanced, sophisticated/naive, to name a few possibilities, the dualities align in no consistent way to support one another or to facilitate a coherent social narrative. One half of the binary is always marked, delimited, and contained by the possibility of its closeted partner. As Sedgwick notes,

Even at the individual level, there are remarkably few of even the most openly gay people who are not deliberately in the closet with someone personally or economically or institutionally important to them. Furthermore, the deadly elasticity of heterosexist presumption means that, like Wendy in *Peter Pan,* people find new walls springing up around them even as they drowse: every encounter with a new classful of students, to say nothing of a new boss, social worker, loan officer, landlord, doctor, erects new closets whose fraught and characteristic laws of optics and physics exact from at least gay people new surveys, new calculations, new draughts and requisitions of secrecy and disclosure. Even an out gay person deals daily with interlocutors about whom she doesn't know whether they know or not; it is equally difficult to guess for any given interlocutor whether, if they did know, the knowledge would seem very important. (68)

Although the examples Sedgwick gives here find applications or analogues in a wide range of epistemological circumstances, I want to highlight specifically how much this description of the gay closet suggests the informing narrative of the American intelligence community, as it becomes the agency of the policy of containment. As my discussion in chapter 6 of the Bay of Pigs invasion will elaborate, the CIA was embedded in courtship narratives of Other and Same, rival and cohort, whose "fraught and characteristic laws of optics and physics exact . . . new calculations, new draughts and requisitions of secrecy and disclosure." The erection always of new divisions, new walls, even while we drowse, turns containment into the epistemological nightmare of that slumber, a nightmare initiated by the uncontainable knowledge of possible nuclear devastation.

This epistemological nightmare informs much of what has been called nuclear criticism. The coinage "nuclear criticism" generally is ascribed to a 1983 symposium on the topic at Cornell University and a subsequent special issue of *Diacritics* devoted entirely to papers from that conference. As the introduction to that issue explains, the field of nuclear criticism targets a variety of goals and areas out of a felt necessity to alter the discourse surrounding nuclear arms, through the application of contemporary critical theories, including deconstructionist, rhetorical, psychoanalytic, Marxist, and semiotic. At stake is an attempt to construct alternative ways of knowing the atom, its power, and the human or social relation to that power. The most recent addition to the genre of nuclear criticism is Peter Schwenger's

Letter Bomb: Nuclear Holocaust and the Exploding Word; Schwenger tries to find a way to "speak" nuclear power, atomic holocaust, by imagining it in terms of the Derridan postcard, the Lacanian unconscious, Girard's understanding of sacrifice and mimetic desire, and several fictions that thematize these approaches. In this regard, Schwenger convincingly demonstrates that knowing the unknowable of nuclear destruction has become an informing narrative in some postmodern fiction. But the essays in his book, like those in the *Diacritics* issue, also demonstrate the alterity of atomic power, never knowable but always recognizable by the myriad closets constructed to contain it.

This point is well elaborated by William Chaloupka in *Knowing Nukes: The Politics and Culture of the Atom,* which details the textual quality of nuclear weaponry as both the framing narrative and specific fictional product of contemporary discourse: "Like few other issues, nuclearism strains to become more than an instance. It aspires to be context and case, to shape public and private life. It seeks a symbolic position of such force that other concerns would arise within the context of nuclear technology, sometimes even when explicit connections are absent. . . . In short nuclearism organizes public life and thought so thoroughly that, in another era of political theory, we would analyze it as an ideology" (1). These ways of thoroughly organizing public life that Chaloupka identifies as nuclearism and Sedgwick as the closet share many formal traits. They both rely on narratives of Other and Same that construct a site of simultaneous threat and negotiation, with the origin of the threat or danger always indeterminate, impossible to pin down as definitive product of either the inside or the outside. The "dangerous" distributes in a necessarily unbalanced economy. As Michael McCanles points out about the concept of nuclear deterrence, there is "a theoretical gap between each side's accusation that the other is destroying deterrence equilibrium, and the tacit recognition on both sides that only by such destabilization can deterrence be maintained" (18).

In the nuclear, as in the sexual, closet, unaligned dualities abound. As Chaloupka points out: "Opponents argue for controls . . . but also use these controls as arguments against nukes. Nuclear managers justify widespread surveillance and disciplinary measures by their observation that the world is so very dangerous, but they then argue that deterrence has stabilized the world under their leadership, and that this action somehow relates to 'freedom.' Repeatedly, the sign of the paradox presents itself as the characteristic sign of an era that strains to ignore those signs and to present a politics of value in response" (16). Chaloupka explicitly connects, moreover, these forms of control and surveillance, stability and instability, with poststructuralist discourse on the one hand and the closeting of sexual orientation on the other:

> Baudrillard's alerts and Derrida's observation on textuality share a poststructuralist position on power. Earlier, Foucault had identified sexuality as an area of activity that was supposedly repressed (perhaps even "unspoken") but was, in fact, pervasively, compulsively spoken. Indeed, that supposedly "natural" realm of activity has been, he claimed, radically constituted in discourse. There are parallels with nukes; we are said to have repressed our anger at the nuke, or our awareness of it. Lifton gave this psychological phenomenon the name "numbing," which is one of the central theses of contemporary nuclear opposition. . . .
>
> The form of a "nuclear criticism" response—that is, a political line that does not rely on "replacement totalities"—might be suggested by Foucault's studies on sexuality and prison reform. Could it be that we have been talking about nukes constantly? (17)

Yes, I would say we have been, but the form of that talk has, especially until the 1960s, required a great deal of supplementary "talk," talk constructed to perform the task of keeping the informing narratives straight.

2. HISTORY, SCIENCE, AND
HIROSHIMA

If, as I have argued, "nuclear criticism" is the poststructural critique of the context that produced poststructuralism—or at least the context that supplied its substantial nucleus—then the matter energized by that critique is the stuff of history. As Stephen Melville has cogently argued, the rupture between "event" and "history" noted by Derrida marked the site of deconstruction's critique of and border with modernism (3).

In this context, I now want to investigate some theoretical issues concerning the relationship between "history" and "event" that problematize writing in the atomic age, and thus delineate in another way that coastline in American culture where the incoming tide of postmodernism continued to redefine modernism's boundaries. One issue is the relation of scientific discourse (upon which the authority for establishing "facts" relies) to historical discourse (which relies on "facts" for its authority). Another is the way in which the problematics of that relationship make a straight epistemology impossible; like geopolitics and political science, like sexual politics and social surveillance, like historical and scientific research, all disciplined activities require their necessary closet. Drawing particularly on the work of Michel de Certeau, I will discuss the ways in which all discourses depend on their closeted Other, the thing they necessarily exclude and yet upon which they rely for their respective authority. In the case of history, that "thing" is the composite of unrecorded activity for which historical records substitute. This substitution claims to capture or represent events, but instead replaces them with language.

Recognition of this substitution, I think, is one of the important and recurring motifs of postmodern literature, art, philosophy, and critique. For many modernists, time as it equated with history was the enemy of art, because it rendered "reality" unstable. Time had effected a dissociation of sensibilities, which defined the modern world as the privileged position from which this disarray could be seen in perspective, and, therefore, as the position from which reassembly becomes a possible, albeit formidable, task. That task, as John McClure points out, manifests in many instances a revulsion for history, substituting apocalyptic models for political specificity. Despite what McClure accurately identifies as the paradigm of romance informing that apocalyptic vision, modernism projected a vision of reality and a charge to artists who accept that vision. In postmodernist writing, on the other hand, history is not the enemy but the accomplice of the artist, who sees writing not as recording or recollecting history but as creating it. Postmodern writers, in other words, realize they have complete control over history and no control whatsoever over events.

Nuclear criticism is therefore important to understanding postmodernism in general because, as the critics stress, nuclear discourse presumes the rupture between history and event, in that nuclear criticism attempts to historicize an event that will put an end to writing, an event that has not taken place and that, in taking place, will end rather than initiate its historicity. As Derrida points out,

> [We] have to recognize gratefully that the nuclear age allows us to think through this aporia of speed (i.e., the need to move both slowly and quickly); it allows us to confront our predicament from the limit constituted by the absolute acceleration in which the uniqueness of an ultimate event, of a final collision or collusion, the temporalities called subjective and objective, phenomonological and intra-worldly, authentic and inauthentic, etc., would end up being merged into one another. But, wishing to address these questions to the participants in a colloquim on "nuclear criticism," I am also wondering at what speed we have to deal with these aporias: with what rhetoric, what strategy of implicit connection, what ruses of potentialization and of ellipsis, what weapons of irony? ("No Apocalypse," 22)

These questions depend on the power of nuclear war to totalize aporias, to turn the gap or rupture into the plenitude of empty space, consuming both history and event, rendering impossible the conditions for historical narratives. In nuclear holocaust—at least in nuclear holocaust as we imagine it—the rupture between history and event realizes its plenitude; the performance of nuclear holocaust consumes its audience in ways symbolically alluded to by such theatrical experiments as the theater of cruelty, theater without walls, the living theater. Devoid of its symbolic or allusive mediations, nuclear holocaust precludes the possibility of a narrative structure that permits its performance to become historical. Much of the rupture between history and event, as suggested by the relation of writing to history, the questions of speaking for the Other, the arbitrariness of the frame and the fragility of the closet (both of which empower the "real"), are all uncannily anticipated by one of the earliest American attempts to represent nuclear destruction, John Hersey's *Hiroshima*, a text that I will examine closely.

A HISTORY OF THE FUTURE

"Tomorrow and tomorrow and tomorrow," moans Macbeth, "Creeps in this petty pace from day to day / To the last syllable of recorded time; / And all our yesterdays have lighted fools / The way to dusty death." Macbeth is succinctly alluding to a set of issues that comprise what we could call the "historical": the unfolding of sequence, the privileging of chronology, the predictable shape of events, the intelligibility of prediction, the attribution of "greatness" to specific names and offices, the presence of events in conflict with the time frame of writing. Writing history requires negotiating these conditions, and Macbeth does so in the manner that, as Hayden White tells us, all histories are constructed, tropically, equating life to a tale "Told by an idiot, full of sound and fury, / Signifying nothing."[1] As de Certeau or Ricoeur might further point out, Macbeth's equating life specifically to a *tale* suggests that the conditions of history necessitate not only trope but narrative.[2] Macbeth thus articulates not only his sense of chaos but also the frustration of trying to make history, in that "making history" is a phrase that turns two ways, meaning both to shape events and to shape the writing of their story.[3] But knowing the significance of events in such a way as to make possible their shaping is to occupy a privileged position that is prior to their occurrence but retrospective to the story in which they figure.

This is possible, of course, only if we posit a position from which writing precedes the events written about. Macbeth had believed that the witches' predictions put him in that position. When he comes to regard that belief as idiotic, the privileged position shrinks for Macbeth from the macroscopic to the microscopic; the metanarrative that informs his ascent as part of a predictable cosmic order crumbles into uninformed narrative fragments lacking significance, or more precisely, signifying *nothing,* signifying, that is, their own incapacity to signify. In the site from which predictions are uttered—the necessary site for the production of history—he can predict only one thing: that making predictions will be impossible. The one prediction thus allows only one historical event—the event of an utterance declaring the impossibility of both acting and writing, the impossibility, in other words, of historicizing one's own historicity.

In this, Shakespeare anticipates nuclear criticism, that is, the figuring of a site past which historicism is impossible. Although Macbeth personalizes the total annihilation that nuclear criticism universalizes, each points to a site past the possibility of signifying, of representing. Nuclear criticism is the extralinguistic with a vengeance. In taking its revenge for the annihilation of all possible conditions of vengeance, nuclear criticism must acknowledge its own ludicrous situation, a desperate absurdity lodged in the need to write the future in such a way that it will falsify the basis for the criticism. The successful nuclear critic wishes, in other words, to be a Macbeth, a person victimized by false prognostication.

Macbeth could also be described as a person victimized by scientific knowledge or seduced by a scientific sensibility, for it is science that speaks from that site of Macbeth's witches. Science shares with witchery the narrative of prediction; it wishes to write the future, not as science fiction but as history; it wishes to give to predictions the status of events. Science, in other words, seeks to discipline the future in the same way that historians seek to discipline the past.

But what is that historical method that science seeks both to adopt and invert? It is a form of storytelling. In several essays and books, de Certeau has argued cogently for the unavoidable connection between science and fiction, as complementary forms of narrative, with history simultaneously relying upon and attempting to disguise its reliance upon both of the narrative models. History, one could say, is thus a mediation that attempts to efface the poles between which it mediates, and necessarily therefore the interdependence of the poles on one another.

Just as scientific method depends on isolating variables to delimit its method, so too the disciplines of science must isolate the array of possible variables. At each level of differentiation, practices acquire discipline by virtue of breakages that produce an Other: the nonscientific, the nonbiological, the extrasensory, the UFO. The practice of measuring requires the establishment of limits. But as de Certeau points out, since the practice determines its limits, the only thing measured is the practice itself. The postulates of a discipline necessarily become the object of its study at the same time as the study asserts exactly the opposite—that it is about something "real," not just about itself. This idea of the real is crucial to justifying a discipline. It constitutes the object of study without which the study would be meaningless, but as de Certeau points out, it is always an object that exists outside of discourse, for which the discourse must substitute itself in order to make the real intelligible.

"Modern medicine and historiography," de Certeau states, "are born almost simultaneously from the rift between a subject that is supposedly literate, and an object that is supposedly written in an unknown language. The latter always remains to be decoded. These two 'heterologies' (discourses on the other) are built upon a division between the body of knowledge that utters a discourse and the mute body that nourishes it" (*Writing*, 3). But that nourishment is also a form of production, wherein the mute body is the raw material that enables the production of discourse about it. At the same time, however, because the body is mute, is outside of discourse, is located in a place not just physically but temporally different from the site that produces the discourse, we can say that that body is unretrievable. And, more important, we can say that our knowledge of it, which necessarily includes our knowledge that it is unretrievable, makes the mute body a product of the discourse.

The issue, then, is one of production. Rather than reexamine the mute body, de Certeau calls our attention to the way that body is produced or reproduced in discourse. In so doing, he makes us see that our mode of using time only as a principle of classification renders all discourse a form of reproduction. History is the gallery of reproductions for which there exist no originals. It produces only reproductions because it necessarily divides itself temporally from the site it (re)produces. This production reflects a "bourgeois" expansionist economy in which the conception of time serves the uses of production: "Recast in the mold of a taxonomic ordering of things, chronology becomes the alibi of time, a way of making use of time without reflecting on it, a way of banishing from the realm of knowledge the principle of death or of passing (or of metaphor). Time continues to be experienced within the productive process; but, now, transformed from within into a rational series of operations and objectified from without into a metric system of chronological units, this experience has only one language: an ethical language which expresses the imperative to produce" (*Heterologies*, 216).

This is the mode of scientific production, a production that separates the subject creating the discourse from the object of study. Only by means of this separation can "objectivity" be institutionalized. In other words, only when the object of study can maintain its discrete status qua object, discontinuous in kind from its student or observer or historian, can practices of scrutiny and analysis develop. Science, after all, demands detachment. At the same time, however, the human observer is never detached temporally, categorically, or conceptually from nature or history; the observer is only detached spacially. To ensure detachment, therefore, time must be treated as a site, a move made possible by the institution of an alternative site, the site of production, that maintains the spacial configuration of the object through an array of institutionalized procedures that have no effect on the object of study. It is vital, after all, that they have no effect, because an effect would imply that the observer and the observed occupy the same site. Objective distance would disappear and therefore so would the object's status qua object.

Thus, de Certeau argues, "in order to come into being, science must resign itself to a loss of both totality and reality" (*Heterologies*, 214). This may at first seem a shocking or extreme statement, but we must remember that science proceeds not from phenomena but from methodology, and that methodology initiates science not with an event but with a hypothesis, so that scientific authority comes from exploring the hypothetical, not the real. Laws of causality, predictable outcomes, concepts of verifiable experiments and reliable results all share with Macbeth's witches the practice of turning the future into a narrative of the present. If science did no more than describe what had happened, it would be called history; its claim on the real resides in what it can project onto the sites it has not investigated, on the extent to which it can correlate its evidence with a hypothetical object.

Science thus makes a statement about a class from observations of a very small portion of that class. Because the claims of science must attend, in order to be valid, to the members of the class not observed, the range of claims must be very narrow. No experiment can survive the charge of allowing unchecked intervening variables, even though—or we could say especially because—intervening variables constitute the imposition of reality on the hypothetical construction of experimental science. Science demands that its object have traits other than those hypothesized, for the hypothesis is only meaningful as a way of negotiating the invidious. Were there an entity or circumstance or physical relationship with one and only one trait, to identify it would be to know all there is to know about it. We would not, for example, conduct an experiment to discover that red is red. If we didn't already know that red is red, we would be unable to locate a suitable object on which to experiment, and once we know red is red, an object becomes easy to find, but an appropriate experiment impossible to construct. On the other hand, once we assert that red comprises numerous physical traits or that the perception of color is socially constructed, experimentation—the testing of hypotheses that negotiate and organize the social or physical traits of red—becomes possible, and the experimental possibilities become organized by discipline—mass spectroscopy, cognitive psychology, social psychology, and so on—so as to isolate the hypotheses. The totality must reside outside of scientific scrutiny, just as the real must be more than the sum of scientific hypotheses.

Without this residue, however, science would be nothing but a Nintendo game. It would merely and exclusively arrange and rearrange a series of signals in response to a set of rules, with each signal equally meaningless except as determined by the rules. Some of these arrangements correlate with details outside the game, but these figurations do not give the game reality; they instead provide its necessary fiction. The fiction, the narrative construction, creates a means to distinguish—and thus valorize—one arrangement of electrical impulses from many others, although all the arrangements in the real world of the machine's chips, circuits, and relays are neutral and equal. Instead of *emanating* from an ethics, the practices delimiting Nintendo *create* one. An iconographic narrative created by ethically neutral electronic configurations creates, in turn, a means for grouping those configurations ethically, as good or bad.

By mediating between the electronic and the iconographic, the narrative gives the electronic an ethical dimension, but the ethics are grounded in fiction and produced by the pure necessity of computer games. And the practice of making the games is a discipline with its experts, conventions, codes, and journals, just like any other. It differs from science, however, in that it claims no residue. Acknowledging its purely fictive authority, it makes no claims for its procedures other than their efficacy inside the framework of Nintendo. Science, however, must make claims that extend beyond the efficacy of its own rules, lest it be reduced to merely a game. It must make claims about the residue that it has necessarily excluded. As de Certeau points out, "whatever [science] has to give up in order to establish itself returns under the figure of the other, from which it continually awaits a guarantee against that lack that is at the origin of all our knowledge. The specter of totalizing and ontological science reappears in the form of a belief in the other" (*Heterologies,* 214). That Other is comprised by what de Certeau has generically called the "practice of everyday life," by which he means practices never extricated from their temporal dimension and spacialized by discourse.

THE INSTITUTION OF THE REAL

Because the general problem produced by scientific methods is that the subject must contain the site of the object without affecting that site, the institutionalized procedures reinforce difference. Thus, the "historical book or article is together a result and a symptom of the group which functions as a laboratory. Akin to a car produced in a factory, the historical study is bound to the complex of a specific and collective fabrication more than it is the effect merely of a personal philosophy or the resurgence of a past 'reality.' It is the *product* of a *place*" (de Certeau, *Writing,* 64).

De Certeau identifies what he calls "the institution of the real" (*Heterologies,* 200), the dogmatizing tendency of the scientific establishment, as "the construction of representations into laws imposed by the states of things. Through this process," he notes, "ethical tasks are replaced by what is supposed to be the expression of reality" (200).

Since that expression is always substitutional and always in language, following White we could call it tropic. We are substituting language for events, but as White notes, the substitution is not one-directional. Rather, a number of distinctions exist that delimit the "event" and the way it can be figured. "Histories," as White points out, "are not only about events but also about the possible sets of relationships those events can be demonstrated to figure. These sets of relationships, however, are not immanent in the events themselves; they exist only in the mind of the historian reflecting on them. Here they are present as modes of the relationships conceptualized in the myth, fable, and folklore, scientific knowledge, religion, and literary art, of the historian's own culture. But more important, they are, I suggest, immanent in the very language which the historian must use to *describe* events prior to a scientific analysis of them or a fictional emplotment of them. For if the historian's aim is to familiarize us with the unfamiliar, he must use figurative, rather than technical, language" (*Tropics*, 94).

Implicit in White's discussion here is the prior status of the event. Events exist elsewhere, outside of language, outside of presence. From this implicit site, they are recovered, translated by a historian for an audience unfamiliar with the event. The unfamiliarity of the audience serves as the "fact" from which White deduces that the "translation" must be tropic. But how did the translator—the historian—become familiar with the material that is unfamiliar to the historian's audience? At some point in this series of translations—tropic substitutions—there must reside the firsthand, the thing itself, the thing, in other words, as seen from a perspective for which technical language suffices. This is, technically, the "event," which is the technicality on which the tropic substitutions rests. In this context, we could say that "history" is the discipline constituted by the technicality we call an event, and it authorizes a discourse that provides a series of tropic substitutions in the name of that technicality.

When the event is nuclear holocaust, however, the technicality precludes tropic substitution, at least retrospectively. The ascent to nuclear power thus empowers an absurd discourse, one that necessarily elides the distinction between history and science fiction, for it necessitates the understanding of an event that cannot exist retrospectively.

De Certeau points out that an event is "what must be presupposed, in order for an organization of documents to be possible. . . . The event does not explain but permits an intelligibility. It is the postulate and the point of departure—but also the blind spot—of comprehension. . . . Far from being the substantial landmark upon which information would be founded, the event is the hypothetical support for an ordering along a chronological axis; that is the condition of classification" (*Writing*, 96). De Certeau is not focusing on the debate over whether events can be said to have occurred, rather he is emphasizing the point that history is only possible after the occurrence has been treated as a technicality. Accepting White's argument that history is constructed tropically, that it is a figuration, we must also remember that the authority for any figuration is the literal for which it is said to substitute. The literal event is thus a necessary technicality for historical discourse.

It is pointless, therefore, to argue that events have never occurred, rather than to examine the factors that allow activity to acquire the technical status of an event. De Certeau, as Tom Conley explains, "emphasizes how events are described, how they are considered meaningful, how they become worthy of record or notice. The eye that recognizes them is necessarily conditioned by the ideologies, assumptions, and dispositions of the observers and scribes from the past, of the chroniclers who have created the modern historian's archives. This background inevitably inflects the ways historians select and interpret events" (xv).[4] This helps focus the question of what historical narratives recover. For White, they have the power to be historical content. They represent the mediation between contemporary discourse that produces the available rhetorical forms and the events that those forms interpret. For de Certeau, they provide the method for obscuring that corporal existence by speaking on its behalf.

At stake is the power of history, which is another way of rephrasing Macbeth's dilemma with which I started. Macbeth feels empowered by history because he believes he knows its story. Based on that belief, he acts, he makes history. His actions, in other words, depend on his belief in a power of history independent of his actions. In acting, he participates in a story that he did not construct and, more important, cannot alter. A sense of unalterable history—fate, prophecy, science—is indeed the mandate for his actions. Were he to believe that actions would alter history, then prophecy itself would be impossible. At the same time that he believes history prophetic, he believes in the agency of his own actions, that is, in his potential to act historically. A historical act for Macbeth, then, is one that (implicitly, unlike most) contributes to the unalterable course of history, which by its nature is indifferent to such contributions.

I am raising this discussion not to develop an interpretation of Shakespeare's play but rather to use Macbeth to illustrate the workings of a dominant historical narrative. As the narrative structure that transcends specific events, it enables him to presume the significance of events he cannot test, and it makes it possible for him to perform—in his case, perform acts of murder—because those acts are already events in a larger narrative, recognizable through its sundry cultural instantiations. The witches are simply the most palpable, current, and cogent instance of what Richard II calls "the sad story of the death of Kings" as they are also the card-carrying agents of the dark sciences within whose scope the story of the future is said to fall. Had these narratives no currency, were their structure unrecognizable, Macbeth would have no more capacity to listen to the witches than his audience would have to eavesdrop. The entire legibility of his story emanates from the narrative that allows Macbeth to constitute the witches' roadside performance as an event, just as the entire legibility of Shakespeare's play, *Macbeth*, depends on the tropic substitutions that allow its acts to be recuperated by the culturally privileged narratives of its respective and successive audiences.[5]

Because the culturally privileged narrative is never the overt social text or the actual performance but the allusion to performance in the echoes of texts, reproduced in fragments—as idioms, figures of speech, folk tales, gossip, fiction, drama, epic, to name a few—it can never claim the authority that it exerts; it always functions as fiction. Macbeth therefore is not just confronted with the fictionality of the witches' prediction but the potential fictionality of his status within their narrative. And yet that status is one that coincides, as the course of the play demonstrates, with the narrative that Macbeth has constructed about his own life. In the Lacanian sense, then, the witches are symptomatic, giving language to the letter that Macbeth has already sent and marking its true destination. But the dilemma of its arrival is the dilemma of the historian, who is always as well the historical subject, even though he or she may not know how that role is defined. Does history exert a force to which humans are subject, or does history name the discourse through which human subjectivity is constituted? Is history the story that organizes—by whatever mode of organization—known events, or is it the process by which events are created so that they can be organized? Does an event have a special status within the realm of human activity, or does it signify the smallest unit of human activity, whether recorded or lost? If the former, then what do we call the rest of human activity? If the latter, then how do we negotiate the relationship of the saved to the lost?

The issue is one of atomizing. What is the smallest knowable unit of any substance, and how does it empower the whole that contains it? Just as in breaking matter into its atomic elements, breaking events into the myriad actions that comprise them creates a surfeit of phenomena and a dearth of comprehension. In the realm of history as in the realm of atomic energy, the power to bind the elements is also the power to subsume them, and the knowledge of that potential is the informing excess of the atomic age. I mean by this that, as Lyotard has cogently argued in *The Postmodern Condition,* the contemporary (Western) world defines and organizes knowledge in "scientific" and in "narrative" forms. Because narrative knowledge therefore can no longer be totalizing, metanarratives are impossible, and, confronted with the "scientific" tests for truth, narrative knowledge faces a legitimation crisis. That crisis, which comprises one of the characteristics of postmodernism, arises out of the nonreciprocal relationship between the two forms of knowledge, such that narrative knowledge always occupies a supplementary position; it is the historical waste, the by-product of the insular and atomized truths of scientific activity, even though that activity is meaningful only when contained by an informing narrative.[6] The narratives thus inform without a legitimating claim to the status of information; they contain the truths by which they are discredited. If the great metanarratives allow us to constitute a whole in the name of some territorial site—heavenly, national, ideological—they do so always in jeopardy of destruction by the binding energy upon which they rely for their integrity.

This line of reasoning suggests that the power of history is inextricably connected to what it contains. Macbeth believed that history contained— meaning valorized—his actions, but the sense in which it did came from a narrative of his own construction, and that narrative in turn had the power to contain—meaning limit—his actions. And in turn history contained more than he imagined, more *for* him and less *of* him. In one sense the prophecy had a residue, an excess; it contained more than it appeared to. In another sense, it contained less than Macbeth thought it would; he and the narrative he constructed became the residue, the discarded excess.

At all points, Macbeth, as our prototypical historian, confronts excess. Either his sense of the power of history was excessive, or his actions were. Either his actions created an excess, or the historical narrative ignored one. To be excessively ambitious is to ignore the excessive quality of history by attempting to contain it inside a narrative structure that makes clear the process by which an event becomes eventual.

The mire of eventualities that comprise nuclear criticism emanate from the oxymoronic oddity of atomic excess: that it is the accelerated production of decay. Nuclear power is harnessed decadence, and part of the problem in controlling nuclear arms proliferation is that nuclear waste is also nuclear fuel. The atomic bomb is fueled by large, unstable atoms of uranium or plutonium, whose decay is so cogent at the molecular level as to accelerate exponentially the decay of like elements. The nuclear flash is the simultaneous release of excess energy that had worked to keep millions of atoms whole, and in many instances the reconfigured wholes contain similar potentials, latent waste/energy.

The power of excess is also an informing principle of the postmodern condition. Excess marks not only the style of Derrida's rhetoric but more importantly its subject matter. Repeatedly he demonstrates the definitive dependency of that which is central—that which passes for essential—on that which occupies the rhetorical position of its marginalized supplement.[7] Similarly, out of his deconstruction of tropes, de Man generates an excess that forms the matter for his allegories of reading. Excess characterizes Lyotard's understanding of contemporary knowledge, populates the Foucauldian library, constitutes the Lacanian unconscious, and stimulates Jameson's recognition in postmodernism that the crisis in historicity inscribes itself as a formal feature, that pastiche replaces parody. In postmodern architecture, that pastiche includes historical references in timeless settings, forms that have no function (which is their function), buttresses that do not buttress, clichés that signify "cliché," illusory foregrounds set in artificial backgrounds, windowless frames, and archways to nowhere. Postmodern architecture recognizes its own excessiveness by privileging the vulgarities of kitsch over the myths promoted in the name of nature, simplicity, or harmony.[8] To make the point excessively simple: Less ain't more no more, no more, no more.

We may get some sense of how the postmodern sensibility constitutes a significant reconfiguring of the romantic conception of a centered subject if we consider briefly the first quatrain of Wordsworth's famous sonnet, "The World Is Too Much with Us": "The world is too much with us; late and soon, / Getting and spending, we lay waste our powers; / Little we see in Nature that is ours; / We have given our hearts away, a sordid boon!" Implicit in these lines is the idea that "nature" is constituted in large wholes, while the quotidian world is composed of small, particular, and insignificant acts. The getting and spending participate in economies of waste antithetical to the production of power. The world of economics—human distributions of value—creates false economies, economies of waste, of sordid exchange, that comprise the general trading away of nature, the site where human powers can be realized.

The phrase "Nature that is ours," of course, conflates the mark or mirror of our selves discovered by examining nature with the nature of the selves that produce that mark. We possess nature and/or produce it; nature produces, mirrors, and/or absorbs us. Nature is everywhere part of a system in which nothing is lost but, as Darwin tells us, the natural is also selective. It is, in other words, just like art, in that it continually shapes its product according to principles. The loss thus becomes redeemed within a narrative of natural progress. In nature, things waste with a purpose, and hence they are not waste. The romantic and modern artists reflect according to their own codes their complex understandings of these complex economies.

But when an uncontrolled nuclear chain reaction occurs—and especially when it precipitates an uncontrolled exchange of worldwide bombardments—the natural ceases to be selective. If we lay waste our powers, everything we see in nature will be ours, marked by the proliferation of waste, wasted by the mark of nature's power. The product and the producer will indeed merge in a reciprocity of power and waste. The human condition, understood through a play of differences, will be subsumed by a universal sameness. This is, at least, one narrative that can be authorized by the ascent to atomic weaponry: in the atomic age, waste, often unarticulated as such, occupies the valorized position that nature did in earlier traditions.[9]

The pastiche of the postmodern, the factitious bounty, for example, of some of Pynchon's catalogues, or the proliferation of incomplete interpretive systems that his work suggests (and equally the proliferation of incomplete analyses that the work generates) can be read as manifestations of a cultural narrative in which the natural is no longer selective. Progress, or for that matter any form of historical narrative, when framed by such a cultural logic blends generically with science fiction.

As Brian McHale points out, the relationship between "postmodern fiction" and "science fiction" is symbiotic: "Just as postmodernism has borrowed ontological motifs from science fiction, so science fiction has in recent years begun to borrow from postmodernism" (69). To the extent that we can delimit and stabilize—or at least stipulate—such generic categories as "postmodern fiction" and "science fiction," McHale is correct and well-supported by other discussions of the issue.[10] Critique of genre stability, of canon formation, of taxonomic arguments, or of essentializing moves, however, helps typify postmodernism in ways that exemplify the legitimation crisis Lyotard describes. The conflict between scientific knowledge and narrative knowledge destabilizes the contextualizing frame upon which genre criticism depends: genres borrow and blend; conventional referents don't attend the convention; surfaces swim out of their depths; time lines tangle in knots, trip people in doorways, loop, fray, or snap; causes mingle unchaperoned with effects; mutants proliferate. If an argument at least as old in English as Spenser's "Mutability Cantos" holds that mutability is the world's most pervasive and knowable constant, the postmodern twist on that argument is that constancy itself is merely a mode of representation, one whose privileged position is historical, not essential. When I used the term *science fiction,* therefore, I was not referring to a historically established genre but rather to the condition that allows a genre to establish its historic identity. Generic mutations, hybrids, deformations become interesting not because they represent a falling away and/or progress toward some essentialized ideal of representation/expression, but rather because they help identify the cultural narratives that permit the appearance of generic stability.

Because it is about the *appearance* of generic stability, the term *postmodern* as a generic term is always problematic in that it asserts the stability it is critiquing, or at least it *appears* to assert that stability (or it only *appears* to critique it). Out of this hall of mirrors I am seeking no path. As Brenda Marshall says, in her introduction to *Teaching the Postmodern,* "I'm not here to get it [the definition of *postmodern*] right, once and for all. No, *that* wouldn't be very postmodern" (2). Rather I am first going to agree with Andreas Huyssen that the postmodernism of the 1960s was initially an American product, "a revolt against that version of modernism which had been domesticated in the 1950s, become part of the liberal-conservative consensus of the times, and which had even been turned into a propaganda arsenal weapon in the cultural-political arsenal of Cold War anti-communism" (190), and that the term *postmodern* "accrued its emphatic connotations in the United States" (190). Next, I am going to suggest *some* conventions and motifs—consistent with my argument that postmodernism makes excess visible—that have been identified by what have become a loose group of widely cited texts, without attempting either to find consensus or to carve out a radical niche in the field.[11]

Postmodernism scrutinizes authority in all its manifestations by making visible the implicit assumptions on which any form of authority must necessarily rely, although it cannot necessarily reveal all of the assumptions in any given form of authority. It does so by undermining frames of reference, for example, appeals to "human nature," history, "common sense," objective facts, narrative closure, notions of progress, national, racial, or sexual "types," science. It destabilizes perspectives so as to make visible the specific assumptions of privilege involved in such distinctions as foreground/background, surface/depth, profound/superficial, central/marginal. It considers the ways in which language is involved in the construction, reinforcement, and disguising of these hierarchies; it does so particularly by suggesting the problematics of treating language as referential, fiction as mimetic, reality as unmediated by language. Postmodernism, therefore, often foregrounds the unstable historicity of all production—grammatical, artistic, industrial, scientific—through a self-conscious recognition that representation is as much, or even more, dependent on its genre than on its referent for the "meaning" it is said to communicate.

HIROSHIMA

In light of all this, John Hersey's *Hiroshima* is a very interesting text for several reasons, not the least of which is that it creates a generic innovation, and does so, moreover, in the name of truth. It attempts, in other words, to resolve the legitimation crisis between scientific knowledge and narrative knowledge that has not yet become visible as a crisis, and of which this attempted resolution may be one of the earliest symptoms. In the extended discussion that follows, I will analyze Hersey's text as a response to America's atomic power and also as a subtle anticipation of the principles of postmodernism. The connection between these two strains, of course, is important to my overall argument, in that one of my goals is to suggest that American postmodernism is a cultural product of the conditions caused by containment's failure to reconcile and discipline the disparate narratives upon which it relied for its authority. If Hersey's attempts to deal with the atomic bomb require a new medium—the nonfiction novel—his formal innovations can be read as implying their own failure. They imply, in other words, the *formal* failure of containment.

Originally published as virtually the complete text of the August 31, 1946, issue of *The New Yorker, Hiroshima* was introduced by the following editorial statement:

> *The New Yorker* this week devotes its entire editorial space to an article on the almost complete obliteration of a city by one atomic bomb, and what happened to the people of that city. It does so in the conviction that few of us have yet comprehended the all but incredible destructive powers of this weapon, and that everyone might well take time to consider the terrible implications of its use. (15)

To "comprehend the all but incredible" is *The New Yorker*'s oxymoronic rationale for its own all but incredible editorial decision, and near totalities abound in this explanation: the *"almost complete obliteration"* requires the almost complete issue of *The New Yorker,* so that *"everyone* might well take time to consider." These totalities are tempered by a striking sense of the fragmentary: "the people of that [almost obliterated] city," the "few of us [who] have yet comprehended." To bridge this gap between the people and their obliterated city, between the magnitude of the event and the small number who comprehend it, *The New Yorker* devotes an editorial space, a space, in other words, for writing.

Although Hersey's text does effectively raise consciousness about some of the implications of the atomic bomb and creates a significant emotional impact on many readers,[12] it can never realize the full goal to which *The New Yorker* had devoted its space; it can never create a totalizing narrative, one that will tell us what happened to the people of Hiroshima, or enable us to comprehend the "all but incredible destructive powers." In examining Hersey's attempt to fill that gap, we may get some insight into the relationship between writing and reality, between history and event foregrounded in postmodern arts and discourses that start to proliferate roughly two to three decades later. In pursuing my analysis, however, I will be interested not merely in noting the postmodern implications of *Hiroshima,* but more importantly, in suggesting that this book's failure helps us view those implications as produced by a narrative occasioned by the cold war and the idea of nuclear containment/proliferation that it entailed.

Hiroshima, as Hersey constructs it, is about the beginning of the atomic age, an age that alters our understanding of time and space, cause and effect, and consequently our methods for measuring and for recording. The first chapter concludes: "There, in the tin factory, in the first moment of the atomic age, a human being was crushed by books" (21). Elevating to a symbol the bookcase that tumbles onto Miss Sasaki, Hersey implies a transformation in the status of knowledge from intellectual weight to physical heft, just as theoretical physics had been transformed into a megaton of concrete destruction. An initiating mark of "the atomic age," as Hersey calls it, is that books serve a new function, one that suggests a reversal in the evolutionary model by which intellectual prowess replaces brute force.

The atomic age, as presented in Hersey's version of its nascence, alters the meaning of allegiance and loyalty (both its principles and manifestations), and it alters the organization of power in the physical, emotional, and psychological sense—particularly as power is grounded in ethnocentric and logocentric assumptions. As such, the age represents a profound decentering of authority, not only in the political, scientific, or social arenas, but also in the realm of writing—the authorizing voice of any text—and in the voice of history itself.

Almost from its opening sentence, *Hiroshima* seems to suggest that the new age demands a new way of writing. The title of the first section—"A Noiseless Flash"—immediately calls into question the cause-and-effect relationship, as old as thunder and lightning, between sound and light. The first sentence also calls into question the relationship between historian and subject: "At exactly fifteen minutes past eight in the morning, on August 6, 1945, Japanese time, at the moment when the atomic bomb flashed above Hiroshima, Miss Toshiko Sasaki, a clerk in the personnel department of the East Asia Tin Works, had just sat down to her place in the plant office and was turning her head to speak to the girl at the next desk" (1). What can the historian know, and by what process does the "knowledge" justify ascribing to some everyday practices the status of historical event? In this one sentence, Hersey invokes three narrative frames. The first, suggested by the title of the essay/book, is the American bombing of Hiroshima, a major event in American history, organized and measured according to American time lines. Equally the sentence places the bombing in the very different time frame of Japanese history, embedded as it must be in its sequence of privileged events that are selected by, and reciprocally constitute, Japanese national and cultural narratives. Finally, the sentence evokes the biographical time frame of Miss Sasaki's life. Focusing on Miss Sasaki and five other survivors of the explosion, Hersey takes us in four chapters from the initial moments of detonation to the hours immediately thereafter, then to the following days, and finally to the point of Hersey's writing, a year later.

The book's opening thus resembles a series of photos on the verge of becoming animated, each character locked in a gesture, like the figures on a Grecian urn or those trapped in the lava of Pompei. The resemblance, however, is inverse: the lava freezes Pompei's subjects in their last moments, and the historian, having unearthed the figures, reports his or her find. Since the cataclysmic event in *Hiroshima* animates rather than freezes the figures, Hersey's implicit metaphor is one of coming to life; the book even reminds us at the outset that these people will live: "A hundred thousand people were killed by the atomic bomb and these six were among the survivors. . . . And now each knows that in the act of survival he lived a dozen lives and saw more death than he ever thought he would see. At the time none of them knew anything" (2). Hersey thus attempts to bridge the 16,000:1 ratio between the victims and his principals (or 40,000:1 ratio between these six and the total prebomb population of Hiroshima) by making each person stand for a dozen lives and stand as witness to an infinite amount of death. But the span between six dozen lives and innumerable deaths neither delimits adequately the subject nor makes it adequately representative, a point emphasized by Hersey's immediate need to distance his "historical" perspective from his subjects' limited knowledge ("At the time none of them knew anything"). Because those limitations are circumscribed temporally and spacially, the representative authority of Hersey's text comes not from his witnesses but from his rhetorical position as omniscient narrator.

The narrative voice not only brings the characters to life but also knows all and sees all, giving characters life in a new era which that voice has named and created. In short, Hersey frames his narrative not with its historical, geographic, or temporal dimensions, but with a narrative voice, one that has more authority than it is entitled to, the authority that we cede to fiction writers with the comfort that their works are bracketed by the caveat "fiction," in the same way that we cede a Nintendo game its informing fictions.

Hersey's authorial authority thus becomes an implicit critique—as all excesses do—of the power it asserts, the power to write history. Hersey tells us, for example, not only very precise and minute details and actions but also his subjects' thoughts and emotions. Even if their memories were precise enough to relate those details to Hersey, he still chooses to present them unmediated. Nor does he even explicitly indicate that his knowledge came from interviews and, consequently, is mediated by recollection. The rhetoric of the text thus omits at least five mediating frames. The first is the context for having access to this information, the second that it represents Hersey's interpretive distillation and organization of the represented material. The interviews also reflect mediation by the speakers' prior distillation and organization of the material—surely they must have told their story to many others, before speaking to Hersey, and that distillation has additionally passed through the mediation of the speakers' speech. Their conscious and unconscious language choices contribute to narratives already mediating their memories. Shouldn't we suppose that some of the speakers found some of the events too horrible to remember or simply impossible to describe accurately? And what of the language differences? Even the bilingual Mr. Tanimoto cannot be expected to share Hersey's realm of nuance and connotation.

Finally, what of the material Hersey omitted? Wasn't the editing process a mediation demanded not by fidelity to "truth" but by the necessity of narrative form? That form provides the perspective that his subject matter will not allow. The motion in the first sentence, from time to space, and from the wide space above Hiroshima to the confined space of Miss Sasaki's desk, typifies Hersey's techniques aimed at unifying the narrative of the city's fragmentation and creating continuity that can focus the reader's attention, by privileging specific characters and actions.

If the opening sentence's continuity implies a universal perspective, one that can situate an event of American history within a narrative that embraces both national and personal Japanese experience, it does so by drawing on the narrative formula of classic Hollywood cinema.[13] That style demanded efficiency and continuity based on the foregrounding of specific characters, motivated by specific, privileged desires. The classic style disdains ambiguity, open mystery, loose ends. This explains, for example, the improbable way in which the six "heroes" of Hersey's saga know one another. Father Kleinsorge, a German Catholic priest, is a friend of Mr. Tanimoto, a Methodist minister, and Dr. Fujii. During the night following the explosion, his path frequently crosses that of Mr. Tanimoto, who during that night helps Mrs. Nakamura; she later gets guidance from Father Kleinsorge, and he is also referred to Miss Sasaki, meets her when she is under the care of Dr. Sasaki, and later assists in her conversion to Catholicism.

The neat interweaving of these lives, such that they alternately, albeit loosely, foreground and backdrop one another, thus substitutes the economy of narrative film for the documentary vastness of the destruction Hersey is attempting to represent. Shunning the generalized perspective that tends to diminish suffering on the human scale, Hersey opts to particularize. But exactly that particularization diminishes the scale of event. How can one hundred thousand dead and fifty thousand injured be represented by six interrelated people when interrelationships characterize narratives of causality, while in every dimension Hiroshima's destruction is a narrative of randomness? From the random collisions of beta particles and nuclei that initiate a nuclear chain reaction or the random factors that impelled the decision to drop the bomb or to drop it on Hiroshima, to the factors that determined who survived or died, randomness was the governing principle.

The effect of randomness, in fact, constitutes a motif in *Hiroshima.* Although soldiers tunneled into the hillside to be safe during the anticipated bombing raid and thus to be able to protect the city from the invasion assumed to follow it, the tunnels functioned as concussion chambers that maimed or killed the soldiers in the "safe" place, while Mrs. Nakamura and her children escaped more serious injury because she ignored the air raid warning and let her children sleep rather than move them to a "safe" place. Cotton air raid helmets, air raid drills, civil defense leaders, water tanks in front of houses to fight fires, referred to throughout the first half of the book, are all part of an implied narrative filled with assumptions about causality.[14]

Hersey uses these for ironic effect. Just prior to the explosion, for example, Hersey describes Mrs. Nakamura observing a neighbor systematically breaking down his own home: "The prefectural government, convinced, as everyone in Hiroshima was, that the city would be attacked soon, had begun to press with threats and warnings for the completion of wide fire lanes, which, it was hoped, might act in conjunction with the rivers to localize any fires started by an incendiary raid; and the neighbor was reluctantly sacrificing his home to the city's safety. Just the day before, the prefecture had ordered all able-bodied girls from the secondary schools to spend a few days helping to clear these lanes, and they started work soon after the all-clear sounded" (9). The ironies here abound. Knowing as we do that the whole city is about to be destroyed, the neighbor's "tearing down his home, board by board" (10) becomes a meaningless sacrifice, one that distinguishes him only momentarily from Mrs. Nakamura. His loss will be no more or less than hers or that of thousands upon thousands of others, even though many of them had not intended to make comparable "sacrifices," for the concept of "sacrifice" requires a predictable narrative, one that can construct an exchange relationship with the future: in order to get X later, I give up Y now. Like science, sacrifice needs to colonize the future, as Macbeth's relationship with the witches reminded us. In this case, the authorized narrative of the future comes not from witches but from the prefectural government that anticipated the nature of the attack and the methods to contain its damage. In the name of that narrative, the conclusion of which was to minimize loss of life and property, the prefectural government issued orders and requested sacrifices. By universalizing *loss,* however, the atomic bomb rendered *sacrifice* impossible, and by altering the narrative of warfare, it rendered prefectural authority meaningless. The idea of human volition, which is based on the ability to differentiate meaningful acts from meaningless, explodes in the same blast that obliterates the physical distinction between housing block and thoroughfare upon which the neighbor's "sacrifice" was based.

The concept of safety is also destabilized in this passage. The secondary school girls were sent out, according to the official narrative, when it was safe ("after the all-clear") in order to make the city more safe. By accepting that narrative, however, they gave up much safety without helping to safeguard the city at all. Like the debate over the dual nature of atomic power that would be initiated by the bombing of Hiroshima, this passage anticipates a significant social, political, and psychological problem of containment, discussed at length in the preceding chapter: that there is no reliable way to distinguish dangerous from nondangerous activity.

The book also anticipates the problems of stabilizing symbolic meaning. Evacuating the site of her home, Mrs. Nakamura wonders what to do with the heavy sewing machine on which her meager livelihood depends: "[S]he unthinkingly plunged her symbol of livelihood into the receptacle which for weeks had been her symbol of safety—the cement tank of water in front of her house, of the type every household had been ordered to construct against the possibility of a fire raid" (27). The construction order she had received represented a social order whose symbolic status she had not questioned. That social order, in attempting to meet its responsibilities, relied on an assumed order of events, wherein fire *causes* widespread destruction rather than *follows from* it. From the chain of causality came the order that produced the water tank; faith in that order—in the authority that issued it—converted the concrete tank into the symbol of safety. The concrete is connected to the symbolic by an order, a temporal, causal, and social order of things. In presenting the order to construct the tank ironically, Hersey collapses the tank's concrete and symbolic functions in such a way as to challenge the symbolic order of Mrs. Nakamura's world.

Hersey draws repeatedly for his ironies upon instances like this one which illustrate the ways in which the atomic bomb destroyed the ability to apply accepted notions of causality, to make traditional distinctions, or to classify events historically. But these are the very distinctions upon which his narrative structure depends, as it attempts to give a symbolic order to the disorder of Mrs. Nakamura's experience, and through it to represent symbolically the experience of tens of thousands of people. Although we learn briefly of Mrs. Nakamura's nameless neighbor that his house is torn down and that he lay dead, we learn nothing about comparable death and destruction that must extend in every direction from Mrs. Nakamura's house; even at the level of personal history—the level that authorizes our minute examination of Mrs. Nakamura—in the interest of focusing the narrative, some losses are sacrificed and most sacrifices are completely lost. Hersey's narrative requires foregrounding while his argument requires generalizing and his mode of mediation, the nonfiction novel, calls into question the author's ability to frame the narrative and at the same time to make necessary distinctions within it.

Hiroshima not only manifests this problem but also thematizes it in several ways that suggest the arbitrariness of the frame, the failure of metanarratives, and the instability of writing. We can see all three of these issues at work if we examine the competing time frames in the book. Although the opening announces that we are situated in Japanese time, repeatedly the narrative voice finds that time inadequate to frame the story.

The first alternative is the substitution of space for time. Starting with the simultaneity of the explosion's effects, the book measures differences not in terms of *when* they occurred but *where,* that is, how many yards from the center of the explosion. Although this motif is picked up again in the fourth chapter, as scientists determine from the myriad forms of damage the exact center of detonation, from the second chapter on alternative representations of time come primarily in two forms: as medical pathology and as theology. Time manifests itself as pathology in terms of the pattern of symptoms that characterize postnuclear wounds and ailments, and it is introduced as theology through two of the principals, who are clergymen.

Mr. Tanimoto, a Methodist minister educated at Emory University, for example, is described after the explosion running toward the city to see his family and church: "The wounded limped past the screams [of the people trapped in rubble], and Mr Tanimoto ran past them. As a Christian he was filled with compassion for those who were trapped, and as a Japanese he was overwhelmed by the shame of being unhurt, and he prayed as he ran, 'God help them and take them out of the fire'" (39). For several reasons, it is impossible for us to know, or perhaps for Mr. Tanimoto himself to know, whether he is praying here as a Japanese or as a Christian, and whether that changes the meaning or the effect of the prayer. The first reason is that Mr. Tanimoto, who authored the prayer, did not author its explanation. His relationship to that explanation, therefore, is unclear: Is the passage intended to *personalize* Mr. Tanimoto's response to the events or to *generalize* Christian and Japanese responses? And what is the relationship of the multiple audiences suggested in the passage: Is Mr. Tanimoto speaking to himself, his society, his God, Hersey, or the American audience that Hersey represents? How does that American audience situate itself in relation to the competing cosmologies in the passage, the two represented overtly as Japanese and Christian and the third represented implicitly as Hersey's omniscience, that is, the cosmology of the fictional world in which Hersey has staged Mr. Tanimoto's conflict?

These questions do not admit answers but rather foreground the ways in which Hersey's attempt to create rhetorically an unmediated gaze on the "reality" of Mr. Tanimoto's consciousness, in the interest of conveying the immediacy of Hiroshima to an American audience, emphasized the arbitrariness of the frames that Mr. Tanimoto himself used to delimit that consciousness. By implication, they all call into question the frame that Hersey constructs to investigate it.

Hersey's juxtaposition of pathological and theological time frames can be seen most dramatically, and most problematically, in the cinematic death of Mr. Tanaka. Distrustful of Mr. Tanimoto because of his Christianity and American education, Mr. Tanaka, a retired businessman, had accused Mr. Tanimoto of spying. Critically burnt, "face and arms . . . covered with pus and blood, . . . eyes swollen shut" (79), Mr. Tanaka realized he was dying and sent for Mr. Tanimoto because he "was willing to be comforted by any religion" (79). From a Japanese-language pocket Bible, Mr. Tanimoto read:

> "For a thousand years in Thy sight are but as yesterday when it is past, and as a watch in the night. Thou carriest the children of men away as with a flood; they are as asleep; in the morning they are like grass which groweth up. In the morning it florisheth and groweth up; in the evening it is cut down, and withereth. For we are consumed by Thy anger and by Thine wrath are we troubled. Thou has set our iniquities before Thee, our secret sins in the light of Thy countenance. For all our days are passed away in Thy wrath: we spend our years as a tale that is told. . . ."
>
> Mr. Tanaka died as Mr. Tanimoto read the psalm. (79)

The passage Mr. Tanimoto chooses—or the excerpt that Hersey repeats— disrupts the pathological time of Mr. Tanaka's ailments with comfort and release by taking the pathology out of the context of Japanese time, which ostensibly frames *Hiroshima*, and putting it into an explicitly different time frame, one in which Christian eternity makes a thousand years "but as yesterday." With this frame, however, comes a vision of God's wrath with implicit parallels to the fury from the sky that fell on Hiroshima, thus re- storing a notion of causality to the random destruction of the city: "For we are consumed by Thy anger and by Thine wrath are we troubled" (79). Mr. Tanaka lay consumed by his burnt and festering flesh because he, like his fellow citizens, had offended the Christian Almighty. They committed the sin, in other words, of living in Japanese time, from which perspective their fate was inexplicable. Mr. Tanaka acknowledges the failure of his time frame by sending for Mr. Tanimoto, just as the cinematic coincidence of these words and Mr. Tanaka's death gives formal closure to the scene and thus assent to the sentiment.

Father Kleinsorge's meetings with the permanently crippled Miss Sasaki make similar points. Visited in the hospital, she asks him:

> "If your God is so good and kind, how can he let people suffer like this?" She made a gesture which took in her shrunken leg, the other patients in her room, and Hiroshima as a whole.
>
> "My child," Father Kleinsorge said, "man is not now in the condition God

intended. He has fallen from grace through sin." *And he went on to explain all the reasons for everything.* (106; emphasis added)

Although we never get his explanation, once again we see the ways in which the limited perspective of Japanese time is subordinated to the total-izing perspective of Christian theology. It is, of course, hard to miss the ironic tone of this passage's concluding sentence, but it is much harder to gloss that irony or identify absolutely its target. Is Hersey pointing out the gullibility or vulnerability of Miss Sasaki et al.? Perhaps he is deriding the self-assurance of Father Kleinsorge or perhaps he is praising Kleinsorge's unflinching faith. In order to focus the irony, we need to contextualize it within a stable narrative frame, a knowable metanarrative. But the inform-ing metanarrative is illusive because of the fictional omniscience that Hersey has constructed. Posing as transparent reality, Hersey's fiction does not allow us to anchor the "everything." Is the authorial voice quoting Father Kleinsorge? paraphrasing him? summarizing him sympathetically? unsym-pathetically? Did Hersey witness this discussion or is he editing someone else's eyewitness account? Since in the book Miss Sasaki and Father Klein-sorge are Hersey's principals, from which one, if either, does the sentiment expressed in that (ironic?) sentence emanate?

This passage thus suggests that if Hersey is trying to be ironic, he can-not control the irony or even fully realize it, and if he is not trying to be ironic, he cannot purge the ironic connotations from the very irony that he cannot realize. This effect is succinctly described by Jameson when he char-acterizes postmodernism as being a condition in which pastiche replaces parody. Lacking the control of a knowable or stable frame, the perspective upon which background and foreground depend becomes impossible, and with it the means for distinguishing a parody from its referent.

The inadequacy of Japanese time is rendered in secular terms as well, through the fragments of news and rumor that filter into Hiroshima. Like Father Kleinsorge, these rumors explain everything. The bomb is thought of as a "self-scattering cluster of bombs" (31), gasoline sprayed on the city and somehow set aflame "in one flashing moment" (51), or "a kind of fine mag-nesium powder sprayed over the whole city by a single plane, . . . exploded when it came in contact with the live wires of the city power system" (77). This last explanation, a rumor reported by one of the survivors "on the best authority" (77), is presented in contrast to the "vague, incomprehensible rumor . . . that the city had been destroyed by the energy released when atoms were somehow split in two" (81). But the best authority in this book is the authorial voice, which has already informed us of the truth and its relationship to the Japanese victims: "Those victims who were able to worry at all about what had happened thought of it and discussed it in more primitive, childish terms—gasoline sprinkled from an airplane, maybe, or some combustible gas, or a big cluster of incendiaries, or the work of parachutists; but, even if they had known the truth, most of them were too busy or too weary or too badly hurt to care that they were the objects of the first great experiment in the use of atomic power . . ." (64). As presented in this passage, the business, the weariness, the pain are not obstacles to the victims' concern about the explosion when it is described in "childish" or "primitive" terms, but they are impediments when it comes to focusing that concern on the sophisticated truth. Bomb victims who are able to care about cluster incendiaries are rendered by their victimization largely incapable of caring about being objects in a nuclear experiment.

Repeatedly, therefore, Japanese time has to be framed by historical time —a time that is neither Japanese nor American but constituted in the timeless omniscience of the narrative voice. Invoking his fictional omniscience, Hersey captures Japanese time, but his captive makes an illusive prisoner just as it made an inadequate frame. Everywhere we see Japanese time in its questionable remnants, chipped away by technology, Westernization, political and social upheaval; even its religious grounding—the tenets that connect corporal measurements with eternal—is rendered dubious by alternate versions of the eternity: Catholic, Methodist, and authorial.

The authorial authority, however, that repeatedly tries to subordinate with irony the authority of rumor also depends on rumor almost exclusively for its representation of the events in the text. If the rumor is the excess or extraneous speech, redeemed only as excess, as rumor, as the ironic supplement to the "truth," then by what means in this text can truth be sorted from rumor? How does Hersey's status as outsider change from marginal to central, and how does that change affect the principals whom Hersey attempts to represent? In converting his absence from the events of Hiroshima into the omniscient historical presence that represents it, Hersey thus relies on a fissure between "history" and "event" in order to invest history with the rhetorical authority of fiction. In so doing, he necessarily anticipates important assumptions of postmodernism. Making the authority for writing dependent on its unreliability, he calls into question the process of framing, the validity of metanarratives, the relationship of the particular to the general, the nature of causality, and the process of representation.

Hiroshima's self-consciousness, its cognizance of itself *as document*, is strikingly marked in the last pages, through the self-referential use of a letter written to an American friend by Mr. Tanimoto, describing some of his experiences on the night of August 6, 1945, that have already been described "objectively" in chapter 3. The letter gives a very different impression of the events, emphasizing a stoic and orderly quality that gives the caring for the numerous wounded an almost ritualistic quality. In Tanimoto's version, the victims, moreover, are united even more by their nationalism than by their catastrophe. One person is quoted as saying, "Look I lost my home, my family, and at last my-self bitterly injured. But now I have gotten my mind to dedicate what I have to complete the war for our country's sake" (112). Tanimoto tells of going to sleep and waking to find many whom he had aided dead. "But, to my great surprise, I never heard anyone cried in disorder, even though they suffered in great agony. They died in silence, with no grudge, setting their teeth to bear it. All for the country!" (112). He tells of a father and son trapped under a collapsed, burning house, who decide to "give *Banzai* to our Emperor," in consequence of which the father reported, "I felt calm and bright and peaceful spirit in my heart, when I chanted *Banzai* to Tenno" (112–13). After his son subsequently got out and then saved him, the father repeated: "What a fortunate that we are Japanese! It was my first time I ever tasted such a beautiful spirit when I decided to die for our Emperor" (113). Finally, Mr. Tanimoto describes a group of thirteen-year-old girls, crushed by a heavy fence and being asphyxiated by smoke, who died singing the national anthem in unison. The letter concludes: "Yes, people of Hiroshima died manly in the atomic bombing, believing that it was for the Emperor's sake" (113). Steeped as it is in extreme patriotism, differing at least in tone, foregrounding and omitting a different set of details, Tanimoto's version stands in sharp—possibly ironic, were irony completely possible—contrast to the version we have already witnessed through Hersey's authoritative mediation.

Now Mr. Tanimoto speaks for himself. But only as a supplement, meaningful only in that he has already been spoken for. His document stands for the partisan, impure, falsified version of the objective reportage in chapter 3. But this false document is also the source of Hersey's objective document, or at least it is issued from the same site, Mr. Tanimoto's memory, approximately one year after the bombing. Although the structure of the book suggests that the details in chapter 3 are the immediate records of the events as they unfolded and those in chapter 4 are reconstructions—of the story and of the city—from a year's distance, both chapters are reconstructions, from the same temporal distance, and both represent Mr. Tanimoto's *re*capitulation.

The difference is that the letter asserts Mr. Tanimoto's agency as writer. Is Hersey's point that writing corrupts? that national interests intercede, make witnesses unreliable, impose stilted narratives? Or is his point that Mr. Tanimoto was not really a reliable source? In other words, is he trying to discredit writing in general or Mr. Tanimoto in particular? Since Mr. Tanimoto is not just *a* source but *Hersey's* source, and since *Hiroshima* is, like the letter it contains, writing based on Hersey's source, the implicit distortion marked by the letter must be placed neither on Mr. Tanimoto nor on writing itself.

Instead, I think, Hersey attempts to attribute the excess of meaning to memory, so that the last pages of *Hiroshima* distance the destruction as far temporally as a year's worth of *re*membering will allow. Memory thus becomes another arbitrary frame, one that is valorized to elide the more problematic instability of the other frames. The difference between memory and fact, however, is that, by definition, memory is allowed to forget. It is defined within a tolerance of distortions, to compensate for which writing exists. Writing makes records of that which memory cannot hold reliably; writing makes permanent that which memory renders ephemeral; writing makes pure and simple that which memory interprets and rationalizes. In order to settle disputes, therefore, we turn in the modern world to the written record—the primary document, the print medium, the history book, the encyclopaedia, the dictionary.

We thus have two versions of writing presented here: writing as the documentary evidence and writing as the transcription of memories. The latter is derived from recollection while the former is derived from the event itself. Like atomic power, like the Soviets, like time, writing has a dual nature: as the source of truth and as the process of distortion. When we realize, however, that the documentary writing of chapter 3 is the distortion of Mr. Tanimoto's written record, we are forced to realize as well that, as in the case of atomic power, observation is inadequate for distinguishing the good version from the corrupt. What we "saw" in chapter 3, Hersey ironically implies, has been muted in Mr. Tanimoto's writing a chapter later. But for this irony to work we must equate the span of the book with the span to which it refers, seeing chapter 3 as a product of August 6–7, 1945, and the end of chapter 4 as a product of early August 1946; chapter 3 has authority as a piece of writing only to the extent that we forget that it is writing and let it replace the testimony that produced it, and we are assisted in that forgetting by *Hiroshima*'s rhetoric of fiction. The suspension of disbelief that fiction can evoke functions here to distance the narration of August 6–7 from its source. The genre decisions that Hersey makes in constructing his history result in the marginalizing of the event through its replacement with a document. When the traces of the event surface in the form of a letter from a speaking subject through whose corporal experience we posit the event, those traces sound like distortions. But the normative version, in this case, is not the event itself; the normative version is the history that has performed the replacement of that event with its representation.

Throughout the cold war, as I will demonstrate in the next three chapters, the strategy of containment required a marginalizing of the narrative problems raised by *Hiroshima*. The fixed relationship between events and their historical frames had to be stable, and had in turn to stabilize the differences between Other and Same in global and domestic scenarios, personal and political relationships, social and sexual economies.

If the failure of containment as a foreign policy or a political philosophy is most dramatically illustrated by the Vietnam War, its failure as a discursive practice is marked by the rise of American postmodernism, a form that makes visible the excesses of atomic power with which containment necessarily struggled, from that moment when the citizens of Hiroshima were, in Hersey's words, "the objects of the first great experiment in the use of atomic power, which . . . no country except the United States, with its industrial know-how, its willingness to throw two billion dollars into an important wartime gamble, could possibly have developed" (64–65).

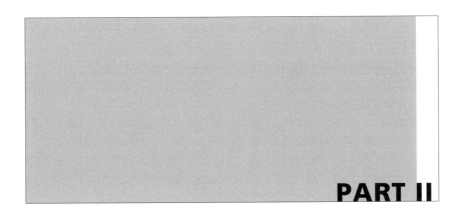

PART II

Containment Culture

3. RHETORIC, SANITY, AND THE COLD WAR

The Significance of Holden Caulfield's

Testimony

The first aspect of containment that I want to discuss has come to be known as McCarthyism, a term that describes generically the growing fear of subversion and the extreme measures to counter it, that developed and heightened from the end of World War II to the early 1950s. My primary focus will be on one of the classic literary works of the period, J. D. Salinger's *The Catcher in the Rye,* whose narrator, Holden Caulfield, voices many of the domestic themes of containment and also demonstrates the impossibility of articulating those themes while speaking veracious speech. Donning his red hunting hat, he attempts to become the good Red-hunter, ferreting out the phonies and subversives, but in so doing he emulates the bad Red-hunters, those who have corrupted the conditions of utterance such that speech itself is corrupt. Speech, like veracity, like the Soviets, like atomic power, has a dual nature, one that implicates the speaker equally with the spoken, allowing only a religious resolution to the closeted life of containment and the web of contradictions that makes it impossible to keep the narrative straight.

Caulfield's rhetoric, in other words, becomes, in the Lacanian sense, the political unconscious. If, as has been widely noted, *The Catcher in the Rye* owes much to *Adventures of Huckleberry Finn,*[1] it rewrites that classic American text in a world where the ubiquity of rule-governed society leaves no river on which to flee, no western territory for which to light out. The territory is mental, not physical, and Salinger's Huck spends his whole flight searching for raft and river, that is, for the margins of his sanity. A relative term, however, *sanity* merely indicates conformity to a set of norms, and since rhetorical relationships formulate the normative world in which a speaker functions, a fictional text—whether or not it asserts an external reality—unavoidably creates and contains a reality in its rhetorical hierarchies, which are necessarily full of assumptions and negations.[2]

Caulfield is an obsessively proscriptive speaker, and his essaylike rhetorical style—which integrates generalization, specific examples, and consequent rules—prevails throughout the book, subordinating to it most of the description, narration, and dialogue by making them examples in articulating the principles in a rule-governed society. In one paragraph, for example, Caulfield tells us that someone had stolen his coat (example), that Pencey was full of crooks (generalization), and that "the more expensive a school is, the more crooks it has" (rule) (4). In a longer excerpt from chapter 9, we can see how the details Caulfield sees from his hotel window—"a man and a woman squirting water out of their mouths at one another"—become examples in a series of generalizations, rules, and consequent evaluations:

> The trouble was, [principle:] that kind of junk is sort of fascinating to watch, even if you don't want it to be. For instance [example:] that girl that was getting water squirted all over her face, she was pretty good-looking. I mean that's my big trouble. [Generalization:] In my *mind* I'm probably the biggest sex maniac you ever saw. Sometimes [generalization:] I can think of *very* crumby stuff I wouldn't mind doing if the opportunity came up. [Generalization:] I can even see how it might be quite a lot of fun, [qualification:] in a crumby way, and if you were both sort of drunk and all, [more specific example] to get a girl and squirt water or something all over each other's face. The thing is, though, [evaluation:] I don't *like* the idea. It [generalization:] stinks, [qualification:] if you analyze it. I think [principle arrived at through a series of enthymemes:] if you really don't like a girl, you shouldn't horse around with her, at all, and if you *do* like her, then you're supposed to like her face, and if you like her face, you ought to be careful about doing crumby stuff to it, [specific application:] like squirting water all over it. (62)

Caulfield not only explains his world but also justifies his explanations by locating them in the context of governing rules, rendering his speech not only compulsively explanatory but also authoritarian in that it must demonstrate an authority for *all* his statements, even if he creates that authority merely through rhetorical convention.

With ample space we could list all the rules and principles Caulfield articulates. Here are a few: "You have to be in the mood to talk to a girl's mother on the phone"; "It's really hard to be roommates with people if your suitcases are much better than theirs"; " 'Grand' is a phony word"; "Real ugly girls have it tough"; "Some things are hard to remember"; "People don't ever believe you"; "People never notice anything"; "If you do something *too* good, then, after a while, if you don't watch it you start showing off"; "All morons hate it if you call them morons"; "People always clap for the wrong things"; "The movies can ruin you"; "Seeing old guys in their pajamas and bathrobes is depressing"; "Some people you shouldn't kid, even if they deserve it"; "It's nice when somebody tells you about their uncle"; "Don't ever tell anybody anything, if you do you start missing everybody." We could easily find scores more to prove the book a virtual anatomy of social behavior. The book, however, also anatomizes Caulfield's personal behavior: he lies, he has a great capacity for alcohol; he doesn't understand sex; he hates to go to bed when he's not even tired; he's very fond of dancing, sometimes; he's a pacifist; he's a virgin; he's a very light eater; he hates ministers; he always gets those vomity kind of cabs if he goes anywhere late at night; he would have a rule that nobody could do anything phony when they visited him.

As the author of the two anatomies, Caulfield thus manifests two drives: to control his environment by being the one who names and thus creates its rules, and to subordinate the self by being the one whose every action is governed by rules. To put it another way, he is trying to constitute himself both as subject and as object; he is trying to read a social text and to write one. When these two drives come in conflict, his autobiographical narratives betray the same structural authority as that of the historical narratives he critiques, and there are no options left. Although reified in the body of Holden Caulfield—a body, like the combined corpus of Huck and Jim, that longs for honesty and freedom as it moves more deeply into a world of deceit and slavery—this lack of options reveals an organization of power that deeply reflects the tensions of post–World War II America from which the novel emerged.

The novel appeared in 1951, the product of ten years' work. Especially during the five years between the time Salinger withdrew from publication a ninety-page version of the novel and revised it to more than double its length, the cold war blossomed.[3] Richard and Carol Ohman have related *Catcher's* immense success to the political climate of the cold war by trying to show that Caulfield provides a critique of the phoniness "rooted in the economic and social arrangements of capitalism and their concealment" (29). Although they tend to oversimplify the text and the relationship between literature and history,[4] *Catcher* may indeed be a vivid manifestation of the period's political unconscious, a narrative in which, as Jameson defines it, "social contradictions, unsurmountable in their own terms, find purely formal resolution in the aesthetic realm" (*Political*, 79). *Catcher's* cogency, in this regard, comes from the fact that Caulfield not only speaks the speech of the rule contradictions impelled by his cultural narratives but also displaces them by internalizing them. In Foucauldian fashion, he thus internalizes the mechanisms of surveillance—social, sexual, political, economic, and theological—that comprise the privileged domestic security devices of containment. Converting his rhetoric into mental breakdown, he becomes both the articulation of "unspeakable" hypocrisy and its critic. Finally, through the theological symbology out of which Salinger constructs his resolution, Caulfield becomes for his audience a sacrificial escape from the implications of such an articulation.

THE SEARCH FOR PHONIES

Victor Navasky describes the cold war as a period having "three simultaneous conflicts: a global confrontation between rival imperialisms and ideologies, between capitalism and Communism . . . a domestic clash in the United States between hunters and hunted, investigators and investigated . . . and, finally a civil war among the hunted, a fight within the liberal community itself, a running battle between anti-Communist liberals and those who called themselves progressives . . ." (3). These conflicts took the form not only of the Korean War but also of lengthy, well-publicized trials of spies and subversives; they were apparent in the form of ubiquitous loyalty oaths, Senate (McCarthy) and House Un-American Activities Committee (HUAC) hearings, in Hollywood and academic purges, in extensive "anticommunist" legislation. Even three years before Senator Joseph McCarthy's famous Wheeling, Pennsylvania, speech, alluding to fifty-seven communists in the State Department, President Truman created a Presidential Commission on Employee Loyalty and the Hollywood Ten had been ruined by HUAC.[5] Constantly legislation, hearings, speeches, and editorials warned Americans to be suspicious of phonies, wary of associates, circumspect about their past, and cautious about their speech. A new mode of behavior was necessary, the president's commission noted, because America was now confronted with organizations that valorized duplicity: "[these organizations] while seeking to destroy all the traditional safe-guards erected for the protection of individual rights are determined to take unfair advantage of those selfsame safe-guards" (*The First Loyalty,* 20).

Since uncovering duplicity was the theme of the day, in thinking constantly about who or what was phony, Caulfield was doing no more than following the instructions of J. Edgar Hoover, the California Board of Regents, *The Nation,* the Smith Act, and the Hollywood Ten, to name a very few. The president's loyalty commission, for example, announced as its purpose to protect the government from infiltration by "disloyal persons" and to protect loyal employees "from unfounded accusations." The commission's dual role, of course, implied dual roles for all citizens: to be protected *and* exonerated. Living in the epistemological closet reflected in the commission's dual charge, each citizen was potentially both the threat and the threatened. And in one more way, the necessary surveillance was also inadequate to its task. Because the enemy was "subversive," one could never know whether one had been misled by an enemy pretending to be a friend; without a sure test of loyalty, one could not sort the loyal from the disloyal and therefore could not know with whom to align. The problem—cutting across issues of sexual license, sexual orientation, and theological commitment, elevated to the level of national security and dramatized most vividly by the Hiss case—was to penetrate the duplicity of phonies.

This problem manifests itself in Caulfield's rhetoric not only in his diatribe against "phonies" but also in a chronic pattern of signifiers that indicate the truthfulness of Caulfield's testimony. He regularly marks his narration with such phrases as "it really does" (4); "if you really want to know the truth" (1, 5, 80, 92, 99, 100, 134, 184, 201, 204); "I really do" (9); "I really didn't" (10); "he really was" (14); "I'll admit" (18, 27); "he really did" (26, 90, 108); "I have to admit it" (26, 126, 129); "I really was" (31, 97); "I really don't" (39, 214); "he really was" (40, 112); "I really did" (42, 76, 196, 198, 204); "they really do" (54); "she really did" (55); "if you really want to know" (56); "she really was, too" (58); "no kidding" (58); "I swear to God" (63, 84, 103, 124, 125, 134, 141, 165); "she really is" (68, 156); "I'm not kidding" (69, 70, 85, 85, 140, 142); "they really can" (73); "I mean it" (73, 80); "I really had" (75); "I swear" (85, 125, 141); "it really isn't" (89); "I really am" (92); "she really was" (94); "it really was" (95, 188); "to tell you the truth" (111); "they really are"

(119); "I admit it" (124, 184); "it really is" (143, 190); "he really did" (145); "she really does" (168). The word "really" additionally appears at least two dozen more times in the narration, often italicized. These signifiers, along with those that emphasize the intensity of an experience (e.g., "boy!") or the speaker's desire for clarity (e.g. "I mean . . .") make Caulfield's speech one that asserts its own veracity more than once for every page of narration.[6] Because it is so important to Caulfield that the reader not think he is a phony, he also constantly provides examples and illustrations to support each assertion, even his claim that he is "the most terrific liar you ever saw in your life" (16).

Examples of such rhetorical performances abounded in the media during the novel's five-year revision period. Like that of many ex-communist informers of the period, Caulfield's veracity rests on the evidence of his deceitfulness. This paradox is especially foregrounded by a discussion Caulfield has on the train with Mrs. Morrow, the mother of another boy at Pencey. In that discussion, he convinces the reader of his truthfulness with the same signifier he uses to make Mrs. Morrow believe his lies. Although Caulfield feels her son, Ernie, is "doubtless one of the biggest bastards that ever went to Pencey," he tells her, "He adapts himself very well to things. He really does. I mean he really knows how to adapt himself." Later he adds: "It really took everybody quite a while to get to know him." Having used "really" as a false signifier, Caulfield, in confessing to the reader, italicizes part of the word: "Then I *really* started chucking the old crap around." The evidence that follows should thus convince the reader that the italicized "real" can be trusted, so that the more he demonstrates he has duped his fellow traveler, the more the reader can credit the veracity of the italicized "real." The *real* crap is that Ernie was the unanimous choice for class president but wouldn't let the students nominate him because he was too modest. Thus Caulfield proves his credibility to the reader: he *is* a good liar, but when he italicizes the "real" he can be trusted. In trying to convince Mrs. Morrow, however, he adds "Boy, he's *really* shy" and thus destroys the difference between italicized and unitalicized signifier (54–57).

Although presented as a trait of Caulfield's character, formalized in his speech, these inconsistencies reflect as well the contradictions inherent in a society plagued by loyalty oaths. Swearing that something is true doesn't make it true, except at the expense of anything not sworn to. There exists, in other words, some privileged set of "true" events marked by swearing.

The swearing, of course, marks them not as true but as important to the speaker—the things that he or she wants the audience to believe, cares about enough to mark with an oath. In this way, Caulfield creates a rhetorical contract—the appeal to ethos—that legitimizes the discourse. It does so, however, at the cost of all those items not stipulated: they reside in the margins by virtue of being so obvious that they can be taken for granted or so unimportant that they need not be substantiated. Thus grouped together as the "unsworn," the taken-for-granted and the not-*necessarily*-so become indistinguishable parts of the same unmarked set. This is exactly what, as Americans were discovering, loyalty oaths did to the concept of loyalty. For all constitutions bind those loyal to them, and the failure to take that for granted becomes the failure to grant a group constituted by a common social contract. It leaves the "we" of "We the People" without a known referent and makes it impossible to distinguish the real American from the phony—the one so disloyal that he or she will swear false allegiance, will italicize *real* commitment in order to dupe others.

Since social contracts rely upon rhetorical contracts, the problem is one of language. But communism, according to its accusers, acknowledged neither the same social nor rhetorical contracts. According to a major McCarthy witness, ex-communist Louis Budenz, communists often used "Aesopean" language so that, "no matter how innocent the language might seem on its face, the initiate understood the sinister underlying message" (Navasky, 32). Because no court recognizes a contract binding on only one party, in dealing with those outside the social and rhetorical contracts the traditional constitutional rules no longer applied. In his 1950 ruling upholding the Smith Act, under which eleven leaders of the American Communist Party were sentenced to prison, Judge Learned Hand indicated that when challenged by an alternative system, "our democracy . . . must meet that faith and creed on its merits, or it will perish. *Nevertheless,* we may insist that the rules of the game be observed, and the rules confine the conflict to the rules drawn from the universe of discourse" (emphasis added). Because the communists did not function in the same universe of discourse, the same rules did not apply to them. But, as the need for loyalty tests proved, it was impossible to distinguish those for whom the rules did not apply from those for whom they did.

To do so requires a position outside the system, from which to perceive an external and objective "truth." In other words, one needs a religion, which as Wayne Booth implies, is the only source of a truly reliable narrator. All other narration must establish its credibility rhetorically by employing conventions.[7] One of Caulfield's conventions is to acknowledge his unreliability by marking specific sections of the narration as extra-reliable. As we have seen, however, marked thus by their own confessions of unreliability, Caulfield's oaths become one more series of questionable signs, indicating not reliability but its myth. Roland Barthes has astutely demonstrated that a myth is an empty sign, one that no longer has a referent but continues to function as though it did, thus preserving the status quo. The loyalty oath is such a myth in that it preserves the idea of a "loyalty" called into question by its own presence, and in that it is executed at the expense of the field in which it plays—the constituted state to which the mythical loyalty is owed.

THE NAMES OF BETRAYAL AND THE SIGNS OF TRUTH

Like Caulfield's oaths, loyalty oaths in the public realm also proved insufficient. In a truly Orwellian inversion, the "true" test of loyalty became betrayal. Unless someone was willing to betray friends, no oath was credible. With the tacit and often active assistance of the entire entertainment industry, HUAC very effectively imprinted this message on the public conscience through half a decade of Hollywood purges. As has been clearly shown, investigating the entertainment industry was neither in the interest of legislation nor—as it could be argued that an investigation of the State Department was—in the interest of national security. It was to publicize the ethic of betrayal, the need to name names.

If the *willingness* to name names became the informer's credential, the *ability* to do so became his or her capital. Thus the informer turned proper nouns into public credit that was used to purchase credibility. Caulfield too capitalizes on names. The pervasive capitalization of proper nouns marks his speech; he compulsively names names. In the first three chapters alone, the narration (including the dialogue attributed to Caulfield) contains 218 proper nouns—an average of nine per page. They include people, places, days, months, countries, novels, cars, and cold remedies. Many of the names, moreover, are striking by virtue of their unimportance. Does it matter if "old Spencer" used "Vicks Nose Drops" or read *Atlantic Monthly?* Is it important that these items are named twice? Caulfield's speech merely mirrors the conventions of the Hollywood witness by demonstrating that its significance lay in alacrity, not content: "A certain minimum number of names was necessary; those who . . . could convince HUAC counsel that they did not know the names of enough former comrades to give a persuasive performance . . . were provided with names. The key to a successful appearance was the *prompt* recital of the names of a few dozen Hollywood Reds" (Ceplair and Englund, 18; emphasis added).

Nor was the suspicion of Hollywood one-sided. Suspected by the right of being potentially subversive, it was suspected by the liberals of being inordinately self-censored. Carey McWilliams, writing in *The Nation* in 1949, bemoans the effects of the "graylist." Intimidated out of dealing realistically with social issues, the moveis, McWilliams fears, were becoming more and more phony.

Not surprisingly, throughout the novel Caulfield too expresses disdain for Hollywood, repeatedly equating it with betrayal and prostitution. The prostitute who comes into his room, furthermore, tells him she is from Hollywood, and when she sits on his lap, she tries to get him to name a Hollywood name: "You look like a guy in the movies. You know. Whosis. *You* know who I mean. What the heck's his name?" When Caulfield refuses to name the name, she tries to encourage him by associating it with that of another actor: "Sure you know. He was in that pitcher with Mel-vine Douglas. The one that was Mel-vine Douglas's kid brother. *You* know who I mean" (97). In 1951, naming that name cannot be innocent, because of its associations. Douglas, a prominent Hollywood liberal (who in 1947 supported the Hollywood Ten and in 1951 distanced himself from them) was, more importantly, the husband of Helen Gahagan Douglas, the Democratic congresswoman whom Richard Nixon defeated in the contest for the California Senate seat. Nixon's race, grounded in red-baiting, innuendos, and guilt by association, attracted national attention and showed, according to McCarthy biographer David Oshinsky, that " 'McCarthyism' was not the exclusive property of Joe McCarthy" (177).

If Caulfield is guilty by virtue of his association with Melvyn Douglas, then guilty of what? Consorting with prostitutes? Naming names? Or is it of his own hypocrisy, of his recognition, also inscribed in his rhetoric, that he hasn't told the truth in that he actually loves the movies, emulates them, uses them as a constant frame of reference? The first paragraph of the book begins "if you really want to know the truth" and ends with the sentences:

"If there's one thing I hate it's the movies. Don't even mention them to me." Despite this injunction, Caulfield's speech is full of them. He acts out movie roles alone and in front of others, uses them as a pool of allusion to help articulate his own behavior, and goes to see them, even when he believes they will be unsatisfactory.[8]

This marked ambivalence returns us again to the way historical circumstances make Caulfield's speech, like all public testimony, incapable of articulating "truth" because the contradictions in the conditions of public and private utterance have become visible in such a way as to mark all truth claims "phony." In their stead come rituals of loyalty, rituals that do not manifest truth but replace it. In presenting advertised, televised confessionals, which were prepared, written, and rehearsed and then were performed by real-life actors, the HUAC Hollywood investigations not only replicated the movies but also denied the movies distance and benignity, in short, their claim to artificiality. The silver (and cathode-ray) screen is everywhere and nowhere, presenting an act of truthtelling hard to distinguish from its former fabrications, stories for the screen that may or may not have been encoded, subversive messages. So too in "real life"—the viewers of these confessions may have been duped, made inadvertently to play a subversive role, followed an encoded script produced by a secret conspiracy of the sort they're used to seeing in the movies. And of course the movies *can* be believed, for if they cannot, what is all the worry about? Why bother investigating the harmless? This was the mixed message of the HUAC hearings: Movies were dangerous because they *could* be believed and movies were dangerous because they *could not*. One cannot escape the message by discovering the "truth," but only by performing the ritual that fills the space created by the impossibility of such a discovery.

In this light, perhaps, Phoebe Caulfield's role in her school play should be read. When Caulfield asks her the play's name she says: " 'A Christmas Pageant for America.' It stinks, but I'm Benedict Arnold. I have practically the biggest part . . . it starts out when I'm dying. This ghost comes in on Christmas Eve and asks me if I'm ashamed and everything. You know. For betraying my country and everything . . ." (162). The passage accurately summarizes the ideal HUAC witness: the former traitor now starring in a morality play that honors the state through a form of Christian ritual, the goal of which is not the discovery of truth, but the public, "educational" demonstration of loyal behavior, in which the fiction's paragon of innocence and the nation's historical symbol of perfidy validate one another by exchanging roles. The narrative structure that informs the novel also informs Phoebe's school play. The performance of treason, like the performance of a redemption ritual, has necessarily been replaced by its representation, a knowingly fictitious representation, constructed out of allusions to other representations—American folklore, Christian salvation stories, *A Christmas Carol*—each of which marks the others with an accentuated fictionality. The play can claim no "veracity" and yet in its overtly fictional mode it reenacts the structural paradigm for truthful testimony played out in contemporary historical media: *The Congressional Record,* the newspapers, the live telecasts, the newsmagazines. And it is this structural paradigm that gives meaning to Phoebe's. Conversely, the proliferation of cultural narratives through media such as Phoebe's play facilitates the recognition of specific performances as *acts* of loyalty, even when they were performed by professional actors, before cameras, actors whose personal histories might raise questions about the sincerity of their performances.

EDUCATION, TESTIMONY, AND SELF (-INCRIMINATION)

Phoebe's play, moreover, unites two central loci for phonies in Caulfield's speech, the worlds of entertainment and of education. In questioning the phoniness of all the schools and teachers he has seen, Caulfield again articulates doubts prevalent in the public consciousness, especially as he is most critical of the Eastern Intellectual Establishment. That establishment, with Harvard as its epitome, came to represent for the general public, as typified by the readers of *Time,* a form of affluence and elitism that could not be trusted. In their education section the week of June 5, 1950, for example, *Time* quoted I. A. Richards at length on college teaching:

> You are never quite sure if you are uttering words of inspired . . . aptness, or whether you are being completely inept. Often you will find yourself incompetent enough to be fired at once if anybody was intelligent enough to see you as you are. . . .
>
> Am I, or am I not, a fraud? That is a question that is going to mean more and more to you year by year. At first its seems agonizing; after that it becomes familiar and habitual. (65–66)

Again we have the same confessional paradigm. Richards gains credibility by confessing he is a fraud. He also suggests an encoded language meant to deceive the average person—anybody *not* "intelligent enough to see you as you are"; by implication, those who are intelligent enough participate in the conspiracy to keep the fraudulence hidden.

This issue becomes particularly germane in a period when teachers and professors were being forced to sign loyalty oaths and/or were being dismissed because of present or past political beliefs. The central issue, many faculty argued, was that academic personnel were being judged by non-academic standards.[9] Yet Richards's statement could suggest that "true" academic standards were really a myth created by those intelligent enough to know better. Intelligence thus signified the capacity for fraud: only someone intelligent enough to see them as they are had something to hide. Because they knew more, intellectuals were more likely to know something they should confess, and hence not confessing signified probable disloyalty rather than innocence.

Time in 1950 made the same inferences about the psychiatrist who testified in Alger Hiss's defense, pointing out that Dr. Murray (like Dr. Binger and Hiss) was a Harvard graduate: "He backed up his colleague, Binger. Chambers . . . was a psychopathic personality. . . . He had never seen Chambers but this did not faze him. He had psychoanalyzed Adolph Hitler *in absentia,* correctly predicting his suicide" ("Trials—Some People," 14).

If, filtered through *Time*'s simplifying voice, these doctors seemed foolish accomplices, Hiss himself came to stand for everything that needed exposure and rejection. About his conviction, *Time* wrote: "[Hiss] was marked as a man who, having dedicated himself to Communism under a warped sense of idealism, had not served it openly but covertly; a man who, having once served an alien master, lacked the courage to recant his past, but went on making his whole life an intricate, calculated lie" ("Trials—The Reckoning," 12). Thus the past existed to be recanted, not recounted. The recounted past—the truth of one's past—became living a lie, while recanting revealed Truth, discovered not in past actions but in ideological enlightenment, enlightenment that reveals that one's life is a lie. Analysis is intellectualized lying, *Time* had suggested in its treatment of Hiss's "authorities," part of the intellectual conspiracy that did not revere the Truth but rather suggested that facts could be contravened by an unseen, subversive presence, knowable only to a trained elite whom the general population had to trust without evidence. For *Time*, truth was less ambiguous, existing in a transparent connection between physical phenomena and accepted beliefs and with its authority lying outside the speaking subject. Hiss had transgressed by seeking to intervene, to analyze, to apply principles not grounded in Truth but in the trained intellect of a fallen mortal, fallen because he believed in the power of human intervention, the ability of the intellect to discern and interpret.

This too is Caulfield's failing, and he must recognize the error of locating himself as the discoverer, interpreter, and arbiter of truth and phoniness. In other words, if his speech constitutes him both as subject and as object, it also constitutes him as testifier and judge, accuser and accused. It has the quality of testimony—the taking of oaths and the giving of evidence to support an agenda of charges. And like much of the most publicized testimony of its day, it has no legal status. As Navasky pointed out about the Hollywood hearings: "[T]he procedural safeguards . . . were absent: there was no cross examination, no impartial judge and jury, none of the exclusionary rules about hearsay or other evidence. And, of course, the targets from the entertainment business had committed no crime . . ." (xiv).

In such a context, it was hard to regard testimony as a form of rhetoric in a forensic argument. Although sometimes masked as such, it rarely functioned in the way that Aristotle defined the concept, resembling more often testimony in the religious sense of confessing publicly one's sins. Caulfield's speech, thus simultaneously steeped in conventions of both forensic testimony and spiritual, reveals the incompatibility of the two in terms of their intended audience, their intended effect, and their relationship to the speaker. Most important, forensic testimony presumes truth as something arrived at through the interaction of social and rhetorical contract, whereas spiritual testimony presumes an external authority for truth; its rhetoric *reveals* the Truth, doing so in such a way as to exempt the speech from judgment and present the speaker not as peer but as paragon.

These distinctions apply particularly to the concept of incrimination. A witness giving forensic testimony always risks self-incrimination; recognizing this, our laws allow the witness to abstain from answering questions. The paragon, who gives spiritual testimony, however, is above such self-incrimination; the paragon knows the truth and has nothing to fear. Exercising the legal protection against self-incrimination (as many HUAC witnesses chose to do) meant that the speaker was offering forensic testimony, not spiritual, and therefore had not found the Truth and could not be trusted. Designed to protect the individual from self-incrimination, the Fifth Amendment then became the instrument of that self-incrimination.

In a society that determined guilt not by evidence but by association and/or failure to confess, people often found that the only way not to incriminate others was to claim that they would be incriminating themselves. Since that claim became self-incriminating, they purchased silence by suggesting guilt. They thus internalized the dramatic conflict between social contract and personal loyalty, with the goal not being catharsis but silence. Autobiography, always potentially incriminating, had become recontextualized as testimony, but testimony had become freed of its evidentiary contexts and become an unbound truth-of-Otherness. It potentially revealed the Other—the subversive—everywhere but in the place he or she was known to be, even in the audience of investigators and/or in the speaker. The speaker, by virtue of testimony's two voices and self-incrimination's merger with its own safeguard, was as much alienated in the face of his or her own speech as in the face of his or her silence. Confronted with the "dual nature" of speech, the speaker was, in the terms I developed in the preceding chapters, forced into a closet, a form of self-surveillance circumscribed by the ubiquitous possibility of appearing Other and/or the unspeakable fear of being what one appeared.

THE CASE FOR SILENCE

The battle waged internally by so many during the cold war—between spiritual and forensic testimony, public and personal loyalty, recounting and recanting, speech and silence—created a test of character. No matter how complex and self-contradictory the social text, the individual was supposed to read it and choose correctly. This is exactly the dilemma Caulfield's speech confronts from its first words: "If you really want to hear about it, the first thing you'll probably want to know is where I was born, and what my lousy childhood was like, and how my parents were occupied and all before they had me, and all that David Copperfield kind of crap, but I don't feel like going into it, if you want to know the truth. In the first place that stuff bores me, and in the second place, my parents would have two hemorrhages apiece if I told anything pretty personal about them" (1). Caulfield will try to tell the truth to his "hearing" without incriminating himself or his parents. But at every turn he fails, constantly reflecting rather than negotiating the contradictions of his world. Against that failure weighs the possible alternative, silence in the extreme, as suicide. The memory of James Castle's suicide haunts the book. Castle, the boy at Elkton Hills, refused to recant something he said about a very conceited student, and instead committed suicide by jumping out a window. Caulfield too contemplated suicide in the same manner after the pimp, Maurice, had taken his money and hit him (104). This image of jumping out the window not only associates Caulfield with Castle but also epitomizes the fall from which Caulfield, as the "catcher in the rye," wants to save the innocent.

The image of jumping out the window also typified, as it had during the stock market crash of 1929, admission of personal failure in the face of unnegotiable social demands. In 1948, for example, Lawrence Duggan fell or threw himself from the window of his New York office. Immediately Congressman Karl Mundt announced the cause was Duggan's implication in a communist spy ring; along with five other men he had been named at a HUAC meeting. The committee would disclose the other names, Mundt said, "as they jump out of windows."

On April 1, 1950, F. O. Matthiessen, "at the time," in the words of William O'Neill, "the most intellectually distinguished fellow traveler in America" (173), jumped to his death from a Boston hotel window. In his suicide note, he wrote: "as a Christian and a socialist believing in international peace, I find myself terribly oppressed by the present tensions" (qtd. in Stern, 31). Although Matthiessen did not commit suicide solely for political reasons, for the general public his death symbolized the culpability and weakness of the Eastern Intellectual Establishment. His powerful intellect, his political leanings, and, especially, his longstanding affiliation with Harvard identified him clearly as the kind of analytic mind that typified the intellectual conspiracy *Time,* Joseph McCarthy, et al. most feared and despised. Like Hiss, he was led astray by his idealism which, in true allegorical fashion, led to deceit and, ultimately, the coward's way out. *Or:* Like many dedicated progressives, he was hounded by witch hunters forcing him to choose between the roles of betrayer and betrayed and leading him ultimately to leap from melodrama to tragedy. Hero or coward, Christ or Judas, in either case, in the morality drama of his day, he graphically signified the sort of fall from innocence against which Caulfield struggles.[10]

In the end, Caulfield renounces this struggle, allowing that one cannot catch kids: "if they want to grab for the gold ring, you have to let them do it *and not say anything. If they fall off, they fall off, but it's bad if you say anything to them*" (211; emphasis added). The solution to Caulfield's dilemma becomes renouncing speech itself. Returning to the condition of utterance stipulated in his opening sentence, which frames his testimony, he says in the last chapter: "If you want to know the truth . . ." (213), this time followed not with discourse but with the recognition that he lacks adequate knowledge for discourse, "I don't *know* what to think about it" (213–14). From this follows regret in the presence of the named names: "I'm sorry I told so many people about it. All I know is I sort of *miss* everybody I told about. Even old Stradlater and Achley, for instance. I think I even miss Goddam Maurice. It's funny. Don't ever tell anybody anything. If you do, you start missing everybody" (214). These last sentences of the book replace truth with silence. The intermediary, moreover, between Caulfield's speech—deemed unreasonable—and his silence is the asylum, and we could say that the whole novel is speech framed by the asylum. It intervenes in the first chapter, immediately after Caulfield asks "if you want to know the truth," and in the last, immediately before he says he does not know what to think. In this way, the asylum functions in the manner Foucault has noted— not to remove Caulfield's guilt but to organize it "for the madman as a consciousness of himself, and as a non reciprocal relation to the keeper; it organized it for the man of reason as an awareness of the Other, a therapeutic intervention in the madman's existence" (*Madness*, 247). "Incessantly cast in this empty role of unknown visitor, and challenged in everything that can be known about him, drawn to the surface of himself by a social personality silently imposed by observation, by form and mask, the madman is obliged to objectify himself in the eyes of reason as the perfect stranger, that is as the man whose strangeness does not reveal itself. The city of reason welcomes him only with this qualification and at the price of his surrender to anonymity" (249–50). In this light, we can see that the asylum not only frames Caulfield's speech but also intervenes throughout as an increasing awareness of his Otherness, marked by such phrases as "I swear to God, I'm a madman." Given the novel's frame, it is not astonishing that Caulfield's speech manifests traits of the asylum. In that his speech also manifests the contradictions of McCarthyism and the cold war, the novel more interestingly suggests that the era in many ways institutionalized the traits of the asylum. To prove the validity of his "madman" oaths, Caulfield must again assume the dual roles of subject and object, for as Foucault demonstrates, the intervention of the asylum (and by extension we can say the cold war) functioned by three principal means: perpetual judgment, recognition by the mirror, and silence.[11]

Given the political mandate to keep the narratives straight, it is not surprising that this idea in the early Foucault, so apt for Caulfield's situation, is an idea that also applies to, or at least anticipates, Foucault's understanding of the homosexual closet. It further helps us to see the disparate aspects of Caulfield's adventures as participating in a cultural narrative that typifies the cold war.

These issues converge in Caulfield's visit with Mr. Antolini, his former teacher, who lectures him on the value of formal education and the efficacy of adhering to social expectations. He particularly cautions Caulfield against a "fall": "This fall you're riding for—it's a special kind of fall, a horrible kind. The man falling isn't permitted to feel or hear himself hit bottom. He just keeps falling and falling. The whole arrangement's designed for men who, at some time in their lives, were looking for something their own environment couldn't supply them with. Or they thought their own environment couldn't supply them with. So they gave up looking. They gave it up before they ever really got started. You follow me?" (187). Mr. Antolini's description figures in several different narratives. Because Mr. Antolini was the teacher who "finally picked up that boy that boy that jumped out the window . . . felt his pulse and all, and then . . . took off his coat and put it over James Castle and carried" the dead boy to the infirmary without caring "if his coat got all bloody" (174), his concern about Caulfield's fall again associates Caulfield with Castle. But Mr. Antolini's concern is that Caulfield not turn out like Castle, not experience what the culture would define as a fall from grace. But he described that fall in language that typified the fate of Hiss or Matthiessen, language, in other words, that signified communist in the lexicon of the McCarthy period.

The "terrible oppression" to which Matthiessen alluded in his suicide note, moreover, as we now know, was not only the red-hunting of the period, but also the homophobia, and if Mr. Antolini's discussion with Caulfield argues for accommodation of the social and political order, it argues equally well for the efficacy of the sexual closet, an association underscored by the homoerotic overtures that the married Mr. Antolini makes—or at least

Caulfield believes that he makes—later that night. If, as Duane Edwards has argued, Caulfield is still uncertain of his sexual orientation, that uncertainty is one manifestation of his more pervasive inability to speak truthfully his orientation about anything, even to himself; it is, in other words, a manifestation of his condition as subject of the cold war.

THE SYMBOLIC RESOLUTION

The final issue I want to discuss here—since I am concerned not only about containment but also about its relationship to postmodern literary conventions—is Salinger's way of contextualizing Caulfield's angst and resolving the novel's narrative. Avoiding duality of speech, as I indicated earlier, requires a position outside the novel, one that allows a reader-author economy dependent upon a symbolic exchange: the world represented in the novel becomes the currency through which the author delivers a message, idea, perception, sensibility about a text other than the one we have been reading. We could call this package the theme, or the social commentary, or the allegorical or symbolic quality. In any case, this quality (or these qualities), perhaps an aspect of all writing, is one foregrounded, through many specific devices, by much of high modernism. The use of allusions, the evocation of earlier texts and traditions, and these particularly in conjunction with the "mythic" turn of Eliot, Joyce, Yeats, Hemingway, Faulkner, and others, foregrounded the role of symbolic representation.

For numerous reasons—too extensive and elaborate to document here—aspects of modernism by the 1950s had become institutionalized and modernism was itself the sign of "serious" art. The vilification of naturalism, of social realism, and of mass culture by modern critics on both the left and the right has been extensively discussed. Donald Pease has made an important and powerful case for the manifestations of the cold war in the canonized American literary criticism of the postwar period, and most recently, Tobin Siebers has pointed out that although "New Criticism appeared in the 1920s and 1930s, . . . it is most associated with the postwar world, when it acquired an institutional status with the help of the postwar boom in population and education" (30).[12] That institutional status is concomitant with the institutionalization of the "modern" throughout American culture, as reflected in the taste for Danish modern furniture, modernist architecture, and the Museum of Modern Art. In the 1950s much decorative art displayed a cubist lineage, and many suburban living rooms, spotted with mock Picassos, showed equally the influence of Mondrian.

In this world, T. S. Eliot was a particular intellectual-class signifier. What well-educated person in 1951 did *not* know that April was the cruelest month or that the modern condition was one of alienation? What writer could be taken seriously without symbolically questing for a grail, replaying a vegetation rite, situating, however subtly and skillfully, the current work within the great mythic quest for the understanding of human nature? In this context, a number of American authors tended to look backward toward classic American texts, the most common being *Adventures of Huckleberry Finn.* In addition to Salinger, Ellison, Updike, and Bellow were among the most canonized of the writers emerging during that period to draw consciously on Twain's novel. Their works also alluded heavily to Eliot and to the concerns central to *The Waste Land:* loss, failure of human relationships, alienation, the search for "genuine" qualities, the search for faith.[13]

The Waste Land is also, as has been noted, very important to Salinger.[14] Particularly important, in this regard, is the way in which this connection allows Caulfield's experience to be read as a quest for faith, realized symbolically when he recognizes that one has to have faith in the innocent— let them grab for the ring—and rewarded immediately by *The Waste Land*'s privileged commodity, rain. After the redemptive rain, Caulfield can yield himself to silence and the asylum, a sacrifice that, within the symbolic context framing the novel, renders Caulfield a figure of sacrifice rather than one who has been disciplined in the Foucauldian sense. The novel's Christ imagery[15] thus provides *containment* for the dualities—the dual and doubly impossible conditions of speech under McCarthyism—by providing readers an outlet for the transgressions they have mouthed in the name of Caulfield.

In this way, the novel manifests thematically and formally an ultimately theological context: appeal to an authority in touch with truths that remain opaque within the world of the text, such that a character's recognition— even partial, elliptical, or implicit—can qualify as an epiphany. This formal principle and its reciprocal—that formal recognition of religious authority can signify truth—typify not only much late modernist writing but, as we have seen, cold war discourse.

4. GOD'S LAW AND THE WIDE SCREEN

The Ten Commandments

as Cold War "Epic"

Even in light of President Eisenhower's oft-quoted statement, "Our government makes no sense unless it is founded in a deeply felt religious faith—and I don't care what it is," or of the fact that Bishop Fulton J. Sheen's weekly religious lecture was a hit prime-time television show, it is hard to emphasize adequately the importance of religion at the height of the cold war.[1] The formal privileging of spiritual testimony over forensic, which I discussed in the last chapter, manifested only one—albeit important—way that religion united issues of veracity with those of national security. Just as the formal qualities of *The Catcher in the Rye*'s symbolism imply a theological authority ideologically consistent with the goals of containment, so too, do the large-screen formats of the 1950s.

The wide-screen movie format developed in the 1950s as a response to the growth of television, which by 1953 had entered two-thirds of American households. To recapture an audience that had declined by 25 percent from 1946 to 1953, the film industry attempted to provide a grandeur unattainable on the small, black-and-white television screens. But more than offer larger images, the wide screen signified a kind of truth inaccessible to television. Live drama, live game shows, and especially live coverage of congressional hearings underscored television's claim to be the privileged site of "real" life, but this reality was limited to a small segment of what the eye could see. In response, filmmakers widened the movie screen to accommodate the perception of the viewer, so that the visual capacity of the audience, not the object of scrutiny, defined the scope of cinematic reality.

The larger screen resulted in such an extreme diminution of detail that director George Seaton said producing intense dramas on a wide screen was as silly "as staging a chess match in the Rose Bowl" (Dowdy, 55). At the other extreme the wide-screen format created an equally grotesque intimacy. One previewer of *The Robe,* for example, referring to a close-up of Victor Mature, suggested that the picture was "about a guy with thirteen-foot lips" (Dowdy, 53). Both of these extremes, as Susan Stewart argues, represent forms of longing. In the case of wide-screen technology, the longing is for a world commodified to shape a visual field determined by human anatomy; it defines "reality" as being "larger than life" and extending "as far as the eye can see." Technologically, the wide screen signified expansion without modification, because the view it presented was determined not by the size of the film but by the expanse onto which its vision could be projected. For example, VistaVision, the wide-screen format used for *The Ten Commandments,* achieved its expansive perspective by photographing sixty degrees' worth of horizon onto 70mm film (a double frame running horizontally), then transferring that onto the standard 35mm reels for distribution.[2]

Although the resulting VistaVision image did not have the extreme width-to-height aspect ratio achieved by the triple-screen cinerama negative or even the standard CinemaScope negative, it was still a wide-frame image that valorized as a form of visual power the expansive economic and technological growth of America in the 1950s. From 1949 to 1960, for example, the American economy showed a rise in *real* gross national product of 51 percent, and one-fourth of all the housing in America as of 1960 had been built during the preceding decade (Leuchtenburg, 63).[4] In the ten years from 1946 to 1955, automobile production increased 400 percent, to eight million a year, and the 1956 National Defense Highway Act authorized constructing over forty thousand miles of new limited access roads.[5]

Inherently acquisitive and global, the wide-screen format attempted to suggest the sublime through the proliferation of mundane details, thus participating in the same cultural narrative as American foreign policy. Especially as interpreted by Secretary of State John Foster Dulles, containment oxymoronically entailed "spreading" the American vision globally. Like the wide-screen camera, containment squeezed what the public saw into the format that could accommodate and then project that version of reality globally. And like the wide-screen format, American foreign policy— a cornerstone of which was our nuclear capacity—celebrated technological supremacy as the appropriate mandate for its vision, a theological as well as political mandate. Dulles, for example, "publicly claimed that 'there is no way to solve the great perplexing international problems except by bringing to bear on them the force of Christianity'" (Miller and Nowak, 91).

Dulles thus expressed the way America's image of itself assumed epic proportions, measured not only economically but also geopolitically and theologically. In 1953, to cite just a few examples, a "float for God" led the procession at President Eisenhower's inaugural parade. In 1954 Congress created a Prayer Room for congressmen, and America became a nation—according to its newly modified Pledge of Allegiance—"under God," thus distinguishing it from the totalitarian, atheist bloc of communist-dominated countries; in 1956, without debate, the House and Senate unanimously made "In God We Trust" the national motto.

This confluence of economics, politics, and religion helps explain why, in the 1950s, the biblical epic was the particularly privileged product of the American movie industry, including three of the five biggest grossing films of the decade: *Ben-Hur, The Robe,* and Cecil B. deMille's *The Ten Commandments,* until the mid-1960s one of the three most financially successful films ever made.[6]

Commenting on Hollywood's "fever of epics," Michael Wood notes that a "certain style of cinema—De Mille's roughly—thus comes to stand for the American cinema itself" (169). Ceding deMille that representative status, I assume that large, collaborative, commercial ventures reflect a consensus about how to commodify a culture's values, and that commercial success indicates an audience's confirmation of that consensus. In this light, *The Ten Commandments* can be read as a major product of American cold war ideology, one that highlights and localizes the foci of America's political, theological, and economic conflicts.[7] In the film, the apparatus of wide-screen technology resolved these conflicts visually by mediating a series of gazes in an economy that equates God's perspective with American global interests.

THE REAL MOSES

Since veracity was a crucial issue in the 1950s because of its relationship to ferreting out "subversives," and since only a speaker testifying before a sacred rather than a secular judge could be trusted, national loyalty, as we have seen, was signified by loyalty to God's word. Understandably, then, deMille's biblical epic starts with this conflating of truth and religion. When curtains rose and lights dimmed in the posh theaters where *The Ten Commandments* began its first run, on the giant screen appeared not the film's credits but instead a projected curtain very similar to the one in the theater. In perhaps the film's most "realistic" moment, the audiences witnessed the truth as a kind of miracle: a curtain disappeared and out of the darkness reappeared; the "real" world that gave way to the imaginary world was not discarded but resurrected. While some films discard the real world, this projected curtain suggests that *The Ten Commandments* provides its simulacrum.

The film further underscores the idea that the curtain is the image of truth and the film its vehicle, when the bottom of the curtain divides to reveal Cecil B. deMille. Because the camera does not cut immediately to middle-distance or close-up, for a few seconds deMille remains a man of ordinary stature, as if he, like the curtain he parts, were "really" on the stage. His speech also emphasizes his commitment to the truth, but to a truth, the speech reveals, based upon what the Bible omits, based not, in other words, upon the authority *of*, but the authority *behind* the words:

> Ladies and Gentlemen, young and old, this may seem an unusual procedure–speaking to you before the picture begins, but we have an unusual subject. The story of the birth of freedom. The story of Moses. As many of you know, the Holy Bible omits some thirty years of Moses' life from the time he was a three-month-old baby and was found in the bullrushes by . . . by [sic] Bithiah, the daughter of Pharaoh, and adopted in the court of Egypt, until he learned that he was Hebrew and killed the Egyptian. To fill in those early years, we turned to ancient historians such as Philo and Josephus. Philo wrote at the time that Jesus of Nazareth walked the earth and Josephus wrote some thirty years later, and watched the destruction of Jerusalem by the Romans. These historians had access to documents long since destroyed, or perhaps lost, like the Dead Sea Scrolls.

The subject of the film is the birth of freedom. That is the truth about Moses, whose largely unknown story must be true because it is part of the Holy Scriptures. The film replicates not the Scriptures, however, but the truth behind the Word. To discover this unrefutable truth, deMille must supplement the sacred Word with the secular historians. But as Derrida has pointed out, the secular cannot supplement the sacred without contaminating the sacred with the evidence that it cannot be sacred—omnipotent, complete—because it requires (secular) assistance. To rescue the historians from their secular status, deMille associates them with sacred events—one coexisted with Jesus, the other saw Jerusalem destroyed—but these associations only defer the problem to another site, one at which geographic or temporal proximity to the sacred events of the New Testament qualifies the historians to account for Old Testament events. Because associating the historians with sacred history also situates them in secular time, deMille must again redeem their credibility by substituting for their position in secular time their access to the eternal Word—"documents . . . like the Dead Sea Scrolls." The tainted historians thus reveal the untainted Word. This untainted text that we lack and hence must imagine, however, necessarily impugns the text we do have, the Holy Scriptures. These become impure versions of Moses' story, purified by deMille using impure historians to recuperate the possibility of an imaginary pure text.

Just as the imaginary scriptures replace (and discredit) the Holy Scriptures, the imaginary Moses replaces (and discredits) the scriptural Moses. Needing more purification, deMille's speech resorts to another authority:

> The theme of this picture is whether men ought to be ruled by God's law or whether they are to be ruled by the whims of a dictator like Rameses. Are men the property of the state or are they free souls under God? This same battle continues throughout the world today. Our intention was not to create a story but to be worthy of the divinely inspired story created three thousand years ago: The Five Books of Moses.

The story is now true, according to deMille, because it replicates a struggle in the contemporary world. At the same time, of course deMille's interpretation of the contemporary world gains veracity from its biblical source. The parallels between the cold war and the Scriptures, with the film—the imaginary version of each—as the mediator, provide the necessary empirical evidence. The imaginary version thus allows the Scriptures to supplement the cold war and the cold war to supplement the Scriptures. Each subsumes the other in a symbiosis that revises the First Amendment so that freedom is not a prerequisite for religious practice, but rather religion is a prerequisite for freedom; the Bill of Rights—the first ten amendments—conflates into the Ten Commandments. To have rights means to be commanded, if the commander is the True commander, the proof of which the film provides for contemporary audiences, as Moses provided proof for the ancient world.

As deMille's filmed introduction indicates, however, the film's story derives its truth neither from the Bible nor historical documents, but from the way it supplements those documents with the truth of the world today, that is, from the narrative of containment. As a supplement to this supplement, moreover, deMille's researcher, Henry S. Noerdlinger, published concurrent with the film's release *Moses and Egypt: The Documentation to the Motion Picture "The Ten Commandments"* (with an introduction by deMille). If not the most outstanding example of pseudohistory published since World War II, then it is at least, one hopes, the singularly most bogus work ever published by a reputable university press.

Space does not permit a full examination of this supplementary book, but it is worth noting that its method relies on a few basic strategies. First it gathers every possible source without any attempt to authenticate one over the other, to discover points of corroboration, or to reconcile points of contradiction. It then selects eclectically and conveniently from among them. It also makes admittedly arbitrary choices and then treats the choices as established facts in order to legitimize subsequent choices. After acknowledging, for example, that there is no way to determine the actual pharaohs with whom Moses dealt, the book explains that a precise historical period had to be established because "This is a motion picture. The characters who bring it to life must have actual names. They must live and perform in reality. An historical void cannot be portrayed on the screen" (5). Therefore they decide to agree with the two scholars who "have rendered an opinion which establishes Rameses II . . . as the pharaoh of the Exodus" (8). From that point on, any details of Rameses II's life depicted in the film are used to indicate the film's probable accuracy. One historian's belief that he acquired the throne by intrigue, for example, inferentially supports the film's depiction of his intrigue against Moses.

Opposite the book's title page, a black-and-white photograph, a bit dark and grainy, shows a bearded man, probably in robes, definitely clutching what look like stone tablets. Beneath the photo is a one-word caption: "MOSES" and, to the right, in small italics, "Photo by Karsh." Although deMille tells us in the introduction that he had "consulted some 1,900 books and periodicals, collected nearly 3,000 photographs, and used the facilities of 30 libraries and museums in North America, Europe and Africa" (2), I do not think he intends that readers believe he unearthed a photograph of the great leader, one that uncannily resembles Charlton Heston; such a claim would mean deMille was obviously a lunatic. Rather I think that the photo, in some ways like the portrait of the royal couple in Velázquez's *Las Meninas*—so deftly analyzed by Michel Foucault—is meant to signify the consolidation of power through the creation of an artificial gaze in an artificial space.[8] It does not mean to show us Moses but rather to reveal the power of the film to construct the true Moses by having a camera mediate between the inadequate Word and the ignorant audience. As Wood notes, "De Mille liked to insist how much Charlton Heston as Moses resembled Michelangelo's rendering of him, but that is hardly the point. The point is not that Heston looks like an accepted and well-known version of Moses, but that Moses now, for generations of people all over the world, looks like Charlton Heston" (177). Only in the composite, to which the film testifies, can we see the true Moses. "Here, I hope," deMille writes in the introduction, "Jewish, Christian, and Moslem believers and the clergy of all faiths will find the light of archaeological and historical science illuminating the Word of God" (2). God's Word needs deMille's illumination, a point he emphasizes yet again at the conclusion of the introduction: "research does help bring out the majesty of the Lawgiver and the eternal verity of the Law" (3).

So does deMille's visual presence. When he parts the opening curtain, he parts the space where we will later see projected the parting of the *Red* Sea, the image demonstrating the power of monotheism and the doom it spells for atheistic totalitarianism. The parted curtain thus not only supplements but prophesies, anticipating what the film shows: the truth of the contemporary world, the incontrovertible truth of the one Maker of all images, whose values are unmistakably Western and whose home is the West rather than the East, with the Middle East forming the disputed margin between.

The dialectic of West and East had long formed an important dimension to deMille's metanarrative of the American epic, particularly in the films he made after the silent era. That metanarrative exemplifies perfectly what Edward Said has called "orientalism," that is, the discourse that divides the world into the "superior" Occident and the "inferior" Orient, the site of the racially, religiously, culturally "inadequate" other, in the name of whose "inadequacies" the Occident subjugates it. DeMille's manifestation of this orientalism emphasizes the religious "inferiority" of the Orient by showing a Christian world that originated in the East dislocated and forced west. As Charles Wolfe has aptly noted, "[H]istory [for deMille is] simply the ever repeating struggle of God's people against the forces of evil. Jew and Christians must contend with Egyptians and pagans, while American settlers battle Indians and pirates, but these godless enemies are essentially interchangeable" (98). Attempts at civilizing or reclaiming the East (e.g., as illustrated by *Sign of the Cross* [1932], *Cleopatra* [1934], *The Crusades* [1935], and *Samson and Delilah* [1949]) have proven less successful than those of civilizing and unifying the West (*The Plainsman* [1937], *The Buccaneer* [1938], *Union Pacific* [1939], *Northwest Mounted Police* [1940], *Unconquered* [1947]).[9] In *The Ten Commandments,* of course, deMille does redeem the Orient by converting it into the setting for an Occidental film, that is, by giving the name of the East to a composite of Western analogues, conventions, and idioms. In the process of marking the East as Christianity's other, he also performs on that Eastern site what Michel de Certeau identifies as the basic act of colonization—creating a discourse that makes the Other the Same.[10]

CORPORATE EGYPT

The ancient Egypt of *The Ten Commandments* thus strikingly resembles America after World War II. Like postwar America, it is undergoing massive expansion as marked by an increase in construction. Less like a nation than a corporation, deMille's Egypt is a construction company that builds pyramids, with the pharaoh as CEO. Linking government to industry as it does, the film presents an image of ancient Egypt very similar to an image of America promoted by government and big business in the early 1950s.[11]

Appropriately, this epic of the American postwar era introduces the adult Moses returning triumphant from war. Although he is not from the correct background and does not seem someone likely to take over corporate Egypt, his military experience indicates his leadership potential, a point not lost on the pharaoh, Sethi, who announces to his own son, Rameses, that he will select the next pharaoh based on merit. Moses, like many Americans not born to privilege, earns access to it by virtue of successful military service. Benign and apolitical, Sethi resembles President Eisenhower, and all of the women of the Egyptian court bear the unmistakable bangs that distinguished Mamie Eisenhower's hairstyle.

The women's participation in this fashion code uniformly marks their subordinate status—as potential "first ladies"—in the rigidly gendered distribution of power, as does more generally the cinematic gaze of classic Hollywood productions. As Laura Mulvey notes, the conventions of classic Hollywood cinema deny female subjectivity by forcing the viewer to totalize his or her view in a nonreciprocal relationship to the object of the gaze, which is constructed as feminine. In *The Ten Commandments*, the subordination of women consistently demonstrates that the wide-screen gaze—and the social and political power it both projects and signifies—are the property of men. From the outset, the plot gives the proprietary interests of women a subordinate status: they achieve through the men they acquire. Bithiah, having lost one man, a husband, and therefore unable to acquire another, a son, is derided. Nefretiri, introduced as the woman who will marry the next pharaoh, is also defined by the man she will acquire. She is destined for the CEO, whoever he may be, because, for someone of her class, a life with middle management is out of the question. With her role set, her only freedom comes in helping the right man to acquire Egypt so that she may acquire the right man. This dependence on acquiring the appropriate man identifies Nefretiri with Bithiah, a connection reinforced by a strong facial resemblance, itself reinforced by the curtain of Mamie Eisenhower bangs that they both wear.

If the classic cinematic gaze, as Mulvey argues, provides pleasure voyeuristically, it is not surprising that these women must acquire pleasure through their men. Their method of acquiring the men, through manipulation and deceit, is equally indirect. To keep Moses, Bithiah removes the truth of his origins by ordering her servant, Memnet, to destroy the Hebrew cloth. But Memnet, practicing one woman's deceit to counter another's, instead hides it. Years later, to save the adult Moses, Nefretiri kills Memnet. Both Bithiah and Nefretiri use deceit to win their man; for the same man, in fact, they practice the same deceit: the covering up of his Hebrew origins. They must keep this secret not only because it threatens his corporate advancement but also because it identifies the source of the exotic Otherness.

The sexual dimensions of that Otherness are underscored by the prize he brings of Ethiopia. Jewels, ornaments, exotic dancing girls follow the Ethiopian king and his sister, who come not as hostages but as friends. The Ethiopian princess, highly salacious in her gaze, announces her affection for Moses, who, as her brother's ally and her sexual object, becomes the

exotic's exotic. Moses thus colonizes the blacks at the same time as he titil-
lates the fair Egyptian women beneath their dark Mamie bangs and, with
his swarthy, hirsute appearance, shows up the pale, bald Egyptian men.
Just as his Jewishness is the *dark* secret beneath his Caucasian cover, the
oddity (and, from the film's perspective, beauty) of that white cover is the
seductive appearance that colonizes Ethiopia. But Ethiopia itself, as the distinctly American accent of its black royalty makes clear, is a cover, a code
name for black America, subordinated even in its sexual exoticism to Moses'
Caucasian virility.

The 1950s' anxiety and fear about black American culture, so vividly
manifested in the work of Norman Podhoretz, Leslie Fiedler, and Norman
Mailer—and in the case of the latter two about sexuality itself—here is resolved as the blacks not only "come back to the raft ag'in" but become (in
Twain's ironic understanding of the term) "sivilized."[12] If we read Podhoretz,
Mailer, and Fiedler, moreover, as expressing a specifically *Jewish* anxiety
about the racial and sexual Other, that is, as expressing a displacement of
the American Jew's own sense of Otherness, then Moses' colonization of
the Ethiopians signifies the elimination of that anxiety by simultaneously
making Jewishness more exotic than blackness yet also fully disguisable.[13] It
thus becomes an exoticism always apparent but always apparent as something else; the covering up of the Hebrew cloth is itself a cover for a larger
truth that the successive parting of curtains both prophesies and reveals.

This exoticism, however sexual—that is, however much represented by
the Ethiopian princess's and Nefretiri's leers, or by the Hollywood-style
close-ups of Moses and Nefretiri in romantic clinches—is more important as
a source of industrial capital, a point Moses makes when he reveals to Sethi
"the full count of Ethiopia's tribute": a sampling of the barges full of wealth
still in transit, to adorn Sethi's new city. Moses' potential to service Nefretiri sexually thus becomes synonymous with his potential to be of service
to Egypt. The wide-screen close-ups that make parallel the gazes of Sethi
and of Nefretiri on Moses triumphant over Ethiopia thus signify a visual
contract to commodify the dark secrets of Moses' origins. Since the wide
screen is an extreme version of classic Hollywood cinema's totalizing gaze,
it is the apotheosis of what Teresa de Lauretis has termed a "technology of
gender," by which she means the "techniques and discursive strategies by
which gender is constructed and hence . . . violence is engendered" (38).
In this light, if Sethi's and Nefretiri's shared gaze marks the commodifi-

cation of Moses' sexuality, Sethi's and Moses' shared gaze will in return commodify Nefretiri's.

But the wide-screen gaze, signifying America's global designs and its theological mandate, is itself a commodity. The film thus makes Moses the possessor rather than the object of the gaze and through Moses casts that gaze on the appropriate site to fulfill its theological mandate. This process identifies the gaze as divine, male, and Christian. The ultimate object of the gaze, furthermore, is the West as indicated by its suitability of Western vistas for the wide screen. To the extent that the wide screen represents America's global vision, and thus signifies veracity, the various sites depicted in the film become more or less appropriate, depending on their suitability for wide-screen representation.

Moses thus proves his managerial potential through his ability to direct and fill the screen with Sethi's city. He succeeds because he relates to labor, showing compassion for the elderly and overworked, improving safety, giving a day off, and increasing pay by dipping into the pharaoh's reserve (of grain). Productivity rises, deadlines are met, Egypt prospers, and Sethi is honored with great monuments. Again a drawn curtain reveals the truth, this time at Moses' construction site headquarters, situated on a pavilion in an undefined space, both close enough to direct the construction (by waving a series of flags) and far enough away to view the huge city in its entirety. From this pavilion, Moses busily checks blueprints, shouts instructions to subordinates, and looks through an instrument suggesting a sexton, lensless telescope, and director's viewfinder. In his autobiography deMille, in fact, compares his directing of over eight thousand extras to Moses' organization of subordinates (428), and as Wood has pointed out, the "hero of *The Ten Commandments* is not Moses, but De Mille himself, who set up the whole show, the voice of God and the burning bush and the miracles in Egypt included" (173). Like deMille himself, Moses is involved at all levels of production; his authority is universal and, in keeping with the privileging of cinematic reality, so is his gaze, which becomes the impossible view, constructed through the conflation of distance and the use of suture, to signify what many have identified as the gendered gaze of classic Hollywood cinema.[14]

In order to assert his own truthfulness, Moses thus invites Sethi to share that gaze and, like deMille, does so by drawing back a curtain, two curtains in fact, each running the length of a wall. The drawn curtains reveal

1   The perspective from picture windows, which the perspectives from Moses' pavilion anachronistically replicate.

a wide-screen panorama of the sort seen from the huge picture windows that represented the sublime in 1950s' residential architecture. In fact, as it is not too hard to see, the views, shaped like picture windows, are movie projections, simulating the perspective from picture windows that the openings in Moses' pavilion anachronistically replicate (figure 1). The projected vision, moreover, signifies industrial expansion made efficient not through the struggles of labor but through the benevolence of big business.[15] In 1951 the editors of *Fortune,* promoting the idea that Moses' management style puts into practice, wrote that modern management "exhibits a sense of responsibility toward its employees, not only to prevent or anticipate the demands of labor unions . . . but for the simple, obvious, and honest reason that a satisfied loyal group of employees is at least as much of an asset as a modern plant or a vital piece of machinery."[16]

Once again the drawn curtain reveals truth—the truth of a simulated perspective uniting the gaze of Egyptians with that of Americans looking through a real picture window and discovering a view sublime because it simulates wide-screen movies, which in turn comprise the only medium through which America can be "truly" apprehended. If, as deMille has indicated, Rameses personifies communist totalitarianism, Moses effectively wins the cold war when he gets Sethi to share his wide-screen gaze, his global vision. But such a victory belongs to a nation that does not yet exist, and the film subsequently distances itself from the Egyptian sites by demonstrating their subsequent unsuitability for wide-screen projection, substituting panoramas associated with Christianity and with the West as a western movie.

DOMESTIC LIFE IN METROPOLITAN AND SUBURBAN EGYPT

The Egyptian world, which occupies about three-quarters of the film, has three chief sites of conflict, corresponding to class distinctions. The Egyptian court signifies the upper management/country club set; the Goshen hovel of Moses' family, the working class; and the suburban patio of Baka the master builder, middle management.

Goshen in the film is something like the rough equivalent to Brooklyn—the place where the Jewish people live. The Goshen hovel, although associated with sincerity, comfort, and family values, visually signifies confinement, not only because the set affords few entrances and surrounds the screen with a thick brown border of stone and earth, but also because deMille refrains to a large extent from suturing together a totalizing view, relying on the actors' movements and crosses to provide visual variety. Although this results in long takes that Andre Bazin has associated with "realism," it does so by substituting the visual conventions of the theater for those of the wide screen.

If the hovel fails to fill the wide-screen gaze, Baka's suburban patio dissects it. Only a small section of the house behind is revealed through an opening identical in size and shape to the sliding glass doors that connected patio with den in the architecture of countless 1950s' single-story, "ranch"-style houses, and "split-level" ranches. And even Baka's outdoor fire suggests the barbecues that adorned such patios.[17] These houses, inextricably connected to the massive growth of suburbia during that decade, were promoted, according to Clifford Clark, with a family philosophy in mind. The 1950s' housing crusade was, as Clark notes, "a central part of a larger perfectionist impulse that swept through postwar American society. Like the crusade to halt communism and the belief that antibiotics would eliminate germs forever, the justification for the postwar housing boom was part of a one-dimensional frame of mind that stressed the possibility of creating the perfect society" (171).[18]

That society, however, was marked by a widely noted lack of privacy.[19] John Keats, in *The Crack in the Picture Window,* characterizes the constant flow of intrusion and lack of privacy as a corrosive social ill caused by economics, demographics, and architectural and social design. He is particularly critical of a universal and uniform air of sexual desire, noting that the "atmosphere of brooding sexual anxiety and frustration lurking over the thirty-two to thirty-eight-year-olds of Rolling Knolls," his fictional and paradigmatic suburban development, "was accentuated by the fact that it was a common problem. . . . Further, this atmosphere was deepened for everyone, every day, through the resources of TV, radio, newspapers and magazines . . ." (102).

In keeping with the conventions of the style, Baka's patio, walled off but still too close to the street to afford complete privacy, has a hinged gate that reminds us of the proximity of neighbors and of the vulnerability to intrusion and violation, which the plot bears out: First Baka attempts to violate Lilia, but Joshua intrudes. When Joshua is subdued by Baka's intruding soldiers, Moses, still coated in the mud of his brickpit, intrudes to save Joshua by killing Baka. Just before he dies, however, Baka penetrates Moses' disguise and reveals his identity. Joshua violates the secrecy of that revelation, and when Moses reveals to Joshua his Hebrew origins, the privacy of this revelation too is violated, this time by Dathan, who eavesdrops over the gate from the alley. The final gaze thus belongs to Dathan, looking in from outside, positioned such that the audience can neither assume his point of reference nor incorporate it into a unified view of the patio. The patio, in other words, fragments rather than confirms the wide-screen gaze, and thus cannot be confirmed by that gaze.

Its potential for allowing promiscuity, coupled with its vulnerability to intrusion, moreover, puts Baka's patio in distinct contrast to the royal palace, but marks it equally as a class signifier. In the palace, Bithiah may adopt a child with the same secrecy that Nefretiri may bring a paramour to her suite or kill to protect that paramour. Although both patio and palace are sites of murder and sexual encounter, the patio lacks the privacy and hence impunity of the upper-class domain. The middle-class patio mediates between the upper- and lower-class settings, sharing the drawbacks of both: like the royal suites it permits sexual indiscretion, deceit, and murder, and like the lower-class hovel it is vulnerable to intrusion.

Securing neither the values of the poor nor the impunity of the rich, the suburban patio, the film tells us, contains danger—the danger of an economy that depends upon, no matter what else, the commodification of women. From the outset, Nefretiri is the commodity that accrues to the throne; Lilia, her counterpart in the subplot, as a slave is also a commodity. The question for both of them is in what economy they will function. When Dathan sees Moses kill Baka, that economy is established. To purchase this information Rameses not only gives Baka's estate to Dathan but also gives him Lilia, and in so doing Rameses acquires the estate of Egypt and Nefretiri. In realizing the potential to which they were born, each of these women has financial comfort in unhappy marriages, and the "unhappy marriage" from this point on becomes the film's signifier of evil. It represents both the cause of Egypt's downfall and the sign of subversion within the Hebrew camp.

HOW TO CATCH A JEWISH HUSBAND

In contrast, Moses' marriage to Sephora seems ideal. When she speaks with Moses, for example, she compares herself to the women of the Egyptian aristocracy in a way that articulates a system of middle-class values for 1950s' wives: "Our hands are not so soft but they can serve, our bodies not so white but they are strong. Our lips are not perfumed, but they speak the truth. Love is not an art to us; it's life to us. We are not dressed in gold and fine linen; strength and honor are our clothing. Our tents are not the columned halls of Egypt, but our children play happily before them. We can offer you little, but we offer you all we have."

Although, of course, the 1950s' housewife would not have needed a strong body to herd sheep (any more than she would live in a tent), like Sephora she was expected to privilege utility over pleasure. Sephora's speech thus stands her in direct contrast not only to Nefretiri (the "woman of Egypt who has left her scar upon your heart") but also to all those in Bithiah's country club who associate wealth with the ability to acquire a man. As one of them says, to the laughing approbation of the others, "I'd rather have gold than a man—with enough gold I could have any man." For a woman to pursue wealth overtly or to make a man her acquisition instead of trying to be his is to violate the gender rules of the 1950s. Stressing her role as homemaker and procreator, Sephora articulates postwar values. As Elaine Tyler May aptly put it,

> Procreation in the cold war era took on almost mythic proportions . . . for individuals, parenthood was much more than a duty to posterity; the joys of raising children would compensate for the thwarted expectations in other areas of their lives. For men who were frustrated at work, for women who were bored at home, and for both who were dissatisfied with the unfulfilled promise of sexual excitement, children might fill the void. Through children, men and women could set aside the difficulties of their sexual relationships and celebrate their procreative results. In so doing, they also celebrated their loyalty to national goals. . . . (136)

Reflecting this 1950s' cult of domesticity, Sephora lauds not her home's splendor but its suitability for family life. In explaining that her children could play happily before her "tents," moreover, she echoes the rationale promoted by Levittown and subsequent suburban developments, and explains implicitly why the picture windows faced the streets, where they afforded the sublime view not of landscape but of domesticity.

In characterizing her sexual desires, as well, Sephora adheres to the conventional wisdom as reflected, for example, in *Modern Woman: The Lost Sex*, a Freudian justification for the domestication of women after the war, by Marynia Farnham and Ferdinand Lundberg. One of the most influential postwar books on the role of women, it was "paraphrased ad nauseam in the magazines and in marriage courses," notes Betty Friedan, "until most of its statements became part of the conventional, accepted truth of our time" (119). Invoking the authority of science, its authors made proscriptive assertions about all aspects of women's experience. About sexual fulfillment, for example, they declare: "The rule [is]: The less a woman's desire to have children, and the greater her desire to emulate the male in seeking a sense of personal value by objective exploit, the less will be her enjoyment of the sex act and the greater her general neuroticism" (265). "Of all the conditions met with in marital sexual difficulties of women," they explain clinically, "[having clitoral orgasms] would certainly rate highest" (267). Clitoral orgasm is problematic, they indicate, because it "[bespeaks] a very definite lack of acceptance of femininity" and also "contributes to a feeling of insufficiency in the man and is derogatory of his organ" (266–67). They consider "feminist ideology" "an expression of emotional sickness, of neurosis" (143) caused by penis envy (140–67). They further recommend that *"all spinsters be barred by law from having anything to do with the teaching of children on the ground of theoretical (usually real) emotional incompetence. All public teaching posts now filled by women would be reserved not only for married women but for those with at least one child, with provision made for necessary exceptions"* (364–65; emphasis *not* added).[20] They are adamant that every aspect of a woman's psychological and sexual health and happiness depends on her desire and ability to have and raise children. Sephora's speech reflects these beliefs by indicating that, for her, sex does not serve diversion—an "art"—but reproduction—"life."

Having thus renounced her need for beauty or sexual pleasure, Sephora has of course defined herself as lacking. All that remains is for her to accept her inadequacies, which she does by responding, when Moses asks whether she would fill the emptiness in his heart, "I could never fill all of it, Moses, but I shall not be jealous of a memory." She has now established the economy of her role as completely commensurate with the political economy of the cold war. By relinquishing her right to jealousy, she compensates for her failure to provide the qualities of which she might be jealous, and thus she allows Moses to desire what she cannot provide—soft hands, white bodies, perfumed lips. In exchange for agreeing to live with this unrequited desire, he acquires the reward of suburban domesticity—a private home, a safe neighborhood, an undemanding wife.

Most significant, all the intimate interchanges between Moses and Sephora take place outdoors, with the panoramic terrain of desert and mountain filling the wide screen, and the mountain in the background identified as God's "temple." Implying the frontier as much as the Holy Land, these scenes use the wide screen to suggest American geographic and theological manifest destiny as the appropriate context for the 1950s' cult of domesticity.

In contrast, the visual context for Rameses' marriage underscores the folly of marrying a woman who offers neither love nor support. Sethi's festive and airy court—identified as we have noted with Eisenhower's America—was visually valorized by filling the wide screen, as was the city Moses constructed for him. Rameses' muted and diminished interiors, on the other hand, preclude expansive physical activity and, despite numerous entrances, reveal few open spaces. In thus acquiring a marriage that cannot fill the wide screen—Moses and Sephora *only* speak together in outdoor scenes—Rameses indicates his poor management potential.

Nefretiri's biggest fault is that she puts her own desires above her husband's (and her husband's corporation). When those desires are frustrated, she subordinates everything—including her firstborn—to revenge. Nefretiri, therefore, not Rameses, causes the plagues and deaths because Rameses' actions respond to Nefretiri's emasculating taunts. Her subordinating maternal concerns to sexual is represented as a compact with Satan, a connection emphasized by Rameses' serpent allusion: "I would not let his people go because your serpent's tongue hardened my heart. You only thought to keep Moses here. You cared nothing for my throne or my son." The Satanic compact is manifested visually when she dedicates Rameses' sword before the slain son, still lying on the altar of the Dread Lord of Darkness. Nefretiri thus becomes the medium of exchange connecting doomed son to damned father and illustrates her role in connecting the son of the pharaoh's body— as Rameses has been called—to the body of the pharaoh's son. When Rameses in response promises to mingle Moses' blood with hers, he makes her success equal her self-destruction. She thus renders her life worthless other than as a functionary in a plan larger than her own. But that is exactly how deMille sees her. As Noerdlinger explains, "A difficulty arose in the writing of the script of *The Ten Commandments*. How can a man, a creature of God, make the choice between good and evil of his own free will, if God hardens his heart? Our solution is given, when Nefretiri says to Moses, 'Who else can soften Pharaoh's heart—or harden it?' To which Moses replies that it may well be *she* through whom 'God will work his wonder' (27; emphasis added). DeMille's strategy is acutely glossed by Christine Froula's insightful analysis of Milton's treatment of Eve: "in order for her to serve as the idealized currency of patriarchal culture, Eve's intrinsic value must be denied; her self, her subjectivity, must be *de*valued to resemble the worthless paper on which the inscription designating money, or credit, is stamped. Eve's subjectivity, her being-for-herself, is the paper upon which patriarchal authority imprints its own valuation" (335). Making Nefretiri the agent of evil at the same time as he denies her agency—in other words, making her Eve—deMille reinscribes the Christian myth of Original Sin in the body of the woman.

THE REAL JEW

The film also reflects Christian ideology by manifesting a theory of Christian typology, that is, a system of biblical interpretation designed to show "history's relations to its fulfillment in Christ" (Charity, 1). Under the theory's circular relationship between prefiguration and fulfillment, the New Testament acquires its validity by fulfilling Old Testament prophesy. The Old Testament thus acquires contingent status as prefiguring the true Savior. In this context, as Jean Danielou points out, "universal Christian tradition has seen, in the people, events and institutions of the Exodus, types of the New Testament and the Sacraments of the Church" (153).[21]

The film emphasizes these connections by referring to Moses as the Deliverer. Although Noerdlinger indicates no precedent for this term, as the film presents it, a Deliverer prophesied to lead the Jews from bondage creates constant fear for the Egyptians and hope for the Jews. Contrary to the account in Exodus, deMille makes this prophesy the motive for the order to kill the male Hebrew children, the order that initially caused Moses' mother to set her infant son adrift. The film skips over the period from Moses' nativity, allegedly predicted by the stars, to the events that lead to his recognition as Hebrew and as prophesied Deliverer. Although Exodus does not supply the number of years between Moses' nativity and his first flight from Egypt, deMille indicates that the period was roughly the first thirty years of Moses' life. At age thirty, then, he disappears into the desert. When Moses returns to Egypt, he returns a changed man, the self-proclaimed savior of the Jews.

To help the film visually underscore these parallels to the life of Jesus, deMille wanted for his scenic designer "a powerful artist who knew how to create dramatic religious works" (Schwarz, 59). He chose one of the leading proselytical artists in America, Arnold Friberg, who was at the time completing a series illustrating the *Book of Mormon,* one of the goals of which was to represent Amerindian, Native American, and Polynesian peoples as lost tribes of Israel that prefigure Christian redemption.[22] The film is invested with Friberg's expertise in typological reinscriptions of the New Testament. In order to create these powerful proselytic images, deMille had Friberg illustrate scenes from the story in much the way he illustrated the *Book of Mormon,* that is, "painting the unknown and portraying it in a way that evokes in the viewer a feeling that the images are authentic . . . that the events were not allegorical; they really happened to real people who have names and jobs and grandchildren" (Schwarz, 53). Like deMille's film, in other words, Friberg's paintings—and the look they gave to *The Ten Commandments*—found their truth in the way they mediated between the sacred Word and the world today, so as to sanctify deMille's secularizations.

Before his initial exile from Egypt, for example, Moses, betrayed by the Judas-like Dathan, is arrested by Rameses and presented before Sethi. At that presentation, Moses, clad in a loincloth and chained to a crossbar, replicates the T-shape of crucifixion. Sethi, unable to condemn Moses, turns him over to Rameses and washes his hands of the matter. When Moses crosses the desert on foot, wearing long robes, carrying a staff, and sprouting a beard, he resembles traditional representations of Jesus, and when he arrives at the oasis and saves the daughters of Jethro, Sephora washes his feet in a scene that replicates the iconography of the New Testament, not the Old.

A similar anachronism juxtaposing New Testament iconography with Old Testament events occurs on the night that the Angel of Death passes over houses marked by lamb's blood. In the home of Moses' family, his nephew asks the Passover questions to which Moses, of course, cannot give the traditional answers because the ceremony commemorates an event that has not yet occurred. DeMille's researcher tries to account for this by indicating that the Passover service in Egypt, according to some of the commentaries, differed from later versions (Noerdlinger, 28–31), but the visual representation—the long table with Moses at the center and his followers clustered at either side, leaning, eating, listening—suggests a different explanation for the anachronistic scene: that it represents another Passover centuries later, at which the "true" Deliverer of the Jews had his last supper. The film merges the two saviors to reveal the greater truth of the imaginary Moses: beneath his Hebrew robes he was Jesus in disguise, and his role is to facilitate the revelation of truth in the coming of Christ. Thus the film ends with Sephora reminding Moses, as he watches the tribes cross to the Promised Land, that he taught them—as Jesus would reiterate—that man does not live by bread alone.[23]

The validity and implicit connection of that reminder are affirmed when the film's closing sequence sutures two panoramic gazes, both including Moses and both attributed to him. The viewer first looks *at* him and then *with* him, over his shoulder, at the Hebrews heading for the River Jordan between two vast expanses of mountains (figure 2). The scene replicates the familiar image of wagon trains taking "civilization" to the West. In the next shot, Moses, flanked by Joshua and Sephora, bequeaths his staff to Joshua (figure 3). Then a close-up shows Joshua and Lilia in costumes that suggest the Crusades more than the Old Testament (figure 4). Next Moses makes his farewells, then walks further up the mountain to answer God's call. When Moses looks back, the film cuts to a close-up as he delivers his benediction. We then see the object of his wide gaze: the panoramic vista of river and mountains, the distant wagon-train-like migration of Hebrews, and the near cluster of Moses' friends and family (figure 5). This view is complemented by an equally vast and equally sublime shot of Moses on a higher mountain ledge, against the horizon of textured and darkly tinted clouds cut by broad rays of sunlight (figure 6). Moses looks up and turns partially back. In this totalizing sequence, the viewer sees Moses from both directions, looks over his shoulder from both directions, and sees what he sees in both directions. Jean-Pierre Oudart and Daniel Dayan have argued that suture always implies the "absent one." If, as Stephen Heath points out, for Oudart the "absent one" is a theological construct and for Dayan an ideological one, this sequence—constructing Moses at both ends of his gaze as the omnipresent absent one who, even in his absence, owns and distributes 360 degrees of the screen's panorama—closes the film by underscoring the intersection of theology and ideology.

When the wide screen emphasizes Moses' role as the corporal figure with a divine gaze, moreover, it contributes to the film's general process of effecting exactly the assimilation that its character, Moses, resists. It resolves the problem of unassimilated Jews in corporate Egypt/America by redefining them as proto-Christians.

The relationship validated by Christian (and Mormon) typology finds its parallel not only in the film's rendition of Moses as Jesus but in its rhetorical structure, as it uses the past both to anticipate the cold war and to prophesy it. The cold war's similarity to the conditions of deMille's Egypt attests simultaneously to the truth of deMille's representation of the past and the religious mandate for containment. Once more the "truth" of the film itself transcends that of its sources by mediating between the Holy Scriptures and the contemporary world, the world in which Hollywood produced films, organized labor, created false images, and, if HUAC was correct, sometimes participated in subverting the public. That subversion—both political and

2 The Hebrews heading for the River Jordan. **3** Moses, flanked by Joshua and Sephora, bequeaths his staff to Joshua. **4** Joshua and Lilia in costumes that suggest the Crusades.

5 The object of Moses's gaze is revealed.

theological—effected through the worship of false images threatened all "loyal" moviemakers by tainting their false images with the charge that left them defenseless. As producers of falsity they were most vulnerable to the charge of corrupting the public with lies. DeMille, an avid red-hunter, was particularly aware of this. According to Victor Navasky, his Cecil B. DeMille Foundation "regularly provided information to California's 'little HUAC,' The Tenny Committee, and to the real HUAC in Washington" (179). In another effort to keep the movies "safe," he led a campaign to require mandatory loyalty oaths of all members of the Screen Directors Guild and, at one point, introduced a motion that would have forced directors to file reports with the SDG summarizing whatever they could find out about the political beliefs of all those who had worked on the film.[24]

In light of these political beliefs, deMille's obsession with the truthfulness of his production can be viewed as his evoking transcendent authority to vindicate his professional practice, a practice not to be measured by the financial bottom line, but by the moral.[25] As such, the film can also be viewed as an autobiographical statement. Although deMille never mentions the fact in his autobiography, devoting only one circumspect sentence to her origins, his mother Beatrice was Jewish.[26] She abandoned that faith to marry Charles

6 Moses on a higher mountain ledge.

deMille, who studied for the ministry but before being ordained changed careers and became a successful playwright. Charles deMille continued to see this as a theological calling, subsequently passed from father to son: "[my mother] told him that . . . in the church he might be able to speak to thousands—through the theater he might be able to speak to hundreds of thousands—and then when I came along the mantle fell upon my shoulders in a new form which was the motion picture, and I was able to reach hundreds of millions" (Koury, 49). Disseminating that Christian message, however, depended upon Jewish businessmen, and just as his father owed his career to the Jewish theatrical entrepreneur David Belasco, deMille owed his to the vast array of Jews who built Hollywood.[27]

So not just American business in general but deMille's life work in particular were redeemed through this refiguring of Moses as, on the one hand, the forerunner of Christ and, on the other, the champion of the cold war. By presenting this Truth on the wide-screen production financed by Adolph Zukor's Paramount Studio, deMille disciplines the infusion of Jews into corporate America with the myth of Christian redemption. Just as Christianity becomes the category that validates Judaism, deMille's film validates the Jewish origins of its own production by subsuming them under the rubric of cold war Christianity. Jews in high places need not be feared, the film indicates, because such Jews are proto-Christians, *not* like those Jews that are actually disguised atheist intellectuals, that is, communists. In this scheme, the "free world" is safe because true Jews are Christians and subversives are false Jews.

Lest we have any doubt that this is the way labor "naturally" distributes in the free world, deMille's own deployment of labor makes this graphic. For his original *Ten Commandments,* he brought several hundred Orthodox Jews from Los Angeles to the film site in Guadalupe because, he explained, "we believed rightly that, both in appearance and in their deep feeling of the significance of the Exodus, they would give the best possible performance as the Children of Israel. . . . They *were* the Children of Israel. This was their Exodus, their liberation. They needed no direction from me . . ." (de-Mille, 252–53). In the making of *Samson and Delilah,* deMille also attended closely to the appropriate Jewishness of his players, insisting, according to producer Jesse Lasky, that Samson's female companion, Miriam, be "the hometown-girl-next-door, the honest Hebrew maiden that Samson should have married" (Erins, 226). "Unfortunately," Patricia Erins notes, "among the contract actresses only 'pure Irish-Americans' were available and director deMille was insisting on a 'Jewish Jewess,' [so they] found Olive Deering, a former actress from the Jewish theater" (226).

In casting the 1956 *Ten Commandments,* however, deMille found no need to place actual Jews other than one—in this light, particularly significant—exception. The only Jew cast in a major role in *The Ten Commandments* is Edward G. Robinson (whose real name was Emanuel Goldenberg), playing Dathan.[28] The other leading "Jews"—Charlton Heston as Moses, John Derek as Joshua—mark their non-Jewishness with strikingly blue eyes. A blue-eyed Canadian actress named Peggy Middleton, whose stage name was Yvonne DeCarlo, plays Moses' wife. Robinson's role, therefore, is particularly significant because it turns out to be the role of the false Jew—the Jew who betrays the Deliverer (Savior), who rejects Moses, who subverts his followers, who worships the golden calf, and who must, therefore, be purged so that the Jews might be delivered to freedom rather than live under the rule of a godless tyrant like Rameses (or his counterparts in the world today). The only real Jew is the dead Jew, the Jew who in betraying his Deliverer is not Jew but Judas.

In the context of the geopolitical conflicts of 1956, *The Ten Commandments* thus reclaims the Middle East not as a Jewish homeland but as part of the Judeo-Christian tradition, that is, the American sphere of influence. *The Ten Commandments'* production period, 1953–1956, saw the rise of Nasser in Egypt, increased tension in the Suez area leading to multinational crisis and conflict, and Egyptian overtures to the U.S.S.R. At stake was the policy of containment and the increasingly valuable Middle Eastern oil supply. Until the 1950s, the West in general and the United States in particular had little need for imported oil, but the massive postwar expansion in American industry, housing, and auto production reorganized priorities and dependencies. In claiming the Middle East for the American/Judeo-Christian free world, deMille contributes to America's global economic policy by claiming the site of oil in the name of God. To put it another way, he was justifying containment by uniting America's political, economic, and theological interests in the West's claim on a Middle Eastern site.

Less than two decades earlier, America had been a staunchly isolationist nation, but the experience of World War II and, more significantly, the technological advances in transportation made Americans dependent on a global economy, as well as vulnerable to foreign assault. The ability to import and export, to deliver goods and services, to deliver nuclear warheads, to transport and to be transported: these created the privileged pavilion for America's global view, and that pavilion rested on a field of oil.

It is not surprising, therefore, that in claiming the Middle East, *The Ten Commandments* participates in a global vision shared by many of the major motion picture productions of 1956. In 1956, the economic boom of the 1950s hit its peak. The Academy Award nominees for best picture that year contained no small or moderate productions like the 1955 Best Picture, *Marty,* or the 1954 Best Picture, *On the Waterfront.* Instead, in addition to *The Ten Commandments,* the list included *The King and I, Friendly Persuasion, Giant,* and the winner, *Around the World in Eighty Days.* In addition to being large, extensive, elaborate, and long movies, each was a period piece.[29] All, in other words, grapple with history and its representation and thus unavoidably reinvent the past. The goal of that revision, like the goal of the VistaVision and CinemaScope lenses, was to shed the light of new vision over the wide expanse made possible by the confluence of technology and consumption. If *Friendly Persuasion*'s Quaker saga set in the Civil War is about the coexistence of hot and cold wars, *Around the World in Eighty Days* about technology and global dominance, *The King and I* about the civilizing (i.e., colonizing) of the East, and *Giant* about the new power of oil in the West, *The Ten Commandments* makes more legible than any of the others the religious authority by which all these makers of 1956 cultural images let there be (wide-screen, Technicolor) light.

5. LADY AND (OR) THE TRAMP

Sexual Containment and the

Domestic Playboy

As Elaine Tyler May has well documented, America in the 1950s practiced the cult of domesticity as a form of political and social containment for the sexual energies of post–World War II teenagers and young
adults, congruent to and commensurate with the American foreign and
domestic policy of containing communism. This containment of sexuality
permeated the full spectrum of American culture in the decade following
the war and contributes to explanations of such varied cultural phenomena
as strictly censored television programming, the drop in average marriage
age, the suburban housing development, the public elaboration of dating
etiquette, and the rigidly constrictive and restrictive structure of female
undergarments. As many have noted, moreover, the responsibility for this
containment in the postwar era fell on women, whose role was to resist and
channel the "natural" sexual energies of men. Female sexuality thus had the
burden of supporting the monolithic goals of cold war America through the
practice of duplicity: the woman had to attract and stimulate male sexual
drives but not gratify them. Female sexuality was thus always double—it
had to be the thing that would gratify a normal male's sexual desires for
the rest of his life while not doing so during courtship; it had to signify
abstinence and promise gratification; it had to indicate its presence through
absence.

Necessarily internalizing this duplicity, American women in the 1950s
became the conflicted site upon which the nature of sexual license was both
encoded and delimited. Two of the most popular films of the 1950s, *Lady
and the Tramp* (1955) and *Pillow Talk* (1959), can be read as articulating the
conflict over the role of female sexuality by simultaneously valorizing and
domesticating male sexuality, as represented by the "playboy." Each does

so, moreover, by focusing on the female, situating the sexually active male in relation to her, such that his sexuality becomes contingent on her sense of role, her female identity.

DOMESTICATED PETS AND DOMESTIC SECURITY IN DISNEY'S AMERICA

Even the title *Lady and the Tramp,* for example, marks this double role. Ostensibly the names of the two central characters—a domesticated female spaniel named Lady and a street-smart male mutt named Tramp—the names also identify the two sexual roles available to 1950s' females, "lady" or "tramp." As in the etiquette books of the day, the health education films, and the advice manuals for teenagers, in the film's title we are reminded that male sexual activity depends on the role the woman plays. The woman's ability to contain the man's sexual drives, in other words, was synonymous with her ability to preserve her good name.

In the movie we watch Lady move rapidly from puppyhood to maturity, that is, the point at which she acquires a license. As a condition of the plot, the license indicates not a birth registration but a coming of age. It signifies her physical maturity and thus, unavoidably, her sexual license. But Lady, true to her name, is still innocent, a point underscored by her inability to understand her mistress's pregnancy and her confession to her two older male protectors, Trusty and Jock, that she has never been told about the birds and the bees.

Exactly at this point, when she has acquired her license and been told about reproduction, she meets Tramp, who does not identify himself by name but as "the voice of experience." He has all the experience she lacks, knows exactly what pregnancy signifies, and also rejects domesticity. If she is innocent and domesticated, he is experienced and undomesticated. He thus forces Lady to compare her form of license with his. Hers entails accepting domestic obligations, the clichés of bourgeois life, and a socially stable role—all things that Tramp debunks, for Tramp associates domestication with loss of personal freedom. When he first wanders into Lady's neighborhood, he says "So this is life among the leash and collar set," clearly associating the collar not with the license that dangles from it but with the leash that controls it. He similarly identifies the prospect of a baby with the loss of freedom and comfort and dismisses the cliché uttered by Jock that "Man is a dog's best friend."

Even after this encounter, Lady maintains her innocence with a long contemplative song wondering what a "baby" is, but after the birth, Lady, reincorporated into the family scheme, accepts with alacrity her gendered responsibilities within the traditional distribution of domestic power. For a weekend, Jim Dear and Darling leave Lady and the baby in the care of a cat-loving maiden aunt who, in effect, treats dogs as undomesticated animals, thus denying Lady her domestic role of protecting the baby. In Lady's altercation with the aunt's Siamese cats, in which the cats destroy the domestic setting of the parlor, attempt to eat the goldfish—another domesticated pet—and try to steal the baby's milk, Lady is seen as the threat, driven out of the house, and taken to be muzzled. In the aunt's eyes, in other words, Lady has been given too much license; she has been given access to the domestic setting which that license threatens; she has, in short, failed to live up to her name. The contrast between Lady and the aunt becomes especially marked in regard to their understanding of what it means to be a "lady." By showing the treachery of the cats, the film too critiques the aunt's definition. Not Lady's license but the aunt's interpretation of it poses the real threat to the domestic scene.

Thus, in trying to muzzle Lady instead of trusting her, she drives Lady into the hands (or paws) of Tramp. The second half of the film shows Lady's adventures on the other side of the tracks, the site where unlicensed behavior occurs, the world of the "tramp." The sexual implications of this escape from domesticity are emphasized repeatedly. First Lady is pursued and trapped in a blind alley by three brute mutts, in a scene that suggests attempted rape. What, after all, could these pursuing dogs be after? Dogs don't eat other dogs, and she has nothing they could steal. Clearly their eye has been caught and their passions inflamed by the sight of a vulnerable female. After rescuing her, Tramp rids Lady of the muzzle the aunt had put on, thus freeing Lady to have a romantic, candlelit dinner, wander freely through the city, and spend the night with an attractive young male—in other words, to experience the life of a tramp.

At dawn, after they have spent the night together, Tramp invites Lady to live with him, an invitation she finds attractive but about which she has a crucial reservation. "That sounds wonderful," she says, "but who will take care of the baby?" Were it not for this one consideration, she could

7 Gathered in the pound are an international set of social outcasts.

succumb to the temptations of a tramp's life. But the "baby," the responsibility attached to her sexual license and the cult of domesticity that that responsibility entails, defines the difference between Lady and Tramp.

Acknowledging this difference, Tramp agrees to take Lady home, but before he gets her there she is caught by the dogcatcher and interred briefly in the pound where she sees the darker side of unlicensed behavior. Gathered in the pound are an international set of social outcasts (figure 7). Crude, vulgar, and unkempt, they represent the lower classes, trapped between poverty, desperation, and death. The futility of their situation is represented in several ways. The Chihuahua, like Sisyphus, digs, refills, and redigs the escape tunnel, a tunnel that at best will provide only temporary escape, a point underscored by the fact that some of the dogs now incarcerated were the same dogs Tramp had freed from the dogcatcher's wagon earlier. Victims of the unfortuitous confluence of heredity and environment, these pound creatures represent the world naturalist drama. The philosophical Borzoi, in fact, quotes from Maxim Gorki's great naturalist drama, *The Lower Depths*. Lady has moved from the middle-class world of romance—

the genre implied by her name—to the lower-class world of naturalism, the genre implied by Tramp's name.[1] There she sees the futile and tragic implications of Tramp's undomesticated and unlicensed behavior. This includes the "putting to sleep" of one dog, Nutsy, whom we only see represented by his shadow as he takes "the long walk" to the execution chamber. The sequence's strong allusion to prison films of the 1930s and 1940s obscures the fact that this animal—one of the few to die in the entire Disney opus[2]— is guilty of no crime other than homelessness. To be homeless, to promote homelessness, is to manifest behavior that challenges the social order. The sexual implications of that behavior are made explicit by the male dogs who list Tramp's sexual conquests and by the female dog, Peg, who explains in a song that "He's a tramp and I love him." And, although the song is about Tramp, in praising his sexuality while accepting its prodigiousness, it actually explains why the lady is a tramp. Accentuated by Peg's accent, the song strongly connects the gender and class implications of Tramp's name, so that the license of the hobo or bum merges with the license of the slut.

For Lady, these implications are profound. Silently she can add herself to the list of Tramp's conquests, that is, the list of tramps. She can also identify with Peg's positive appraisal; after all, she had already told Tramp that living with him sounds wonderful. Lady, in other words, has shared Peg's Tramp and can see herself in Peg's trampiness, an identification emphasized by the fact that the same actress, Peggy Lee, does both Peg's voice and Lady's. Despite this identification and/or because of it, Lady can also see the other tragic implications of such undomesticated license, of allowing herself to permit a liaison in which there is no one home to look after the baby.

Having a license, she is allowed to return home, a chastened woman, chained to her doghouse outside the domestic setting. She is also morally tainted by having tramped around. Her good name has been lost, and in an attempt to help her redeem it, her two male friends (and confirmed bachelors), Trusty and Jock, agree to propose marriage, thus underscoring that Lady's shame comes not from her day in the pound but from the night that preceded it. She indicates the same thing by rebuking Tramp—who arrives with an apologetic bone—not so much for his allowing her to be caught by the dogcatcher as for his promiscuity.

The moral implications are clear. Lady has failed the responsibilities that come with legitimate sexual license, that is, failed to domesticate the male and channel his sexual energies toward the interests of the baby *before* she spent the night with him. This failure has been acknowledged by Lady and her friends, and now the only way to redeem herself, to be worthy of her license, is to renounce Tramp on the basis of his unlicensed sexuality. No compromise here can be allowed, and the only possibility for the happy reconciliation of lovers must come from Tramp's proving he will renounce his former life for the license that comes with domestic responsibility. He must be willing, in other words, to be the answer to Lady's question: "Who will look after the baby?"

And that is exactly what happens. When the rat sneaks into the baby's bedroom, beyond the reaches of Lady's chain, Tramp responds to her call, enters the house through the trapdoor, pursues and destroys the insidious rat in a violent fight that results in his being wounded. Tramp is then mistaken for the attacker, trapped by the aunt, and sent to the pound where he will, the catcher implies, be immediately put to sleep. Tramp's redemption, his salvation from wrongful execution, and his eventual entrance into the domestic setting of Jim Dear and Darling's home, as a licensed husband and father, not only represent Lady's triumph as the domesticater of the American male and hence the licensed channeler of his and her own sexuality, but also indicate the political dimension of her role and, in general, of the cult of domesticity in 1950s' American ideology.

The film is divided into roughly two halves, the first focusing on Lady's life as a lady and the second on her life as a tramp. Both end with assaults on the baby by intruders that result in the ravaging of a domestic setting. In the first, the Siamese cats destroy the parlor as Lady tries to prevent them first from eating the goldfish (figure 8) and then from stealing the baby's milk. The visual representation of the cats draws heavily on the images of the Asian associated with World War II and Korean War propaganda. They are slant-eyed, shifty-eyed, insidious, grinning creatures, wearing expressions of predatory obsequiousness. True to the image of the "yellow menace," they are conspiratorial, subversive, malign. Although ostensibly domesticated, their goal is to subvert and exploit the domestic scene to their own ends. Although aggressors, they pose as victims.

Most important, in the lexicon of the 1950s, they are un-American, their un-Americanness emphasized from the outset, when they announce: "We are Siamese if you please; we are Siamese if you don't please." Everything about this announcement—the insidious reversal, the overly polite "if you

8 The Siamese cats destroy the parlor.

please" and the brashly rude "if you don't please," the false parallelism of the syntax, the clearly foreign accent of the voices and the music—everything tells us that these cats are double agents. Although they pose as domesticated, they are not domestic; they are foreign. Both their duplicity and their accents put them in direct contrast with Tramp, who is, as his speech demonstrates, quintessentially domestic. Although he can imitate an array of accents and ethnicities, his true identity is composite, an all-American product of the melting pot, able to tolerate and accommodate all of them without retaining a foreign allegiance that he places above domestic concerns. As he puts it, he has all of these (ethnic) homes, "But none of them have me."

His domestic character thus marks his potential for domestication, a potential that not only distinguishes him from the inscrutable Siamese in the first half of the film but also from the benevolent but pathetic pound animals in the second. Almost all the male dogs there are marked not only by their inability to obtain a license but by their foreign accents. (A few are marked

by distinctly lower-class American accents, thus suggesting an equation between the lower classes and potentially subversive immigrants.) More the
source of pathos than animus, they nevertheless fall outside the margins of
the domestic and cannot acquire licensed domesticity. The film thus uses
the potential for domestication to differentiate between "American" and
"un-American" activity. The "American" activity, in the final analysis, is to
look after the baby, to protect the domestic setting from, on the one hand,
the unassimilated underclass who weaken it, and, on the other, from the
subversive aliens who threaten it: the Siamese and the rat.

Not only their trashing of the domicile but also their physical representation link the cats to the rat. Like the rat, the cats are drawn with large
rear haunches, elongated tails, foreshortened front paws, slanty eyes, and
large teeth. The cats who want the baby's milk thus become subversive fore-
runners of the rat who wants the baby itself; their undetected subversion
gets Lady out of the way and paves the way for the more overt enemy, the
rat. Even in its death, moreover, the rat nearly succeeds in causing Tramp's
execution and completely discrediting Lady, who is blamed with abetting
Tramp's alleged assault on the baby.

In order to save Tramp from the injury fomented by these subversives
(and their naive dupe, the aunt, who always wears some pink garment or
trim), another American coalition must be formed, this time not ethnic but
regional. Recognizing their misjudgment of Tramp's character, Trusty and
Jock pursue and detain the dogcatcher's wagon. Both Trusty and Jock have
accents, but they are somewhat distinct from those of the pound inmates.
Jock's Scottish (terrier) accent, first of all, links him to WASP aristocracy, and
his frugal pragmatism, paired with Trusty's Southern drawl and manner-
isms and his nostalgia for a glorified past, suggest that Jock represents the
Yankee aristocrat and Trusty the Southern aristocrat. With slightly conde-
scending compassion for Trusty's lineage and lost youthful prowess, Jock
confides to Lady that Trusty has lost his sense of smell. But Trusty in unison with Jock marshals his faculties and rises to the cause of saving Tramp,
saving Tramp from the fate of the tramp. The coalition of North and South
thus recognizes the suitability of the ethnic composite for domestication.

The sexual license awarded to Tramp at the end—as evidenced by the
litter—becomes synonymous with the marriage license, both signified by
his new collar and tag. Tramp has protected the baby, been accepted by

9   This issue of domestic security is identified as a gender problem.

the Northern and Southern purebreeds, and been licensed by Jim Dear and Darling to mate with their Lady. By domesticating Tramp, Lady has earned the right to sexual activity and thus domesticated the tramp in herself. The duped aunt, ostensibly disabused of the ruses worked on her, also endorses the union with a Christmas gift. The national agenda too has been served, with Tramp assimilated into the stable domestic setting, adding extra protection against the future subversion by cats, or invasion by rats, and forever divorced from the ethnically or socially marginal, who are left to be purged by the elements, both natural and social.

In its final representation, moreover, this issue of domestic security is identified as a gender problem. For Lady and Tramp's litter consists of four females, all of whom resemble Lady's appearance and behavior, and one male who replicates exactly his father (figure 9). This mischievous pup needs constantly to be disciplined in ways that his female siblings do not. Prior to coming of age and receiving their own licenses, the sisters can allow their parents to discipline the male; following their mother's example, we can assume, by the time they receive their own licenses they will be well trained to handle him, knowing that, as *Lady and the Tramp* indicates, boys will always be playful and girls will always become ladies by domesticating the playboy.

DOES SHE OR DOESN'T SHE?

By situating this message in the context of animals, Disney found the license to talk about the responsibilities of female sexuality for a general audience. *Peyton Place* (1957), for example, would explore this issue as a seamy drama typifying aberrant rather than normative behavior—behavior, in other words, that falls outside normal American domesticity. The problem, of course, is that within the dominant discourse of the 1950s, female sexuality was almost always not reconcilable with domestic security. Or if it was, there seemed no acceptable discourse that could make the concept consistent with domesticity.

It is this problem—the problem of talking about female sexuality without, by definition, suggesting "trampiness," deviance, the threat to domesticity—that *Pillow Talk* confronts directly in its title and title song. The title *Pillow Talk*, like the title *Lady and the Tramp* (and like, as we have seen, atomic power), has a double meaning. Like appropriate female sexuality itself, as the lyrics of the title song make clear, "pillow talk" is a euphemism standing both for sexual activity and for its absence. "Pillow talk" means "another night of hearing myself talk, talk, talk, talk." It signifies, in other words, talking to one's pillow instead of one's lover, sleeping alone, being all talk and no action. But that form of pillow talk is a performance of the desire to do away with it, replacing it with its opposite—having "someone to pillow talk with me." That desire is further framed by two quandaries: "I wonder how" and "I wonder who." As in *Lady and the Tramp,* female sexuality is thus delimited by two voices—that of innocence and that of experience—both of which are "pillow talk." Jan (Doris Day), significantly more mature than Lady, is concerned less for the baby than for herself. For her, legitimate sexual license is the end, not the means, an end that nevertheless sees the marriage license as the only socially acceptable form of sexual license.

The song repeatedly attempts to reject "talk" ("another night of being alone with talk, talk, talk"; "All I do is talk to my pillow"; "another night of getting my fill of talk, talk, talk"), but in favor of what? Each time the speaker tries to articulate a pragmatic agenda, a list of hows and whos, that list becomes inextricably linked to the unimaginable: "I *wonder* how it would be"; "I *wonder* how"; "I *wonder* who"; "the boy I'm gonna marry *some*day, *some*how, *some*how, *some*time" (emphasis added). Between unsatisfactory talk and unimaginable acts lies the pillow, the site where dreams are constructed and the site of the dreamer whose dreams are socially constructed. The pillow thus marks the site at which talk fails to reconcile personal desire to social imperative. The song acknowledges this failure by contrasting her voice with the voice of society: "Two heads together can be better than one—That's what they say. They always say." Simultaneously she quotes conventional wisdom and distances herself from it both by ascribing it to "them" and by countering one cliché that asserts a truth with another that asserts doubt.

The song resolves with an extended play of clichés—the empty voice of social wisdom—that contrast personal desire with social imperative in a manner that throws into doubt the validity of either. The clichéd belief that "there must be a boy for me" is followed by another cliché that questions it, "I hope I'm right," and then another that casts it further into doubt, "I better be right." The word *better* suggests that the word *must* signifies not a condition of possibility but an imperative. The conclusion of the song reiterates and underscores the imperative tone. The phrase "there must be a pillow-talking boy for me" is reduced to "there must be a boy" so as to place increased emphasis on its imperative form. Then a male chorus echoes "there must be a boy," identifying the imperative as social, not merely personal. Finally, the song ends with the phrase reduced to pure imperative, "there *must!*" But rather than bridge the gap between talk and action, between desire and fulfillment, this imperative underscores it by making personal imperatives and social imperatives inseparable under exactly the conditions in which the social is the obstacle to the personal. As such the imperative, like all clichés, is all talk, an empty sign, a Barthean myth. The assertion that there must be a boy for her in no way tells her how to speak in order to find him. The same imperatives that tell her she must find a boy tell her that she must not speak this desire. If "pillow talk" is a euphemism for sexual intercourse, it is talk that cannot be talked about by a lady, lest she lose the status of lady and with it the opportunity for socially condoned pillow talk. Only in talking alone to her pillow, therefore, can she manifest her sexuality, and only as a literal act desiring its own eradication in favor of its euphemistic Other.

The point I am making is that the dominant discourse circumscribing the cultural site constructed by *Pillow Talk* rendered female sexuality at a double remove from the fulfillment of its own desire, that fulfillment being an act replaced by a euphemism replaced by talk about that euphemism. The song thus delineates the point of departure for the film, a point more than a decade after the institution of the social, political, and theological agenda that attempted to contain sexual activity in the same manner that it attempted to contain communism. Jan is attractive, independent, well past the age of consent, and actively interested in men. She has followed the social prescriptions throughout the entire period of the cold war and she has successfully contained her sexual activity. But she has failed to reap the promised rewards of following the prescribed social agenda and, more significant, the containment of her own sexuality (and that of others like her) has failed to have the commensurate effect on male sexuality.

Put simply, the restricted sexual license of the female has not had the domesticating effect implied by Walt Disney. Instead it has disciplined female sexuality into a form of duplicity, as an organization of itself as the lady's internalized and silent Other, reinscribed as a social question implicitly attached to the representation of all women, about the relationship between lady and license. The question found its public articulation in the infamously successful 1959 advertising campaign for Clairol hair coloring: "Does she or doesn't she? Only her hair dresser knows for sure." The object of the campaign was to give women the license to dye their hair by promising that exercising that license would not taint their images.

The slogan both gave women the license to be promiscuous and reassured us that it would not be abused. For if *only* her hair dresser knows, then we know she has no lover (who might also be in a position to know). The emphasis falls on the cohort who creates the image of purity, not on the cohort who penetrates the disguise. At the same time, of course, the hair dresser is the surrogate for all the intimates who can conspire with a lady to help her disguise her duplicity. The campaign thus lauded the virtue of the natural as an ideal to be achieved by equally lauded unnatural means. The natural thus becomes a version—the successful version—of the artificial. The natural comes to stand not for the undisguised but for the impenetrable disguise, impenetrable because it *may* be natural. What the commercial campaign does is make legible the point of sexual license—that it was always already available so long as it could remain disguised. Natural female sexual license was available, the ads implied, because of the efficacy of unnatural disguise.

LICENSING THE PLAYBOY

If female sexuality became overtly marked by this 1959 ad campaign as a form of disguise and duplicity, the range of legitimate sexual license for the male, by 1959, had steadily increased, a point best illustrated by the growing cultural acceptance of the "playboy," as promoted by *Playboy* magazine and as reflected in its general success. Started in December, 1953, *Playboy* rapidly became the most successful "men's" magazine in America, and by the late 1960s its circulation was surpassed only by *TV Guide* (Stern and Stern, 36). Although this might be attributed to its revealing "girlie" pictures, the magazine constructed its image and appeal out of being the antithesis of the "girlie" magazines of its day. Such magazines as *Whisper, Flirt, Eyeful, Titter, Wink,* and *Beauty Parade* all differed from *Playboy* (and resembled each other) in that they were cheap both in their newsstand price (25 cents) and their production values. The interiors were not composed of color glossies but of black-and-white newsprint, sometimes augmented by a second color, like the back page of a tabloid newspaper. Equally cheap were their representations of women, almost all of whom were posed in skimpy clothing—clearly costumes—acting out fantasy scenes in artificial settings, thus resembling prostitutes rather than lovers. These pictorials, which included no complete or even partial nudes, moreover, comprised virtually the entire content of the magazines, other than advertisements, most often for acne creams, bust-developing creams, hair-restoring creams, muscle-building programs, and trusses. With virtually no articles, and absolutely no verbal substance, the magazines appealed exclusively to "readers" interested in participating in these prostitute fantasies, fantasies that saw the women as tramps, foreign from and alien to the readers—or anyone's—domestic setting.

At the upscale end of the spectrum, *Playboy*'s major competition was Hefner's former employer, *Esquire,* the leading men's magazine in America. But *Esquire*'s claim to "respectability" mandated its divorcing men's interest from its sexual focus. As *Time* noted in *Playboy*'s third year of publication, "*Esquire* has paid the ultimate compliment by shedding some of its latter-day respectability. But *Esquire* still cannot keep abreast" ("Sassy," 71). Indeed, in that year, *Playboy* dethroned *Esquire* as the nation's leading men's magazine; more important, according to a 1958 independent survey of fifty magazines, it was able to attract an upscale audience rivaled only by *The New Yorker* and *U.S. News and World Report* in most upscale indicators, including median income and travel, clothing, appliance, and automobile expenditures.

Esquire, as Mike Wallace noted in a 1957 interview with Hefner, began with much the same philosophy as *Playboy.* But Hefner's locating sexuality as central to masculinity critiques the notion implicit in magazines like *Esquire* that women comprised one of an array of interests—including, for example, sports, outdoor recreation, and carpentry—around which men bonded. When Wallace demands Hefner explain "what's wrong with muscle in men's magazines? . . . What's wrong with outdoor sports? With hunting and fishing and human adventure?" ("Mike Wallace," 83) at stake is the definition of masculinity. Throughout the hundred years leading up to this interview, a dominant culture heavily invested in the idea that men and women who showed significant interest in sexuality were perverted and socially unacceptable was equally invested in maintaining rigid gender roles. In consequence, gender difference had to be maintained by marginalizing exactly the roles that explicitly distinguished the sexes. When Hefner makes sex roles central rather than marginal to gender roles, he is forcing his audience either to acknowledge the normative nature of sexuality or to do something neither Hefner nor his audience was willing to consider—dismissing completely the concept of gender roles. As Hefner explained to Wallace,

> I don't believe there is anything within the pages of the magazine that would be harmful to a normal, healthy American child. . . . There's nothing dirty about sex unless we make it dirty. A picture of a beautiful woman is something that a fellow of any age ought to be able to enjoy. If he doesn't, then that's the kid to watch out for. Our Associate Publisher . . . observed that when he was young, there were two kinds of boys—those who liked to pull the wings off of flies and those who liked girls. We confess to a preference for the latter. The deviates, the perverts, the serious juvenile delinquents—they're not interested in healthy boy-girl relationships. It is the sick mind

that finds something loathsome and obscene in sex. For us sex is neither dirty nor a sacred cow. ("Mike Wallace," 83)

While both the "girlie" magazines and the "men's" magazines (along, of course, with the "women's" magazines) reinforced the dominant ideological classification that promoted rigid boundaries between "lady" and "tramp," *Playboy* used numerous rhetorical and semiotic strategies to elide the boundaries between these categories.

Hefner astutely understood, for example, the connection between idea and representation, and therefore that the first way to disassociate sexuality from cheapness, from trampiness, was to make it look expensive. "*Playboy* charged into the battle of the sexes," as Barbara Ehrenreich aptly states, "with a dollar sign on its banner" (46). Walt Disney's sexually active Tramp thus changed not his behavior but his income level and his milieu, suggesting that, for the male at least, sexual license was a class privilege. Hence the name "Playboy" was attached to a visual environment that signified expensive taste, from its glossy pages to its slick layouts and award-winning graphics. Its spectacular nude centerfolds, featuring completely naked women against a richly textured and bright-colored cloth background, were photographed, highlighted, muted, and retouched with the care of the highest-class fashion magazines. The treatment resembled less that accorded a pinup girl than that accorded a Miss America.

The wholesome "Miss America" type, in fact, was exactly what *Playboy* wanted to suggest. As David Cort wrote in *The Nation*, "Instead of being an unattainable, and in that sense undesirable mannequin, as in *Esquire* she is the girl next door or at the next desk with her clothes off and looking very well, thank you" ("Playbill," 2). The point, not lost on Cort, was that the distinction between the women a man knew and the ones he found desirable was a distinction maintained by *Esquire* and assaulted by *Playboy.*

Playboy found many ways to make this point. After a year, it switched from the lush cloth backgrounds for the centerfolds to "natural" settings. The magazine started to recruit the centerfold models from all walks of life and eventually started to provide brief descriptions of how they were found and recruited. One issue, for example, printed a short story authored by the woman featured as that month's centerfold. *Playboy's* centerfold photographer thus assumed the persona of a wandering eye, at large in society, appreciating the seductive potential of women in even the most mundane settings. The reader was both implicitly and explicitly urged to share in this universal gaze through lenses no longer polarized by the bifurcation of female roles.

This traditionally polarized gaze was undermined in other ways as well. One of their photographers, Bunny Yeager, posed nude for a special feature, and another feature presented a woman photographed by her husband. In this way, the magazine sought to establish a rhetorical equivalent between gazer and gazed-upon and thus to universalize the perception and appreciation of sexuality. One particularly significant "playmate" was Janet Pilgrim, a woman who worked in *Playboy*'s subscription department. From directing a subscription department of three people to directing a larger unit of the *Playboy* corporate empire, concurrent with her rise as a nude pinup celebrity, Ms. Pilgrim's progress constitutes a *Playboy*-style morality tale, chronicled by numerous appearances in photo features through two decades. One feature detailed Janet's weekend as an honored guest of the Dartmouth student body. "As the Weekend came to an end, the Dean remarked," *Playboy* tells us, "that he had never met anyone 'from the outside' who comported herself more creditably or better represented her organization than our girl Janet." In the strategy orchestrated by *Playboy*, Janet not only made the office worker sexy but, in charming an Ivy League school, made the sexy office worker respectable.

Perhaps equally important was *Playboy*'s willingness to return to Janet periodically, as it did to many of its "playmates" with annual recaps and return photo features. With this continuity, they demonstrated their willingness to "call again" after a woman acknowledged her sexuality, to respect her, so to speak, in the morning.

UPWARD MOBILITY IN A CLASSLESS SOCIETY

These strategies also had important class implications. While the hedonistic life associated with its founding editor, Hugh Hefner—and typified by the acquisition of expensive paraphernalia such as audio equipment, cars, fine clothing—suggested that the playboy lifestyle was limited to the upper class, the magazine actually had a double message, the second part of which was that a man didn't have to be upper class to have a classy life. As it was in so many aspects of the middle-class boom of the 1950s, the message was that the pie was very large and that every American could have a piece of it.

The concept of upward mobility—the myth that enables members of a population to identify with those economically above them rather than those below, that enables them to construct the narrative of their lives in terms of what they imagine they will be rather than what they know they have been—was crucial to *Playboy*'s argument. Its essays, its articles, its advertisements all indicate that the magazine's intended audience was upwardly mobile middle-class men who were acquiring increasing spending power in the economic boom of the 1950s. For it told its readers that they could acquire some of the goodies between its covers, and with the correct aspirations they could acquire more and more. If they couldn't acquire the fine clothing, they could at least acquire the ability to buy tastefully and dress stylishly, or certainly at least to recognize what was or was not stylish. *Playboy*'s first essay on men's attire, appearing early in their second year of publication, was a brief two-page article gently acclimating the reader to the idea of men's fashion: "assuming our man is not totally color blind, possesses most of all the necessary appendages upon which to hang assorted articles of apparel, earns more than $60 a week, and takes a shower at least as often as he receives a paycheck, there's no reason he can't look as tastefully attired as that fellow who sells Schwepps" ("Newsletter," 39). The emphasis here clearly is not on fashion but on convincing the reader that he can be fashionable.

Even as surveys indicated that *Playboy* rapidly acquired a relatively affluent readership, the magazine maintained its—albeit sometimes tongue-in-cheek—instructional tone, often with various charts to help the reader develop his wardrobe or later to help the college student start the fall semester appropriately attired for his particular school and budget.

Playboy's first full-page advertisement (appearing in the middle of its second year of publication) is an ad for an LP record club called "Music Treasures." The club's introductory offer gave the subscriber two virtually free LPS, recordings of Beethoven's Fifth and Schubert's Unfinished Symphony. These are obviously intended for subscribers unlikely to own any classical recordings. But more significantly, the club provides, with these and subsequent LPs, what it calls a Music Appreciation Course—a set of guidebooks to instruct the reader in appreciating the classical recordings he has purchased.

Playboy took the same approach to the array of reader interests—cars, wines, furniture, audio. Treating the reader always as a neophyte rather than a connoisseur, it constructed an implicit narrative, starting with knowledge, taste, style, followed by modest acquisitions and the promise of more and more. Serving almost as a do-it-yourself manual for a growing class, *Playboy* schooled its readers in grooming, music appreciation, and leisure activities.

Between what the reader had and what the reader desired—in other words, at the margins of the reader's class—lay the magazine to supplement what the reader could not (yet?) attain. But the supplement was limitless, thus implying the paradoxical boundary without a margin. The playboy lifestyle was presented as a representation of the reader's life and a representation of the difference that delimited that life. But this doubleness has always haunted American mythology because that mythology embraced two tenets that were mutually exclusive: that America was a classless society and that upward mobility—the American Dream—was possible for everyone. The paradox arises when we realize that the only way to demonstrate upward mobility is to measure it against class markers, the very markers whose existence militates against mobility. Put simply, without stable classes mobility is impossible, and with mobility stable classes are impossible. Class requires a monolithic order, while mobility threatens it; class by definition must be exclusive; democracy by definition must not.

The Playboy Clubs, created in the early 1960s, reinscribe the same double message about class. They were simultaneously elite, because they allowed admission only to key-carrying members, and egalitarian, because anyone with the money could purchase a key. The description of the original Chicago club explained that membership "is limited to the men of substance and influence in each urban area; the initial fee is fifty dollars, which assures membership for life." Even factoring three decades of inflation into the formula, we still have a relatively meager means test for becoming a lifetime man "of substance and influence." But even within this realm of lifetime elitism, one finds stratification. Descriptions and photographs of the clubs, which become a running feature of the magazine, both in the form of "Playboy Club Newsletters" and pictorial features about specific clubs, all reiterate the several *levels,* organizational and economic, into which the clubs' interiors stratify. One newsletter headline described the St. Louis club as having "4 Levels of Fun" ("Newsletter," 1962, 33). And the pictorials always featured shots of elaborate staircases, as if to signify the ubiquitous potential for upward mobility afforded by membership in the club. The

New York Club is featured in another newsletter as housing "Seven Stories of Joie de Vivre" (ibid.) and described as a "SEVEN-STORY WONDER" in the newsletter devoted to its long-awaited (or long-delayed) "closing" ("Newsletter," 1963, 37). ("We cannot say 'open for business,'" the editors explained, "because the club doors will *always* be closed except to members.") That club also featured, as the subhead announced, a "VIP Room, for the Very Important Playboy." The room, also known as the "fourth level," is distinguished from the others not by the clientele but by the price and selection of the menu, and hence the quality of the entertainment, the length of the shows, and the quality of service. All of the club levels, in fact, are identified by their menu items, from bar food and drinks to roast beef on one level, filet mignon on another, and the right to menu selection at the VIP level. The right to have mass service from one-item menus thus becomes a keyholder's privilege as well as a way of measuring himself against other "members" of the club. Within this stratified key-holding world that makes status a form of consumption, the only consumable class signifier available at all levels is the service of bunnies.

In this context, the role of women in the magazine is particularly interesting. The gorgeous actresses and models, with little or no clothing, made up, touched up, photographed in perfect light, constituted in many ways the most unattainable of all the "acquisitions" folded between *Playboy*'s covers. Particularly in 1953, at the height of the cold war, under the strict moral and political censure of the period, the beautiful women were pure fantasy, even for the reader who could afford a good "Hi-Fi." The argument *Playboy* made, from the outset, however, was exactly the opposite—that sexual intimacy was one aspect of the *Playboy* lifestyle available to everyone.

Central to *Playboy*'s argument were the ideas that the sexual double standard was destructive to male and female pleasure, that marriage was not the only appropriate—or even the most pleasurable—relationship for sexually active adults, and that pursuit of pleasure was not the privilege of the upper class. At the same time, however, it made this argument by treating women as acquisitions. The idea that women could and should be acquired as part of a fulfilling life, a premise essential to the magazine's concept, would ultimately doom its astonishing success. From the perspective of the 1990s—when Hugh Hefner's daughter, who now runs the magazine, makes feeble attempts to describe the journal as in some way feminist while she watches the once ubiquitous bunny insignias disappear from the American landscape, save for the occasional yard sale or costume party—it is hard to imagine a cultural milieu in which the magazine could look in any way progressive in its attitude toward its most valuable acquisitions. But the 1950s, I think, was such a period, one whose dominant gender narrative was well represented by *Lady and the Tramp,* and women, like those vying for Moses in *The Ten Commandments,* acquired men by performing acts of manipulation and/or self-subordination. With its unprecedented financial and technological growth, the American 1950s were acquisitive times. But the personal price was high, and by the end of the decade it is not surprising that an alternative cultural narrative was emerging, any more than it is surprising that it would most privilege male heterosexist pleasure.

DOES HE OR DOESN'T HE?

The popularity of *Playboy* thus reflected—and no doubt contributed to— the increased tolerance for male sexual license by 1959, thus modifying the narrative of containment, putting the "playboy" in direct conflict with the woman whose sexual license is still delimited by the cult of domesticity, the woman whose "pillow talk" consists of talking alone to her pillow and wondering how and who. This conflict is the focus of the plot of *Pillow Talk,* initiated when the ladylike Jan is forced temporarily to share a phone party line with "playboy" Brad Allen (Rock Hudson). Because he chronically talks on the phone to an array of lovers, she overhears and/or interrupts conversations between him and his "tramps." He thus forces her to confront the threat of unlicensed sexuality, a threat that pervades Jan's world, made all the more threatening and pervasive by virtue of her own desire "to find a pillow-talking boy."

   Equally at stake are their similarities. They both work at home, are professionally successful, physically attractive, musically talented. They both are consenting adults over the age of thirty. They are also both middle class and upwardly mobile. She has clearly earned her status as a successful interior decorator, as he has earned his playboy status. As the script makes clear, not born to luxury, he worked his way through college, struggled to achieve his goals, and acquired his wealth by doing good work, that is, by writing commercially successful songs. And they both desire sexual relationships.

Brad's middle- (or lower-middle-) class origins and his debt to work rather than inherited wealth are emphasized through a series of contrasts. He stands in every way, for example, in direct contrast to Jan's client's rich son, a Harvard student who is short, blond, immature, and attempts to molest Jan in his sports car. And Brad's college roommate, Jonathan (who is also Jan's suitor), compares Brad favorably to himself by reminding Brad that Brad had the advantage of starting off with nothing and being able to make something of himself, whereas he (Jonathan) was burdened by starting off with $8 million. Although traditionally the model for the playboy, Jonathan desires to be anything but a playboy. He is guilt-ridden, neurotic, heavily dependent on his psychiatrist, three times divorced and now desperately seeking to marry Jan. In an elaborate extended metaphor, Jonathan compares single men to trees in the forest and married men to domesticated wood, hewn, processed, and turned into interior decor. When Brad confronts Jonathan with the apparent unattractiveness of the meta-phor, Jonathan's only retort is "With Jan, you look forward to having your branches cut off." The problem, of course, is that Jan doesn't want a man without all his limbs any more than Brad would want his cut off.

These similarities between Brad and Jan make the differences all the more telling. Whereas Brad's professional success has garnered him sexual license and sexual gratification, Jan's has left her talking to her pillow. This point is underscored by their respective relationship to song. The title song, "Pillow Talk," sung by Jan as the credits appear, is presented as an interior monologue; the audience overhears the plight that she confesses only to her pillow. The movie makes an audio transition from the opening titles to a shot of Jan putting on her stockings by having Jan hum the song she has just sung. The song is hers, but in the daytime world, she must withhold, interiorize, the lyrics. Trying to use her phone, she overhears Brad talking with a woman about the preceding night's lovemaking. He then plays for the woman a song that he claims to have composed for her. The song tells her that she is beyond compare.

The respective status of each song is revelatory. Jan's song represents a truthful expression of unfulfilled desire, which she can speak only to her-self, while Brad's song represents a duplicitous expression of fulfilled desire that he can speak not only to the object of that desire but also, as it turns out, to eavesdropping third parties. Brad's seductive song further illustrates his capacity to integrate professional and personal success, exactly the ca-

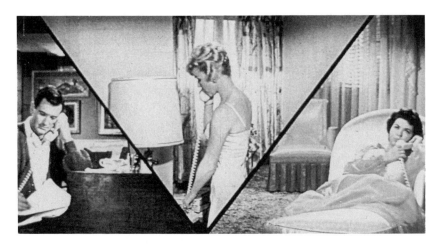

10 Inserted as a wedge in the trisected CinemaScope screen, Jan comes between Brad and the woman, creating not one but three triangles.

pacity Jan lacks. (All of her professional creating of domestic settings has failed to create a domestic scene for her.) Inserted as a wedge in the trisected CinemaScope screen, Jan comes between Brad and the woman, creating not one but three triangles (figure 10), a visual representation not only of the way her third-party intervention breaks up Brad's party but also the way in which the sexual double standard has become triangulated.

We have the same triangulation, in effect, suggested by the title *Lady and the Tramp:* the lady, the tramp, and the man who could be attracted to either or both. This of course can be reduced to a set of three unsatisfactory pairs: the man and the tramp, unsatisfactory because the tramp never satisfies the man enough to make him forego other women and the man never satisfies the tramp by making a lasting commitment; the lady and the tramp, unsatisfactory because each represents what the other cannot have, license or respect; the man and the lady, unsatisfactory because they cannot talk to each other without pervasive duplicity. The same desire that the man and the lady cannot admit respectably to one another they find in the tramp, so that she is both the other woman and the woman's Other. Jan's intervention makes clear the nonsymmetrical and nonreciprocal nature of sexual relations, for the triangulation requires the women to see themselves as Other while it allows the man to remain self-contained.

The plot of *Pillow Talk* develops so as to instantiate the symmetry by forcing the man to experience the same estrangement, to adapt the persona of earnest suitor to complement that of playboy. In creating the Other of his own desire, Brad becomes feminized, that is, forced to create a self that cannot acknowledge his own or the woman's desires. Like the Foucauldian madman, he functions always as the Other in the face of his own observation, always worried that his Otherness will make itself visible. The fear is legitimate because that desire, as Jacques Lacan has shown, is always already present in the speech of the subject that tries to repress it. Thus the script is filled with sexual double entendres that do not demonstrate a coy attitude toward sex so much as represent it as the common narrative, informing activities as diverse as phone repairs and foreign policy.

The double meanings are not only apparent to the audience but also to the characters who are forced repeatedly to confront in their own speech the very desire that the speech is not allowed to articulate. For Jan, recognition of this speech becomes a disciplining factor, a way of reminding herself of her own Otherness, of the self she cannot speak.

Finally, the double speech takes the form, for both Jan and Brad, of interior monologue that comments and translates overt speech. This mode of speech develops in the crucial scene at the nightclub where Brad first meets Jan. Although they do not know what one another looks like, Brad and Jan already know, by virtue of their party line and their acrimonious interchanges about it, a great deal about one another. Brad also knows about Jan from Jonathan's obsessive praise of her. The nightclub itself, neither a domestic nor work place, is a special site because of the way it permits the fluidity of roles. Brad is seated with one of his girlfriends, who is part of the floor show, and in the next booth Jan is seated with the drunk Harvard boy. (She has agreed to have a drink with him in order to stop him from molesting her in the car.) Thus before Brad and Jan meet one another, we know that they are in a place where class and gender roles are not rigidly fixed: the performer can be the guest, the Harvard man a vulgar drunk. Overhearing the conversation in the next booth, Brad realizes that the woman is Jan, but he also realizes, as he tells himself, "The minute you tell her who you are you're dead." In so doing he has articulated the central dilemma of the movie, because who he is is the playboy, that is, the person with overt sexual desire and the license to pursue it. Linking the playboy to the madman, Jan had reported to the phone company that she was sharing a party line with a "sex maniac," but his mania is no less pervasive, only less overt, than hers as expressed in her talk to her pillow. As we have already noted, however, within the cultural framework of the film, the minute she tells the world of her mania she would be called a nymphomaniac and her chances for domestic bliss would be dead. When he realizes, in other words, that the minute he reveals his sexual side he disqualifies himself as a partner, Brad has put himself in Jan's position.

Thus in order to seduce Jan he adopts a falsely earnest role of the wholesome Texan, Rex Stetson. In so doing, he must efface his sexuality in order to assert it, and always risks losing his potential lover should he reveal his true desires, his true identity, even when those are exactly the desires Jan wishes him to have. As a result their courtship now acquires the symmetrical duplicity absent from the tripartite party line talk earlier. Brad and Jan both talk to each other and comment independently to themselves (and the audience) about their true desires, the ones they may not express to one another.

This level of duplicity is complicated by yet another in which Brad, disguised as Rex, calls Jan and then calls her as himself to offer advice and commentary on her relationship with Rex. In this way, he helps facilitate Rex's seduction of Jan by setting Rex up as the antithesis of Brad. With Brad playing the tramp to Rex's "lady," these conversations effectively invert and balance the three-way party line interchanges at the outset. Here Brad and Rex exist as each other's Other, while Jan remains whole, aware and in charge of her own duplicitous, seductive goals.

Being forced into a role analogous to Jan's, Brad becomes feminized—a point underscored by a running gag about an obstetrician who believes Brad may be pregnant—and the experience changes him. When Jan discovers (in the nick of time) his duplicity, he still cannot put her behind him. Hoping to win her back, he hires her to redecorate his apartment by making it the kind of place she would feel comfortable in. As a form of revenge, she instead makes it look like a vulgar bordello. Like everything in the film—or everything, we might posit, in the normative courtship practices of the 1950s—the revenge is duplicitous. If Brad's experience has forced him to discover the female role, Jan's has forced her to recognize her desire for sexual license. If the decor she chooses parodies Brad's sexual activity, it projects equally her sexual desire. Thus when Brad announces that he wants to marry her, she locks the door and drags him down onto the "trampy" bed. As in *Lady and the Tramp,* the lady domesticates the playboy, eliciting a commitment to marriage and family. Here, however, it comes not from his masculine bravado meeting her concern for the baby, but from his feminizing experience creating a site for the recognition of her sexual desire. If *Lady and the Tramp* thus reflects cold war concerns, *Pillow Talk* reflects concern with the possibility of personal fulfillment that anticipates the 1960s. Both films affirm the cult of domesticity, but they do so in the interest of resolving different social problems.

POLITICS MAKES STRANGE BEDFELLOWS

The films, of course, do not resolve the problems, but they do help make legible the shifting sites of conflict in the culture as those problems undergo redefinition. By the end of the decade, *Playboy*'s message for many seemed not merely compelling but prophetic. For the growth in American affluence coupled with the technological explosion that produced a vast array of affordable creature comforts, and with a seemingly endless expansion in the class of upwardly mobile men, lent credibility to *Playboy*'s argument that any man could be a playboy. If this were so, however, then a corollary was that any woman could be a playboy's "playmate," and the magazine's "philosophy" (as Hefner pretentiously called its editorial positions and policies) thus held the potential of freeing middle-class women from having to choose between the rigid classifications of lady and tramp. Noting, as we have, that those classifications were crucial to far more wide-reaching ideological concerns in cold war America, we can see the complex problems that the playboy image posed to American culture when no longer disciplined by class boundaries.

This is particularly so because the "philosophy" also entailed challenges of censorship in all forms, championed blacklisted authors and performers, attacked racism, demanded the strong separation of church and state, and urged tolerance for deviant lifestyles. In 1954, accompanying shots removed from the American versions of European movies because of censorship, came the statement that *"Playboy* has a strong aversion to any minority (or majority, for that matter) forcing its opinions, tastes, and attitudes on the rest of us. We make a habit of thumbing our nose at censors, because we feel they have no place in a democracy" ("Nudity," 44). And in 1960, in the first—perhaps the only—designated "editorial," as such, in the magazine's history, the editors pointed out the dangers of radioactive fallout and called for an immediate halt to nuclear bomb testing. *Playboy*'s treatment of the arts also had distinct political implications. A continuous promoter of jazz, through record reviews, reader polls, all-star bands, and regular columns and features, *Playboy* was not only championing black art and helping black (and white) artists. It was also promoting a racially integrated array of musical artists in a nation that still practiced numerous forms of segregation, not limited to Southern schools and facilities but also including national tendencies toward separation of the races through discrimination in housing and compartmentalization in the media. The first of the magazine's regular interview features was a 1962 interview with Miles Davis, the overwhelming bulk of which was devoted to his critique of racism in his own life, in the music and entertainment industries, and in America in general. Less than a year later, it ran an even more polemic interview with Malcom X. The magazine also ran, in the late 1950s, features on and/or by counterculture critics such as Jack Kerouac, Allen Ginsberg, Ralph Ginzberg, Gregory Corso, and Lenny Bruce. In 1959, it ran a long article explaining and attacking the Mann Act and, in 1960, an essay by Dalton Trumbo debunking the Oscars. Trumbo, *Playboy* explained without embarrassment, had been a blacklisted screenwriter in the 1950s and thus he was unfairly denied credit for an Oscar he won writing under a pseudonym. In 1960 it also ran a long feature article on Charlie Chaplin, who had been vilified in America because of political views and was living in self-imposed exile.

In fact, in the very late 1950s, *Playboy* seems to have made an editorial decision to deal more directly with political issues. Perhaps this indicates a general thawing in the politically repressive 1950s, or perhaps, bolstered by a circulation of well over one million copies per month, a plethora of advertisers,[3] and a strong line of ancillary products, they felt they could safely make more explicit the beliefs implicit in the magazine from the outset. In any case, as Hefner later pointed out, he thought it was "important to have a magazine of considerable circulation establishing and reestablishing these basic concepts of freedom upon which our nation is built. If *Playboy* hadn't spoken up on behalf of Chaplin in 1960, no one else would have. At any rate, no one else *did*—no other major magazine—either before or after" (49). Starting with its anti-nuclear-testing editorial, *Playboy* thus encouraged an array of political positions on such issues as race relations, censorship, separation of church and state, and the right of consenting adults to unrestricted sexual license.

This was encouraged not only through numerous feature articles by such people as James Baldwin, Lenny Bruce, and Nat Hentoff, but also a new set of features. The "Playboy Advisor," for example, begins in 1960, as an offshoot of the letters column. Answering reader questions on anything from stereo equipment and sports cars to etiquette and romance, it becomes a podium, with some regularity, from which the anonymous voice of objective authority could denounce censorship and laws or social codes inhibiting free speech or sexual license. The magazine also started articulating these views in a regular editorial column, somewhat pretentiously called the "Playboy Philosophy," and an additional feature, the "Playboy Forum," composed of letters responding to these columns.

SEXUAL LICENSE AND LICENSE TO KILL

Instead of a repression of the magazine or its ideas, however, the early 1960s effect a rereading of *Playboy* by grafting its liberal, libertarian, antiestablishment values onto the conservative, repressive, pro-establishment movie image of James Bond.[4] The James Bond of the early 1960s' movies is both the quintessential playboy and the renunciation of almost everything for which *Playboy* argued. He is in fact the magazine's perfect mirror image, that is, a one-to-one correspondence that reverses everything.

Whereas for *Playboy* good taste compensated for and was more important than unlimited finances, for Bond judgment was inextricably linked to an apparently limitless expense account, such that he was regularly derided by the technical experts for his cavalier attitude toward the high-tech gadgetry with which he was supplied. Whereas technology for *Playboy*, moreover, was the means to leisure, for Bond it was the fetishized end in itself, a point that becomes clear in the format of the films which present Bond at near the beginning with special devices that he does not so much use as use up, often to no effect—as is the case with the super-equipped, super-armed Aston Martin in *Goldfinger*—other than to demonstrate to the audience how they work. Bond is not an operative in relation to these items but—like the Playboy Club member or the reader of the men's gifts display

11 *From Russia with Love:* What was in *Playboy* sexual license for Bond became license to kill.

in the annual "For Dad and Grad" feature—a consumer, one whose interest is not in acquiring but, as Jean Baudrillard would say, in participating in codes of consumption. After one use, therefore, the items hold interest neither for Bond nor for his audience. For their interests are synonymous—equally vicarious and equally fictive.

Whereas *Playboy* considered sex an appropriate topic of discussion for mature adults and urged frankness and openness, Bond specialized in the coy double entendre that made sex a topic always present but never frank and never open to discussion, and whereas *Playboy* emphasized trust and openness as the cornerstones of true eroticism, Bond always regarded women with distrust, seeing each woman as a potential assassin. In *Dr. No,* for example, he visits a woman, knowing that the rendezvous is a trap, makes love to her repeatedly, timing their sessions so that he can dispense with her before the assassin arrives, kills the assassin and has her arrested. *From Russia With Love* starts with a similar rendezvous/trap, and they become running motifs in James Bond series. The underlying premise of all his sexual encounters is that they are framed by the question, Is she acting like this because she wants to kill me (and therefore will I have to kill her first)? (Figure 11).

What was in *Playboy* sexual license, for Bond thus became license to kill. In *Thunderball*, after the woman captures him, he explains that in their sexual encounter he performed in the interest of Queen and country and received no pleasure from the experience. The same act of sexual intercourse between affluent, consenting adults is thus historicized by a narrative that reads the performance of a sexual act as the performance of one's duty to the national interests. Even in the intimacy of a sexual act, the autobiographical experience is subsumed by the national narrative, with any disparity between the two constituting a form of political error. The pleasure principle privileged by Hefner thus becomes the pretense of passion to service the woman in Her Majesty's secret service. And the smugness of that "secret" service signifies the degree to which it is really self-serving. All the gadgets, all the women, all the gourmet delights simply serve as the media through which Bond services himself. In the interest of the national narrative he restores the closet by performing his *secret* service, secret not because it is private or unknown, but because it is completely contained by the national narrative. The autoerotic nature of Bond's adventures becomes clear, and thus so does the way in which he most stands for the *Playboy* reader whose experience of *Playboy* is masturbatory, not because of its women but because of its self-serving lifestyle to which they contribute.

SELF-SATISFACTION AND THE IMPOSSIBLE ELSEWHERE

In a particularly absurdist moment in the film *What's New, Pussycat?* (1965), dressed in black tie, Woody Allen, playing a sexually frustrated incompetent named Victor, late at night opens a bridge table on the bank of the Seine and serves himself an elegant meal, complete with chilled Champagne. He does this oblivious to the mad Dr. Fritz Fassbender (Peter Sellers), an equally frustrated German psychiatrist who is trying to commit suicide in a Viking manner by wrapping himself in a Norwegian flag doused in gasoline and setting himself aflame while floating down the river in a skiff. When Victor refuses to change the site of the meal—a birthday present to himself—Dr. Fassbender calls him "a selfish gourmet"[5] (figure 12).

12 A selfish gourmet.

Perhaps no term more aptly reveals the way in which the Bond and *Playboy* images merge to define and delimit the autoerotic sensibilities of viewers and readers, wherein they are given the license to love and to kill with the same self-serving stroke. The idea of the "license to kill," moreover, not only redisciplines sexual license and reconnects it to the global politics of the cold war, but also it reasserts class values, because the license to kill, a form of law above the law, must by definition be elite.

This conflation of sexual license with license to kill focuses on two themes central to Woody Allen's work, themes that explicitly constitute the title of his 1975 film, *Love and Death*. It is not surprising, therefore, that Allen's first two film endeavors, *What's New, Pussycat?* and *What's Up, Tiger Lily?* deal respectively with the image of the playboy and of the secret agent. Both films, as the titles imply, question the images, exposing the myths and contradictions upon which they rely and, in so doing, some of the contradictions in the mid-1960s' concept of masculinity.

Pussycat shows the ways in which the foregrounding of the role of play-

13 Michael James (Peter O'Toole) seeks the help of a psychiatrist (Peter Sellers) who is in effect his antithesis.

boy as a positive social value unavoidably makes "masculinity" the site of the same objectification and commodification to which the male gaze had subjected women. Its focus is a handsome Paris features editor of a fashion magazine, surrounded by beautiful women, all of whom, like all the women he has met since puberty, want to seduce him. Fearing that his inability to resist these overtures renders him incapable of making the long-term commitment demanded by his regular girlfriend, he seeks the help of a Dr. Fassbender, who is in effect his antithesis, a homely, married, relentless pursuer of women (figure 13). Michael James (Peter O'Toole) is the quintessential playboy—the sexually active, financially independent man, living in a comfortable, well-decorated bachelor apartment. Handsome, well-groomed, tasteful, he is an object of desire for every woman he meets. Equally, he is the object of every man's envy. Cutting short their first session, Dr. Fassbender says, "Fifteen minutes of you is all I can take." He then bolts to his phone and black book to make a date. The implication is that James has not only aroused Dr. Fassbender's envy but also his sexual desire. James thus provokes male and female (hetero)sexual desire. He has become, in other words, a sex object in the eyes of everyone, including, as his foray to the psychiatrist makes clear, himself.

Watching O'Toole/James in this movie is thus like reading a copy of *Playboy* in that he makes visible the persona constructed by the magazine as the medium through which the array of sensual pleasures become accessible to the reader. For *Playboy* may egalitarianize or universalize the pleasure principle but only at a remove, through a form of mediation that could be called the image of the playboy. It is not surprising, therefore, that the announcement of the Playboy Club highlights the closed-circuit televisions that "permit you to catch other members with the camera, or come in for entertaining close-ups on the Bunnies." The potential playboy approaches his potential through the recognition of his own two-dimensional simulacra, as mediated by newsprint or by the voyeuristic camera lens. To the extent that the reader can participate in that mediation, identify with that image, he can enjoy the pleasures available to it, but always therefore as a third party. For a reader, that third-party enjoyment is always voyeuristic, but as James's dilemma makes clear, that voyeurism does not supplement first-hand pleasure but rather delimits it by making the image of the playboy, as defined by the voyeuristic experience of reading *Playboy,* the consciousness of the male self as pleasure-seeker. For the potential playboy, all experience is textual, a form of reading measured against the possibilities suggested by *Playboy* and the capacity to fill the roles created by it. The feminizing that the playboy underwent in *Pillow Talk* thus becomes not the distance between his speech and his desire but the distance between his desire and his ability to articulate it even to himself—the distance created, in other words, by his objectification of his own image.

Tiger Lily similarly reveals the preposterous quality of the James Bond figure through a series of defamiliarizations. The film, a Japanese James-Bond-style adventure, was not made by Allen but rather acquired by him, savagely recut, and then overdubbed with a script having no resemblance to the original, so that the suave, Japanese superhero identifies himself as "loveable rogue Phil Cohen" and is given the task of recovering a stolen egg salad recipe. The point of reference for the film, as Allen makes clear in the introduction, is all those "James Bondian things." And implicitly Phil Cohen's point of reference, like Bond's, is *Playboy* or the image of relentless womanizing that, more than his other adventures, defines his prowess. Because of one sexual encounter with Bond, in fact, Pussy Gallore abandons her until then willing complicity in a scheme to kill sixty thousand people and nuke all the gold at Fort Knox, and instead contacts the Feds and betrays Goldfinger. Alluding to that miraculous conversion, the villainess in *Thunderball*, after a session in bed with Bond, tells him that he had overestimated his powers of conversion; shortly thereafter he throws her in the way of an assassin's bullet.

One of Allen's techniques, particularly in the first half of his film career, is to juxtapose clichés from two completely incompatible realms so as to create an impossible space—a kind of extended mixed metaphor—the dissonance of which reveals the absurdities of each realm. In an early monologue, for example, he merges the sacred with the mundane in recounting a conversation he had with a nun in which they agreed "that He was pretty well-adjusted for an only child." In *Take the Money and Run*, the punishment for an inmate on a Southern prison work farm was to spend three days in a windowless hole with an insurance salesman, and in *Bananas* the duped American, invited to an opulent dinner at the palace of the presidente, arrives at the door with a packaged cake.

The dissonance in *Tiger Lily*, however, takes on a particular twist because the film in its original version has already merged two incompatible realms in making a Japanese imitation of the film James Bond, who is himself a merger of a British superhero and an American playboy. Allen's voice-overs at points merely underscore the already present incongruous connections. On one occasion, for example, one character offers to bribe another with "a naked picture of Hugh Hefner." In addition to connecting the actions to the governing value system that informs them, the joke, like the pretext of *Pussycat*, suggests the ways in which the playboy himself becomes the object of voyeuristic pleasure. In turning that into a literal object—a nude picture of the Playboy himself, that eliminates the middlewoman, so to speak—Allen reveals the emptiness of the image. He shows, in other words, how much the playboy depends on the woman not for pleasure but for the constitution of his own subjectivity. Always at one remove from objects, the playboy remains trapped in an economy of images, a code of consumption in which people may participate but that never meets their needs.

Far from meeting their needs, their participation highlights their inadequacies as a form of distance from the image, a point made by another of Allen's jokes in which one of the villains intimidates a rival gang by telling them that he has photographed them with a special camera that goes through their clothing to take pictures of them naked. "You better not mess around with me," he tells them, "unless you're all completely unashamed of your bodies!" Once again he is holding the men—each a potential playboy, a Hugh Hefner in his heart—to the same standard that the playboy holds the centerfold woman: being the person who is completely unashamed of her body. The problem, of course, is that being paradigmatic the image necessarily defines an ideal. The mediating image of the playboy, necessary to liberate both men and women from the shame-ridden classifications of "lady" and "tramp," thus creates an alternative shame, the shame of falling short of the ideal. The incompatible realms exposed by Allen's dubbing are those of the masculine image and the man's image of himself.

The resulting dissonance can be no more apparent than in the dubbing itself—the disparity, independent of the words, between the lip movements and the voices. The impossible site of Phil Cohen's Japan is further removed, however, to an Eastern monarchy that has no place in the world, where an oriental monarch informs Cohen that his country is on a waiting list (and the egg salad recipe must be recovered because it is written that whoever makes the best egg salad sandwich cannot be denied a place in the world). But this exotic elsewhere is just another overdubbing that glosses all the impossible sites at which James Bond's adventures take place. The Paris of *Pussycat* is similarly—although more subtly so—an impossible elsewhere, a Paris populated chiefly by German, British, and American actors, with the Swiss Ursula Andress parachuting in. There is also a more subtle "dubbing" of the British Peter Sellers using a German accent to play the psychiatrist and the Austrian Romy Schneider speaking English with a French accent to play the French heroine.

This impossible elsewhere, like Bond's elsewhere, is the elsewhere of sexual license, a connection underscored by Ursula Andress, arriving late in the film, as incongruously, inappropriately, and inconveniently as she does walking out of the water on Dr. No's island (figure 14), to demonstrate that whatever the intrigue, whatever the circumstance, wherever James Bond goes, beautiful, seductive women arrive. It is the proof that whatever his occupation Bond is foremost a playboy. The role defines his prowess and thus promises the success of his nonsexual adventures, adventures not only penetrated by but framed by sexual encounters. At the outset of *Dr. No*, for example, Bond is pursued by a woman whom he beats at baccarat, and at

14 Ursula Andress walking out of the water on Dr. No's island.

the outset of *From Russia with Love* he is picnicking with the same woman. In both cases, he is called away immediately by "M," and in both cases he fails to respond until he has finished having sex with the woman.

For Bond it appears everything is subordinated to sex, but this subordination is only apparent. His work as a secret agent is never compromised despite his refusal to forgo sex for work. Given the perfection with which he controls every situation, one is loathe to criticize any of his decisions. All the decisions create the image of James Bond, the superhero in perfect control. It is that image that inspires our confidence in him, that tells us that he will not panic, succumb to torture, betray a friend, or trust an enemy. His heroism—which distinguishes him from the would-be playboys in the audience—thus comes from his ability to discern these things impeccably. It is, in other words, a matter of good taste, a matter of knowing how to enjoy fine wines, fancy sports cars, and beautiful women.

Bond re-creates, in this way, the impossible doubleness associated with the lady and the tramp, this time by inverting it. If the lady had to use discretion to signify indiscretion, Bond converts sexual indulgence into a form of self-control. He makes it, in fact, the definitive form of self-control, so that his ability to avail himself of every attractive sexual opportunity without a loss of power or control promises us that he will be able to withstand any ordeal devised by a Dr. No or a Goldfinger. In this way, we could say that his sexual encounters become the true test of his ability to deal with torture.

In making this connection, the image of James Bond reconciles the implications of *Playboy* to the politics of the cold war. No longer is it the woman's role to fight communism by containing the sexual energies of men; in the world of James Bond the men continue the fight even more effectively by making their indulgence a form of containment. This is achieved by reading the playboy as the apotheosis of image, the seamless representation of a role that substitutes taste, reason, judgment for any display of—or for that matter any noticeable sign of—passion or any other form of interior life.

The introduction of the idea of an interior life complicates this Bondian reading of *Playboy* beyond salvation because it makes the "honest" Bond unremittingly duplicitous and turns his sexual prowess into at best shallowness and at worst indifference. Exactly this attention to the relationship between an interior life and an imaginary or illusory one has been one of Woody Allen's longstanding concerns. (Think, for example, of *Interiors*.) And this confrontation between the image of the playboy and his interior is exactly the situation that initiates *Pussycat* when James goes to the psychiatrist and thus converts the seamless image of James Bond's playboy into the conflicted site that contains not foreign, alien powers but internal passions, contains them in the interest of preserving an impossible image that is itself the foreign power, the alien constructed by his own objectification.

James has thus turned himself into the fetishized alien whose passions he must contain lest he subvert the image. For James, therefore, the arrival of Andress—the beautiful woman falling out of the sky—after he has made his commitment to Carole (Schneider) is a problem because it portends his loss of control rather than, as it does for Bond, prove his prowess. The problems Andress creates for the playboy are directly associated with the image of James Bond when, in the midst of the fracas at the hotel, James says of Andress, "She's a personal friend of James Bond," alluding to Bond in this movie about the playboy in the same way that Allen alludes to Hefner in the "Bondian" *Tiger Lily*.

For by the mid-1960s the two are inseparable, with the image of the playboy, ostensibly constituting the supplemental aspects of Bond's character, the margins of his identity, forming instead the source of his power and the limits of his control. And yet it is Bond who has taken control of the playboy image by creating a reading of it that deprives it of an interior life. The problem for James, for any would-be playboy, is to gain control over Bond without having to assume Bond's powers of control by relinquishing a sense of his own interior life.

Focusing as it does on controlling Bond himself, this struggle replicates the plots of the James Bond movies, wherein the plans to acquire secrets or weapons become subordinate to plots for dispensing with or acquiring Bond himself. As the goal of all the other players, he becomes not only the seamless image but also the completely fetishized object. But Bond can never be acquired because he is an object that always exists elsewhere.

And that elsewhere, James makes clear when he enters the shower where Carole is bathing, is an imaginary—a cinematic—space. Carole asks James if they are going to make love by asking, "Is it foreign movie time?" To what country's movies is she referring? Since she is in France, she couldn't mean French movies, but certainly she doesn't mean American movies, which allow much less sexual license. As actors in an American (pro-duced/financed) film, of course, they are incapable of making it a foreign movie, for even if they were to perform in a way that revealed their ex-plicitly sexual relationship and showed that they were not ashamed of their naked bodies, this would still not be a foreign movie, but rather an Ameri-can movie living up to the image signified by the phrase "foreign movie." Despite James's assent to "foreign movie time," however, it fails to live up to its (necessarily impossible) promise, as James only partially disrobes and Carole never removes her bathrobe before "foreign movie time" becomes a comic fight about James's refusal to make a commitment, driving him back into his clothing and out of her apartment.

Within the context of the film, of course, this means that it does become a foreign movie, that is, a non-French film. For the audience, however, it remains what it was, a nonforeign film, set in a foreign place, made familiar not only because of its language and situations but also because it locates explicit shameless sexual relations as taking place elsewhere, in a foreign place. But the foreign place created for sexual license is the foreign place foreign to the foreigners, who are themselves foreign to their own for-eign environment: a British actor playing a British character in France, an

Austrian actress playing a French woman (with French parents). The site designed by *Playboy* for the playboy to be the playboy is thus constructed here as a foreign movie place—in other words, as a place always foreign and always imaginary.

This is a kind of visual bad dubbing that complements the bad dubbing in *Tiger Lily*. The characters in *Pussycat* speak as if they were in France, in language foreign to its environment, made all the more unnatural by the presumption of naturalness, in speech that is accented often in accents adapted to signify the ways they are speaking on behalf of the Other. But in many ways bad dubbing is just the most graphic representation of the levels of estrangement between speech and signification involved in constructing the American playboy, who is potentially exotic and domestic, elite and egalitarian, lover of women and their adversary, image and voyeur. The image of liberation, of license, becomes internalized as a man's unarticulated recognition of his Otherness, represented in the films as an inexplicable foreignness, an alienation that the valorization of the playboy embedded in "masculine" discourse by the mid-1960s.

PART III

Double or Nothing

6. THE INVASION OF POSTMODERNISM

The Catch-22 of the Bay of Pigs and

Liberty Valance

In March of 1960, John F. Kennedy hosted a dinner party at which one of the guests was Ian Fleming, the author of the James Bond novels. Kennedy was an acknowledged fan of the novels,[1] and probably of the figure of Bond himself, who was in many ways the apotheosis of the kind of leader Kennedy most admired—one who furthered the cause of containment with unlimited license, whose sexual prowess, as we have noted, was testimony to his political fitness, whose amorality was a sign of goodness. Perhaps, as Kennedy's actions surrounding the Bay of Pigs invasion suggest, Bond provided the ideal resolution of the conflict between his inclinations toward action and toward restraint. As the biographers of the Kennedy family, Peter Collier and David Horowitz, point out, "If he was cautious himself, Jack was impatient with the caution of others, which he saw, typically, as effeminacy" (268).

To put it another way, the James Bond novels were stories that allowed a happy ending to the gendered courtship narrative that informed the strategies of containment as figured originally in George Kennan's 1948 essay. The character of Bond gave public legitimacy to sexual agency and to political agency—the two forms of secret agency that fostered the narrative of the cold war. This may account for what James Giglio characterized as Kennedy's initially "overtly exalted view" of the CIA (54).

This romance with the CIA was, as John McClure has convincingly argued, completely consistent with the romantic narrative constructed by Kennedy's speeches:

the romance elements . . . introduced as part of a process by which Kennedy constructs a grand romance of contemporary history: he defines the world as a battlefield where "freedom and tyranny" contend, emplots the times as ones of grave crisis but also great possibility, and casts America, a collective actant, now as a prisoner in need of rescue (by Kennedy, of course), now as a heroic protagonist in the global struggle. . . . The story he tells again and again has two parts. In the first Kennedy himself appears to remind America of her high destiny, to rescue her from the debasing preoccupations of quotidian materialism and the stupefying reassurances of the Republicans. In the second, the reawakened nation, led by Kennedy, goes adventuring across the new frontiers of the times. (43)

Kennedy's romance with the CIA, however understandable, was also of course doomed, ostensibly by the Bay of Pigs invasion, but moreso by its own impossible contradictions, for which the invasion became a legible cypher. Even though much has been written about the invasion, it still remains mired, like the Vietnam war, in a web of accusation and blame, with even its most rudimentary goals remaining unclear. Although at the time of the invasion, for instance, certainly everyone behind it hoped it would result in the overthrow of Fidel Castro, much evidence indicates that the invasion's plans assumed that by the time the U.S.-backed Cuban expatriates actually landed, Castro would have been assassinated. A box of Castro's cigars was impregnated with a hallucinogenlike substance. Another was contaminated with a botulism toxin lethal on contact. Later a Mafia contract on Castro was taken out by the CIA.[2]

JUST LIKE THE GUATEMALAN COUP

Planned during the Eisenhower administration, the invasion was modeled on the "successful" 1954 covert operation in Guatemala that overthrew Jacobo Arbenz, the democratically elected president. That plan was psychological and political more than military. Fictitious radio broadcasts to a nonexistent Guatemalan underground and six months of "leaked" secrets about a U.S.-backed invasion force across the Nicaraguan border panicked the Guatemalan government into a spate of repressive measures, including murder of suspected collaborators. Then a small insurgent army (150 troops) invaded from Nicaragua. "Technological tricks," Lloyd Etheredge explains, created "the impression that a small invasion force was large and ominous.

[The CIA] selectively jammed the communications of the Guatemalan army and fed false orders and reports of a larger invasion over its radio network. Thus believing his country under major attack, Arbenz found himself unable to learn what was happening or even to control his own troops. The army was not eager to fight, *especially faced with the possibility such resistance would only bring invasion by American troops"* (6; emphasis added).

This model relied, as the strategies of containment had from the outset, on the image of the United States as the aggressive leader of the West. It relied on the cultural narrative of the traditional American western, wherein the lone stranger, working outside the law, bringing to bear superior martial expertise, tames part of the West by enforcing typical "Western values"— the authority for which can be found back East—in a manner unique to the uncivilized West. At stake in the western genre, as in all issues of settling and colonizing, is the struggle between Other and Same, the construction and understanding of difference. The West, these narratives repeatedly remind us, is different from the East. It is more dangerous, tough, and lawless. Its lawlessness comes in three forms: indigenous people—humans who live in contradiction to the codes of civilized behavior—who are culturally and possibly biologically aberrant; outlaws—humans who knowingly disregard the laws of back East—who are biologically similar but legally aberrant; and nature. These three forms of lawlessness create the warrant for extreme countermeasures. Lawlessness, unruliness becomes generic to the West— the law of the West—and, as Derrida points out, the law of genre must always be obeyed. Only within the generic boundaries of Western behavior can the West be made to conform to the Western values that originate in the East.

The conflict in the West, in other words, is between those in the West who represent the East and those in the West who represent the West. But mastery over the West—the successful remaking of the West in the name and image of the East, the elimination of difference—comes from the triumph of the representative of Eastern values who can successfully reject those values and master the law of the West, the law, so to speak, of lawlessness. So long as the representative of the East—the site of Western values— remains the same as the Easterners, he cannot fulfill his colonizing goal, which is to make the West the same as the East. Only when he differentiates himself from the Easterners, when he becomes Other, can he make the Other—the West—the Same.

The East thus depends for its agency on a form of double agent, someone who can be both Other and Same, who can meet the generic demands of the law of the West so as to incorporate the West under the rule of the law of the East. This outlines one informing narrative of the CIA: responsible for incorporating the unruly world under the law of the Eastern establishment, which governs the Western bloc and represents the Western hemisphere, the agency seeks to become the same as the Others so that it may make the Others the Same, and to control Others who will acknowledge their similarity. The Guatemalan insurgents acquired credibility by virtue of their having been Guatemalan, that is, other than U.S. forces, but they succeeded by virtue of representing those U.S. forces through a process that was simultaneously covert and overt. If covertly merely actors in a CIA-conceived, CIA-financed, CIA-staged fiction, overtly they were, via the CIA, precursors to full U.S. armed intervention. At issue then was not whether the United States was involved in the actions, but rather what aspects of the action and the involvement were fictitious.

The issue, in other words, was the CIA's ability to control the narrative that made its actions legible to the Guatemalans. The CIA wanted Guatemalan leaders to believe that the insurgent forces were large and represented — were large *because* they represented — the full commitment of the world's preeminent nuclear power. The CIA assistance for the insurgents was thus the supplement upon which the insurgency depended and hence could not be a secret. The secret was that the insurgency itself was a fictional supplement to the overt CIA support for it. Because much U.S. prestige and credibility, in other words, foreign policy, depended upon that secret in the 1950s, the United States was willing to risk war to cover it up. In sum, the strategy was to create a fictional insurgency with real CIA support that implied massive real U.S. support, support that would become real only if the fictional status of the insurgency were in danger of being revealed.

This model seemed perfect for dealing with what had become a serious problem with Cuba, as summarized in a State Department memo:

> When Castro came to power in 1959, the United States looked upon it with sympathy, recognized it almost immediately, and welcomed its promises of political freedom and social justice for the Cuban people. We made clear our willingness to discuss Cuba's economic needs. Despite our concern at the Cuban regime's mounting hostility toward the United States and its grow-

ing communist tendencies, we attempted patiently from early 1959 until mid-1960 to negotiate differences with the regime.

Elements in the Castro movement engaged in anti-American activities during the revolution against Batista. Soon after it came to power in 1959, the Castro government turned away from its previous promises, permitted communist influence to grow, attacked and persecuted its own supporters in Cuba who expressed opposition to communism, arbitrarily seized U.S. properties, and made a series of baseless charges against the United States. It ignored, rejected, or placed impossible conditions on repeated United States overtures to cooperate and negotiate. In 1960, Cuba established close political, economic, and military relationships with the Sino-Soviet bloc, while increasing the pace and vehemence of measures and attacks against the United States. We did not take measures in our own behalf to isolate Cuba until July 1960. (qtd. in Etheredge, 1–2)

The document lists America's repeated attempts to court Castro and grounds American policy in his ignoring, rejecting, or placing impossible conditions on "repeated United States overtures." In addition to rebuffing U.S. overtures, he made increasingly clear his preference for partnership with the Sino-Soviet bloc. This meant that a dozen years after articulating the strategy of containment—that we should make ourselves the more attractive partner for other nations—the United States had failed to convince one of its nearest neighbors that it was preferable to the communists, whose drives it was set on frustrating. To put it another way, instead of finding itself in the role played by Rock Hudson—the playboy whose virility valorized his license and vise versa—the United States was playing Doris Day's role, that of the dutiful woman who had preserved her virginal image at the expense of establishing a satisfying partnership.

It is, of course, on the one hand oversimplifying to reduce foreign affairs to the plot of *Pillow Talk,* but on the other hand, we could argue, the cold war was based on a series of oversimplified narratives of opposition and partnership, invoking the same motifs of innocence and corruption, license and discipline found in American popular culture. The significance of the Bay of Pigs fiasco is that it made legible the failure of those narratives to contain the disparate elements attributed to them. Part of the story of the Bay of Pigs becomes its failure to form a coherent story. Just as *Hiroshima* visibly—albeit often inadvertently—marks its inability to authorize the story constructed in its name, so too the term *Bay of Pigs*, as would *Vietnam* and *Watergate*, signifies not only failed actions or failed policies but also the failure of a narrative that could contain the failures.

One problem, as the State Department memo suggests, is that the difference created by Castro's revolution openly confounds the pattern of Other and Same that stabilized containment. Castro promised "political freedom and social justice," apparently absent from Batista's Cuba. In that way, Batista's Cuba was not like the United States, the leader of the "free world." At the same time, Batista's Cuba was like the United States in that it was part of the "free world" by being party to U.S. opposition to the Sino-Soviet bloc. Geographically, moreover, Cuba was part of the Western bloc, and thus it disturbed the geopolitical polarities—so staunchly asserted by Cecil B. deMille—upon which the distinction between East as Other and West as Same relied. To put it another way, the West's authority to construct its narrative in the name of the West necessitated discovering in itself the same monolithic qualities it attributed to its rival, the East.

The patient and consistent attempt that the State Department notes to "negotiate differences with the regime" is thus the attempt to negotiate the differences *away*, in other words, in what de Certeau would characterize as the quintessential act of colonialism: to make the Other the Same. This was both a test of American attractiveness and a recognition of the threat that the Cuban revolution posed to the narrative that represented America as the world's, or at least the West's, most attractive partner. Having failed to be the Same, Castro was the Other, and in a narrative uncannily resembling *Pillow Talk,* he was the Other reviled and feared because of his promiscuity. The United States was afraid that he might seem too attractive to other Western hemisphere nations or, failing to seduce them, that he might deceive them or even force his affections on them. In any case, he would taint the U.S. image by coupling with our former partners. He had become, as the term applies to Rock Hudson's character, the "playboy" of the Western world.

THE PROBLEMATIC PLAYBOY

The solution in our cultural narrative for the fear of the playboy, I have argued, was to discipline his threatening tendencies through a form of secret political agency, as typified by the prowess of James Bond. It makes sense, then, that our espionage unit, the CIA, should be the agency to counter Castro, and it especially makes sense that such a plan should be attractive to Kennedy. As Collier and Horowitz note, "always something of a secret agent himself, working for his own clandestine desires under cover of respectability, [Kennedy] found the [CIA's] lack of protocol, rhetoric or moral pretense attractive. He liked the elan and efficiency, and told Bundy in his first days in office, 'I don't care what it is, but if I need something fast, the CIA is the place to go' " (264).

Fleming's opinion, therefore, may have had a peculiar authority for JFK when, according to Michael Beschloss, "over coffee, Ian Fleming had said that Americans were making 'too much fuss' about Castro: it would be perfectly simple to take the steam out of him" (134). Fleming recommended ridicule, "opining that the Cubans only cared about three things: money, religion, and sex. Cuban money should be scattered over Havana, crosses painted on the skies. Pamphlets should be dropped on the island warning that atomic testing had made the Cuban atmosphere radioactive: radioactivity made men impotent and lingered longest in beards. Cubans should shave off their beards. Without bearded Cubans, revolution would cease" (134). This plan bears an uncanny resemblance to plans, before and after the Bay of Pigs invasion, for dealing with Castro, including a plan to dust his shoes with a depilatory to make his beard fall out and one to spray "his broadcasting studio with a chemical that produced erratic behavior, much like LSD" (Wyden, 40).

To some extent, however, the invasion had a life of its own. By the time Kennedy took office, the invasion plans were in their final stages. The same base in Nicaragua on which the 150 Guatemalans had trained was opened to train approximately 1,500 Cuban expatriates. These troops were to sail to Cuba under U.S. escort, land on Trinidad Beach, be greeted by an uprising of the Cuban underground, and set up a government, which would be immediately recognized by the United States; after recognition, the government would, if necessary, be able to ask the United States for assistance. A series of air strikes prior to the invasion, aimed at knocking out Castro's small air force, would facilitate establishing a successful beachhead. In order to avoid the appearance of U.S. involvement, these strikes were to be flown from the base in Nicaragua by a small number of obsolete B-26s that could be called defectors from the Cuban air force. If the landing party failed to establish a site for its government, then it was supposed to melt into the mountainsides, where it would be welcomed by the extant guerrilla forces.

Whatever Kennedy chose to believe or to ignore about the circumstances germane to this plan, it is clear that his perception of them was at great variance from the actual conditions. One reason is that Kennedy was misinformed. Contrary to CIA representations, there was no active guerrilla force in the vicinity of Trinidad Beach, where the landing was originally to have taken place, nor had there been any guerrilla activity in the Zapata region, where the Bay of Pigs lay, during the entire twentieth century. Also missing were the mountains alleged to contain the guerrillas—fifty miles of impenetrable swamps separated the Bay of Pigs from the nearest mountains. If the secluded beach lacked access to the mountains, it also lacked seclusion, as the Cubans were busy working day and night to convert the Bay of Pigs into a resort area. Nearly two hundred bungalows, along with a motel, bath houses, and a recreation center were being constructed on the east side of the bay's mouth. "Hooded twelve-foot lights on silver metal poles in concrete foundations," Peter Wyden points out, "had been installed throughout the new community" (104). These lights made it look to Grayston Lynch, one of the CIA operatives leading the invasion, "like Coney Island" (Wyden, 218). The lights and the active construction work took away the secrecy of a night landing—its only advantage—while leaving all its disadvantages. As William Manchester reminds us, during the course of World War II, the United States had learned a great deal about amphibious assaults, and one of the things it learned was that they were not to be attempted at night (103).

In these areas, Kennedy was clearly misinformed about circumstances and about the efficacy of the tactics. Equally misinformed were the Cuban insurgents. Repeatedly they were promised an umbrella of U.S. air cover; prior to the landing, they believed that Castro's air force had been immobilized; and throughout the planning and execution they were assured that in the advent of an unsuccessful invasion, they could count on full U.S. military support. This was directly in contradiction to Kennedy's explicit instructions, which were that direct U.S. involvement was to be avoided under any circumstances.

The problem here, however, is not merely one of knowable truth and knowing deception. Like the Guatemalan action, the Cuban invasion depended not upon truths but upon a coherent narrative. For circumstances like these, the CIA had developed the concept of "plausible denial," which signified a way of avoiding the creation of statements, documents, or circumstances that make it impossible for a leader to deny knowledge of or consent to an embarrassing and/or illegal act. In ordering that there be absolutely no U.S. involvement, therefore, JFK could easily be read as constructing his plausible denial. At the same time, Kennedy's willingness to approve the action necessitated his trusting his intelligence sources. He had, after all, little direct knowledge of the Cuban exile community, the nature of Cuban resistance, or the details of Cuba's terrain. What he did have was an exalted image of the CIA and, Lloyd Etheredge asserts, an equally "wistful image of the Cubans," that allowed him to conceive of the invasion as "American *support* for Cuban liberators" (37–38). The Cuban liberators, however, were U.S.-organized, U.S.-trained, U.S.-supervised, U.S.-financed, and U.S.-controlled; their participation was thus understandably contingent on the assumption of U.S. involvement in the operation.

The narrative of Kennedy's relationship to the Cuban insurgents thus reveals the catch-22 of the text. By withholding the promise of direct U.S. involvement, according to Etheredge, Kennedy was testing the commitment of the exiles: "Did they *really* want to do this (and accept the risks) on their own, for their own ideals?" (56). The test, however, could not work because no one believed Kennedy, not even his own advisers. The concept of plausible denial made it impossible to differentiate between a president telling the truth from one merely saying something he wants to be believed or one communicating an encoded contradiction, a covert text that doubles and undermines the overt text. Or, to put it in the terms of the last chapter, there is no way to distinguish "pillow talk" from "pillow talk."

This is one of the central problems not just of politics (or any other form of governance) but of postmodern discourse. Whereas many of the encoded texts of modernism were constructed (or at least read as though they were) to suggest a central, "universal," coherent metatext, the possibility foregrounded by postmodern texts is that the codes do not condense under the authority of a metanarrative or the figure of authorial authority but rather produce an infinite doubling of texts that undermine even the authority of grammar itself. What happens in the Bay of Pigs incident, I shall argue at some length, is that the return to monologic authority becomes impossible, producing not an authorized coherent version but a catch-22 that makes authority incompatible with coherence. At the same historical moment and in the same way, moreover, Joseph Heller's novel, *Catch-22*, and John Ford's film, *The Man Who Shot Liberty Valance,* manifest, I believe, the same conflicts between authority and coherence that typify postmodern discourse. Both works, moreover, locate those conflicts in the attempts to establish a coherent national narrative, as American foreign policy did during the cold war, out of the desire to use limitless force in the interests of establishing the peaceful limiting of force. This is the double message of atomic power — not that it could be used for good *or* destructive ends, but that its good use *was* U.S. willingness to use it destructively.

We have seen from the outset how containment required figuring the "dual nature" of the atom as producing discrete effects; at the same time, the foreign policy of containment continued to merge the differences rather than keep them straight.[3] If, as I have argued, this contradiction — the warrant for what would much later be called "nuclear criticism" — was inherent in American assent/ascent to atomic power, until the Kennedy era, these contradictions were contained through the appeal to the monologic, monotheistic discourse so typified by *The Ten Commandments*. Similarly, many literary conventions, as they had throughout the modern era, invoked a symbolic metatext, so that, for instance, Holden Caulfield's inability to speak during the McCarthy period, as we have seen, is resolved in mythic terms. The symbolic redemption in the form of rain becomes Caulfield's recognition of himself in Christ, and his failings shift from the untenable politics of discourse to the realm of human frailty. Caulfield, Salinger ultimately suggests, has been plagued not by a political unconscious but by a lapse in faith. He therefore suffers a nervous breakdown, which signifies the internalizing of his inability to understand a higher power.

In the atomic age, however, the highest power becomes the nuclear power — the power to destroy the world with one command, with one word. In this light, it was no doubt reassuring in some ways for Americans to view the U.S. mandate as theological as well as political. So long as the commander-in-chief could be viewed as God's agent, the chances for accident or error seemed slim (or at least slimmer). Conformity to the norms set by the dominant discourse thus became a form of, and a demonstration of, public reassurance. The Bay of Pigs incident acquires significance, therefore, not because it reveals the duplicity of U.S. foreign policy, but because it locates in the seat of authority itself — authority that is supposed to be monologic, theologic, and sexually domesticated — the inability to produce a coherent narrative, because it is, as it necessarily must be, duplicitous, amoral, and promiscuous. And it is this loss of central authority that creates the excess so important to postmodern and poststructuralist discourse. Derrida could well be said to have revealed the catch-22 of language and, like Heller, he could well be seen as owing much to the early Sophists who similarly were regarded as threatening to the state.

FROM THE CATCHER TO THE CATCH

In *Catch-22*, Heller deconstructs the normative assumptions of *The Catcher in the Rye* by shifting the breakdown from the subject to the rhetoric, that is, from the "catcher" to the "catch." If the language of *The Catcher in the Rye* implies a correlation between fact and judgment, an objective way of clarifying actions, the language of *Catch-22* implies just the opposite: normative statements do *not* correlate with their exempla; effects are not the consequence of causes, but causes are rhetorical functions that rationalize and classify events. Set on an American Air Force base in Italy during the final stages of World War II, the novel examines the exploits and the milieu of Captain Yossarian, a bombardier in a squadron led by an egomaniacal, albeit not very bright, Colonel Cathcart who, in his ruthless pursuit of self-aggrandizement and self-interest, will jeopardize or sacrifice anyone in his command. He "was impervious to absolutes. He could measures his own progress only in relationship to others, and his idea of excellence was to do something at least as well as all the men his own age who were doing the same thing even better" (185). In this way he mirrors Yossarian, who is equally self-interested. The relativist colonel, however, differs diametrically from Yossarian, whose self-interest is absolute: he wants to stay alive. Instead of following a traditional plot structure, the novel is intricately organized around the interplay of numerous characters whose conflicts perpetually recontextualize situations from absolute and relative perspectives that ultimately present the "history" of World War II (or history in general) as an expression of power caught in an infinite play of difference.

The world of *Catch-22*, therefore, puts into play the idea of sanity and the objective perspective that it authorizes. For Yossarian and his comrades, there can be no mental breakdown because nothing could be more insane than following the norm—continuing to fly missions—especially when the norm set by Colonel Cathcart was abnormal. Having flown forty-eight missions, Yossarian asks why he cannot go home:

"Catch-22," Doc Daneeka answered [Yossarian] patiently . . . "says you've always got to do what your commanding officer tells you to."

"But the Twenty-seventh Air Force says I can go home with forty missions."

"But they don't say you have to go home. And regulations do say you have to obey every order. That's the catch. Even if the colonel were disobeying a Twenty-seventh Air Force order by making you fly more missions, you'd still have to fly them, or you'd be guilty of disobeying an order of his. And then the Twenty-seventh Air Force Headquarters would really jump on you.

Yossarian slumped with disappointment. "Then I really do have to fly the fifty missions, don't I?" he grieved.

"The fifty-five," Doc Daneeka corrected him.

"What fifty-five?"

"The fifty-five missions the colonel now wants all of you to fly." (58)

Even when the norm is abnormal and arbitrary, any aberration from the norm, according to "catch-22," signifies sanity and therefore is not an excuse for deviating from the norm. A breakdown of the sort Holden Caulfield had, in other words, would not take him out of the war but would prove his sanity and hence his fitness for combat. Unlike the rhetoric of *The Catcher in the Rye*, the rhetoric of *Catch-22* does not allow for the breakdown, location, or relocation of the subject, because normative language does not correlate to an objective reality but rather shows that objective reality is created by the sharing of language. Under such circumstances, insanity is not a personal failure to conform to objective norms but to the demands of an interpretive community.

Perhaps one of the most striking examples of this phenomenon can be found outside Heller's novel, in the CIA's judgment of Castro, formally made by the Board of National Estimates, in February of 1961, which concluded that Castro was a danger to the United States because he was "a psychotic personality," as proved chiefly by his rampant opposition to the United States. His postrevolution allegiance with the Soviet Union was assessed a function of "his own disordered mind, unrelated to any fact of U.S. policy or action," and in a logic as simple and elegant as any application of catch-22, the report reasoned that Castro must be psychotic because "no sane man undertaking to govern and reform Cuba would have chosen to pick a fight with the U.S." (cited in Etheredge, 49). Working from this tauto-logical premise, the board found it confirmed by all the "evidence": Castro's elation when the revolution succeeded, his aggressiveness, and particularly his apparent belief that the United States was out to get him. Castro's be-havior was necessarily interpreted independent of the fact that Castro was aware of the plots against his life, that he knew about the training base in Guatemala, and that "with a network of active agents in Miami as well as Guatemala [he did not] hallucinate that the underground operations and airdropped supplies to terrorists who set fire to sugar cane fields and killed civilians with several bombs a week in 1960 were the sole work of private groups the United States simply had difficulty controlling . . ." (Etheredge, 50). One could, of course, further argue that having the agents who in-formed him of these things proved even more clearly Castro's delusions of persecution.

The logic here, not surprisingly, mirrors the logic manifest by Clevin-ger in *Catch-22*. A liberal idealist, Clevinger typifies the best and brightest young men, many of whom, a decade and a half after World War II, would find themselves in the Kennedy administration and, after Kennedy's assas-sination, as architects of the Vietnam War: "As a Harvard undergraduate he had won prizes in scholarship for just about everything, and the only reason he had not won prizes in scholarship for just about everything else was that he was too busy signing petitions, circulating petitions and chal-lenging petitions, joining discussion groups and resigning from discussion groups, attending youth congresses, picketing other youth congresses and organizing student committees in defense of dismissed faculty members. . . . In short, Clevinger was one of those people with lots of intelligence and no brains, and everyone knew it except those who soon found it out" (67). Clevinger's assessment of Yossarian, uncannily similar to the CIA's analysis of Castro, concluded that Yossarian was crazy, grounded especially in Yos-sarian's "unfounded suspicion that people hated him and were conspiring to kill him" (20). Yossarian's suspicion, however, was founded, like Castro's, on evidence:

> "Then why are they shooting at me?" Yossarian asked.
> "They're shooting at *everyone*," Clevinger answered, "They're trying to kill everyone."
> "And what difference does that make?" (16)

At issue here is the authority to define sets. When Yossarian points out, in another argument with Clevinger, that "It doesn't make a damned bit of difference *who* wins the war to someone who's dead," Clevinger tells him that he "can't think of another attitude that could be depended upon to give comfort to the enemy." "The enemy," Yossarian responds, "is anyone who is going to get you killed, no matter what side he's on" (122). While Clevinger is trying to maintain distinctions of Other and Same, as the major premises from which other distinctions follow, Yossarian has constructed a set that merges Other and Same in ways that reorganize the meaning of "enemy." If, as Clevinger maintains, the enemy is the group that is trying to kill him when he's flying a mission, then Yossarian's failure to distinguish the enemy from those who order him to fly the mission will indeed comfort the enemy. If the enemy, on the other hand, is any group responsible for his getting killed, then Clevinger's insistence on seeing commanding officers as ally rather than foe provides comfort to the real enemy, and Yossarian's accusations provide discomfort.

But who is the "real" enemy? In this situation, as in so many throughout the novel, events do not mandate interpretation but rather interpretation determines perception and thus predetermines "reality." Clevinger's court marshall provides another example: "Clevinger had a mind and Lieutenant Sheisskopf had noticed that people with minds tend to get pretty smart at times. Such men were dangerous, and even the new cadet officers whom Clevinger had helped into office were eager to give damning testimony against him. The case against Clevinger was open and shut. The only thing missing was something to charge him with" (70). Having stumbled while marching to class, Clevinger is then charged with "breaking ranks while in formation, felonious assault, indiscriminate behavior, mopery, high treason, provoking, being a wise guy, listening to classical music, and so on" (74). The outcome, as the tribunal decides, is that "Clevinger was guilty, of course, or he would not have been accused, and since the only way to prove it was to find him guilty, it was their patriotic duty to do so" (79). Clevinger's status—dangerous not benign, guilty not innocent—functioned independently of any action or predisposition he had manifested. It was rather a function of the power to classify. Guilt was not determined by objective criteria—evidence that Clevinger committed a specific offense—but was the product of the accusation, and it was also therefore the origin of the offense. In a final assault on the principle of set theory, upon which traditional logic rests, Yossarian simultaneously employs it and demolishes it in the interest of explaining Clevinger's outcome:

> "You haven't got a chance, kid," he told them glumly. "They hate Jews."
>
> "But I'm not Jewish," answered Clevinger.
>
> "It will make no difference," Yossarian promised, and Yossarian was right. "They're after everybody." (80).

For Yossarian, Clevinger's distinctions "make no difference." Although even their own systems of classification show that Clevinger is not their enemy, Clevinger remains their enemy. The need to differentiate between ally and enemy upon which the officers' status as officers and their identity as soldiers depends takes precedence over any criteria for difference. They need to constitute their identity through the production of an enemy, as Clevinger learns, independent of the criteria for doing so: "[he] understood instantly that nowhere in the world, not in all the fascist tanks or planes or submarines, not in the bunkers behind the machine guns or mortars or behind the blowing flame throwers, not even among all the expert gunners of the crack Hermann Goering Antiaircraft Division or among the grisly connivers in all the beer halls in Munich and everywhere else, were there men who hated him more" (80). The separation of evidence from conclusion is further underscored by Clevinger's subsequent refusal to classify as enemies officers who want him dead, even though his own experience made it impossible for him to differentiate their attitude toward him from that of the Germans.

Clevinger and Yossarian seem to be arguing about the minor premise in a syllogism—who fits the classification "enemy"—but they are actually disputing the authority to establish the major premise, because all wars, hot and cold, require narrative, a chain of provocation, response, and justification, of desires frustrated or fulfilled. Without a set of assumptions, a body of major premises, such as the idea of a "national interest" or the presumption of a "chain of command," that narrative is untenable. In order to challenge the authority of the metanarrative, Heller repeatedly asserts a series of major premises upon which a line of reasoning depends, only to show that the premises comprise null sets. In arguing with Yossarian, Clevinger asserts the trustworthiness of the commanding officers, based tautologically (albeit subtly so) on the premise that they are in positions of trust: "There are men who are entrusted with winning the war who are in a much better position than we are to decide what targets have to be bombed" (122).[4] Yet Clevinger already knows that these are the same positions of trust that allowed the officers to view him as their enemy, and thus he should know that he has created a category based on faith rather than reason.

THE MAJOR, MAJOR, MAJOR, MAJOR PREMISE

If the authority for offices of command relies on null sets, perhaps the exemplary null set in the novel is Major Major Major Major. Even his name is an empty sign, signifying not authority but the name of authority, not power but its absence. His promotion to squadron commander was rendered as a tautology that emphasized its insignificance: " 'You're the new squadron commander,' Colonel Cathcart had shouted rudely across the railroad ditch to him. 'But don't think it means anything, because it doesn't. All it means is that you're the new squadron commander' " (57). Like his promotion to squadron commander, his initial promotion to major, done by an IBM machine with a sense of humor, is an empty gesture indicating the power of signs divorced from their referents. Similarly, Major Major Major's name, secretly given to him as a joke by his father, identifies nothing. Unaware of this name until he started kindergarten, "it was a harsh and stunning realization . . . that he was not as he had always been led to believe, Caleb Major, but was instead some total stranger named Major Major Major, about whom he knew absolutely nothing and about whom nobody else had ever heard before" (84). Bearing a striking resemblance to Henry Fonda, Major Major even lacks his own physical identity and is recognized only as a reference point, an allusion to someone he is not and whose public identity, in turn, is an imaginary referent, coming as it does from roles written and directed by other people. Simlarly, his personality and his personal history, constructed completely out of clichés, are vague references to empty signs:

> He was polite to his elders, who disliked him. Whatever his elders told him to do, he did. They told him to look before he leaped, and he always looked before he leaped. They told him never to put off until the next day what he could do the day before, and he never did. He was told to honor his father and his mother, and he honored his father and his mother. He was told that

one should not kill, and he did not kill, until he got into the Army. Then he was told to kill, and he killed. He turned the other cheek on every occasion and always did unto others exactly as he would have had others do unto him. When he gave to charity, his left hand never knew what his right hand was doing. He never once took the name of the Lord his God in vain, committed adultery or coveted his neighbor's ass. In fact, he loved his neighbor and never even bore false witness against him. Major Major's elders disliked him because he was such a flagrant non-conformist. (84)

Even the clichés that comprise his identity, the passage makes clear, like Henry Fonda's public identity, refer to a null set: a body of fictions, a composite of normative behavior to which conforming is abnormal.

The only perogative that the novel allows to Major Major's authority is ordering that people may see him in his office only when he is out; when he is in he receives no visitors. In this way, the power to assert his own authority becomes synonymous with absenting himself from the site of that authority. A major premise of the novel, then, is that the major (major major major) premise of the syllogistic reasoning upon which war, national narratives, or any form of institutional behavior depends is a null set; its authority derives not from a substantive body of reasons but, like Major Major's rank or any form of cliché, from mechanical and mindless repetition.

This situation helps explain the novel's pervasive critiques of mindless repetition. By challenging the relationship of literal to figurative, for example, Heller undermines the process of referentiality through which words and phrases acquire authority. When we are told that "it was a vile and muddy war, and Yossarian could have lived without it—lived forever, perhaps" (67), we are denied both the figurative and literal meanings of the phrase "could have lived without it." If we are reminded that war is literally life-threatening, we are also reminded that life is always threatened, that death is a matter of unavoidable fact and life its intermittent aberration. The set that comprises the living, as Nietzsche reminds us, is only a small subset of the field of death. Language like "could have lived without it" attempts to make a difference by giving authority to a discrete category—like enemy or ally, playboy or virgin, Other or Same—a category whose status is purely nominal: a null set.

Yet upon these null sets rests the authority to create hierarchies, and, repeatedly, the novel underscores the power of language to create bogus hierarchies. A particularly apt example, because it deals directly with the issue of hierarchy, is the sentence describing Major Major's relationship to Major —— de Coverly: "He knew that Major —— de Coverly was his executive officer, but he did not know what that meant, and he could not decide whether in Major —— de Coverly he was blessed with a lenient superior or cursed with a delinquent subordinate" (90). The very phrase created by the army to designate nominal authority calls that authority into question, and the very character who exercises the greatest nominal authority in the novel is, by virtue of that authority, so intimidating that no one knows his name. De Coverly thus exists simultaneously as the sign of absolute nominalism and the site of namelessness. When Yossarian moves the bombing line that nominally divides Other from Same and makes possible the narrative of progress and setback upon which war history depends, Major —— de Coverly goes into Bologna and disappears, a victim of blind—he was already blind in one eye—faith in the power of nominal divisions.

The nominal nature of these divisions is further underscored by Milo Minderbinder's reclassification of the war based on the right to earn profits. From Milo's perspective, the bomb lines are meaningless, since both the Germans and the Americans are members of the same syndicate. When Milo arranges to have his own bases bombed, his double agency is redeemed under the monolithic discourse of free enterprise, which allows him to escape all charges of treason merely by demonstrating that he made a profit. Similarly, his privileged position as head of the syndicate allows him to sell the position of enemy targets to the Allies and sell the time of the consequent bombing raid to the enemy.

Milo thus becomes the production site of double agency and, under the name of the syndicate, its monolithic redeemer. The doubling of agency, like Milo's process of selling everything twice, becomes synonyous with the single-minded goal of the free world in the cold war: to make the world free for the pursuit of private enterprise. Under the rubric of these clichés, even those who do not own stock in his enterprise have a stock in protecting its profits.

Because the power of Milo's double agency depends on its being seen as contributing to the single goal of profiting the syndicate, to which everyone belongs, the act of *seeing* everything twice threatens his authority. The novel is full of such acts of seeing everything twice, from the recontextualizing of categories or the literalizing of clichés, to obsessive return to places and events, such as the hospital, the target at Ferrara, or the scene of Snowden's death over Avignon.

The novel is also marked by a recurrent sense of déjà vu, the sensation of perceiving as double an event that the normative discourse regards as single and unique. To challenge that norm, as Holden Caulfield demonstrated, calls into question one's sanity. In *Catch-22*, the chaplain comes closest to sharing Caulfield's—or Salinger's—point of view by trying to retain faith in a verity outside of the interpretive community. Like Caulfield, he then ends up internalizing his failure to explain phenomena, and thus he doubts his sanity. He does not know how to cope with the sense of déjà vu he experiences when seeing Yossarian, nor with the sense that he had seen a naked man in a tree while presiding at Snowden's funeral:

> The chaplain felt most deceitful presiding at funerals, and it would not have astonished him to learn that the apparition in the tree that day was a manifestation of the Almighty's censure for the blasphemy of pride inherent in his function. To simulate gravity, feign grief and pretend supernatural intelligence of the hereafter in so fearsome and arcane a circumstance as death seemed the most criminal of offenses. . . . How could he explain [the vision of a naked man in a tree]? It was not already seen or never seen, and certainly not almost seen; neither *déjà vu, jamais vu* nor *presque vu* was elastic enough to cover it. Was it a ghost then? The dead man's soul? An angel from heaven or a minion from hell? Or was the whole fantastic episode merely the figment of a diseased imagination, his own, of a deteriorating mind, a rotting brain? The possibility that there really was a naked man in a tree . . . never crossed the chaplain's mind. (266–67)

On two occasions on the same day the chaplain finds himself in Colonel Cathcart's office. On both occasions, the colonel is trying to devise a way of getting himself into *Life* magazine; his inspiration is a story that the magazine has already run. His first idea—that the chaplain hold prayer meetings before bombing runs—is abandoned when Cathcart is confronted to his astonishment with the major premise of monotheism: "You mean [enlisted men] pray to the same God we do?" "Yes, sir." "And He *listens?*" (191). On the second occasion, Cathcart wants the chaplain and his assistant to write for him sincere letters of condolence, full of personal details, "to the next of kin of every man in the group who's killed, wounded or taken prisoner"

(275). These personal sentiments are to be expressed through the mindless repetition of a form letter. On both occasions, the office is full of bushels of ripe plum tomatoes, from Cathcart and Korn's farm in the hills, tomatoes that Milo buys and sells twice.

Standing for the second time before the colonel, who for the second time is trying to use the chaplain to get into *Life* magazine, surrounded by bushels of tomatoes that come from the Cathcart's second occupation—supplying Milo with food he sells twice—hearing a plan for duplicating personal letters, the chaplain "was almost convinced that he had stood in Colonel Cathcart's office on some similar occasion deep in the past and had been surrounded by those same bushels of those same plum tomatoes. *Déjà vu* again" (276).

Or once again "déjà vu" rationalizes the perception of duplicity that penetrates the aura of monolithic authority. In this situation, as in the chaplain's view of the naked man in the tree, Heller suggests that events do not mandate interpretation, but rather that interpretation determines perception and thus predetermines "reality." This point is emphasized when, to the chaplain's horror, Cathcart decides to volunteer his men to bomb Avignon a second time because "the sooner we get some casualties, the sooner we can make some progress on this. I'd like to get into the Christmas issue if we can" (277). If the first mission over Avignon was caused by a military strategy, the enactment of which caused high casualties, in the second mission the casualties would cause the mission.

The double purposes—one aimed at diminishing the enemy's resources, the other at diminishing one's own resources—suggest the reversibility of cause and effect, as does the case of the "soldier in white." Covered in gauze from head to toe, the soldier in white has one intravenous tube entering above his elbow, "through which he was fed clear fluid from a jar" (10). Another tube from his groin dripped clear liquid into a stoppered jar on the floor. "When the jar on the floor was full, the jar feeding the elbow was empty, and the two were simply switched so that the two could drip back into him" (10). When Dunbar wonders, at one point, why they couldn't connect the tubes and eliminate the middleman, he articulates exactly the problem of constituting the subject in *Catch-22*—that he is not an individual but a functionary in a flow that is arbitrary and reversible. (Milo's ostensive role as consummate middleman, similarly, turns out to be a linguistic function that disguises his positions at the ends of the chains, as the ultimate buyer and ultimate seller in a syndicated flow that he controls.)

The absence of a predetermined direction to that flow makes any concept of causality—and hence culpability—impossible, a point even further underscored by Yossarian's analysis of the soldier in white's death: "Now that Yossarian looked back, it seemed that Nurse Cramer . . . had murdered the soldier in white; if she had not read the thermometer and reported what she found, the soldier in white might still be lying there alive exactly as he had been lying there all along. . . . Lying there that way may not have been much of a life, but it was all the life he had, and the decision to terminate it, Yossarian felt, should hardly have been Nurse Cramer's" (166). The vital flow in the novel, as this passage makes clear, is not kidney fluid but language. Thus ex-Pfc. Wintergreen runs the army because, having access to a switchboard and a mimeograph machine, he not only controls but generates, redirects, and critiques language. He intervenes in memo wars by informing one general that his writing is too prolix and disrupts phone conversations by inserting, apparently from nowhere, the phrase "T. S. Eliot."

As a censor of letters, Yossarian similarly intervenes anonymously under the names "Washington Irving" and "Irving Washington," thus triggering both imitation Washington Irving/Irving Washingtons and a c.i.d. witch hunt to unearth him/them. The reversibility of the name mirrors the reversibility of the hunt itself, in which suspect and accused constantly change roles, until the innocent chaplain is finally "proved" to be the culprit because his signature looks nothing like that of Washington Irving/Irving Washington. What better proof that he must be a forger? The forger, however, is also not Yossarian, who quickly became bored with the task and, in any case, vacated the job each time he left the hospital. The vacancy was quickly filled by the compendium of vacancies, Major Major Major Major, who does double service as absent authority and bogus censor. Nominal, anonymous, and infinitely reversible, he is the crucial and crucially empty link in the hierarchical system that turns dual purposes into singular actions. To see the double purposes is to challenge the major premises in the logical chain from which the chain of command derives its authority.

The novel suggests, moreover, that the only valid premise for any chain of logic is that all repetition, any form of language, is as Derrida argues in "Plato's Pharmacy," a death rehearsal. Yossarian learns this lesson in basic training when he emulates and then becomes a delirious soldier who claims to see everything twice, although it is unclear whether "twice" refers to double images or chronic repetitions. In any case, the doctors can do no more than argue about who has the authority to diagnose him (which will, of course, determine the diagnosis) and quarantine him. In order to prolong his stay in the hospital (and thus out of the war), Yossarian emulates the ailing soldier: "[Yossarian] knew he was in the presence of a master. His talented roommate was obviously a person to be studied and emulated. During the night, his talented roommate died, and Yossarian decided that he had followed him far enough" (180).

In the rest of the chapter, Yossarian attempts in numerous ways, all unsuccessful, to distinguish himself from the soldier who saw everything twice and was thus bound for death. His attempts to claim he was cured are thwarted by the doctor who knew he was feigning all along. Being cured of the disease thus makes no difference because, as the doctor points out, "Of course you're dying. We're all dying. Where the devil else do you think you're heading?" (181). The doctor wants Yossarian to pretend to be the soldier who saw everything twice for the soldier's grief-stricken family, so that the family won't feel that it has traveled to the dying son's bedside in vain. If Yossarian refuses, furthermore, the doctor threatens to report Yossarian for feigning his liver ailment. At the same time that the doctor asserts his authority, however, he demolishes the distinctions that separate him from Yossarian: "We're all in this business of illusion together. I'm always willing to lend a helping hand to a fellow conspirator along the road to survival . . ." (181). Just as the enemy is anyone who wants to kill Yossarian, the ally is anyone who, like him, wants to keep them both alive. The other distinctions—national, political, professional, military, physical, sexual—are the business of illusion, the process of creating an Other so as to deny the Sameness: "We're all dying."

When the doctor then tells him that all he has to do is "lie there a few minutes and die a little. Is that asking too much?" (181), the implicit question is whether Yossarian can do anything less. No matter how much Yossarian tries to destroy the illusion that he is the dying soldier, he cannot. The fact that he looks nothing like their son, Giuseppe, confirms for the family the gravity of his illness, as does the fact that he uses another name. They even try to honor his wish to be called Yossarian in deference to his terminal condition. Their deference thus makes it impossible to him to assert a difference, so that in his final exchanges with the family, neither he nor they know who is dying. When the brother says they feared that they wouldn't get there in time to see him die, Yossarian asks what difference it would make and the brother explains that they didn't want him to die by himself. When Yossarian once again asks, "What difference would it make?" his question ceases to be substantive, instead becoming one more way of destroying the difference between Yossarian and the delirious soldier who saw everything twice: " 'He must be getting delirious,' the brother said. 'He keeps saying the same thing over and over again' " (183). When the mother is then corrected for calling him Giuseppe, she too demolishes the nominal differences that identify Yossarian: " 'What difference does it make?' the mother answered in the same mourning tone, without looking up. 'He's dying' " (184). The family starts to cry, and "Yossarian remembered suddenly why they were all crying, and he began crying too" (184). When the father's parting remark—"Soon you are going to die" (184)—makes Yossarian cry a second time, it is impossible to isolate the cause of Yossarian's tears because there is no way to differentiate the Yossarian who identifies with the family whose son has died and the Yossarian who identifies with the dead son. He is not Giuseppe, not Italian, not ill, not dead, but neither are these meaningful distinctions when the father gives the same prognosis as the doctor had earlier: "Soon you're going to die."

The fact that Giuseppe is Italian further complicates the reliance on narratives of Other and Same upon which both the war narrative and the act of warfare depend. Giuseppe is the same as Yossarian, so much so that Yossarian cannot differentiate himself from Giuseppe even to Giuseppe's parents or, in some ways, to himself. And yet in the war, Italians are the Other and Italy is the site of most of the bombing missions that he flies. Italians are also the whores who comfort the conquering allies and the whores who disdain them. In a dialogue with Nately in an Italian brothel, the 107-year-old Italian man effectively dismantles the idea of national narratives when he points out that "the trick lies in *losing* wars" (240), that "Italian soldiers are not dying any more. But American and German soldiers are" (238), and that "there are now fifty or sixty countries fighting in this war. Surely so many countries can't *all* be worth dying for" (242). The old man thus puts Nately in the position of defending the unreconcilable premises that inform the cold war. In Nately's discourse, Italy is the Other—the vanquished enemy—while also being a nation of people welcoming American liberation. Thus Italy is the Same. Nately wants both to conquer Italy and to be loved, courted, seduced by it. On a personal level, Nately has been seduced by and fallen in love with an Italian whore, and he wants her to love him in return. To this end, he continues to pay for her services in the hopes that by reinforcing this continuous business relationship he will effect its dissolution. The old man effectively tells him, however, that whoredom—sexual, political, national—is not a subset of lovemaking, a kind of courtship, but the major premise from which all courtship is deduced.

For this reason, control over Nately's whore becomes an essential issue of conflict, upon which the authority of the army command depends. Trapped in a hotel room by an array of "middle-aged military big shots" (346), Nately's whore could not leave until she said "uncle":

> "You still don't understand, do you? We can't really make you say uncle unless you don't want to say uncle. Don't you see? Don't say uncle when I tell you to say uncle. Okay? Say uncle."
>
> "Uncle," she said.
>
> "No, don't say uncle. Say uncle."
>
> She didn't say uncle.
>
> "That's good!"
>
> "That's very good."
>
> "It's a start. Now say uncle."
>
> "Uncle," she said.
>
> "It's no good."
>
> "No, it's no good that way either. She just isn't impressed with us. There's no fun in making her say uncle when she doesn't care whether we make her say uncle or not." (346)

At issue, then, is not her actions but the narrative in which those actions are situated. That narrative, however, is full of contradictions: it demands that she both refuse to submit to their authority and refuse not to, that she both be won over by their power and be paid for her services, that she be relied upon both to accede to their demands and to act of her own volition. Like Holden Caulfield, she is expected, moreover, to internalize the contradictions involved in meeting those demands, for the alternative is to expose their impossibility, and the power of all authority rests in its ability to make demands that can be met.

If Holden Caulfield spoke for the cold war HUAC witness, expressing existential angst over the nature and meaning of his "testimony," Nately's whore speaks what will emerge as a postmodern form of testimony that glosses the superficiality of the binary opposition between spiritual and forensic testimony: "She didn't care about them a bit, and it upset them terribly. They shook her roughly each time she yawned. She did not seem to care about anything, even when they threatened to throw her out the window. They were utterly demoralized men of distinction. She was bored and indifferent and wanted very much to sleep. . . . She wondered vaguely why they wanted her to laugh when they laughed, and why they wanted *her* to enjoy it when they made love to her. It was all very mysterious to her, and all very uninteresting" (346). The relationship between authority and gendered narrative is foregrounded here by the whore, who inverts the role of the McCarthyist witness who is both courting the interrogators and courted by them. The McCarthyist witness, selling betrayal as a form of loyalty, must gain acceptability by suppressing the prostitutional nature of the intercourse. Once prostitution defines the conditions of the intercourse, the interrogation will not be validated but eliminated by the suppression of its prostitutional context. In this way, Heller deconstructs the gendered narrative of the cold war that informed not only George Kennan's "containment" essay but also the courtship roles that, as we have seen, permeate equally the American sense of domestic security and of domesticity, from Hiroshima to the Bay of Pigs.

I am arguing, in other words, that the binary opposition of lady and tramp is represented here not as an opposition but as a continuous surface that comprises one of the superficial representations of the containment narrative. Like the seductions in *Pillow Talk,* the saying of "uncle" has to be both voluntary and coerced, a manifestation of loyalty and of rivalry, a marriage of opposites, for if the history of the CIA proves nothing else, it proves that politics makes strange bedfellows. Those bedfellows, however, are created by the strangeness of containment itself, a policy that can never remain self-contained because it must always promote the courtship and the estrangement of the Other. Recontextualized as acts of prostitution, however, volition and coercion become arbitrary and indistinguishable versions of the same empty sign system. The importance of this passage is not that "uncle" functions as an empty sign, but that, in a move that anticipates

the American reception of Roland Barthes's *Mythologies,* Heller's text foregrounds that emptiness as a vacancy upon which the power/knowledge
system relies and hence that it must deny.

WHY DON'T WE MOUNT AN INVASION IN DENMARK?

The historical specificity of that rhetorical move is suggested by its similarity to discourse surrounding the Bay of Pigs invasion, an action that,
like *Catch-22,* makes legible the double and self-contradictory speech upon
which the logic of cold war discourse depended. As an act of liberation,
for example, the invasion was supposed to free Cuba from communist dic-
tatorship, but the overthrow of Castro functioned independently of plans
for the subsequent governance of Cuba, so much so that the provisional
government to be set up in Cuba was not even conceived until long after the
plans for invasion to establish it were in place. To put it simply, the purpose
of the invasion was to put the rule of Cuba in the hands of a governing
body that did not exist. Although that governing body was to be credited
with planning and directing the invasion, it was itself merely one of the
invasion plans.

At a stage in the planning of the invasion, a liberation government representing Cuba was created by the dictates of the United States, which represented the interests of free Cubans, which the free Cubans were not free to
represent for themselves:

> Jim Noble [an alias], the last station chief in Havana . . . was attending a
> meeting at the State Department run by Bissell and Adolf A. Berle, Ken-
> nedy's Latin American specialist at State. Colonel King, the c1a's Western
> Hemisphere man, was there. Bill Bundy represented Defense. At the end of
> the table sat [Richard Goodwin from the White House]. . . .
>
> Finally Berle said, "Well whom do we have who could become part of
> the Cuban committee?"
>
> King turned to Jim, who said "Well, there's Tony Varona."
>
> "Well," said Berle, "give us a rundown on him."
>
> Jim said that Varona was a former Vice-President of Cuba and head of
> the Cuban Senate. He then mentioned other exile leaders. The men at the
> table seemed to know little or nothing about any of them.

"Why don't we get together four or five of these people and name them?" asked Berle.

Jim said, "Gee, can I make a suggestion? There must be a couple of hundred thousand Cubans in the Miami area to give this thing some substance. Couldn't they have a convention down there? Maybe we could get a few thousand of them together. Whatever it is, at least you would have some basis of popular support."

"We have no time for consulting the Cubans on this," Berle said. (Wyden, 114–15)

Most of the "experts" knew nothing about the old Cuba that Castro had overthrown or the Cuban exiles with which they wished to replace him. Both were completely marginal to the operation. Cuba was defined completely by the presence and/or absence of Castro. Although ostensibly marginal to the true Cuba, Castro had come to define that Cuba such that his absence could restore it to the true blank space that it had otherwise occupied in the perspective governing American strategies of containment.

From that perspective, Cuba itself was the absence that surrounded geographically and chronologically Castro's regime, while the regime was the center of U.S. attention. That attention, however, needed supplementary help from the rest of Cuba: from the forbidding terrain that surrounded Castro's island of power; from the anti-Castro Cuban rebels, whose rebellion the invading exiles would bolster; from the Cuban exiles, who would supply an invasion force and whose interests that force would represent; from a Cuban government in exile, whose authority would legitimize the invasive use of force. The image of Castro as surrounded by the hostile environs—geographic and political—from which he had himself emerged, however, was an essential detail in a narrative constructed in order to create the conditions it professed to describe.

In an inversion of cause and effect that could exemplify a principle of poststructuralism, the United States coerced the formation of the coalition that it was allegedly supporting, so that the coalition was the product of the invasion, not its sponsor. As Etheredge notes, "just *after* his selection as head of the liberation government, Dr. Miro Cardona was requested to ratify the CIA's *earlier* selection of Manuel Artime as Brigade Commander" (39; emphasis added). The selection itself, of course, was the product of the brigade's having been assembled as one part of the invasion plan. Were there no plan, there would have been no brigade, which in turn would have required neither a nominal Cuban brigade leader nor a liberation government to appoint him retroactively. If the coalition government did not represent the Cubans, it was also not allowed to represent itself. Instead, the CIA hired a public relations firm, and the CIA propaganda chief dictated statements to the firm on behalf of the liberation government, which was not even at liberty to write its own liberation manifesto; the manifesto was authored instead by CIA operative (and later Watergate defendant) E. Howard Hunt.

Hunt's manifesto, however, was no less representative of the coalition's positions than the coalition's own assertions. Reviewing with Arthur Schlesinger the land reform package that the White House wanted his group to adopt, Cardona "sighed; it could be put down on paper, but almost any idea, including these bold reforms, was a matter of intense controversy among the politicians temporarily united under his leadership" (Etheredge, 39; see also Wyden, 116). The coalition thus signified the impossibility of coalescing, and the conditions that legitimized the coalition made legitimate speech impossible. The liberation government was either authorizing speech it hadn't authored or authoring speech it didn't believe. Like *Catch-22*'s soldier in white, it comprised the blank space that gave speechless nominal authority to an infinitely reversible flow over whose origins and goals it had no control.

When some of the expatriate Cubans objected to this functionary status, they were, like Dunbar, "disappeared": "about a dozen intransigent troublemakers were kidnapped . . . and held incommunicado by armed guards for three and a half months until the invasion attempt was completed" (Etheredge, 40). At one planning meeting, according to Wyden, the former Havana Bureau Chief Jim Noble (an alias) asked when the Cuban underground would be notified.

> "We're not going to advise them at all," Colonel Hawkins said. "With those dumb bastards over there, it will be all over town. If we tell them it will be on a certain day, the whole goddamn island will know about it."
>
> "The whole goddam island knows about it now," Jim said, "and every newspaper in the United States knows about it. Why should we keep in the dark the guys whose heads are going to be on the block?"
>
> "Well I don't trust any goddam Cuban," the Colonel barked.
>
> "Jack," Jim taunted, "why the hell are we mounting an invasion in Cuba?

Why don't we mount an invasion in Denmark? They're real nice people over there, and I think you'll love it! You'd trust the hell out of them. Don't let's fool around with these Cubans." (Wyden, 115)

If Cubans didn't need to initiate their invasion, didn't need to plan it, couldn't be trusted to speak on behalf of it, and weren't allowed to know when it would take place, the role of the Cuban exile community was solely to function as a sign—a necessarily empty sign—of non-Castro Cubanness, in the name of which American support could be enlisted. This liberation government that the United States would assist, however, like the foreign movie space in *What's New Pussycat?* was the homemade product of U.S. imagination. Helping the liberation government was thus the imaginary means by which the United States could help itself (to Cuba).

If the function of the liberation government was to signify legitimate Cuban authority (as the function of catch-22 was to signify legitimate American military authority), it failed to fulfill its function, becoming instead, like catch-22, a sign of the impossibility of locating the site of authority within a coherent, logical system.

This problem could not be more clearly exemplified than by the Heller-like character of General Charles Cabell, a CIA deputy director, who was left in charge of operations over the weekend of the invasion. Director Dulles feared that deviating from standard procedures by leaving a more capable person in charge would jeopardize the secrecy of the operation. He didn't want, in other words, to risk leaving the operation in competent hands. Instead the weekend operations were handled, as usual, by General Cabell, whom Peter Wyden describes as a taciturn man,

> given to communicating by grunts whenever possible. . . . At meetings he often fell asleep, which worried his colleagues; they thought that with his ever-present cigar still clenched in his teeth, he might burn himself. . . .
>
> Best of all, Cabell liked to go on inspection trips of CIA stations abroad— as many countries in as short a time as possible. Two retired colonels serving in the agency would have to squeeze themselves into their old uniforms to travel in attendance. Elaborate briefings were scheduled in every country. The material in the resulting reports, Bob Amory always said, "you could get out of Section Four of *The New York Times.*"
>
> During the Cuban affair, Cabell became known as "Old Rice and Beans." Having approved a weapons drop for some guerrillas, he learned that the

supplies would take up only part of the plane. He ordered it filled with rice and beans. Dave Philips pointed out that rice and beans, the national dishes of Cuba, were two items that were not scarce. "Son," said the general, "I don't want to have to explain to an appropriations committee why we're flying nearly empty planes over Cuba."

The guerrilla team leader radioed that the heavy bags almost killed his men and questioned headquarters' sanity. (196)

The guerrilla leader was, as *Catch-22* makes clear, raising exactly the wrong question. Since sanity is a function not of logic but of authority, and the authority of officers is presumed, it is illogical to question their sanity. The same logic that thus justified Cabell's decisions to his subordinates justified President Kennedy's to Cabell. When Cabell found himself in the position of having to convince the president to reinstate the air strikes, without which there was *no* chance of a successful invasion, he related the information to Secretary of State Dean Rusk. Rusk called the president, explained the situation, but still advised against the strike. When Kennedy agreed with Rusk, Rusk gave Cabell the opportunity to speak directly to the president, but Cabell declined, saying, "There's no point in my talking to the President" (Wyden, 200).

The point, of course, would have been to question the president's decision, but within Cabell's understanding of authority, that could raise questions about his own sanity; nothing was more questionable than the choice to raise questions. Throughout the Bay of Pigs operation it is clear that questions do not produce answers but blank spots, filled by allusion to some absent authority. The liberation government, for example, was established to answer the same question that the invasion was supposed to answer but, even before D-Day, could not: Who represents Cuba? The Bay of Pigs invasion, similarly, was supposed to solve the problem of representing Cuba, but instead the invasion merely made clear the array of competing agents asserting representative status and the dubiousness of their authority to do so. In addition, and perhaps more important, the invasion also made clear the confusion about the audiences for whom the representation was aimed. The liberation government, claiming to represent Cuba *for* the expatriate community, in fact represented Cuba *to* that community and represented the expatriate community *to* the larger U.S. and world communities. The liberation government represented Cuba to these audiences *for* the CIA, whose interests it served. To some degree—perhaps a crucial degree—the liberation government also represented Cuba to JFK, for whom the commitment of the expatriates was an important (perhaps decisive) factor in supporting the operation. In this way, the exile government was doing overtly what the CIA was doing covertly: representing Cuba to the president of the United States.

The covert (intelligence) reports, however, as the actual invasion made clear, were misrepresentations. The underground was not ready to rise up; there was little support for insurgency; there was no substantial force of guerrillas in the mountains; there were no mountains near the bay; the bay was not secluded; the dark coastal blotches on the aerial photos (analyzed by CIA experts) was not seaweed but coral; the landing could not be effected at night; the air strikes could not possibly be large enough to immobilize the Cuban air force while still being small enough to be successfully represented as the work solely of Cuban defectors; the coalition liberation government could not be relied upon to promote reform or democracy, nor could it be relied upon to have the support of the Cuban people, especially since some of its members were former leaders the Cubans had thrown out.

The one thing the liberation government could be relied on to do, however, was to ask military assistance of the United States, which planned to recognize the government as soon as it landed on Cuban soil. This meant that the exile government was supposed to represent Cuba to the world (O.A.S., U.N.), even at the exact moment that it was demonstrating its inability to represent Cuba to the Cubans. But the Cubans, as we have noted, were the blank space onto which would be written a narrative of representation that the United States could recognize as true. That recognition would come from the fact that the United States had served not only as reader but as author of the narrative.

Attempting to assume the role of quintessential playboy—both charmer and trickster, Rock Hudson and James Bond—JFK was thus implicated, like the ideal *Playboy* reader, in the autoerotics of reading his own narrative. But as Woody Allen's recontextualizing of the playboy makes clear, his role as ideal reader is necessarily framed and hopelessly complicated by his sense of his own image. And thus, exactly because JFK, like all would-be "playboys," could not extricate his self-serving goals from the sense of image that framed them, he was the worst possible reader of the narrative that the CIA prepared and that the liberation government represented.

Castro's rise to power in Cuba thus created a crisis in representation for the United States, one that could not be contained to the representation of Cuba, because U.S. representations of Cuba became inextricably connected to U.S. representations of itself. The intelligence agencies, for example, could not represent Cuba without also representing themselves as reliable sources of intelligence and also as strategists who have efficaciously represented U.S. interests. Because these strategies were covert, moreover, the United States had the additional problem of representing itself to the world as differing from the image implied by the strategies it pursued. These dual goals of representing its interests and representing its image were discrete and intertwined. The United States had to represent itself as acting overtly in a way that differed from its covert actions, but that difference could not be so great as to be recognizable as such, lest the U.S. image suffer to the extent that it would not be good for U.S. interests.

To this end, the U.S. government replicated inside itself the same strategies of duplicity and containment that it practiced to the outside world. The most infamous consequence of this doubling was Adlai Stevenson's aggresive lying on the floor of the u.n., when he emphatically denied that the B-26 pilot who had landed in Miami was on a U.S. mission (as were the other B-26s that attacked Castro's air bases) rather than the Cuban air force defector he claimed to be. When Stevenson called Washington to check the defector story, the assistant secretary of state was lied to when he contacted the cia on Stevenson's behalf. "In the cia's view," Etheredge explains, "an assistant secretary of state had no right ('need') to know his part was a cover-up. A cover-up was *better* if believed by its defenders: why uncautiously open the door to complication or entrust national security only to their acting ability? If the assistant secretary or Stevenson should have known, they would have been briefed by their bureaucratic superior (Rusk) who did know" (85). The fact that Stevenson did not know proved that he did not need to know, and since (we could say, according to catch-22) it was necessary not to do anything that was unnecessary, if Stevenson did not need to know then he needed not to know, a necessity sufficiently proved by the fact that he did not know. Asking the question thus proved that he should not get the answer. (The converse of this rule is stated explicitly in *Catch-22*, when Headquarters expresses alarm about the questions at Clevinger's educational sessions, "for there was no telling what people might find out once they felt free to ask whatever questions they wanted to" (35). Colonel Korn, in response, creates the rule that "the only people permitted to ask questions were those who never did" (35).

This secret manipulation of Stevenson manifested what Roger Hilsman identified as a more general rivalry between the State Department and the CIA, with jealousy on both sides.[5] It also reflected divisions within the CIA, where there was a felt pressure to give Bissell the information he needed to support the case for invasion and to recruit the Cuban exiles who would support the claims Bissell had made for them.[6] During the course of the training and invasion, moreover, the Cuban exile recruits were chronically misinformed about the level of promised U.S. support, so as to keep them committed to the task.[7]

It is important to understand that these misrepresentations were not merely lapses or errors. Rather, they were understandable failures to differentiate between those misrepresentations that were inherent to the strategy upon which the operation was based and those that might undermine it. Misrepresentation was at every level part of the logical system that enabled the planning, not an invidious or parasitic element in a coherent structure.

For the invasion to succeed, for example, prior air strikes immobilizing Castro's air force were deemed essential, but these strikes could only be possible if they could be successfully misrepresented as having been carried out by defectors from the Cuban air force. Although this misrepresentation may have been necessary to convince other nations of U.S. noninvolvement—and did convince Adlai Stevenson—it certainly could not convince Castro, who of course would know if any pilots or planes were missing from his own small air force. The result of this misrepresentation was that it tipped off Castro to the imminence of the invasion, and he rounded up and detained thousands of possible subversives before the invasion. Since the Cuban population, moreover, was supposed to think that there was a massive underground rising to join the rebels, the scope of the resistance was supposed to be misrepresented by encoded signals broadcast to Cuba. Because U.S. misrepresentation of the air raid had motivated Castro to order the mass detentions, however, the members of the Cuban population most likely to respond to the misrepresentations were those rendered least capable of doing so by them. And many of those not incarcerated saw no point in quixotic gestures. When the CIA operative in Oriente province received the coded message "to 'interrupt communications,' 'blow bridges' and arrange for an uprising . . . He wired back: 'Impossible to rise. Most patriots in jail. Thanks for your damned invitation. Closing transmission.' . . . He collected two of his friends from the local underground and said 'Let's go to the beach' . . . and went swimming" (Wyden, 246).

A series of diversionary landings was also supposed to misrepresent to Castro not only the site of the actual invasion but also the scope and the source: he was supposed to think it was a U.S. invasion, which it would not be (although of course it was). These somewhat questionable diversions, assisted by a sound and light show designed by former Walt Disney employees, were further hampered when the man who was supposed to lead a small group that would mark the beach "was teaching the group how to use hand grenades. One of the grenades went off, killed him and injured several others" (Wyden, 163). As another part of the diversion, Castro was supposed to respond in some way to nonsense messages meant to imply a code: "Alert! Alert! Look Well at the rainbow. The first will rise very soon. Chico is in the house. Visit him. The sky is blue. Place notice in the tree. The tree is green and brown. The letters arrived well. The letters are white. The fish will not take much time to rise. The fish is red" (Manchester, 1101–2). As Hunt explained, the encoded message was a substitute for planned direct calls for sabotage, which Bissell canceled for fear of exposing "our teams" (200). Thus Hunt and Knight, the authors of the bogus messages, had created a situation that could virtually gloss much poststructuralist critique of language and much postmodern fiction: the meaningless message was a decoy for a real message that did not exist. All code with no referent, it was code language for the presence of code language, and that code was meant to be broken by the same audience for whom the message's opacity was designed. No other audience, in fact, existed, except, it was hoped, in the minds of the actual audience, for whom the message's meaning depended on its not knowing it was the audience.

This complex play of message and code was at work even among the planners of the invasion, up to and including the president, so that even today much debate exists among historians not only about what JFK knew but also about how he interpreted what he knew and how others interpreted his responses. The very fact that he was in charge of approving the operation belied his most emphatic precondition for approval: that there would be no direct U.S. involvement. The invasion thus could only take place without the direct U.S. involvement that was necessary for it to take place. Did the president mean then that there could be no *appearance* of

U.S. involvement, or only that there would be no *admission* of involvement (regardless of appearances), or that there would be *limited* involvement (regardless of appearance or admission)? If so, was the limitation fixed and rigid, regardless of circumstances, or was there flexibility to respond to changes in circumstances? If one of the changes was a change in the appearance of involvement—that is, if the world believed that the United States was involved—would that allow the United States to become more directly involved? Under those conditions, what would "more directly" mean?

If the president answered—or even asked—some of these questions, would that compromise his ability to deny knowledge and/or involvement? Would that compromise endanger national interests or his own political interests? Framed as it was by these uncertainties, the word of the president and commander-in-chief was not the source of authority but of its infinite deferral. With the emergence of poststructuralist critique, many would argue that this problem is endemic to language. Whether or not this is so, the historically specific conditions of this period not only made this indeterminacy visible within the realm of public discourse but also connected it to the conditions of governance and the strategies of containment that had constructed the monologic discourse of the cold war.

WHO REPRESENTS THE WEST?

The crisis in representation that emerged from the process of representing Cuba became inextricably implicated in the problems of representing the United States to the United States, to the Western bloc, and to the Eastern bloc as representative of the West. The same crisis of representation is thematized in the 1962 John Ford western, *The Man Who Shot Liberty Valance*, a film that in numerous separate ways examines the problem of representing the West. The story chronicles, from the perspective of thirty years, the events that made Ransom Stoddard (James Stewart) the representative of the unnamed Western territory, who led that territory to statehood, became its governor, then served as its representative in the U.S. Senate, and later represented the United States as ambassador to England. His success originated in his having gained fame as the person who rid the territory of Liberty Valance (Lee Marvin), a notorious villain, brute, and criminal, a man in short who represented the lawlessness and independence that was the code of the Old West. Stoddard, a young lawyer, had gone West with a different code, as part of a new generation, expecting to make of the Old West a New Frontier, one ruled by law rather than force, supported by books rather than guns.

Before Stoddard arrives in the town of Shinbone, where the bulk of the action is set, his stagecoach is held up by Valance, and when Valance steals from a widow the broach given her by her husband, Stoddard intercedes, angrily asking Valance, "What kind of a man are you!" Valance responds, "Let's see what kind of a man *you* are" and beats Stoddard severely. This interchange frames and informs most of the action in the movie, for a central issue of the film is the *kind* of man to represent the West, with the showdown between Stoddard and Valance coming because Stoddard defeats Valance in an election to the territorial convention.

But the story does not give us a set of simple bifurcations: new versus old, good versus bad, law versus brute force, writing versus guns. Although Stoddard promotes literacy, disdains violence, and advocates the rule of law, none of these defeat Valance. While Stoddard becomes the advocate of Eastern values (literacy and law) and adopts the domesticating roles of food server, dishwasher, and teacher, he also teaches himself to use a gun in preparation for what seems an inevitable violent confrontation. When that confrontation comes, however, his skills are inadequate. Valance taunts, wounds, and prepares to kill Stoddard when Stoddard manages to fire off a round that appears fortuitously to kill Valance. His reputation as the man who shot Liberty Valance subsequently becomes the credential that can assure his election as territorial representative to Washington; not wishing to benefit from having killed a man, he is about to turn down the nomination and leave the territorial convention when Tom Donophon (John Wayne) tells Stoddard that he, Donophon, had actually killed Valance, ambushing him from a nearby alleyway at exactly the moment that Stoddard took his ineffectual shot. "Murder, plain and simple," Donophon explains, "but I can live with it and you can't."

Donophon is thus the other hero in this western, the other man who shot Liberty Valance. A tough, powerful, independent horse rancher, he exemplifies, like Valance, the code of the Old West. As such he is Stoddard's antithesis, having little faith in the rule of law, the power of the pen, or the value of education. Although at several points he saves or protects Stoddard, initially rescuing him after Valance's beating left him near death and later protecting him from Valance's assaults, much in the film associates Donophon with Valance. Stoddard first notes the similarity, telling Donophon he is just like Valance when Donophon advocates getting a gun as the only way of dealing with Valance. Donophon himself also draws parallels between their prowess, saying that "Valance is the toughest man in the Territory . . . except me." His ability to live with being a murderer also associates him with Valance rather than Stoddard, as does the fact that they both see Stoddard as a rival, Valance for the right to represent Shinbone at the convention, Donophon for the love of Hallie (Vera Miles).

These parallels are further underscored by a series of parallel gestures. In the restaurant, when Donophon thwarts Valance's attempt to kill Stoddard, Valance leaves, throwing down coins, drinking whiskey from a bottle and hurling the bottle through the window. After he kills Valance, and thus facilitates Stoddard's courtship of Hallie, Donophon replicates these gestures in the saloon. At one point, to humiliate Stoddard, Donophon soaks him with paint by shooting a bucket on a post above Stoddard's left shoulder. In their showdown, Valance replicates the scene by shooting a water jug perched in exactly the same relationship to Stoddard.

These thematic and visual parallels make us ask about Donophon the same questions Valance and Stoddard raised about one another: What kind of a man is he? Is he the same kind of man as Valance or is he the kind of man necessary to rid the West of Valance's kind? The answer of course is both, which takes us to a central problem that Ford explores about the myth of the West and its implications for an American national narrative. The West is the site of masculine activity, the place where one proves one's manhood; at the same time, the success of that masculine endeavor is the settling—domesticating, feminizing—of the West. The success of the Western man, therefore, is measured by his ability to create a place in which there is no longer any place for him, at least none that can be acknowledged.

Although it appears to be a single act, the shooting of Liberty Valance is really a double act—an official narrative and a covert act of murder which that narrative depends upon and, equally, which it depends upon suppressing. The man who shot Liberty Valance is both myth and fact, hero and murderer, Valance's antithesis and his double, the man who represents Eastern values in the West and the man who represents the adoption of Western values. I am arguing, in other words, that the western narrative formally and thematically duplicates the containment narrative of U.S. foreign policy: in order to make the world safe for democracy we must resort to antidemocratic measures. Just as the Bay of Pigs incident and *Catch-22* make legible the double and self-contradictory premises necessary to authorize the narrative of democracy, *The Man Who Shot Liberty Valance,* a product of the same historical moment, makes legible the ways in which these same double messages inform the western. In drawing these parallels, we can see how interrelated the two narratives are, a point the film itself emphasizes by repeatedly connecting its story to the formation of a consensus that will incorporate disparate territories into a coherent narrative under the rule of American law and of the Eastern establishment.

The doubling in the film is most obviously represented as the two men who shot Liberty Valance, but it is much more pervasive: Stoddard identifies himself as a figurative disciple of Horace Greeley, and later the newspaper editor identifies himself as a literal disciple. Donophon twice tells Hallie that she's "mighty pretty" when she's angry. Valance has two confrontations with Stoddard, both of which lead to standoffs with Donophon, who is in each case aided by his black assistant, Pompi (Woody Strode), appearing in a doorway with a pointed rifle. There are two exchanges of a cactus rose, one given at the outset from Donophon to Hallie and the other placed by Hallie on Donophon's coffin. Twice Valance injures Stoddard, and twice Hallie tends to his wounds on the daybed at the rear of the restaurant. Although these repetitions suggest the mythic status of the tale that draws on infinitely repeatable elements, it also suggests the ways in which the story with a single name is always a double story: the two men who shot Valance, the two men who loved Hallie, the two codes of order, the two modes of resolution.

There are also two versions of Shinbone. The one in the present of the story, seen at the outset, is "modern." It is part of a state in the Union, represented by senators and congressmen, ruled by federal and local laws, accessed by telegraph, telephone, and train. The old Shinbone, the site of most of the film's action, predates the railroad and is accessed in two ways — from the East by stagecoach and from the present by memory, storytelling. Thus in the opening sequences of the film, we see Stoddard enter Shinbone twice, initially in the film by train, to attend Donophon's funeral, and shortly thereafter by stagecoach as part of the flashback that recounts the time thirty years earlier when he first came to Shinbone.

That flashback is part of an interview he gives to the local reporters, and that interview frames the story of Stoddard's becoming the man who shot Liberty Valance. But that story, which takes nearly two hours to unfold, is the second part of the interview. It had been preceded by two hours of talk that we don't see, which is characterized as the typical opinionating of a politician. Like the two men who shot Liberty Valance, there are two two-hour stories. One is implicitly the cliché-ridden, insincere speech that typifies political interviews, and hence not worth the viewer's time. The other is the true story that has never been written down, the true speech that is one with its speaker. It participates, as Derrida would say, in the myth of presence, the idea that a speaker not disrupted by the mediation of writing can be one with his or her meaning.

Everything that follows, of course, demonstrates the fallibility of that assumption, showing Stoddard's chronic inability to give authority to his assertions or to construct a coherent identity until he becomes the man who shot Liberty Valance, in other words, until he becomes the person he's not. Even then, he cannot accept the authority that accrues to that representation until he learns that it is a misrepresentation. Only with the knowledge that his authority is based on misrepresentation does he feel qualified to represent the territory. We thus learn that the representation of the old Shinbone and the re-presentation of the story of the shooting of Liberty Valance is authorized by the speaker who has misrepresented himself. Not in the presence of his speech, the film makes clear, but in the interdependence of its representation and misrepresentation resides Stoddard's authority. Representation is not at odds with misrepresentation but rather depends upon it, frames it and is framed by it.

This suggests in many other ways as well the idea that meaning is frame-dependent. There are, for example, two election conventions, one a microcosm of the other. The first elects Shinbone's delegates to the territorial convention; the second elects the territory's representative to Washington. In this way the meaning of the specific, local acts in the town of Shinbone become recontextualized within the framework of regional and national agendas. The shooting of one lawless villain in one small town thus becomes representative of the national narrative that draws on every act of brute vigilance to support the story of manifest destiny. It is very significant, therefore, that the story of the shooting is retold by Donophon at the site of the territorial convention, so that the reinterpretation of the shooting serves the purpose of westward expansion. Visually, moreover, the story

15 Visually the shoot of Liberty Valance is represented as a reframing of the same event seen earlier.

of the shooting is represented as a reframing of the same event, so that we see not only Valance and Stoddard on the street but also Donophon in the alley across the street (figure 15). This perspective, belonging to Donophon, not Stoddard, frames Stoddard's version of the events. At the same time, situated as a flashback within Stoddard's flashback, it is also framed by Stoddard's version and necessarily relies for its authority on Stoddard's version.

These reframings, therefore, are neither arbitrary nor neutral. They are situated within the political context of deciding territorial interests, of deciding how to represent the West to the nation. In the film, Stoddard represents the current state and the old territory, and thus he does not provide contrast between the present and the past but rather demonstrates continuity, and that continuity is based not on the triumph of law over brute force but rather by the co-optation of legal means by physical, of direct action by covert, of self-defense by murder, of speech by action. It is also the co-optation of event by legend, that is, by writing.

Stoddard's present—the turn of the century—which frames the earlier days in the Old West, is itself framed, of course, by the present of the film, 1962, during the New Frontier administration and at a moment that marked the end of the golden age of the western genre. From its early beginnings (roughly the moment when Stoddard retells his story) until the 1960s, the western had been a mainstay of the movie industry. In the 1959–1960 television season, moreover, the appeal of westerns peaked with over thirty separate shows on the networks or syndicated. Among the most popular were *Maverick,* starring James Garner, *Wanted Dead or Alive,* starring Steve McQueen, *Rawhide,* co-starring Clint Eastwood, *Gunsmoke,* starring James Arness, and *Have Gun Will Travel,* starring Richard Boone. Others included *Wyatt Earp, Cheyenne, Sugarfoot, The Rifleman, Restless Gun, Tales of Wells Fargo,* and *Wagon Train,* to name a few. From 1960 on, interest in TV westerns declined until, for a period, they disappeared completely from the television screen and from the movie screen as well. Retrospectively, we can see that the serious western as a movie genre enjoyed its greatest popularity during World War II and throughout the height of the cold war 1950s.

In that period, it served in many ways the same function that Stoddard does—to represent the Old West in such a way as to reconcile it to the rule of the Eastern establishment and suppress the acts of brute murder upon which the spread of a democratic nation was predicated. The television westerns, the prolific multiplication of which mirrors almost perfectly the proliferation of television itself, guaranteed that at the time virtually all Americans acquired television sets, all their prime viewing time would be dominated by performances of the western narrative. The performances of that narrative not only found their echo in JFK's New Frontier campaign, but more importantly made his speech legible as the ubiquitous voice of America, for what could have been more ubiquitous, more common to more American homes in 1960 than the western?

John Ford and his favorite hero, John Wayne, are often credited with elevating the status of the western with the film that made Wayne a star, *Stagecoach*. It is particularly significant, therefore, that Stoddard is brought to Shinbone by Donophon's (Wayne's) death, and that the icon stimulating Stoddard to tell his story is a stagecoach, now standing as a dusty relic. Brushing the dust away, he establishes himself as Ford's alter ego by alluding to the film *Stagecoach,* saying that this was the very stage on which he had arrived. The shooting of Liberty Valance thus becomes a collaborative effort between Stoddard and Donophon, just as the shooting of so many westerns was a collaborative effort between Ford and Wayne. But the effort now is framed by a self-conscious awareness of the event as story, as film, as genre.

That self-consciousness is manifest not only in the film's self-referential allusion to *Stagecoach*, but in a foregrounding of its own artificiality. After developing a reputation for vast outdoor panoramas photographed in stunning color, almost all of the black-and-white *The Man Who Shot Liberty Valance* is shot in claustrophobic interiors or unmistakably artificial sets, such as the clearing where Valance ambushes the stagecoach or the streets of Shinbone. In this way, Ford implicates the shooting of *The Man Who Shot Liberty Valance* in its own historicity. The western genre is clearly the product of a myth as well as the producer of one. And the elegiac quality of the film marks not the loss of the Western hero but the era when truth and falsehood could be distributed in an economy that allowed a coherent narrative.

A particularly important aspect of the film's examination of the western narrative and its relationship to national interests is its foregrounding of the issues of gender and courtship. At the center of the film is Hallie, who was Donophon's "girl" but who is eventually won over by Stoddard. Donophon kills Valance, not out of concern for Stoddard but out of an interest in pleasing Hallie. In the elaborate play of Other and Same that incorporates the West into the East or, during the cold war, nations into the Western bloc, a series of narratives give ostensive stability to the fluid identity of the Other. Similarly, the question "What kind of man are you?" that surrounds Stoddard from the moment he meets Valance is only answered when Donophon kills Valance, thus making Stoddard the kind of man who shot Liberty Valance. Until that point, he assumes a large variety of names and roles. Donophon calls him "pilgrim"; he is also identified as an attorney, a schoolteacher, a reporter, and a dishwasher. His refusal to carry a gun raises questions about his manhood, as does his serving tables in an apron. Even in his showdown with Valance, he still wears the apron. After the showdown, he assumes a new set of roles, roles that serve the state and the nation: delegate, senator, governor, ambassador. He also becomes Hallie's husband, and he takes her from the West to the East, which for Stoddard has always remained the authoritative source of meaning. Early on, for example, when Hallie notes the beauty of the cactus rose, Stoddard says with astonishment, "You mean you've never seen a real rose?" Hallie responds that she's never been East, making the East for both of them the implicit site of the "real" rose, and Stoddard's superior Eastern experiences even with nature clearly impress her. He also clings to the rule of Eastern law, referring to the authoritative power of the law books he has brought with him, despite Valance's illustration of their uselessness, tearing up pages before he nearly beats Stoddard to death.

Hallie, nevertheless, is seduced by literacy, by writing, despite all the evidence that it doesn't supply what it promises. At one point, while washing dishes, Stoddard summons Hallie, saying, "I've got Valance just where I want him." Because his hands are wet, he asks her to read the passage aloud and thus discovers that she can't read. The scene illustrates Stoddard's illusions about the power of writing. He says that he has Valance where he wants him, when all he has are some laws about jurisdiction, to be read by someone who is illiterate, in a town where the word of the law does not affect its enforcement. Although Stoddard thinks he has Valance contained by the law books, the books only contain writing, and the real problem of jurisdiction is the relationship of the code of the West to the word of the law. While Stoddard seems to think that writing will stabilize meaning and contain lawlessness, it can only create differences that will defer the problem to another site.

This point is made repeatedly. In the schoolroom that Stoddard runs, the bulk of the learning is done through recitation rather than reading. Even the newspaper editorial that Stoddard praises for its writing is never read to or by the students; instead Stoddard summarizes it orally. Pompi, the only black in the class, is asked to recite from memory rather than read the beginning of the *Declaration of Independence*. When Stoddard points out that Pompi left out the part about men being "created equal," Pompi says,

"I always forget that part," to which Stoddard responds, "That's all right Pompi, a lot of people do." The point about the United States' failure to effect civil rights for black Americans applies equally to the moment in which Stoddard speaks, contemporaneous to the institutionalization of segregation in the South, and the moment in which the film is made, nearly a century later, which is witnessing the South's violent attempts to block the end of segregation. This double-edged civil rights point, however, is made at the expense of the written word. As the scene makes clear, written declarations and the laws that follow from them have little effect on the practices of everyday life.

For the newspaper editor, Mr. Peabody (Edmond O'Brien), too, writing is discrete from speech, a point schematized by his two roles, journalist and town drunk. When he is drunk, we are told, he can out-talk any man, and indeed his eloquent public speech at the territorial convention makes Stoddard the representative of the territory. When drunk, however, he also becomes inept at writing, a point illustrated by the fact that the headline composed and proofread when he was drunk had a serious misspelling. That headline reports the delegate election in which he and Stoddard were selected as representatives. Valance, who lost the election, does not, however, feel bound by the official record of that meeting, made by Peabody, any more than he does by Stoddard's law books. His challenge to the outcome takes the form of his threatening Stoddard, his brutally beating Peabody, and his destroying the press. When Stoddard finds Peabody, beaten and barely conscious, Peabody gasps, "We really showed him, didn't we?" and then passes out. The point, of course, is that they didn't *really* show Valance anything, because all they showed him were words.

In recognition of the gap between reality and writing, Stoddard goes to confront Valance with a gun. As he walks down the dark main street of Shinbone, Stoddard pauses momentarily in front of the wrecked newspaper office, and we see him crosshatched by the shadows of the small squares that comprise the office's front window frame. Valance had knocked out most of the panes, and the light inside projects the few stenciled letters from the remaining panes across Stoddard's white, aproned body. Fragmented and inverted, these letters form the trace of a message no longer decipherable that named the site of writing, of news, no longer functional. Whereas for Stoddard writing had once signified a stable and knowable center, a source of authority, a link between the nation and its territories, a mode of containment, it now becomes a site of violence and disruption that additional writing cannot mend.

Nor can the violence caused by an assault to writing ever be mended, the film suggests. What started out as a tale of how the West was tamed by the rule of law reveals another tale about the inability of written law to tame or stabilize. That tale, the story of the covert lawlessness, the ineffectuality of writing, however, cannot be told, for when Stoddard finishes trying to speak the true story in the present, the interviewers refuse to print it. "This is the West," the new editor says, "and here when legend becomes fact we print the legend."

This legend, as I have pointed out, has not only served the interests of the national narrative but also stabilized the gender roles that made Stoddard's coupling with Hallie possible. The film ends with Hallie's admitting that she had placed the cactus flower on Donophon's coffin and, implicitly, Stoddard's recognizing that Hallie knew he was not the *man* who shot Liberty Valance. This recognition destabilizes a premise of their relationship, and that instability is immediately connected to a renunciation of the national narrative: Stoddard on the verge of receiving a vice presidential nomination tells Hallie he wants to withdraw from national politics and go back West. This renunciation, however, cannot alter the official record. The closing lines of the film, therefore, come from the train conductor who says "Nothing's too good for the man who shot Liberty Valance."

In that it foregrounds the arbitrariness of the frame, the instability of writing, the absence of centered meaning and authority, an awareness of its own artificiality, a self-referential recognition of its own historicity, and cognizance of the fissure between "history" and "event," *The Man Who Shot Liberty Valance,* like *Catch-22,* manifests many of the formal traits that characterize American postmodernism. These works, I am arguing, can be read as historically specific products of American culture at the moment when such events as the Bay of Pigs invasion were making legible the contradictions and duplicities embedded in the gendered, monolithic narrative of containment.

In this light, it is particularly significant that "history" is not represented as the history of events but rather as the events that are saved and fashioned by records. In *The Man Who Shot Liberty Valance,* as we have seen, the history of the West is represented by the genre of the western and the legends upon which it is based. In *Catch-22,* the whole history of World War II is up for grabs, with the competitors waging a war of memos and directives, maps and bombing lines, inventories and ticker tapes. Perhaps the book's most striking assault on the idea of documentation is Danby's revelation, in the last chapter, that "They can prepare as many official reports as they want and choose whichever one they need on any given occasion" (432). Writing, therefore, and not some objective reality, is the source of facts. For that reason, Doc Daneeka's death, proven by his name on the flight roster of a plane that had crashed, remains uncontradicted by his physical, animate presence. At the same time, the dead man in Yossarian's tent (actually, the dead man's possessions) cannot be sent home; having died before he officially checked in, he had created no record of his life and hence no way of recording his death. The parade-obsessed automaton, Colonel Sheisskopf, put in charge of special services as the result of one directive is promoted to general and put in charge of his superiors when another directive reclassifies "combat" as a special service. "After all," says General Peckem, who initiated the directive, "if dropping bombs on the enemy isn't a special service, I wonder what in the world is" (316).

From Holden Caulfield's perspective, constructed within the parameters of cold war norms, General Peckem's reasoning would seem phony, even insane. The belief in a referential reality (however complex) and in the possibility of transcendence provides Salinger's informing narrative, one both manifesting and disciplining the contradictions embedded in containment. Whereas Salinger presents events and, by extension, "history," as the product of objective reality, compromised by the imperfection of language and speakers, postmodernism, as typified by *Catch-22* and *The Man Who Shot Liberty Valance*, represents "history" as a discourse created by language. Postmodernists, as I stated in the introduction, thus assert complete control over history while relinquishing all control over events.

In viewing these works as products of a national narrative, it is particularly important, I think, to note the territorial nature of the issues. The cold war was a global board game, with the object being a chronic mapping and remapping to be done in the absence of the overt conquests allowed under the earlier version of the game, called imperialism. Attempts in the cold war to replicate the quintessential colonialist move—that of making the Other the Same—had to be performed in the name of *anti*-imperialism (or "democracy"). The cold war thus created a double agency that often found itself in conflict over the same territory. The disruption of the narratives that attempted to contain this doubleness thus reveal territorial conflicts.

In *The Man Who Shot Liberty Valance,* the fate of the territory connects all the other conflicts. In *Catch-22,* Snowden's body becomes the territorial site that effectuates Yossarian's traumatic refusal to play the territorial game. Attending to a deep wound in Snowden's thigh, Yossarian fails at first to discover the mortal disemboweling caused by shrapnel that entered under Snowden's flak jacket. In trying to comfort Snowden, Yossarian says, "There, there," repeatedly. The pronoun literally referring to a place, "there," when said twice becomes a cliché that refers to no place. The emptiness of this phrase is emphasized by the fact that Yossarian says it as he addresses the wrong place; the wound, like the phrase, is double, and the serious one is not *there* on the thigh, where Yossarian thinks it is, but *there* under the flak jacket, where it is so serious that Yossarian couldn't treat it even if he knew it was there. When finally the flak jacket can no longer contain what is left of Snowden's insides, and Yossarian discovers what is there, he wonders "how in the world to begin to save him" (429). Still he continues, automatically, habitually, to mutter "There, there," suggesting the double sightings and also suggesting nothing at all. Cited by the doubling of meaningless referents, Snowden's body becomes one more territory, mapped by a bomb pattern that Yossarian can neither read, nor affect, nor refer to accurately. Snowden becomes, in other words, the topos of Vietnam.

7. THE RULES FOR FREE SPEECH

Speech Act Theory and the

Free Speech Movement

On September 30, 1965, Roger W. Heyns, the newly appointed chancellor of the Berkeley campus of the University of California, issued the following letter "To the Berkeley Campus":

> During the past two weeks Professor John R. Searle has been meeting with students and faculty to discuss the proposals for student participation in developing and reviewing rules on student conduct. He has also reviewed practices on other campuses. On the basis of his work to date, Professor Searle recommends creation of a Campus Rules Committee. . . .
>
> The main task of the Committee would be to review our present rules and recommend a permanent set; to propose policies for administering rules, both provisional and permanent, to review questions posed by any member of the campus community about the rules; to consult with the Chancellor on matters relating to the rules, and to propose further revisions in the permanent rules as needed.
>
> This proposal would complete our grievance mechanisms. Grievances about the enforcement of a particular rule would go to the Faculty Committee on Student Conduct, or a hearing officer.

This committee was formed more than a year after the turmoil over "free speech" originally developed on the Berkeley campus. The turmoil had virtually closed down the campus for several days during the preceding academic year and had caused numerous rallies, sit-ins, and police actions. It resulted in the effective overhaul of the University of California administration and in the arrest and conviction of a number of students and nonstudents. The successful prosecution of the leaders of the Free Speech movement focused attention on the young prosecuting attorney, Edwin Meese III, who was shortly thereafter hired by California gubernatorial hopeful, Ronald Reagan.

This earliest of 1960s campus revolts, which would anticipate a decade of acrimonious conflict at Berkeley and numerous other campuses, began as a local territorial dispute of sorts that escalated into a complex and multifarious struggle over rules and the legitimate authority to create or enforce them, over authority and its legitimate boundaries or implicit margins. On August 10, 1964, a few weeks prior to the initial Berkeley conflict, the Gulf of Tonkin Resolution was passed and, by the time Searle's Campus Rules Committee was established a little over a year later, America had given Lyndon Johnson a landslide presidential victory, started bombing North Vietnam, and sent over a quarter of a million combat troops to South Vietnam. During the same one-year period, Martin Luther King was awarded the Nobel Peace Prize, Malcolm X was assassinated, and, two days after the first anniversary of the Gulf of Tonkin Resolution, the Watts riots started.

On resonating levels that replicate the shifting registers of postmodern fiction and/or the labyrinthine networks of hypermedia information systems, these simultaneous sequences illustrate the breakdown in the cold war system of social, racial, political containment. On the Berkeley campus, as elsewhere, the attempt to settle territorial disputes through the appeal to rule-governed authority had revealed, and would continue at an exponentially increasing rate to reveal, not the failure of the rules but the dubious authority upon which the rules relied.

In Vietnam, the dual roles for nations outside the Western and Eastern blocs, defined by the gendered narrative of containment, were distributed geographically. As stipulated by the Geneva Accord of 1954, the South, unlike us and thus a suitable mate but also like us and thus suitable for mating, assumed the role of the courted Other. The other courtier—the rival whose courtship energies we were to frustrate and thus contain—was stipulated to be the North. Vietnam was divided in order to keep these energies discrete, separated by a rigid boundary, the DMZ, that was neither North nor South. As Lyotard has argued, however, the boundary that establishes difference can never be either separate or rigid. Rather it is, itself, the site of dispute, always in flux and always having the traits of both sides. If we apply it to George Kennan's informing trope for the narrative of containment—that of rival suitors—the border is the hermaphrodite, always already Other and Same, functioning not to separate the two sides but to taint each with the trace of that which it would strategically identify as Other. The history of America's role in the Vietnam War—from biased neutrality to advisory to combatant, from policies of pacification to Vietnamization, from tactics of search-and-destroy to protective reaction strikes—could, in fact, be read as the failed attempt to maintain this impossible boundary between Other and Same. The historiography of the war, similarly, could be described as a debate over the rhetorical strategies to bolster or reconfigure the shape and border of difference, just as the principals of the war debated for months over the shape of the negotiating table in Paris.

These debates made legible the ways in which history was not a rule-governed activity but a rule-governing one, concerned necessarily, as I have discussed earlier, with its own disciplinary border maintenance. The authority of a discipline, like the authority for pursuing containment, cannot survive exposure as a form of purely self-interested border maintenance. Thus history must always claim to be about events (even historiography must treat the writing of history as the event[s] that comprise its "legitimate subject"). So too the pursuit of containment must always claim to be about the interests of the free world—the spreading of democracy—not about the interest of the United States in preserving its authority to make rules in the name of the free world; it must appear to be about the story of democracy, not about claiming the authority to tell the story.

Thus the Geneva Accord must appear to reflect history by giving names and boundaries to a historical difference between Vietnamese. But that difference was one that did not exist *in* Vietnam. Rather it was a difference between the inside (Vietnamese) and outside (French). The French struggle to maintain control of Vietnam was a struggle to blur those distinctions by reinforcing them within Vietnam's borders. When this struggle failed, the French were thrown out. But because the French autocratic control of Vietnam represented metonymically the power of the free world and the defense of democracy, French withdrawal threatened the strategy of containment by showing the Eastern bloc a more attractive partner than the Western bloc, or at least by suggesting that the East was the more powerful aggressor. The only counterevidence within the narrative of containment was the use of nuclear supremacy, since that supremacy and U.S. willingness to use it was supposed to provide the authority for containment and the deterrence necessary to protect the free world. In order to prevent that authority from being tested, it thus became necessary for the French to stay in Vietnam until they could replicate the same difference inside the country that they had used to delimit the entire country during the days of their colonial prowess.

Instead of replicating that difference, however, the Geneva Accord doubled it, so that the North became the site of Vietnamese self-determination *or* the site of communist aggression, and the South became the site of Vietnamese self-determination *or* the site of colonial and postcolonial influence. The accord, moreover, was simultaneously supposed to maintain the distinction between North and South and also to allow time—a two-year period—for those distinctions to materialize so that they then could be dissolved, in the name of democracy, by a national election. It was in the name of democracy, however, that the Vietnamese were denied their right to vote, because it was clear—in a logic straight out of *Catch-22*—that the antidemocratic forces of the North would win and therefore, in the interests of democracy, a democratic election could not be allowed. At the same time, a democratic distinction between North and South could not be maintained, and the forces of democracy needed military advice and assistance to rebuff the will of the undemocratic Vietnamese majority. Because the accord to segregate inside from outside, Other from Same, had failed, the military assistance attempted to bolster democracy by replicating *inside* the South the same strategies of division that the accord performed on the country as a whole. Moving from site to site, village to village, within the South, the forces of democracy sought to identify, delineate, and eradicate opposition.

The authority for this search-and-destroy policy was the Geneva Accord, which created the South as a homogeneous representative of anticommunist, pro-Western democracy. In order to legitimize that difference and thus preserve the democracy it stipulated, the Other within had to be destroyed. Otherwise, the authority of the accord itself would be open to scrutiny, and finally so would the authority of U.S. nuclear capability, which did not have to be demonstrated, so long as the differences created by the accord remained intact. In their turn, the search-and-destroy pacification programs also failed because they relied on the distinction between Other and Same within the South, which in turn depended on the reliability of speech acts, the rules for which Professor Searle was formulating shortly after he helped formulate the rules at Berkeley for "free speech."

Before I return to Berkeley and the attempts to fix territorially freedom and speech, I need to look briefly at another set of simultaneous events. In 1954, at the same time that the Geneva Accord was attempting to further the interests of democracy by segregating Vietnam's South, the Warren Court was attempting to fulfill the mandate of democracy by *de*segregating America's South. Under contention, similarly, were territorial rights. Did a state have the right to determine its own rules? Did the North have the right to exert over the South its claim to represent the nation, or was the Constitution an accord that established segregated boundaries? Did these boundaries that segregated the South from the North (and West) permit the South to replicate the acts of segregation at local sites—buses, restaurant counters, washrooms, schools—within its delimited borders? Like the 1954 Geneva Accord, the 1954 Supreme Court decision led to a decade of conflict and violence over the configuration of difference, creating a plethora of categories such as legal, illegal, extralegal, violent, nonviolent, peace-keeping, duly elected, improperly elected, legitimate authority, corrupt authority, local authority, outside authority, outside agitator, civil rights organizer. These categories were applied in an array of narratives to local police and/or federal marshals, the attorney general of the United States and/or the governor of Arkansas, the national guard and/or the Ku Klux Klan, Martin Luther King and/or Bull Connor, to name a few.

By July 2, 1964, five weeks prior to the passage of the Gulf of Tonkin Resolution, when President Johnson signed into law the 1964 Civil Rights Bill, the focus in the civil rights movement, like the focus in Vietnam, had fallen on the right to self-determination, and in the summer of 1964 a massive voter registration drive, conducted by hundreds of college student volunteers from the North and West, swept the South. These civil rights workers returned to their campuses in the fall, invigorated by a sense of accomplishment and toughened by adversity, setback, and violence. They had also learned, as their noncollege counterparts were starting to learn in Vietnam, the topical and logistic nature of authority. They had learned that circumstances acquired meaning not because they were rule-governed but because they were allowed to authorize the rules governing their boundaries. Even students who did not participate directly in Freedom Summer witnessed on the nightly news the ways in which the "legitimate" authorities clashed over the legitimate nature, function, and application of the legal system. The "one nation under God" to which these students had grown up pledging allegiance was becoming *visibly* incapable of containing the universal claims to liberty and justice within the monologic, theologic narrative of containment.

At Berkeley, some of the students who had participated in Freedom Summer and were members of the Berkeley Friends of the Student Nonviolent Coordinating Committee were soliciting members to carry on the fight for civil rights by coordinating efforts to oppose racial discrimination in employment and housing in the San Francisco Bay area. To this end they set up a table outside the Sather Gate of the Berkeley campus. Nearby were tables from a variety of groups, including the Young Socialists and the Young Republicans. The area had been the traditional site for this kind of activity because it had been technically off campus and therefore not subject to the university rules against political activity. When it was discovered that the small piece of land had been ceded to the university by the city of Berkeley, the university officially banned recruitment for any form of political action, and the students quickly violated the ban. This led to attempted disciplinary actions, which were subsequently protested by further, larger, more blatant violations of the ban, which in turn led to attempted arrests. These attempted arrests became impossible when masses of students surrounded the arresting patrol car. In order to disperse the students, the administration negotiated a settlement with the leaders of the Free Speech movement, which in less than a month it violated in several crucial areas. This led to a confrontation, sit-in, and the arrest of eight hundred students.[1]

At issue, in the largest sense, was a disagreement about the appropriate place for the appropriate activity. The United States allowed freedom of speech, assembly, and petition, but the university had rules governing uses to which these rights could be put within the boundaries of the university. In the words of University President Clark Kerr, "The University will not allow students or others connected with it to use it to further their non-University political or social causes, nor will it allow those outside the university to use it for non-University purposes" (Heirick, 94). Like the leaders of the American South, Kerr had created a geographic boundary by which to segregate the university from politics and society, which constituted an outside. This inside/outside distinction further worked to segregate the population inside the university, creating a distinction between those with and without nonuniversity purposes. Although he could not prevent members of the community from having nonuniversity purposes, he could prevent them, he felt, from using the university to further those purposes.

In the preceding year, Kerr had delivered the Godkin Lectures at Harvard on "The Uses of the University," in which he attempted to articulate the modern university's role in society, one coextensive with the needs of industry, as a research organ and supplier of trained personnel. He also explained at length the ways in which government funding had dictated the direction of much university research, and while in the introduction to the published version of these lectures Kerr asserted that "in the discussion that follows, analysis should not be confused with approval or description with defense" (v), the book makes clear that these are acceptable purposes for what he calls the "multiversity." Like the political rhetoric of the cold war and of the Southern segregationists, Kerr's writing attempts repeatedly to delimit the boundaries between inside and outside at the same time that the process marks the impossibility of such boundaries. The professor, for example, "has a choice of roles . . . as never before," he tells us. "He may even become . . . essentially a professional man with his home office and basic retainer on the campus of the multiversity but with his clients scattered from coast to coast. He can even remain the professor of old, as many do" (44). If many professors see their work as coextensive with industry and society, where are the boundaries of the multiversity, since those boundaries thus cannot logically be restricted either physically or intellectually to the work done or the clients served within the geographic limits of the campus?

Even before the contemporary advent of a national electronic network, the boundaries of the university were at best fluid, tainted, seeping, leaving distant and barely perceptible traces and residues across an unmappable space. (It was indeed much like the military and political topography of the Vietnam War that allowed little of the geometric mapping—bombing lines, fronts, liberated territory—that characterized much World War I and World War II reportage.) Given this questionable topography, moreover, we can no better locate the professor who, in Kerr's words, "need not leave the Groves for the Acropolis" (44) than the one who stretches its limit. Some professors may choose to remain inside, but inside of *what?*—inside something whose boundaries cannot be determined. (Again, the presence of a similar rhetorical problem helps explain the persistence, during the second half of the 1960s, of the seemingly unanswerable questions: How did we get *into* Vietnam? and Why can't we get ourselves *out?*) In answering his question, "What justification is there for the modern American multiversity?" (44) Kerr asserts, as the proponents of or apologists for the Vietnam War did, "History is one answer." Kerr goes on: "Consistency with the surrounding society is another. Beyond that, it has few peers in the preservation and dissemination and examination of the eternal truths; no living peers in the search for new knowledge; no peers in all history among institutions of higher learning in serving so many segments of an advancing civilization. Inconsistent internally as an institution, it is consistently productive. Torn by change, it has the stability of freedom. Though it has not a single soul to call its own, its members pay their devotions to truth" (45). Failing to construct geographic, social, or intellectual boundaries, Kerr tries to impose temporal boundaries—appeals to history and eternity. Time—ultimately an implicitly theological time, devoted to universal and eternal truth—attempts to mitigate the temporal truth in which Kerr's argument finds its consistency: *that the multiversity is a form of production.* "Inconsistent internally . . . it is consistently productive." Its modes of production constitute its consistent outside, regardless of its inconsistent inside.

If its margin, its outside, its border, facade, or identity is constituted by its mode of production, what the university must *not* produce, Kerr subsequently makes clear, is direct political action. In a press conference in the fall of 1964, in response to the Sather Gate controversy, Kerr explained, "The University is an educational institution that has been given to the Regents as a trust to administer for educational reasons, and not to be used for direct political action. It wouldn't be proper. . . . It is not right to use the University as a basis from which people organize and undertake direct action in the surrounding community" (Heirick, 115–16). Revealing perhaps unintentionally an inability to separate the abstract principle from the geographic boundary, Kerr uses "basis" to mean "base"; the *basis* for action is the *base* of action, and the university can provide neither. As de Certeau has made clear, however, all colonization must take place from a site. Only after the establishing of boundaries does it become possible to authorize an action, to move on that which is outside or Other. When Kerr thus conflates the denotation of authority with the connotation of a geographic site, he expresses a geographic metaphor that informs the philosophical territoriality of the university's mandate. Its realm is synonymous with its rules. To become the base of action is to become the basis for action. The university is thus a bastion of freedom but also the universal adjudicator of what acts may be freely performed within its limits.

This role raises questions not only about the possibility of making such adjudications but also about the possibility of delimiting the site from which they can be made. A memo by a member of the Berkeley administration made this clear. In regard to the historical status of the Sather Gate area as a space for free speech, Alex Sherriff noted: "In several committees we discussed turning over the small area concerned as a gift to the City of Berkeley. This somewhat wild idea was discarded . . . because it was believed embarrassing to ask Berkeley to allow a function that we could not allow" (Heirick, 95). The rules governing the multiversity thus extend beyond its territory, becoming implicitly coextensive with the city of Berkeley. If not inside the campus and not outside the campus, then where could the "function" be allowed?

As a *basis* for its position, the university had cited article 9, section 9 of the state constitution: "The University shall be entirely free of all political or sectarian influence and kept free therefrom in the appointment of its regents and the administration of its affairs." This requires, of course, an impossible purity, the impossibility of which is made all the more clear when applied to specific actions. In 1963, for example, Kerr had removed the ban on communist speakers on a university campus (after three years of petition and protest and the threat of a suit) but proclaimed new rules "aimed at *all* 'controversial' speakers. Henceforth, the administration could require, at its pleasure, that any meeting with outside speakers be chaired by a tenured professor" (Draper, 21). In December, 1963, at the UCLA campus of the university, a specific rule sought to purify the general concept signified by the word "controversial" by requiring the tenured professor "only in the case of speakers representing social or political points of view substantially at variance with established social and political traditions in the U.S." (Draper, 21–22). The problematic question is how a university "entirely free of all political or sectarian influence" can make what must be a political distinction between those points of view that are or are not "substantially at variance with established social and political traditions in the U.S." Since one of the principles of democracy is the right of the people, through the act of political consent, to alter their social and political practices, to what extent is the privileging of established tradition consistent with the traditional principles of democracy? One of the privileged principles—both traditional and juridical—that provides people with the means to alter traditions democratically is freedom of speech. Is it possible then for the university to make the distinctions it felt necessary in order to remain "free from all political and sectarian influence" without undertaking actions "substantially at variance with established social and political traditions in the U.S."? And further, could it make an argument defending this rule without demonstrating "political or sectarian influence"?

Outside every corner of the campus, the world is tainted by politics. Political candidates continue to run for offices that determine the status not only of the streets that surround the university but also of the people who enter it, the funds that support it, the funding that supports its faculty. Higher education bond issues are floated as public referenda, endorsed or decried by newspapers, some of which, like the influential Oakland *Tribune*, may engage in racially discriminating hiring practices and also express curiosity about the legitimacy of students who recruit for political action at the Sather Gate, especially when those actions might entail picketing businesses in the Oakland area that practice discrimination. The newspapers and the television are saturated with politics—global, national, local—and the students, not fully assimilated into the search for universal truth, are vulnerable to becoming politicized and in the process tainting the university of which they are products. In order to protect the university, institutional practices are necessary, the creation and enforcement of rules. Acceding to political pressure, arrived at through political means, these rules must nevertheless insulate the university from politics.

This attempt to preserve or restore or protect the apolitical university has surfaced again more recently in the array of "political correctness" debates which similarly hold that politics taints or corrupts the true university's charge. As I have noted elsewhere, however, even those who staunchly believe that the university can be apolitical can hardly doubt that it is composed of people who behave politically. In department committees and meetings, on hiring committees, in tenure and promotion proceedings, in line and budget allocations, in vying for course assignments and enrollments, in appointing deans, directors, department heads, in ordering textbooks—just to name a small sample of university activities—people behave politically. In positing the apolitical university, therefore, we must imagine the rampant deployment of markedly political behavior to effect apolitical ends. This is not a logical impossibility, but it certainly is an improbability of monumental proportions today, as it was in 1964 or at any other time.

The problem, however, is not with the university but with speech itself, which cannot be rule-governed in the way John Searle would wish. In attempting to demonstrate that speech performs acts that are rule-governed, Searle develops a speech act theory that, as the university did, tries to privilege the traditional center so as to avoid dealing with the problems of the margin. Repeatedly in his opening chapter of *Speech Acts* he underscores the centrality of traditional usage—what we already know—as the basis for a theory of language, asserting that "we could not recognize borderline cases of a concept as borderline cases if we did not grasp the concept to begin with" (8). Rather than challenge the center, the fuzziness of the border for Searle affirms the center. Similarly, he needs to exclude from his analysis language use that is not serious, that is parasitical, that is fictitious, that is a joke. In order to perform the speech act of making a promise, for example, it is necessary, Searle explains, that "normal input and output conditions obtain" (57). He further explains that this condition "excludes *both* impediments to communication such as deafness and also parasitic forms of communication such as telling jokes or acting in a play" (57). Implicit in this analysis is the sense that the basis for speech action resides in a central, but not fully knowable, set of rules. When he tells us that his analysis will focus upon "institutional facts" and that "institutions are a system of constitutive rules" (51), he is ascribing normative power to the institutions whose rules he has undertaken to describe and that he admits are never fully describable.

Like Searle, Kerr uses the central idea of the institution whose rules he is in the continual process of revising to define the border between university and nonuniversity purposes and the fuzziness of the resulting borderline cases to affirm his act of definition. The rules of the University of California created the institutional fact that specific actions were prohibited, that specific students were transgressors. This institutional fact applied, despite the university's inability to distinguish between violators and other students, between legitimate student groups and outside agitators, between its negotiated agreements and its failure to implement them. When over three hundred students signed petitions indicating that they had staffed the illegal tables and requesting to be treated in the same manner as the five cited students, the administration responded by adding three names to its list of offenders. When this administration response multiplied the protests and led to a massive sit-in, to avoid a potential confrontation between the students and 450 police, a negotiated settlement with the students included adjudication of the student cases by the "Student Conduct Committee of the Academic Senate." Since the Academic Senate had no such committee, the administration, following a script that might have been written by Joseph Heller, therefore announced that "since the committee named did not exist, the suspension cases would be taken up by the only committee which did exist—namely, the same administration-appointed committee on student conduct which the pact had pointedly *not* assigned to the task" (Draper, 66).

It may be asserted that this simply indicates bad faith, dishonesty, some set of conditions that make speech acts dysfunctional, but much of the rhetoric supporting the administration suggested that the behavior was motivated by the institutional need of the administration to fulfill its role: to preserve order and enforce its rules, to be taken seriously. If the institutional facts necessary for Searle's theory can be preserved only by the playing of roles, and the playing of roles constitutes the form of parasitical speech that makes Searle's paradigmatic speech act—the promise—impossible, then is it ever possible to have an institutional fact that creates the norm and eliminate the parasitic speech that makes it impossible? If we can say that Kerr is at one moment speaking as an individual and at another in his role as president of the university, then can we determine the set of rules that would allow us always to segregate the two speeches, and if we could, wouldn't that also be a means for knowing when speech act theory did not apply, that is, when Kerr was assuming his institutional role?

Searle might well argue that our ability to make this distinction proves that we already have a system of rules for differentiating, and that the few occasions that render the distinctions fuzzy prove that we have the knowledge to distinguish, but Derrida points out that the fuzziness of the margins is the function of a process reproduced at the center of Searle's—and by extension we might say Kerr's—attempt at rule-governed activity. Much of Derrida's critique has already been incorporated in my discussion of both Searle and Kerr, and I shall just emphasize the main points here because my interest is not in analyzing Derrida's critique of speech act theory but in suggesting how much Derrida's critique in *Limited Inc.* of Searle glosses, as well, not only the free speech controversy at Berkeley but also the civil rights and Vietnam conflicts that contextualized it. *Limited Inc.* thus replicates the critique of syllogistic reasoning that pervades *Catch-22*, a novel produced at roughly the same cultural moment, in which the major (major major major) premise of a syllogism, upon which the authority for all deduction relies, is represented as a vacant office, a null set whose presence is an absence. Like the soldier in the novel who sees everything twice, Derrida points out the forms of death rehearsal at work in the pervasive and uncontrollable doubling that characterizes writing.

In regard to Searle specifically, Derrida argues that parasitic speech is not the marginal or borderline case but rather endemic to all speech because of its iterability, that is, its ability to be cited, repeated, parodied, recontextualized, a process that *Catch-22* thematizes. Nor is this a marginal aspect of writing but rather the quality that makes it intelligible, and thus it cannot be expunged to create a normative set or instance that comprises "serious, literal" speech, the acts of which can be fixed and the rules for its fixations discovered. In order to make this point, Derrida plays with Searle's name, so as to distinguish between the biological John Searle and the name that appears in the copyright of his essay, the *Reply* to Derrida. Playfully demonstrating the problems with making the two synonymous, Derrida limits himself to the text and thus assigns limited liability to the biological Searle: "I decide here and from this moment to give the presumed and collective author of the *Reply* the French name 'Société à responsabilité limitée'—literally, 'Society with Limited Responsibility' (or Limited Liability)—which is normally abbreviated to *Sarl*" (*Limited Inc.*, 36). The liability—for error, bad faith, misrepresentation, misreading, or muddled logic, all of which possibly taint *Reply*—should be limited to Sarl, and would be if we could find a way of disassociating Sarl from Searle. But the rule-governed activity of limiting legal liability breaks down in the attempt to fix linguistic boundaries. An error in the text always bears the trace of its author, a point Sarl makes about Derrida, whom he accuses of misreading the work of J. L. Austin. Sarl thus tries to protect a rule-governed operation that affixes context and stabilizes meaning in such a way as to allow language to be consistent with the established social traditions of English. At the same time, Sarl attempts to demonstrate that Austin's writing has failed to make clear its context or stabilize its meaning in such a way as to prevent Derrida's misreading and misunderstanding. In light of the logical problem caused by this argument and in light of Sarl's apparent misreading of Derrida's essay,

Derrida wonders how one can take Sarl seriously. Sarl insists, of course, on the seriousness of his own activity, for it is only for "serious" speech that he makes his theoretical claims. "Because the model speech act of current speech act theory claims to be serious," Derrida points out, "it is normed by a part of its object and is therefore not impartial. It is not scientific and cannot be taken seriously" (72). Nor can Derrida be taken seriously, according to Sarl, if one were to detect in Derrida's writing a lack of seriousness. But how is seriousness to be judged, and can Searle regard as serious Derrida's refusal to give him a serious response?

To the extent that Searle holds Derrida accountable for the lack of seriousness in *Limited Inc.*, he proves that ink can never be limited, that writing will never maintain rigid boundaries that will fix or delimit meaning or damage or responsibility. To do so would be to separate the inside from the outside, the principle from the application. But, as Derrida points out, the discourse of speech act theory "finds itself an integral part—part and parcel, but also *partial*—of the object it claims to be analyzing. It can no longer be impartial or neutral, having been determined by the hierarchy even before the latter could be determined by it" (71).

The necessarily partial, partisan quality of speech act theory, although Derrida never says so, renders it political. Similarly, the university, the site of eternal truths, finding repeatedly at its margins sites of political truths, must maintain the purity of the center by attempting to erect a rigid boundary to exclude the political. But to do so it must turn to political means—negotiation, courts, lawyers, committees, the Academic *Senate*—in order to render itself nonpolitical. The university's legitimate authority hypothesizes a political process that legitimately prohibits political speech. This action replicates the strategy, according to Derrida, of Sarl's *Reply*—that of appropriating the arguments of Derrida's essay, "almost literally and with regularity, while pretending to pose them as objections" (105). Derrida refuses to exert his copyright on these arguments, he explains, because "there is always a police and tribunal ready to intervene each time a rule [constitutive or regulative, vertical or not] is invoked in a case involving signatures, events, contexts. This is what I mean to say. If the police is always waiting in the wings, it is because the conventions are by essence violable and precarious, *in themselves* . . . " (105).

Just as Searle would attempt to develop rules for the use of the campus on the one hand and the use of speech on the other, he would anticipate the police action of one sort or another that would characterize the historic specificity of the 1960s. Nor is it surprising, at a time when rule-governed speech should prove incapable of governance, incapable of the centered, monologic discourse necessary to legitimize its own authority, that we see produced a poststructuralist approach to language and a postmodern fiction, both of which thematize that inability. It is perhaps even less surprising, moreover, that the forces of tradition or the dominant discourse should try to discipline the newer approaches to language and literature through a process of appropriation, misreading, and disinformation.

It seems appropriate, moreover, that the political nature of these conflicts should become visible through a process of territorial mapping designed to preserve power through infinite acts of replication and deferral. In regard to Vietnam, the floating boundaries extended to make a monolith of Vietnam, China, and the U.S.S.R. or contracted to the foliage that separated friendly village from hostile; the boundaries expanded and contracted the western border of Vietnam, in accordion fashion, such that Cambodia was part of the Vietnam War ground or the site of incursions from that war ground; in language, the territory of ally and foe, similarly, mapped and remapped the U.S. Senate, the induction centers, courtrooms, and prisons, the mall outside the Pentagon and the Canadian border. In the four decades since the first school desegregation order, territorial distinctions have displaced and preserved various forms of segregation. The end to legal segregation in the South has deferred the preservation of difference to a variety of venues—courts and statehouses, workplaces and colleges—and been represented by a vocabulary of logistics: "busing," "urban flight," "inner city," "sun belt."

It would be fair, therefore, to see the conflict between speech act theory and deconstruction as a battle over turf, but it would be incorrect, I think, to see that turf as exclusively academic, for the battle waged in the pages of the journal *Glyph* and *Limited Inc.* can be read as one encounter in the battle for global turf that made possible the entire strategy of containment, a strategy authorized by the ability to draw lines, create sides, and secure the borders between. It was over the rule of language that could make domestic security simultaneously an internal and an external affair, and containment a "nonpolitical," "bipartisan policy," that was a central goal for all Americans, coextensive with domestic needs. It was over the rules that could *on nonpolitical grounds* make political action inconsistent with the university's purposes. It was, in other words, a battle over Searle's political role on the Berkeley campus to insulate it from politics, which I suspect his Campus Rules Committee never successfully won.

PART IV

Two Nations Too

8. MY COUNTRY TOO

Time, Place, and African American Identity

in the Work of John A. Williams

In the epilogue of Ralph Ellison's *Invisible Man*, the unnamed black narrator meets the white trustee, Mr. Norton, who is lost in a subway station. Norton asks for directions but becomes frustrated when he gets instead cryptic responses, culminating in the rebuke: "Mr. Norton, If you don't know *where* you are, you probably don't know *who* you are" (436). The roots of this relationship between identity and place, which forms a central motif in *Invisible Man*, can be found in the slave narrative. Unlike other travel or picaresque genres, the slave narrative, as Phyllis Klotman points out, positions the central figure not as running away but as running toward. Its goal is not simply the escape from bondage but the reward of freedom. This structure and the situation it reflects imply that, by moving, the black might change not only his or her environment but also the definition of himself or herself. The Mason-Dixon line, the western territorial boundaries, the Canadian border signified not just climate and locale but also a body of legal, social, and economic definitions of humanity. In slave narrative, then, the connection between *where* you are and *who* you are is not metaphorical or metaphysical. It signifies concrete proof that the definition of humanity is not absolute, but rather the matrix of power organized in a given time and place.

As Sidonie Smith points out, however, although the slave narrative is apparently a story of success, "there is also another story implicit, if not actually explicit, within the slave narrative. That story is the story of the failure to find real freedom and acceptance within American society, a disturbing sequel to the successful story of the radical break away from southern society" (24). Frances Smith Foster notes further that this implicit story created generic plot restrictions for the nineteenth-century slave narrative:

"Once the protagonist achieves his freedom the . . . narrative terminates . . . [f]or to continue the adventures of a black in the so-called free states or countries would be to expose the overwhelming prejudice and discrimination which existed therein. The problem would be revealed as more complex and pervasive than would be to the advantage of most narrators to expose, for it would necessarily indict those from whom their narratives sought sympathy and aid" (124–25). The slave narrative implies a promise that American society has never kept: a time and place when and where the humanity of blacks would be assumed.

But time and place intersect only by virtue of a report that can make the intersection legible. A cogent example of this circumstance can be found in Gary Wills's discussion of the 1967 Detroit riot casualties: "Over 25 percent of the young Negro males in America were not tracked down for the 1960 census. Such men can hardly be said to have disappeared in the Detroit fires. They had already disappeared; they were officially invisible. If they do not show up for the death count they are simply keeping their record for being unrecorded" (56). If Wills indicates dramatically the breach between events and history, which has framed much of the argument in this book, he also suggests that the breach can take historically specific manifestations, with political implications.

In artistic endeavors, the attempt to connect events to history, however much marked by fragmentation and failure, characterizes modernism rather than postmodernism, a point I have returned to frequently throughout this book. The stylistic experiments of modernism, as Ellison has pointed out—and as others have argued about Ellison—can be used as a form of protest. As Phillip Brian Harper has noted, "the Invisible Man's failure at self-idealization is rooted not in any fundamental psychic deficiency on his part but rather in the politics that govern his social relations with Norton and other whites" (116). Drawing strongly on the African American roots of slave narrative and the conventions of modernism, the invisible man's interchange with Norton exemplifies the power relationships implicit in much Afro-American literature, that of regarding identity as a function of time and place. Norton, embedded in his ethnocentric vision (trapped inside history, the invisible man would say), cannot understand the decentering implications of the black's remarks. He remains fixed on his desire to find the Centre Street station, as though all locations were defined relative to it. The thousands of miles of New York City tracks and tunnels cannot be navigated by compass or sunrise or North Star; Centre Street is not a direction but an abstraction. Norton, nevertheless, *believes* in that abstraction, and he cannot be untracked by the invisible man's remarks, exactly because Norton so vividly exemplifies his own limitations. A slave to his historical narrative, he acts in full complicity with his bondage.

In this way, Norton resembles the white Americans described by Eldridge Cleaver in *Soul on Ice:* "It is painful that many [whites] do not yet see that their fantasy world has been rendered uninhabitable in the last half of the twentieth century" (80). Cleaver is talking from a perspective outside of the containment narrative, a perspective that not only can contextualize that narrative as politically and historically situated, but that also can understand the ways in which it is sustained by its repeated performance in popular culture:

> The "paper tiger" hero, James Bond, offering the whites a triumphant image of themselves, is saying what many whites want desperately to hear reaffirmed: *I am still the White Man, lord of the land, licensed to kill, and the world is still an empire at my feet.* James Bond feeds on that secret little anxiety, the psychological white backlash, felt in some degree by most whites alive. It is exasperating to see little brown men and little yellow men from the mysterious Orient, and the opaque black men of Africa (to say nothing of these impudent American Negroes!) who come to the UN and talk smart to us, who are scurrying all over *our* globe in their strange modes of dress—much as if they were new, unpleasant arrivals from another planet. Many whites believe in their ulcers that it is only a matter of time before the Marines get the signal to round up these truants and put them back securely in their cages. (80)

Clearly Cleaver does not identify with a narrative based on the technological supremacy of atomic power or the privilege of controlling the images of sexuality, a narrative that can distribute gender roles in the same interest and with the same authority as missile sites, or that can valorize the "playboy" and the "virgin" with the same obliviousness to hypocrisy as it manifests when it legitimizes an Asian dictator in the name of "democracy."

Cleaver recounts having a pinup on his prison cell wall eventually ripped down and torn up by a guard. "Get yourself a colored girl for a pinup," the guard told him, "—no white women—and I'll let it stay up" (8). Cleaver admits, to his shame as well as shock, that he had "chosen the picture of the white girl over available pictures of black girls" (8). What follows is Cleaver's examination of a love/hate relationship with white women that reveals the dominant discourse's ability to control the images of beauty and desirability, and through them the construction of his masculinity. "If I had followed the path laid down for me by the officials," he concludes, "I'd undoubtedly have long since been out of prison—but I'd be less of a man" (17).

"Manhood" is one of the important components of an African American cultural narrative, as it identifies a duality that antedates America's nuclear supremacy and, more importantly, that reflects disempowerment rather than power. Within this narrative, nuclear supremacy becomes just one manifestation of white supremacy, as Cleaver's understanding of James Bond implies. The connection is also implied by actor Ossie Davis in discussing his eulogy for Malcolm X:

> whatever else he was or was not—*Malcolm was a man!*
>
> White folks do not need anybody to remind them that they are men. We do! This was his one incontrovertible benefit to his people.
>
> Protocol and common sense require that Negroes stand back and let the white man speak up for us, defend us, and lead us from behind the scene in our fight. This is the essence of Negro politics. But Malcolm said to hell with that! Get off your knees and fight your own battles. That's the way to win back your self-respect. That's the way to make the white man respect you. And if he won't let you live like a man, he certainly can't keep you from dying like one! (457)

My interest here is not the cultural, and in some cases physical, emasculinization of black American men, practiced over a period of more than three hundred years, the documentation for which is extensive. Rather I wish to focus more narrowly on the way that the issues of black "manhood" help us contrast the narrative of containment with the narrative of black American culture during the cold war. Containment, as we have seen, continued to accommodate and validate growing male (hetero)sexual license at the expense of female sexuality, black "manhood," and homoerotic desire. Perhaps the simplest example of this phenomenon is the facility with which Leslie Fiedler was able—first in his 1948 essay and later in his 1962 book which it germinated—to equate the black and the homosexual as boys fleeing the domesticating power of the feminine.

Foregrounded by the blonde sexuality that pervaded the fifties, the separate narratives for black and white Americans could not be more apparent than in the Clairol hair commercial I discussed in chapter 5. The question, "Does she or doesn't she?" as I noted, encoded female sexual license. What I did not point out, however, is that the commercial also encoded that question racially; for black women, the commercial made clear, the question was irrelevant. The "she" who was the object of the viewer's inquiry and desire was white and, naturally enough, blonde.

In this context, especially given a history of violence against black men who expressed even the most passing attention to white women, what does it mean to be a black American man? One of the most fully developed and articulate examinations of this question can be found in the work of W. E. B. Du Bois, who identifies an important aspect of black American discourse with the phrase "double-consciousness." As he explains in *The Souls of Black Folk,*

> One ever feels his two-ness,—an American, a Negro; two souls, two thoughts, two unreconciled strivings; two warring ideals in one dark body, whose dogged strength keeps it from being torn asunder.
>
> The history of the American Negro is the history of this strife,—this longing to attain self-conscious manhood, to merge his double self into a better and truer self. In this merging he wishes neither of the older selves to be lost. . . . He simply wishes to make it possible for a man to be both a Negro and an American. (364)

The two strains that comprise the double-consciousness become virtually personified, in the 1960s, by the figures of Martin Luther King and Malcolm X. Both men were attempting to change the cultural narrative of the dominant culture. King focused on direct appeal, while Malcolm X worked from the premise that such appeals only confirmed the extant distribution of power. He urged black Americans, therefore, to change their own narratives in such a way as would force white America to accommodate. Summarizing the differences between the two approaches, James H. Cone has succinctly said, "during the time that Martin King was preaching his American dream, Malcolm X offered a challenging critique of him by proclaiming that America, for the vast majority of blacks, was not a dream but a nightmare" (111).

The thesis of Cone's extended parallel biography of the two leaders is that their differences arose primarily from drastically different religious, familial, and geographic backgrounds, backgrounds that spanned much of the broad spectrum of black American experience. From the respective positions created by these backgrounds, they were able to complement one another as well as provide each other necessary critiques. Nevertheless, Cone argues, the similarities, particularly as defined by a common goal, were greater than the differences. Rejecting the differences, Malcolm was emphatic in emphasizing that "integrationist" black leaders were not in opposition to "separationist" leaders. "What you and I are for is freedom," he said in his "The Ballot or the Bullet" speech; "Only you think integration will get you freedom; I think separation will get me free" (Cone, 247). As a basis for his argument that their two positions were moving closer together, Cone points out that " 'Respect as human beings' was the central theme of both Malcolm and Martin in the black freedom struggle. Initially, Malcolm believed that 'respect' was found primarily in religio-cultural identity — affirming blackness (Africa) and rejecting whiteness (America). By contrast Martin, though he believed black people's cultural identification with Africa was important, contended that blacks could achieve 'respect' only by acquiring social and political respect in America, *as Americans*" (247). In both their similarities and differences, in other words, King and Malcolm X manifest the condition described in 1903 by Du Bois:

> From the double life every American Negro must live, as a Negro and as an American, as swept on by the current of the nineteenth while yet struggling in the eddies of the fifteenth century, — from this must arise a painful self-consciousness, an almost morbid sense of personality and a moral hesitancy which is fatal to self-confidence. The worlds within and without the Veil of Color are changing, and changing rapidly, but not at the same rate, not in the same way; and this must produce a peculiar wrenching of the soul, a peculiar sense of doubt and bewilderment. Such a double life, with double thoughts, double duties, and double social classes, must give rise to double words and double ideals, and tempt the mind to pretence or to revolt, to hypocrisy or to radicalism. (504)

That duality contrasts directly with the duality of containment. Containment was the response to excess — too much power, too many political, sexual, social options — while the double-consciousness is based on scarcity, deprivation, fragmentation. The enduring quality of that narrative —

or the failure of the dominant discourse to construct a widely accepted multiracial cultural narrative—can be seen in the ways that Du Bois's comments anticipate what Andrew Hacker as recently as 1992 has described as *Two Nations:* "Black Americans are Americans, yet they still subsist as aliens in the only land they know. . . . So America may be seen as two separate nations. Of course there are places where the races mingle. Yet in most significant respects, the separation is pervasive and penetrating" (3). Hacker characterizes these two nations as the product not only of demonstrable economic and social bifurcations (although these are crucial causes and consequences), but also of different perspectives on American life and their respective roles in it:

> Most white Americans will say that, all things considered, things aren't so bad for black people in the United States. Of course, they will grant that many problems remain. . . .
>
> What white people seldom stop to ask is how they may benefit from belonging to their race. Nor is this surprising. People who can see do not regard their vision as a gift for which they should offer thanks. (30)

Hacker's idea that sight is a form of blindness, worked through so elaborately in 1952 as the controlling metaphor of *Invisible Man,* demonstrates the persistence with which the cultural narratives have remained discrete.

Discrete, but without symmetry. As I pointed out in the first chapter of this book, the pathetic murderer in *Rear Window,* Lars Thorwald, must be removed from the visible field in order to restore the symmetrical relationships mandated by containment. Thorwald's error was to have made visible some aspects of his own narrative, enough of them to make the rest legible and thereby for him to incur scrutiny, persecution, and prosecution. He performs his last act of terror and rage out of desire to protect himself from full exposure and, simultaneously, out of frustration at his inability to do so, frustration at his having become visible as subversive to the domestic order and thus as a threat to domestic security. Thorwald, in some ways unsettlingly similar to Richard Wright's Bigger Thomas, suffers what Hacker describes for black Americans as the "sheer strain of living in a white world, the rage that you must suppress almost every day" (49).

The story of *Rear Window* must, by violence if necessary, remove Thorwald to contain—with the aid of some transparently token accommodations—the disruption of the domestic code that he represents. In the same manner, the disruptions performed by King and Malcolm were violently stopped and, with the similar token accommodations, the cultural narratives remained separate and unequal: so separate and so unequal, and so strongly differentiated by escalating violence, that by 1968 Wills could describe the difference as *The Second Civil War:* "I went out believing in one country," he states, "which was not likely to commit suicide. I continued, however, forced to test a new hypothesis—that a white country already exists; that a black community is rapidly coming into existence; and that the two are on a collision course" (23).

In 1964, writing about Watts for the *New York Times Magazine,* Thomas Pynchon came to a similar conclusion: "lying much closer to the heart of L.A.'s racial sickness is the coexistence of two very different cultures: one white and one black" (35). Like an alternative information system in a Pynchon novel, black America's cultural narratives surface through hints and fragments, implying a not quite accessible relationship between "truth" and "reality":

> But in that white culture outside, in that creepy world full of pre-cardiac Mustang drivers who scream insults at one another only when the window is up; of large corporations where Niceguymanship is the standing order, regardless of whose executive back one may be endeavoring to stab; of an enormous priest caste of shrinks who counsel moderation and compromise as the answer to all forms of hassle; among so much well-behaved unreality, it is next to impossible to understand how Watts may truly feel about violence. In terms of strict reality, violence may be a means to getting money, for example, no more dishonest than collecting exorbitant carrying charges from a customer on relief, as white merchants here still do. Violence may be an attempt to communicate, to be who you really are. (84)

Almost evoking a Pynchonesque understanding, Wills examines the ways in which the Watts riots suggest the codes of that other America, understood as the paranoia *of* the Other and impelling paranoia *about* that paranoid Other:

> In the Watts riot, rumor went everywhere, and was accepted. . . .
> Unfortunately, those who live regularly in this world of "symbolic truth" may find it impossible to accept the standards of a more prosaic truth; they offer their private vision as the objective record of events. . . . What is truly

expressed is the victim's awareness of himself as victim. And that awareness, turned back on itself, leads to paranoia. (141)

In 1952 there was simply no way for Ellison's Mr. Norton to navigate this other world, any more than there was a way for the invisible man to restore Mr. Norton's bearings in the world Norton took to be real. When Ellison's Tod Clifton—a leader uncannily anticipating Malcolm X—falls outside "history," he performs a historical act for which, as the invisible man's funeral oration makes clear, a cultural legibility does not exist. It is this breach that Ellison's modernist techniques attempt to bridge: the fragmentation of the double-consciousness at a double remove from the dualities of containment. Those dualities underlie Norton's confusion, as he confronts the decentering of the postmodern condition, whose explorations of excess will render Centre Street a questionable name for a dubious destination, pursued with unreliable instructions from invisible instructors.

Predicting that Norton's postmodern condition would follow from white America's pursuit of containment, however, does not make *Invisible Man* a postmodern text, as Harper argues, because Norton's condition is a referent, and the political imperative of Ellison's work *as protest fiction* requires that we read it as referential. As Harper himself points out, the fragmentation in *Invisible Man*

> may indeed characterize black experience, and it can certainly be considered . . . an effect of the dominant U.S. racial ideology, in the context of whose early manifestations it was a definite impairment. But within the political-economic context of the late-twentieth century United States, it is not fragmentation *per se* that poses the primary threat to black identity; indeed, it may well represent the closest approximation we have to the "cognitive map" that Jameson proposes is necessary for the effective negotiation of the postmodern condition. Even Ellison's protagonist, in the end, sees nothing at all detrimental in the fact of fragmentation itself. . . . The danger arises when the fact of the essential dividedness, multiplicity, and hence *specificity* of black experience . . . is dissembled beneath signs that suggest black culture's simpleness, and the consequent ease of its containment and assimilation. (143)

In this light, it is fruitful to examine the work of John A. Williams, who, like many African American writers, has used narrative conventions that

reflect a sense of displacement—historical, psychological, and geographic—
endemic to African American experience. In much of his work, he foregrounds the complications of this displacement by destabilizing the point
of view. "Point of view," as Seymour Chatman defines it, "is the physical
place or ideological situation or practical life-orientation to which narrative
events stand in relation" (153). But for Williams the "physical place," which
is linked to the "ideological situation" and the "practical life-orientation,"
neither stands still nor stands the test of scrutiny. In this way, Williams's
narrative poetics explore the locus of Afro-American identity in the matrix
of time and place.

With this in mind, I want to identify the way some of Williams's works
participate in the double-consciousness that critiques the privileging of time
and place as knowable interstices, implicit in the containment narrative
and upon which its history depends. The group for whom history means
exclusion, not intersection, focuses much of Williams's writing.

It is not surprising, therefore, that one of Williams's earliest published
books was the nonfiction work, *Africa: Her History, Lands and People.* Published in 1962, with young readers as its intended audience, it was the first
paperback illustrated history of Africa, and as such it was a significant revision of the concept of "world" history then being taught to high school
and junior high school readers.

Perhaps even more significant in the understanding of Williams's fiction
is another early nonfiction book, *This Is My Country Too.* Based on articles
originally written for *Holiday* magazine as a black man's *Travels with Charley,*
John Steinbeck's account of his car trip through America in the 1960s, *This
Is My Country Too,* written in 1965, differs from Steinbeck's book not only
in its view of America but in its point of view. Despite the assertion in the
title—or perhaps indicated by that assertion—Williams views America very
much from the perspective of an outsider, distanced and alienated from the
scenes he sees. This is more than simply the objective distance of a journalist; it is that of a man who never knows what rights he may exercise in
a given time or place. Since his locale keeps changing, he must constantly
reassess his freedoms, and he makes us see over and over that the question
is not what the outcome of that assessment will be, but that regardless of
the outcome he must constantly reinitiate the tests.

In this way, his experience replicates the epistemology of the closet that
structurally models much cold war discourse. The crucial difference, how-

ever, is that he is not confined by the closet but excluded from it. Denied the option of withholding his blackness, of making it secret, he is made instead the constant observer of closeted attitudes of white America. His double-consciousness, in other words, is a function of the white closet, the local contents of which have immediate political implications for the construction of his "identity." Each time he stops at a roadside diner, Williams has repeatedly to reassess his "rights," a point Hacker reiterates nearly thirty years later: "Suppose, for example, you find yourself having to drive across the country, stopping at gasoline stations and restaurants and motels. As you travel across the heart of America, you can never be sure how you will be received. While the odds are that you will reach your destination alive, you cannot be so sure that you will not be stopped by the police or spend a night in a cell. So you would be well advised to keep to the speed limit, and not exceed it by a single mile. . . . Or if a motel clerk cannot 'find' your reservation, is it because she had now seen you in person? And are all the toilet facilities at this service station really out of order?" (Hacker, 48). For black Americans, as Williams makes clear in the extended detailing of his journey, freedom depended not on the Emancipation Proclamation, the Constitution, or the Supreme Court, but upon immediate logistics. In this way *This Is My Country Too* alludes to the slave narrative, but with perhaps a more sinister or at least sadder turn, in that no *one* direction now promises anything. We have only the search, without a fixed or stable site as its goal.

In 1968, prompted by the visible and violent confrontations between these dual Americas, Wills, on assignment for *Esquire* magazine, travels America, not to produce another travel book but to visit police stations and report on preparations for future riots. This experience gives him a hint of the perspective from which Williams had performed his observations. Describing a black man taking a photograph through the window of a commercial airplane, Wills notes that "he had permission to look at the country through an expensive lens," but that expensive lens becomes Wills's metaphor for the price black Americans have paid for their perspective; as Wills adds, "Unlike whites, he *saw* it, with all its faults" (21). That vision is coupled with Wills's recognition of his own blindness: "I suppose everyone, sooner or later, gets the feeling that, whatever his earlier experience of the country, he is finally 'discovering America.' But this was a discovery that seemed more like a lobotomy: as I found out more things about my country, I knew less. I was discovering an alien armed place, not at all one I had thought

I would be living in; one I knew continually less about, and admired less. My great 'discovery' seemed all a process of erasure" (16). The place that was beginning to disappear for Wills was the same place that had never existed for Williams. These two reporters, crossing the same site in the same decade, on very different journalistic assignments, mark signs of the same narrative. A crucial difference, however, is that the narrative performs for the white reporter a very different function than for the black. For Wills, the narrative of two nations, two formulae for truth, two consciousnesses is a glimpse that decenters the "place" in which he lives, a place he can recover only under erasure. For Williams, the narrative is neither a glimpse nor a discovery but part of a longstanding critique, one with a historically specific target. That target is the narrative that Wills had taken to be normative and universal.

In the concluding paragraph of *This Is My Country Too,* Williams marks the long history of his critique by shifting the quest from *place* to *time:* "I have been to Africa and I know that it is not my home. America is; it is my country too, and has been for generations. As I said, I am committed to the search for its true meaning; I hope what I have found is not it and I have no choice but to meet the challenge of it. Yes, it is true that America has yet to sing its greatest songs, but it had better hurry up and find the key to the tunes" (158). Until such a time as it does, Williams implies, its history will remain incomplete because it excludes Williams, who is, nevertheless, for many generations a part of that history. Since time, not locale, thus creates and defines his America, it is possible to be an American expatriate even when driving through its heartland, especially when one constantly rediscovers, in motels, in restaurants, and even on the superhighways, themselves full of suspicious highway patrolmen, that one cannot drive far enough to locate the definition of humanity that one needs to make his or her patriation whole.

Expatriation thus forms a central motif in Williams's fictional explorations of the relation between history and identity. Iris Joplin, one of the central figures in Williams's early novel, *Sissie* (1962), for example, attempts to escape history by escaping America. For her, America signifies deprivation and rejection, even within the boundaries of her own family. The Great Depression which dominated the economy of her childhood also produced for her numerous sorts of emotional poverty. Her father, shamed by his inability to support a family, by the degrading work both he and her mother, Sissie, had to do, and by the decrepit living conditions he had to accept, eventually abandoned the family. Even before the Depression, however, he had failed to fulfill his promises: "Big Ralph promised me the moon [Sissie recalls]. . . . Well that moon was so far away. . . . We went hungry plenty of times" (177). Sissie's disappointment and frustration increased when poverty led to the death of her first daughter: " 'Juanita started to die when we didn't have money to buy coal and keep the house warm. I got mad, I just got mad' " (177). As a result, Sissie sought comfort with a lover, Albert, and to punish Ralph for his failures and her frustrations she led him to think that Iris was Albert's daughter, not his own. Then, fearing that Ralph would think she loved another man's child more than his, she willfully withheld affection from Iris.

In this way, Williams forges the chain that shackles the failure of public economy to the destruction of emotional wealth. Scarcity of money and opportunity produced in Sissie's family a scarcity of affection. In mediating between these two worlds, Sissie is the consummate middleman(woman), bartering dignity for solace or solace for security, always discovering that for those with impoverished resources, the power to refuse must compensate for not having the power to give or to buy.

This lesson Iris learns well. Responding to her exclusion even from the affection of her own family, she brings the connection between public and private, emotional and political full circle by expatriating herself. Iris, like Williams's other expatriate protagonists, represents an attempt to separate place from history. In this way *Sissie* is a sequel to the slave narrative in that it responds to the narrative's failed promise of a place where the definition of humanity changed for blacks. If the legal definition had changed, the social and economic had not, and history still remained the accident from whose reports Iris, by definition, was barred, both in the broad national sense and, as we have seen, in the narrower familial, in ways that do not allow the safe insulation of her personal narrative.

This theme of expatriation is underscored by the narrative's equally dislocating shifts in point of view. Although the novel begins and ends from Iris's point of view, much of it is presented from her brother, Ralph's, her mother's, or her father's. Although they overlap, their stories are as much discrete and estranged from one another as they are congruent. The novel thus foregrounds not the composite of one family but the fragments of a family no longer containable in one site or under one context.

The expatriation of Max Reddick, *The Man Who Cried* I AM! (1967), can be seen as representing a similar connection between public policy and personal bondage. When his fiancée, Lillian, dies from an abortion that she undergoes because they cannot afford to raise a family while Max continues to struggle as a writer, Max's thoughts make a direct link between the accident of history and those left out of the reports: "They [white America] gave Lillian the photograph, the image of the American Family Group, but when she looked very, very closely, she wasn't in it; she wasn't even the blanked-out one of every ten who would contract polio or clap or pox; nor was she the one who wasn't insured by Metropolitan Life or Allstate. She was nothing and she was not to get that little house surrounded by shrubbery and a white picket fence" (116–17).

Max Reddick too attempts to expatriate himself but, like Iris Joplin, he finds the act of expatriation can succeed only if one is first part of the country one has chosen to leave. Never fully patriated, Max cannot be a full expatriate, and his adventures in Europe become a complicated network of connections with black Americans and black Africans, as if being in Europe were not so much escaping America as discovering the hyphen that connects the phrase "Afro-American." Even his Dutch wife, Margrit, represents for him his entrapment within the limitations of racism, so that he always sees in her the loss of Lillian. At the beginning of the novel, seeing her after an estrangement, he thinks:

> [Her] stride was not the same: he fitted it into the one he remembered watching in Holland, Spain, France, Puerto Rico, St. Thomas, Manhattan, East Hampton, Vermont, Mexico. . . . There was something sad about her stride now. . . .
>
> "Margrit! [Lillian!] Margrit! [Lillian!] Margrit! [Lillian!]," he shouted, coming out of his chair like a shot, the pain grabbing deeply in his rectum, and he was halfway across the street, all the while fighting the urge to grab himself, tear himself inside out. (6–7)

Max's pain, a terminal case of rectal cancer, is a metaphor for the "shafting" he has received. Here it acts up when he tries to move toward Margrit, who should represent escape from national boundaries. Her stride, after all, had remained recognizable on both sides of the Atlantic. But calling out to her, Max only finds in her name his own repressed longing for the Lillian whom he lost to the demands of the impossible-for-them American Dream.

Time, not place, therefore, separates him from Lillian, just as it alters Margrit's stride ("sadder *now*"), a stride that remained unaltered by place. As Earl Cash points out, "instead of a case in which the white woman is the ideal the Black must copy, Lillian is the Black ideal Margrit must live up to" (103). But if Margrit's failure is that she can never do so, Max's failure is that he cannot escape the definitive quality of Lillian's influence, nor can he make anyone else fit the definition. If Margrit is the inverse of Lillian, Max can neither turn her inside out to make her Lillian nor turn himself away from the desire to. The logistics of his life have created only unsatisfying intersections with the racial imperatives of his history. In trying to cross the street, therefore, he can no more regain Margrit than he can regain Lillian. He is left only with the pain of his condition and the desire to escape it through a painfully inverting metamorphosis.

To regain, of course, is a temporal act as much as it is a logistical one, and the time frames of Reddick's life thus signify not only that life's logistical impossibility but also its temporal and hence historical impossibility. This is foregrounded by the disruption of the linear narrative, so that the novel's temporal dis-locations create ruptures foregrounding Reddick's alienation from history as well as country.

Iris Joplin also finds herself estranged equally from history as from her nation. As a successful singer touring Europe, she tries to separate history from time, history being the authorized text of a nation and time being the personal rhythms of a life. Williams almost allegorizes this aspect of Iris's plight, by having Iris divorce the American soldier who brought her to Europe and start singing with a jazz group whose leader is called "Time." Time thus represents alternative art forms, African American tempos, ahistorical chronology. But like Max Reddick's, Iris's attempted escape is illusory, becoming a reminder of its own impossibility. Her performances are another proof that in her artistry she did not free herself from Africa or America but became the link that connected the two, with all their inherent contradictions:

> Iris could not know as she stood in her cones of light from Birmingham to Berlin, Copenhagen to Capri, Bordeaux to Berlin, which of the Africans or Arabs were igniting the torches of nationalism in their homes. When she and Time listened to them they exuded the sense that all of Europe had died and only Africa . . . lived and would be free of the French and the British. They

bellowed it out in club cellars and from the various colleges and quarters to which they had been assigned *de facto*. But they cried, Iris and Time always noticed with amusement, in better French than the French, and in better English than the British. And when they cried, one arm raised to pound against the sky, the other arm lay softly upon the shoulder of a colonial daughter.

"How mad!" Iris said.

Time shrugged. (80)

Iris and Time thus stand apart from American history and from the Africans and Arabs who are trying to replicate that history, complete with the performance of its love-hate act with the colonialists.

Iris differs from Time, however, in her attitude. Throughout her attempted escape, Iris has been trapped in the past. She always wonders how her mother, Sissie, would evaluate her success in Europe, and sometimes, "on the beaches—Algrave, Monte Carlo, Rapallo, Costa Brava—it all seemed to Iris a betrayal of her past" (86). Time, on the other hand, "always looking for the new, discovering new numbers, talking to strangers" (87), is trapped in the future, and when Iris is with him she thus feels "cut off" (87).

Slowly the members of Time's combo begin to return to America, but he and Iris stay on, pick up new sidemen, gain fame, and become lovers. Iris gravitates to Time as though in his embrace she can escape history. The irony of her situation, like Reddick's, is one of time and place. Because she cannot learn to shrug off the madness of history—be it the national history of racial rejection or the personal history of maternal rejection—she has to continue rebelling against it and thus is ever bound up in it. She cannot therefore free herself to marry Time, but when she turns down his proposal, he says: "Listen, I wanted to marry you and maybe go back home. It's something I always looked forward to. I never wanted to be an old jazzman dropping dead from a heart attack. But goddam, Homefolks, why would you do this to me?" (89).

In this speech, Williams captures much of the double-consciousness of Iris's tenuous patriation, as it represents the dilemma of many black Americans. Her inability to shrug, her drive to deny, her need to stay away are exactly the traits that brand her "Homefolks." Because she is Homefolks, she cannot go home. Because he is Time, he cannot look back.

To underscore Iris's paradoxical situation, however, the novel constantly looks back. The "present" covers only a few days in which Iris flies into New

York to see Ralph's play and then with Ralph to Los Angeles to visit their dying mother. Regardless of locale and point of view, however, time does not progress so much as unwind. Thus the moment in Europe when Iris looks back is also one, simultaneously, that Iris looks back upon. The same is true of the sections situated in Ralph's point of view, in Ralph Sr.'s, and in Sissie's. The impossibility of the stable point from which to achieve per-spective—either physical, national, temporal, or historical—is underscored particularly by having Iris's past frame the book and thus seem to "con-tain" her mother's memories that antedate Iris's birth. In this way too the narrative promises motion—perhaps the implicit promise of all narrative—toward a goal of resolution, change, conclusion, rest. It delivers, instead, an awareness of dis-location.

The narrative structure of *Mothersill and the Foxes* (1975) creates the same temporal and spatial dis-locations, in this case focusing on the question of Afro-American identity in a sexual context. Odell Mothersill's life, narrated primarily but not exclusively from his point of view, contains numerous flashbacks and jump-forwards, often underscored by jumps into the present tense. The novel presents his life in terms of thirty-five years of sexual en-counters, without marriage or progeny, marked by former lovers who have, among other things, met violent deaths, gone insane, or tried to kill him. The failure of Mothersill's relationships reflects his inability to fulfill some-one else's image of what he should be, what role he should play. The racial implications of these role conflicts are clear from the outset, when a woman whom Mothersill has brought to his apartment for the first time stops their lovemaking just before he enters her so that she can watch *Cheyenne* on TV:

> For forty-five minutes he watched and listened as Shirley cried:
> "Kick his ass, Cheyenne! ! Whump! Aw, do it, Cheyenne!" She paused between exclamations to smile at Mothersill. He, however, was willing his limp penis to rise, but the flesh was weak, mortified and unable to sustain his imagery. Finally it sulked between his thighs as if seeking a hiding place. (16)

As Shirley's fantasy lover, Cheyenne, the huge, square-jawed, pale-eyed, Anglo-featured cowboy of the 1950s, illustrates the impossible image against which Mothersill's self-image falls flat.

Mothersill's attempts to assert his own image—often comic, sometimes violent or tragic—become historicized in the third section of the book, when Mothersill, visiting the Caribbean, searches for the site of a former slave plantation. Now with a Ph.D. and an administrative position in the Peace Corps, he has traveled through much of the world, both sexual and geographic, without finding what he was looking for. In this case, he is looking for the black history of the plantation, after noticing that a tourist brochure had omitted the slaves: "Don't talk or write about things and they will cease to exist and perhaps never did. If you don't talk about Moses being born in Africa, he wasn't an African. A reedian? Found floating in the reeds?" (130). Mothersill finds overgrowth instead of records and artifacts, as if the blacks themselves, he thinks, had "conspired with the writers of the tourist brochures to produce a void" (130).

This historical search, however, is connected to the personal when we are told that "Mothersill's was to have been a journey of personal discovery" (131), so that the narrative's juxtaposition of these details with the sexual adventures on the island underscore the matrix of the two. In the scenes that immediately follow, for instance, he ends up providing sexual pleasure to an affluent black couple after having refused to be used in the same way by an aristocratic white woman, and he then meets on the beach and has another failed fling with a woman with whom he had lived years earlier in New York.

This section of the book thus focuses our attention on the idea of "the past." Mothersill, having gone to the Caribbean to search for the past, found it in the forms of personal servitude and sexual failure. It is both his personal past reenacted in a historical setting and his historical past reinscribed in his personal/sexual experience. Like so many of Williams's expatriate protagonists, Mothersill travels elsewhere only to find at one more remove the same dis-located perspective. The faces he sees in the Caribbean remind him of American blacks he had known. "Africa always did that to him too. He'd see a face and it would remind him of someone at home, someone he'd grown up with or knew later. Strange" (130).

This sense of a story chronically re-told and re-erased governs even more notably the narrative structure of *Captain Blackman* (1972). Captain Blackman is the eternal black American soldier sacrificed to the interests of "American" history and erased from its pages. The captain, who had been conducting an unsanctioned seminar in black military history for soldiers in his company in Vietnam, is seriously wounded at the novel's outset. The framework for the novel is the series of fantasies he has while being rescued, medicated, and hospitalized. The fantasies merge his experiences as a black soldier with the content of his seminars in such a way that his dreams reenact the history of American wars from the Revolution to the present (or future) on the site of his temporally finite life. At the same time, he lives his life through its infinite repetition at the sites of all American wars. The site is always different and the story is always the same, especially in the way that, in the end, it always sacrifices Blackman to its interests and then erases him from the story.

Like *Mothersill and the Foxes, Captain Blackman* has a structure that is more cumulative than linear, one that moves forward by accumulating the past, such that the weight of the accumulations becomes both the protagonist's and the reader's impossible and inescapable burden. Although the narrative in *Captain Blackman* constantly tries to merge personal and public history, it ends up emphasizing the impossibility of such a merger, for each episode ends with the accident report I have called "history" omitting the casualties—not just the casualties of warfare but those of narrative omission.

Although located within the world of publishing itself, *!Click Song* (1983) reflects the same struggle to find a place not incompatible with the forces of history, and the !click indigenous to many African dialects represents not only speech and speakers outside the range of English (or white) articulation but also the culture that turns these sounds into music. It represents, in other words, not just an art form lost to Western culture, but also a lost audience. Lacking a publishing and consequently reading audience for the !clicking of his culture, Cato Caldwell Douglass must translate the !clicks into a more marketable commodity if he is to "place" his fiction, that is, if he is to find a place as an American writer.

His problem is that in order to make a place for himself, he has to place his fiction, but as a black, in order to place his fiction he has to know his place and not make one for himself. In fact, as the story makes clear, for Douglass, as for all black writers, the publishing world has few places and all of them taken. If the traditional cliché for becoming a successful artist is ⸢ ⸣aking it," *!Click Song* suggests that for the black artist making it is not half as difficult as finding a place for it after it is made.

The reason for this, Douglass is told repeatedly by editors, publishers, and agents, is that it is not the right *time.* Again the fourth dimension of time destabilizes the other three, never permitting a stable place where the people who make the !click songs can be heard and accepted. To frame the issue in the context of that classic conundrum of Western philosophy: If a tree !clicks in the forest, is it a noise if no one hears it? or a song? or a book? or a culture?

Against this context, in which all time and space are relative to the world of publishing, the other movements in *!Click Song* should be measured. Like Reddick and like Iris Joplin, for example, Douglass finds his experiences abroad do not so much free him from the paradoxes of his situation as underscore those paradoxes. When he meets a black Spanish woman in a Barcelona night club, he realizes that "Uncle Sam must have been smiling out of his star spangled heaven . . . because, like all other tourists (though black people are special cases), I was proof that Democracy Works! Never mind Mack Parker and Emmett Till and Little Rock; if it was so bad, how had I managed to get away? I was standing here, my key in the lock, incontrovertible proof that America was indeed the land of the free . . ." (50). Douglass thus becomes proof that the place he left was not the place that he left, and that undermines his place, even before his arrival, in the world he has come to. Like his role with Monica, the black Spanish woman whom he takes in and whose child he fathers, his place in any physical locale is compromised and tenuous. Hence it dissolves when contrasted with concerns about his literary place, and when he sees his book galley, he realizes he must go back to New York, to the world of publishing. About his return to New York, nevertheless, he states: "It's returning to familiar places that after a time takes its toll. I didn't know that then. I was ignorant" (58). Although time does not alter the locale it changes Douglass's place in that locale, and the toll of that alteration is the sapping of his artistic life.

The narrative structure of *!Click Song*, Gilbert Muller has pointed out, conveys "a sense of lives converging, diverging and coming together again in altered forms. Thus even as the primary narrative advances through the stages of Cato's adult life . . . Williams . . . interweaves past, present, and future, often juxtaposing elements or providing information to clarify relationships or events" (145). The pattern of the story, in other words, is that of returning to familiar places so that the narration replicates the events and the toll they take on the narrator.

As the narration moves forward, it shifts Douglass from place to place, against which it measures his shifting place in the publishing world, which in turn is the world that authorizes the narration. Since the decisions, interchanges, and artifacts that create the landscape of that world come from parallels in Williams's own publishing experiences, which made possible the publication of *!Click Song* (a book that returns to those familiar places in its narrative), *!Click Song* in a sense narrates its own publication.

The structure thus extends the conflict between time and place that runs through Williams's work, for if the text, as the narration of its own history, is always one step removed from itself, there is never a time at which the narrative time can stop framing the act of publication that created it. And so long as the frame is also framed, we can have no stable place that we can call inside or outside, only a never-ending Möbius strip.

If the only way to end the Möbius strip is to tear it crosswise, then perhaps the only way to end *!Click Song* is to rupture the narrative structure. This may explain why the narrative shifts at the end into pure fantasy, in the form of a violent, nightmare confrontation with the police. Because *!Click Song*'s ever-shifting relationship between time and space also represents the abstract extension of the expatriation theme in Williams's work, its resolution is particularly important. In violently rupturing the narrative with a fantasy that destroys the voice that created it, Williams seems to be suggesting the paradoxical bind of the black writer—or of any runaway who has arrived at the place that promised to be an end, a resolution, a secure location where one is defined as human, only to discover that the arrival is untimely and the life cannot fit the story that the runaway desired to make of it.

This rupturing also has antecedents in Williams's earlier fiction. In *Mothersill and the Foxes,* after Mothersill is shot at point-blank range by a former lover, instead of dying he appears in a pastoral setting, far removed from any other setting in the novel, and high above them: "One of my pleasures up here is seeing the days begin. . . . Also . . . the stars . . . seem much closer to earth here . . ." (233). In this brief sixth section of the book—the only one narrated in the first person—all of Mothersill's dreams have been realized, and this part of the book contains its only chapter designation, "Chapter One," setting up this section as the only alternative to Mothersill's unfair demise.

This is another version of the World War III holocaust vision that ends *Captain Blackman* and of Max Reddick's violent death in the failed attempt to make public a conspiracy of international genocide of blacks. It is also a version of Iris Joplin's decision to deny her mother's deathbed request, for only in rejecting the force that rejected her can Iris affirm her own tenuous place. To put it another way, we could say that the affirmation through negation typifies for many the historical conditions of African American performance.

9. RACE, RIGHTS, GENDER, AND PERSONAL NARRATIVE

The Archaeology of "Self" in *Meridian*

Throughout this book I have made much of the idea that history is created through the repetition of narratives, in sundry forms, such that they become referential signs of "reality" and of "relevance." These signs allow (or disallow) aspects of human activity (or, for that matter, geologic activity) to become legible as "events" and to be represented in history's hierarchy.

This concept, of course, implies an audience: Legible to whom? Particularly in the contemporary Western world, and especially in the United States, the numerous modes of performance and the numerous means for recording performance and deploying the records make absurd the idea of narratives in a monolithic voice or addressing a uniform audience. Subsectors of the population abound, each with its own accepted (as well as its set of internally disputed) narratives. Since I will address the implications of this situation in the conclusion, at this point suffice it to say that in the previous chapter I discussed at least one important group of narratives at variance with those of the dominant discourse. Even in the midst of the breakdown of containment, the resulting array of dominant narratives in American culture—especially as codified in the 1984 and 1988 presidential campaigns—have accepted as legible only a small fraction of African American narratives.

In this context, I now want to focus on another concept I discussed in the introduction but to which I have returned much less frequently: the personal narrative. This is, in short, the composite of stories that individuals tell themselves so as to construct out of sensation a concept of identity. "Narratives do accrue," and, Jerome Bruner notes, "the accruals eventually create something variously called a 'culture' or a 'history' or, more loosely, a 'tradition.' Even our own homely accounts of happenings in our own lives are eventually converted into more or less coherent autobiographies centered around a Self acting more or less purposefully in a social world"(18).

Bruner's position has much in common with the work of Paul Ricoeur. For Ricoeur, narrative is the mediation without which cosmic time could not enter human experience. As such, in Ricoeur's formulation, narrative is inherently mimetic in that it imitates not actions but rather the forms by which actions can be recognized and contextualized. For Ricoeur, humans exist at one remove from time, conscious of it only by means of the ways they inscribe their actions on it—for example calendars—or by means of the ways it delimits their actions. Human experience, for Ricoeur, therefore, is constituted by the narrative activity that mediates between memory and anticipation so as to bridge the aporias of time, and narrative forms are always imitating that "essential" human activity. Narrative, therefore, is not the escape from reality—the conversion of reality into a story—but rather the form that stories must take for humans to recognize them as real. Narratives themselves are never real, but they are always the necessary access to reality.

In Ricouer's formulation, of course, reality exists in some form that is discrete from its access, and that issue I cannot pursue here.[1] Rather, I want to examine the relation of personal narration to cultural narratives in facilitating that access, because a significant problem foregrounded by African American literature is the question of equal access. How do the narrative constructions of one's identity become legible as part of a group—be it a family, a club, an institution, an ethnicity, a nation—without violence? I mean by *violence* here *not* attacks on the status quo, on the people and institutions whose duty it is to perform the acts that comprise dominant cultural narratives and then who narcissistically read those acts as affirming the narratives that motivated them. I mean violence against the individual who wants to belong or, more precisely, violence against that individual's personal narratives, against the stories by which an individual constitutes the subject who would belong.

This issue has found much currency in legal discussion. The Constitution and, by extension, the legal system and the courts provide, according to Kenneth Karst, the crucial mechanism for belonging to America. Pointing out that "a deep current of egalitarianism has always run through American society, and [that] we have often resorted to law to effectuate our ideals" (1),

Karst notes the disparity between Americans' egalitarian ideals and their behavior, and he argues that the incongruity has been reconciled for successive generations of Americans by defining "the community's public life — or the community itself — in a way that excludes the subordinated groups. The inclination to exclude is not innate; it arises in the acculturation that forms individual self-definition out of attachment to one's own group and separation from other groups. . . . Equality and belonging are inseparably linked: to define the scope of the ideal of equality in America is to define the boundaries of the national community" (2).

The "majority," in other words, to minimize the disparity between itself and its community, constructs narratives that perform exclusionary acts. The "minority" is not the *victim* of these acts, but rather it is the *product* of them, because a minority can only exist after a dominant cultural narrative renders their performances illegible. The "minority" is the victim, in other words, of the process of definition that relegates the performance of their lives to "minority" status. This is a way of describing what Lyotard has called "terrorism" — playing by rules that make the rules of the Other impossible. The point is that African Americans have not been an excluded minority because of black skin, but because of the narratives that rationalized the exclusion (and denigration and abuse) of people with black skin, a point made most clear by the way that narrative has extended to those ethnically identified with African American (or Caribbean or African) experience, regardless of pigmentation. Conversely, the exclusions, as Patricia Williams has made so cogently clear, have not applied to those of African descent who have been embraced by Euro-American history, such as Beethoven; *instead, his ancestry has been disavowed.*

Commenting on a case in which a racist act resulted from an argument at Stanford University between a black and a white student over the fact that Beethoven was a mulatto, Williams, a professor of law, places the dispute in the context of the exclusions I have been discussing:

> The most deeply offending part of the Beethoven injury is its message that if I ever manage to create something as monumental as Beethoven's music, or the literature of the mulatto Alexandre Dumas or the mulatto Alexander Pushkin, then the best reward to which I can aspire is that I will be remembered as white. Perhaps my tribe will hold a candle in honor of my black heart over the generations — for blacks have been teaching white

people that Beethoven was a mulatto for over a hundred years now—and they will be mocked when they try to make some claim on me. If they do press their point, the best they can hope for is that their tormenters will be absolved because it was a reasonable mistake to assume I was white: they just didn't know. But the issue is precisely the appropriation of knowledge, the authority of creating a canon, revising memory, declaring a boundary beyond which lies the "extrinsic" and beyond which ignorance is reasonably suffered. (113–14)

The theme in this example runs through Williams's *The Alchemy of Race and Rights*. In a unique combination of personal essay, legal philosophy, case study, and social commentary, Williams examines numerous instances, like the one above, in which a constructed "difference" defines a social norm from which social and legal "realities" follow. Her work, in other words, is an extended demonstration of the effects of cultural narratives on legal performance. If Karst is correct, moreover, in asserting that legal performance is the mechanism for belonging to America, then Williams is analyzing not only the practices of the American legal system but, through them, the performance of America in the narratives that affect its residents.

Williams analyzes persuasively, for example, the racist assumptions surrounding the debate over the 1986 Howard Beach incident in New York City. In that all-white neighborhood, three blacks were followed from a pizzeria by a group of white teenagers who taunted, chased, and severely beat the men; one of the men was struck and killed by an automobile as he tried to escape. Those who defended the harassment and beating questioned the blacks' motive for being in Howard Beach, pointing to the illogic of their stopping in that pizzeria and to the media's revelation of the "unsavory dispositions the victims had" (6). But this line of reasoning, Williams explains, presumes as *real* a distinction that equates "white" with "good" and "black" with "evil," from which premise follow the unspoken assumptions of the Howard Beach residents: that everyone who lives there is white, has no black friends, employs no blacks, permits no blacks to shop there, because "no black is ever up to any good" (59). Within the narrative of the assaulters (and the community that defended their actions), blacks are in the a priori position of having to prove their difference from the sign of blackness. Like Beethoven, the blacks' best reward would be to escape their own ethnic identity, to become invisible.[2] At stake, in other words, is not merely the different cultural narrative that Williams urges, but for the victims themselves—and thus for any blacks, since they are all potential victims of Howard Beach's narrative and the violence it impels—at stake is their personal narrative, their ability to be visible in the stories of their own lives, lives in which blackness does not a priori equal evil. Failing to define themselves within the cultural narrative of the community that they entered was a way of performing their near, virtual, or actual executions.

One repercussion of the event was an interracial protest march through Howard Beach by fourteen hundred protesters. In trying to explain the hostility of Howard Beach residents to this action, Mayor Koch asked an audience in a nearby black neighborhood how they would feel if fourteen hundred white protesters marched in their neighborhood. Koch's question, Williams points out, "accepts a remarkable degree of possessiveness about public streets . . . that is racially and not geographically bounded. Koch was, in effect, pleading for acceptance of the privatization of public space. This is the de facto equivalent of segregation; it is exclusion in the guise of deep-moated property 'interests' and 'values.' Lost is the fact that the object of discussion, the street, is public" (69).

If we extend the implications of Williams's argument a bit further, however, I think that we could argue that the fact that the street was public was not lost, but was actually an important premise for the assailants and their neighbors. What was *lost* was a meaning of "public" that includes blacks. If the public space is defined as space that is neutral, protected, free to public access, within the Howard Beach dominant narrative that means a space without blacks. It was *because* the white teenagers treated the space as "public" that they felt ire toward the blacks who had violated it. By relating to the streets as public, the gang activity acquired a civic dimension that allowed the public performance of private anger. Like the Nazis, the white teenagers accepted a cultural narrative that permitted their personal narratives to merge with their idea of the public will and the common good. The blacks in the pizzeria that December night turned the small mob into public servants. It did so at the price of the personal narrative of the Other, but that price had already been paid in a nonreciprocal social contract at least in North America as old as the advent of slavery. As Williams points out in another essay, "The blackness of black people in this society has always represented the blemish, the uncleanliness, the barrier separating individual from society. Castration from blackness becomes the initiatory tunnel. . . .

Once castrated they have shed their horrid mortality, the rapacious lust of lower manhood, the raucous, mother-witted passion of lower womanhood, and opened themselves up to participation in the pseudo-celestial white community" (*Alchemy*, 198).

Situating Williams within the conflict between personal and dominant cultural narrative is, I think, in keeping with her own project and the style she has developed to pursue it:

> I am trying to challenge the usual limits of commercial discourse by using an intentionally double-voiced and relational, rather than a traditionally legal black-letter, vocabulary. . . . On the one hand, my writing has been staked out as the exclusive interdisciplinary property of constitutional law, contract law, African-American history, feminist jurisprudence, political science, and rhetoric. At the same time, my work has been described as a "sophisticated frontal assault" on laissez faire's most sacred sanctums, as "new-age performance art," and as "anecdotal individualism." In other words, to speak as black, female, *and* commercial lawyer has rendered me simultaneously universal, trendy, and marginal. I think, moreover, that there is a paradigm at work, in the persistent perceptions of me as inherent contradiction: a paradigm of larger social perceptions that divide public from private, black from white, dispossessed from legitimate. This realization, while extremely personal, inevitably informs my writing on a professional level. (*Alchemy*, 7)

As Williams makes clear, the situation from which she speaks is not only black but female. As such, it is not surprising that some would call her work "performance art," that is, something not recoverable by history. Much of this owes to the historically specific conditions, touched upon in the last chapter, that made the narrative asserted by black men depend upon the valorizing of black masculinity. As the title of John Williams's best-known novel, *The Man Who Cried I AM!* implies, identity and manhood are inextricable parts of the same narrative. Patricia Williams knows this well, as indicated, in part, by her discussion of the situation she was placed in by her father who would give his poetry to her (and her sister) instead of trying to publish it: "I was powerful. . . . What I did was lie, no matter how much I believed in the talent of his poetry. My power was in living the lie that I was all audiences. My power was the temptation to dissemble, either out of love or disaffection. This is the blacks' and women's power, I used to think, *the power to lie while existing in the realm of someone else's fantasy. It is the power* to refrain from exerting the real, to shift illusion, while serving as someone else's weaponry, nemesis, or language club" (200; emphasis added).

Another way to describe "blacks' and womens' power" is to say that it is purchased at the same price as the invisibility of black men in the white world: the cost of the "I AM!" Although, as Patricia points out, "Williams" is the second most common name in America, I suppose we could fantasize that John and Patricia might trace their ancestry back to the same William who reified their ancestors, the proprietary "Bill" that they are still paying off. If so, extending this metaphor, we could say that Patricia has had to pay the estate twice, meeting double interest but never touching on the principal, paying once to the dominant discourse and once to the narrative of black manhood.

This theme, which recurs in the essays of black women writers such as bell hooks, Michele Wallace, and Alice Walker, is marked, as it is in Patricia Williams's, by the stylistic merging of criticism and autobiography. This merger can indeed be seen as a form of postmodern writing: pastiche, or metafictional commentary, or in some cases, writing the body. But I prefer to read it as a referential performance, a use of the personal narrative to critique black masculinist discourse and, through it, the historically specific conditions that have legally, socially, economically, and politically isolated that discourse from history.

As hooks explains, it is inadequate to say that this form of writing affirms the slogan "the personal is political." "If the personal and the political are one and the same," she argues, "then there is no politicization, no way to become a radical feminist subject" (*Talking Back,* 111). Hooks is concerned not with the use of autobiography or confession as a springboard to a political consciousness, but rather with the danger of its becoming the goal instead of the initiation. The problem, as we have been examining it, is not that blacks and/or women do not have narratives that comprise their personal history or sense of identity, but that those stories are not widely legible. If power is the negotiating of illegibility, then the personal becomes political not when it speaks of itself to itself, but only when it affects the dominant cultural narrative.

But that process is complicated by the narratives of black masculinity, which for hooks reinscribe the problems of white patriarchy: "Although the gendered politics of slavery denied black men the freedom to act as 'men' within the definition set by white norms, the notion of manhood did be-

come a standard used to measure black male prowess" (90). Michele Wallace
makes the same point:

> [In 1969, in college,] I discovered my voice, and when brothers talked to
> me, I talked back. This had its hazards. . . . Here was the logic behind our
> grandmothers' old saying, "A nigga man ain't shit." It was shorthand for
> "The black man has learned to hate himself and to hate you even more. Be
> careful. He will hurt you."
>
> I am reminded of a conversation I had with a brother up at City College
> one mild spring day . . . he was telling me what the role of the black woman
> was. When a pause came in his monologue, I asked him what the role of the
> black man was. He mumbled something about, "Simply to be a man." When
> I suggested that might not be enough, he went completely ape. He turned
> purple. He started screaming. "The black man doesn't have to do anything.
> He's a man he's a man he's a man!" (22)

Wallace's first book, *Black Macho and the Myth of the Superwoman,* was attacked for its assault on black sexism as promoted even by black civil rights
leaders and its critique of African American women writers, who Wallace
claimed continued to reinforce the myth of the superwoman. Although
Wallace has subsequently admitted that she was reading some of the fiction
by black women "too narrowly" (226) and that she had not adequately taken
into account the psychological and social ordeals of growing up in segregated America for civil rights leaders such as King, she still finds a problematic duality within African American discourse, prompted by models of
masculinity. If Malcolm X and King, as I suggested in the last chapter, represent alternative strains of the double-consciousness, they feed for Wallace
into a common masculine construction of contemporary leadership.[3] In her
critique of Spike Lee's film, *Do the Right Thing,* she explains that

> [filmakers] entirely miss the mark, that they reinscribe the very thing that
> they aim to dislocate, when they trivialize or deny the importance of
> women's oppression in general, and the problems of black women in par-
> ticular. Moreover, to do so makes no sense in terms of the material reality
> of representations of "race" in American culture, which has always been
> profoundly entangled with issues of gender, sexuality, and the female body.
>
> Although we are geared to focus on the careers of great men, in fact the
> history of black liberation struggles invoked by the photograph of King and
> Malcolm X together is unimaginable without the input of women. . . .

By ending with a quote in support of nonviolent resistance from Martin Luther King, Jr., who is the hero of the integrationist/assimilationist position, and a quote in support of self-defense from Malcolm X, who is the hero of the cultural nationalist position, Lee squarely places the film in the vanguard of contemporary experiments to reinterpret the two approaches. But, beneath the surface, the entire debate spells "history" as great men have made and written it, not as many women and the poor have lived it. If the life-giving processes of the female body and the "family" are not figured into the calculation, what remains is the lifeless, inhuman abstraction of war games. (*Invisibility Blues*, 109–10)

As hooks points out, "the tensions Wallace describes [in *Black Macho*] between black women and men have not abated, if anything they have worsened [in the last ten years]. In more recent years they have taken the form of black women and men competing for the attention of a white audience" (*Black Looks*, 101).

My point here is not to take sides in this argument, to defend or attack black "masculinity," or to echo calls for a new form of black feminism. Rather it is to note the competing narratives that comprise the matrix of African American culture, similar not in the bulk of their arguments but in the way that those arguments have only marginal legibility within the dominant discourse. Just as many black Americans find themselves belonging to dual nations and their speech still circumscribed by the double-consciousness, many women among them find themselves equally invisible within the patriarchal African American world. Many characters in John Williams's novels seem to be looking—like Richard Wright, James Baldwin, and ultimately, W. E. B. Du Bois, to name a fraction of the most prominent writers (not to mention the numerous black artists and musicians)—for a site where their humanity is not a metaphoric or contingent or private assertion in the dubious margins of public knowledge. For many African American women, feeling themselves at one further remove from those dubious margins, the site becomes not Europe or Africa but their own body, as a source of authority and an authorizing text.

All of these issues are at work in Alice Walker's remarkable novel, *Meridian*, a text that rehistoricizes the civil rights movement of the 1960s through the cultural and personal narratives of African American men and women. Like much of the African American writing I have discussed, Walker's presents a continually dichotomous world, the antecedents of which are located in a problem common to slave narratives—a problem emphasized, as I pointed out in the last chapter, in the epilogue of Ralph Ellison's *Invisible Man*—that identity is a function of place. An underlying premise of the slave narrative was that a literal place existed that altered the definition of humanity for blacks. When the North failed to fulfill its promise of being that place, the relationship of place to identity became one more dichotomy embedded in the language and activities of black American existence, one more dichotomy embodying the impossibility of assimilation and the impossibility of continued "apartheid."

The problem is one as well of reconciling the individual and tradition, which means both finding a tradition *and* breaking with one, for "tradition," as it has been handed down, is the tradition of an enslaved or oppressed people who have had many of the direct connections to their native rituals, beliefs, and languages ruptured by violent racial and economic oppression. Under such circumstances, Walker has pondered, "How was the creativity of the black woman kept alive . . . when for most of the years black people have been in America, it was a punishable crime for a black person to read or write? And the freedom to paint, to sculpt, to expand the mind with action did not exist?" ("In Search," 234). Walker concludes that this creativity often manifested itself anonymously, in folk arts and domestic activities ("In Search," 240). The "anonymity," of course, has made the tradition hard to identify, and Walker recalls longing for black anthropologists and collectors of folklore: "Where is the *black* person who took the time to travel the back roads of the South and collect the information I need . . . ?" ("In Search," 11). It is not surprising, therefore, that in the fictional world Walker presents, blacks as a result of this oppression often repress their desires and sublimate their frustrations in ways that enable them to accept the status quo and/or even adopt their oppressors' values.

In addition, Walker explores the problem that, within the black community, the roles of oppressor and oppressed are often reenacted between men and women, so that women must go through the same encoding and sublimation to cope with male oppression that blacks go through to cope with racial oppression. In Walker's earlier novel, *The Third Life of Grange Copeland*, Copeland addresses this issue very directly in his long diatribe, in chapter 45, against his son, Brownfield (205–9). In that novel, "ostensibly about a man and his son," Walker has said, "it is the women and how they are treated that colors everything" ("In Search," 250–51).[4] This leaves black women at a double remove from power and makes them participants in a double encoding system. If black history forms a repressed, encoded, ruptured alternative to published American history, then maternal history—the chain between generations bound by maternal experience, genetic biases, and empathetic subjugation—is an encoded subtext within the black male cultural history.[5]

With this in mind, *Meridian* can be read as an attempt to mend the ruptures and reconstruct an alternative black tradition from its contemporary American artifacts. The novel, in other words, conducts a historical search in that it tries to recontextualize the past in a manner not dependent on the dominant historical narratives or the arbitrary "beginnings" by which they delimit "reality." This requires layering information, information about pre-Christian inhabitants of North America, about the civil rights workers of the 1960s, and much albeit fragmented information about the time between. In conducting this historical search, I will argue, Walker treats narrative as archaeology and thus provides instructions for reading Meridian's life as though it were inscribed on the archaeological site of her body. Such a reading depends on recognizing the relationship between Meridian's body and the body politic, and it reveals the role of maternal history in constructing a personal narrative. This lesson in reading, Walker further suggests, is necessary to reconcile the conflicts between art and activism in black American life.

NARRATIVE AS ARCHAEOLOGY

The first half of *Meridian* moves not only through Meridian's personal history and the history of her parents and grandparents but also through the history of her land and folklore. It moves almost in an archaeological manner, less interested in chronological exposition than in a process of unearthing and reexplaining.

In many ways, this situation can be seen as a structuralist endeavor of the sort applied to cultural anthropology by Claude Lévi-Strauss, among others, in that it attempts to decode cultural phenomena by understanding the implicit system that gives them meaning.[6] "When one takes as object of study," Jonathan Culler explains, "not physical phenomena but artifacts or events with meaning, the defining qualities of the phenomena become the features which distinguish them from one another and enable them to bear meaning within the symbolic system from which they derive" (5). These "defining qualities" only have meaning in terms of the single point of view from which they are gathered. To change the point of view is to restructure the investigation and change the meaning of the constituent phenomena — just as changing the rules of grammar would alter the meaning of specific words in specific sentences.[7]

The first chapter of *Meridian* exemplifies this archaeological approach to narrative by examining Meridian's life and ancestry synchronically, as though they were the strata of one archaeological site at which each unearthing of an antecedent redefines the structure of the whole. The chapter begins in the novel's present, then quickly jumps back ten years to a meeting in New York of revolutionary women taunting Meridian with the question: Would she kill for the revolution? She is unable to answer because she recontextualizes the question in terms of a further past: "what none of them seemed to understand was that she felt herself to be, not holding on to something from the past, but *held* by something in the past: by the memory of old black men in the South who, caught by surprise in the eye of the camera, never shifted their position but looked directly back; by the sight of young girls singing in a country choir, their hair shining with brushings and grease, their voices the voices of angels. . . . If they committed murder [Meridian wonders] *what would their music be like?*" (27–28).

Remembering this black Southern Christianity of her childhood takes Meridian still further backward in time, as her father's singing makes her connect the church music with the pre-Christian beliefs of American Indians. The fruitful interaction of the music, her imagination, and her family thus have taken her to a past that had been distorted by centuries of cultural rape. From the pre-Christian past, Meridian's memory starts moving forward again. It returns to a moment when she sat in church beside her mother. Because she had recognized a sense of pre-Christian spiritualism — the sense that her father did not believe in the same God as her mother did — Meridian was unable to embrace Jesus and thereby forever alienated her mother. From Meridian's childhood, the chapter continues to move methodically toward the present: from the church where Meridian is unable to meet her mother's conditions, to the apartment where she is unable to satisfy the revolutionaries', to her home (set in the novel's present) where she similarly acknowledges her unwillingness to meet Truman's needs.

The chapter works, then, so that the present is embedded with, and thus constantly informed by, various layers of "pastness."[8] It is important to recognize, therefore, that the conversation with Truman, which frames the chapter, is not dramatic in the sense that it engages in a conflict that will effect change. Because at this point in their lives the relationship between Truman and Meridian is beyond change but not beyond understanding, the opening chapter changes the reader's understanding of the relationship by unearthing a succession of historical, cultural, and artistic contexts.[9]

The book as a whole functions similarly, locating black American experience in ultimately pre-American, pre-Christian contexts through a stratified examination of its presence in postcolonial, postbellum, Christian, and white art and artifacts.[10]

This chain of maternal history, marginalized and suppressed by white patriarchal history, connects Meridian, for example, with her great-grandmother, who had had an ecstatic experience while sunning herself on the mound of the Indian Sacred Serpent burial ground. "Later [she] renounced all religion that was not based on the experience of physical ecstasy . . . and near the end of her life she loved walking nude about her yard and worshipped only the sun" (57). Meridian had a similar experience at the same site and another at the ruin of a pre-Columbian altar in Mexico. But this experience connects her with her *paternal* great-grandmother, and, like the pre-Christian spirit in which her father believed, it is associated in the book with an independence rarely found by black women because of their enslavement to men and to maternity.

Meridian grew up, therefore, with the sense that she had stolen something from her mother: "It was for stealing her mother's serenity, for shattering her mother's emerging self, that Meridian felt guilty from the very first . . ." (51). Patricia Williams insightfully links this sense of loss and theft inscribed on the contours of African American maternity as connected to antebellum property laws: emphasizing "the degree to which black history in this nation is that of fiercely interwoven patterns of family, as conceived by white men," Williams points out that even those slaves who were biologically part of the owner's family were strangers to the family circle and treated as commodities. Laws and practices further suppressed any "image of blacks as capable either of being part of the family of white men or of having family of their own" (162). This included antimiscegenation laws, the laws that rendered blacks, as chattel, incapable of entering into contracts, including marriage contracts, and the Dred Scott decision which affirmed black inferiority to the extent that negated all possibility of rights. These, coupled with laws

> restricting the ability of slaveholders to will property or freedom to blacks suspended them in eternal illegitimacy.
>
> The recognition of such a threshold is the key to understanding slavery as a structure of denial—a denial of the generative independence of black people. A substitution occurred: instead of black motherhood as the generative source for black people, master-cloaked white manhood became the generative source for black people. Although the "bad black mother" is even today a stereotypical way of describing what ails the black race, the historical reality is that of careless white fatherhood. Blacks are thus, in full culturally imagistic terms, not merely unmothered but badly fathered, abused and disowned by whites. (*Alchemy*, 162–63)

Within the story of Meridian's family, the context for Meridian's personal narrative, we could argue, are the narratives of theft and usurpation that derive from the legal performance of racial servitude as a knowable cultural verity. That "verity," of course, was not the product of truth but of history, and as such, even when it ceased to perform its function as legal truth it still functioned as cultural narrative, even—unarticulated as such—within black familial relationships.

Within the boundaries of these narratives, acquisition becomes theft; continuity becomes disruption. In the same way that Meridian had stolen something from her mother, her own early pregnancy had stolen something from her: her capacity to be active in the emotional, intellectual, or physical world. She is awakened from her lethargy by the bombing of a civil rights worker's house in her neighborhood: "And so it was that one day in the middle of April in 1960 Meridian Hill became aware of the past and present of the larger world" (73).

To become part of that world, to become an activist, however, she has to relinquish her role as mother. When she gives up, moreover, not only her child but the history of her life so that she can enter college, she thinks of her decision in terms of maternal history: "[Meridian] thought of her mother as being worthy of this maternal history, and she herself as belonging to an unworthy minority, for which there was no precedent and of which she was, as far as she knew, the only member" (91).[11]

The motion from private to public, from personal to political, from artificial to historical, in other words, entails the breaking down of barriers as well as the reconstituting of the existing fragments in a new context. To put it another way, the book presents the enterprise of discovering a synchronic reading that will restructure the contexts through which the artifacts of black American culture are read. Barthes has emphasized this principle of semiological research: "in principle, the corpus must eliminate diachronic elements to the utmost; it must coincide with a state of the system, a cross-section of history. . . . [F]rom an operative point of view, the corpus must keep as close as possible to the synchronic sets. A varied but temporally limited corpus will therefore be preferable to a narrow corpus stretched over a length of time . . ." (98).

MERIDIAN'S BODY

The unique quality of *Meridian,* and its uniquely feminist quality, is that these conflicts—the simultaneous breaking down and reconstructing—take place in the body of Meridian. The "corpus," in other words, that Barthes desires in principle—the "varied but temporally limited corpus"—is Meridian's corporal self. In this way, Walker engages in what has become popularized by French feminist theorists as *écriture féminine,* writing located in and authorized by fundamental female experience: "writing the body."[12] Ann Rosalind Jones's description of this principle, when applied specifically to *Meridian,* provides a very apt gloss on the novel's structure: "to the extent that the female body is seen as a direct source of female writing, a powerful alternative discourse seems possible: to write from the body is to recreate the world" (252).

In regard to this principle, Elizabeth Meese has noted that the "body is the site where the political and the aesthetic interpret the material" (117). This is certainly true of Meridian. The first chapter of the novel makes clear the connection between Meridian's body and the body politic when, after leading a successful protest (by staring down an armed tank), Meridian's body suffers a seizure of paralysis that necessitates her being carried home by four men, "exactly as they would carry a coffin, her eyes closed, barely breathing, arms folded across her chest, legs straight" (24). The protest had been staged to enable some black children to see an ostensibly mummified white woman housed in a circus wagon. Because, as Deborah McDowell has noted, Meridian's paralyzed condition mirrors that of the freakish white woman made inaccessible to the eyes of black children by armed force, the book forces a comparison between Meridian and the mummy, one that suggests an alternative to the untenable roles of womanhood produced by white and male culture and replicated in the mummy woman's alleged history.[13]

Truman, misunderstanding the relationship of Meridian's body to the events, thinks her seizure followed from the protest and asks, "Did they hurt you out there?" (24). As Meridian makes clear, however, social conditions, not social protest, have caused her illness; the protest is part of the cure:

> "They didn't touch me," she said.
>
> "You're just sick then?"
>
> "Of course I'm sick," snapped Meridian. "Why else would I spend all this time trying to get well!" (24–25)

The idea of "trying to get well," of "self-recovery," as bell hooks calls it, constitutes a recognition of the ways in which the double remove from the narratives of the dominant discourse has suppressed the personal narratives of black women. Recovery in the sense of getting well is thus a process of recovering the narratives that allow the idea of an unfragmented self. Describing her first book, *Ain't I a Woman?* as such an act of recovery, hooks explains that "writing this book, I was compelled to confront black women's reality, our denied and buried history, our present circumstances. The thinking, the writing, was an act of reclamation, enabling me to recover myself, to be whole" (*Talking Back,* 30). But by specifically making this recovery a form of corporal articulation, Walker is recognizing a condition that Michele Wallace calls typical of black womanhood: "black women grow up living the reality in their bodies of how sexism and racism intersect, coincide and collaborate, but the representation of that correspondence has barely been written by them except in literature and poetry in which it is heavily coded" (162).

In her encounter with the Wild Child, before Meridian can take any action, her body similarly responds to the initial circumstances. Approximately thirteen years old, "Wile Chile" had grown up without home or parents, haunting the outermost margins of poverty-level civilization. Because she signified not only the inadequacy of social agencies and the breakdown of the family but also the failure of all social codes including language itself, when she is seen pregnant, the neighbors in the slum surrounding Saxon College "could not imagine what to do. Wile Chile rummaged about as before, eating rancid food, dressing herself in castoffs, cursing and bolting, and smoking her brown cigarettes" (36). Upon first seeing Wile Chile, Meridian enters into a corpselike coma on the floor of her bedroom (in Saxon College's honors house). Only after passing through this act of embodying literally all the social paralysis that Wile Chile's presence signifies can Meridian emerge with a method to lure the child into the shelter of the honors house.

Meridian's body also provides the site for sexual conflicts that reflect not only the conflict between the personal and the political but also the conflicts between male and female roles, the mind and the body, the sacred and the profane. In her relationship with her teenage husband, Eddie, for example, "she—her body, that is—never had any intention of *giving in.* She was suspicious of pleasure. . . . Besides, Eddie did not seriously expect more than 'interest' from her. She perceived there might be something more; but for him it was enough that his pleasure should please her. Understanding this, they never discussed anything beyond her attitude" (67–68). Meridian's sexual relationship with Truman necessitates a similar recognition of the antagonism, for Meridian, between mind and body: "She decided to click her mind off, and her body seemed to move into his of its own accord" (113).

Like her relationship with her men, Meridian's political consciousness is described in terms of a mind/body dichotomy, and only after freeing herself from her body does she first come to realize that the demands of the political world require she relinquish her maternal role: "she attempted to meditate on her condition, unconscious at first, of what she did. At first it was like falling back into a time that never was, a time of complete rest, like a faint. Her senses were stopped while her body rested: only in her head did she feel something, and it was a sensation of lightness—a lightness like the inside of a drum. The air inside her head was pure of thought, at first" (74).

As her meditation develops, she focuses on the bodies of young and teenage girls, as they grow from shame to "the beginning of pride in their bodies" (75). Meditating free of her body, with a greater political consciousness, however, Meridian thinks, "for all their bodies' assertion, the girls moved protected in a dream. A dream that had little to do with the real boys galloping past them. For they did not perceive them clearly but as they might become in a different world from one they lived in" (75).

Confronting that "world they lived in" has a profoundly different effect on the body of Meridian, a form of "battle fatigue" that manifests an array of symptoms, from initial uncontrollable crying to the "shaking of her hands, or the twitch in her left eye" (85), and later to the loss of her hair and the paralytic fits. When Meridian admits publicly at Saxon that she is not sure there is a God, the near ostracism she suffers shows its effects on her body. "She began to have headaches that were so severe they cause her to stutter when she spoke" (94).

Finally, her body reflects the conflict between her role as a mother and as a self-fulfilling woman: motherhood, in Meridian's world, reflects the abnegation of personal freedom for the roles defined by men, race, and class, and for the responsibilities mandated by poverty and by children. Or, as it is summarized by Meridian's mother: "The answer to everything . . . is that we live in America and we're not rich" (56). The fertile body, capable of turning a woman into a mother—and of allowing her child to "steal" her life—thus becomes Meridian's obstacle as it impels her out of womanhood and into motherhood: "[Meridian was] disgusted with the fecundity of her body that got pregnant on less screwing than anybody's she had ever heard of. It seemed doubly unfair that after all her sexual 'experience' and after one baby and one abortion she had not once been completely fulfilled by sex" (115). If her fertile body at one extreme is at odds with sexual pleasure, at the other it wars with her spiritual satisfaction. For Meridian perceives it as the obstacle to her mother's acceptance, that is, to the religious traditions and the chain of women's history her mother represents: "Meridian felt as if her body, growing frailer every day under the stress of her daily life, stood in the way between a reconciliation between her mother and that part of her own soul her mother could, perhaps, love" (97). Meridian's body, in other words, must bear the burden for having stolen her mother's life and for having failed to accept the role of her mother, having failed to replicate motherhood.[14]

In these ways, Meridian's body becomes the territory that measures and tests the distinctions between theft and ownership, not only of property but of life, hope, and ambition. In all of these tests, it functions both as subject and as object and thus presents itself as a medium for connecting the contexts rent by relegation to the realm of "oppressor" or "oppressed." This is why Meridian's development as a civil rights worker reflects an inverse relationship between possession and power. The more she is able to shed not only of her personal property but also of her person itself—the flesh of her body, the aborted fetus of her womb—the more power she has to control and heal those around her, most importantly because she turns these renunciations into lessons in reading.[15] For black Americans to read and hence rediscover their cultural ancestry, her story suggests, they must remove the anglicized surface, the framing context of white, Western distortion, in much the way an anthropologist or archaeologist would, discovering from the artifacts the art of a lost culture.[16]

ART, ARTIFACT, AND ACTIVISM

Yet the novel also seems suspicious of its own endeavor, insofar as art has been—in the form of storytelling, for example, or jazz—one of the traditional ways that blacks sublimated frustration and thus facilitated, however unintentionally, their own oppression. One of the central conflicts in the novel, therefore, is between art and politics. Although both are subversive acts, the question is: What is being subverted and how? Because art turns experience into artifact, in some ways it militates against change. For this reason, the novel does not endorse as revolutionary Truman's work as an artist. Furthermore, if we cannot trust art because it serves as a form of sublimation that ultimately removes the artifact from its context, and perhaps the artifacts, especially of an oppressed or destroyed culture, should always be distrusted. They exist, after all, in a context created by the same dominant power that tried to destroy the culture.

The novel presents us with the problem, however, that the active—the revolutionary—is equally untrustworthy exactly *because* it is not stable or predictable. It also is subject to the influence of vested interests, and those interests, likewise, are subject to change. When the students protest, for example, because Saxon College will not permit them to hold the Wile Chile's funeral in the chapel, the event moves back in stages that first permit the anglicized black students of Saxon to connect with their slave and pre-Christian heritage and then lead them to destroy the very roots of that connection. At first they want to use the Christian chapel. Denied access, they stage a replica Christian funeral on the chapel steps, for which the people from the local community wear their "Sunday best outfits" (47). After the community people, intimidated by the austerity of Saxon, flee, the students cast off some of their learned decorum and solemnity: "For five minutes the air rang with shouts and polite curses" (47). Next they move to the more primal responses of booing, stamping their feet, and sticking out "their tongues through their tears," after which they begin to shed their Western garb: "they began to take off their jewelry and fling it to the ground—the heavy three-strand cultured pearl necklaces, and the massive, circular gold-plated chastity pins. . . . They shook loose their straightened hair," all the while glaring at the locked chapel with "ferocity" (47).

As their attire becomes less anglicized and their behavior changes from polite curses to ferocity, "as if by mutual agreement" (47) they shift the site of the funeral to The Sojourner—the tree planted on the site of a slave's buried tongue. With its roots both figuratively and literally connected to antebellum black, African, and pre-Christian spiritual lore, the tree is believed to possess talismanic qualities. Yet after Wile Chile is buried, the students "rioted on Saxon campus for the first time in its long, placid, impeccable history, and the only thing they managed to destroy was The Sojourner" (48). Once again, the novel shows the activist in conflict with the artifact in ways that destroy the latter and render the former suspect.

One reason that activists in *Meridian* are particularly suspect is that they operate within narratives that omit too much. When Anne-Marion assists in chopping down The Sojourner because she associates it with the college that surrounds it, she ignores the fact that the tree predates its current context, that it sheltered blacks long before Saxon College recontextualized it. Similarly, Anne-Marion employs a Marxist version of history to discredit the church. The church she discredits, however, is not one that conforms to traits upon which Marx based his assault. She ends up, therefore, as with The Sojourner, severing her ties to the native traditions that, although disguised with the trappings of white authority, connect her with her own identity.[17]

Anne-Marion's writing is also suspect, and, as with Truman's art, Meridian cannot endorse it as revolutionary. After Anne-Marion breaks with Meridian, she continues compulsively to write Meridian letters: "no one could have been more surprised and confounded than she, who sat down to write each letter as if some heavy object had been attached to her knees, forcing them under her desk, as she wrote with the most galling ferocity, out of guilt and denial and rage" (125). At the same time that Meridian cannot embrace the contents of the letters, she cannot dismiss the anger that produced them or, more important, the history that anger signifies. Therefore, she neither reads the letters nor discards them; instead, she decorates her walls with them.

In many different ways, Meridian's treatment of the letters is an act of recontextualization. First, as she explains to Truman in the first chapter, she looks at them for their appearance, not their content: "I keep the letters because they contain the bitch's handwriting" (32). Because they also contain, in a sense, an action—the hand *writing*—Meridian's perspective demonstrates the way that performance becomes artifact; by putting the letters on the wall, she also demonstrates how artifact becomes decorative art. The act of using the limited materials at her disposal to decorate her sparse surroundings, furthermore, replicates an activity Walker ascribes to her anonymous ancestors, the oppressed black women "who literally covered the holes of our walls with sunflowers" ("In Search," 242). In this way, Meridian makes the letters allusions to the heritage Anne-Marion and she share and, by virtue of Meridian's act, one in which they continue to participate. The letters thereby serve to connect not only Meridian but also Anne-Marion with their pre-Christian ancestry, a connection Walker makes explicit in her essay, "In Search of Our Mother's Gardens":

> Guided by my heritage of a love of beauty and a respect for strength—in search of my mother's garden I found my own. . . .
>
> And perhaps in Africa over two hundred years ago, was just such a mother; perhaps she painted vivid and daring decorations in oranges and yellows and greens on the walls of her hut; perhaps she sang—in a voice like Robert Flack's—*sweetly* over the compounds of her village; perhaps she wove the most stunning mats or told the most ingenious stories of all the village storytellers. Perhaps she was herself a poet—though only her daughter's name is signed to the poems that we know. (243)

By converting performance into artifact into art, Meridian moreover makes the process of this conversion clear so that the decoration cannot be divorced from the action, the anger, and the history that produced it. Anne-Marion's letters decorating Meridian's walls not only allude to their mothers' gardens but also signify the anger and oppression that produced those anonymous gardens. As such, they perform the archaeological re-contextualizing, so prevalent in the novel, both by reconstructing a lost tradition out of the present and by subsuming the present in that tradition.

Finally, because they signify a problem not resolved, an anger not dispersed, Anne-Marion's letters point toward the future as well as the past. For Meridian, they become quite literally the handwriting on the wall, the reminder that there are people who believe they would kill for the revolution. And we must remember that it is Meridian who takes these personal diatribes and converts them into the handwriting on the wall in the same act that connects her with the anonymous artistry of her ancestors. It is Meridian, in other words, who gives these letters their significance. As their addressee, recipient, reader, interpreter, and, ultimately, artist, she becomes the cipher that connects artifact to heritage, personal to historical.[18]

In the same way, her body serves the ciphering function throughout the novel. By making it the receptacle of this unearthing as well as reader of the unearthed, Meridian assumes an androgynous role that makes her an object lesson in both the reading and the authorship of self—the living connection between art and artifact. In this role, she tries to create a context that will revive the rituals of her lost tradition, that will connect the artifactual with the active. The novel is full of stories that have the quality of folk or fairy tales; they possess talismanic qualities also, and they echo the supernatural and/or religious and/or magical. Into which of these categories they fit is a question of reading and an issue of hermeneutics. A folk tale can have roughly the same rhetorical structure as a parable, yet one is given sacred importance, which it can only have based on a preconception about its meaning and context.[19] This is a lesson in hermeneutics and in history. We need a cipher through which to read the lessons (or the absence of lesson) in a fable, a parable, a folk tale, a religious ceremony, or a history book. The cipher that the novel *Meridian* presents is the body of Meridian—the body of her sensations, experience, and language.

LESSONS IN READING AND THE POSTMODERN

But if Meridian is a lesson in reading, she is not a simple one, or one that will lend one sanctioned reading to a text. Rather she is a lesson in alternatives, attitudes, and perspectives, made perhaps most evident by the divisions in the novel and the difference in narrative technique in the respective parts. Whereas the first section of the novel, which identifies Meridian and is named for her, moves backward and forward through a series of juxtaposed findings, unearthed bits of gold (or fool's gold, as one chapter suggests), the section named for Truman Held adheres more strongly to linear narrative. Because even in its temporal interpolations the section never incorporates the parablelike or folkloric details found in the "Meridian" section, Walker forces us to read not only one history against another but also one kind of writing—one way of attributing significance—against its alternatives. The short third section of the book, "Endings," more sharply contrasts Truman's mode of reading with Meridian's. In the book's penultimate chapter, Meridian tells Truman about a poor black woman who left her husband because he was in love with his dog and treated it better than his family. The story, rendered in almost fairy tale fashion reminiscent of portions of the "Meridian" section, ends with the woman's returning to her husband because "alone she could not feed her children. Of course she made her husband promise to kill the dog" (218). Truman, interested in linear narrative, in what happens next, in what the man does (in history), asks if he did kill the dog. Meridian, reflecting a different mode of reading, a concern not with the last act but with the context in which it takes place, the organization of power it reflects, shrugs: "'I suspect that is not the point,' she said" (218).

Through Meridian, Walker tests the ways one gives meaning to activities and to objects, to self and to others. Meridian is a lesson in the power of language, the power to retain as well as to distort, to affect as well as to deny. All of these lessons, moreover, are implicit on the definition page at the outset of the book that presents the myriad ways one can read the word *meridian*:

> mer.rid i.an, *n*. [L. *meridianus,* pertaining to midday or to the south, from *meridies,* midday, the south; *medius,* middle, and *dies,* day.]
> 1. the highest apparent point reached by a heavenly body in its course.
> 2. (a) the highest point of power, prosperity, splendor, etc.; zenith; apex; culmination; (b) the middle period of one's life, regarded as the highest of health, vigor, etc.; prime.
> 3. noon [*Obs.*]

4. in astronomy, an imaginary great circle of the celestial sphere passing through the poles of the heavens and the zenith and nadir of any given point, and cutting the equator at right angles.

5. in geography, (a) a great circle of the earth passing through the geographical poles and any given point on the earth's surface; (b) the half of such a circle between the poles; (c) any lines of longitude running north and south on the globe or map, representing such a circle or half-circle.

6. (a) a place or situation with its own distinctive character; (b) distinctive character.

7. a graduated ring of brass, in which a globe is suspended and revolves.

first meridian: see *prime meridian* under *prime.*

magnetic meridian: a carefully located meridian from which any secondary or guide meridians may be constructed.

mer.rid i.an, *a.*

1. of or at noon or, especially, of the position or power of the sun at noon.

2. passing through the highest point in the daily course of any heavenly body.

3. of or along a meridian.

4. of or at the highest point of prosperity, splendor, power, etc.

5. southern. [Rare.] (13)

The list of definitions is a virtual compendium of the motifs in the novel. It identifies Meridian as a source of power and as a reference point, as an ideal and as something in midcourse ("a woman in the process of changing her mind" [25]). It suggests the spiritual power of the sun that Meridian shared with her great grandmother, and the secular power of a civil rights mediator. It also unites two poles of attraction in the novel, the character of Meridian and the South.

If, in applying noun definition 6, the "distinctive character" is Meridian and "the place or situation with its own distinctive character" is the South, the site where those two aspects of the definition meet is Meridian, Mississippi, a site crucial to understanding the intersection of personal and historical narratives that give this novel its distinctive character. Completely demolished by General Sherman in 1863 as a dry run for his march to the sea, Meridian, Mississippi, less than a decade later was the site of bloody race riots resulting from Klan activities. "Reports of the Meridian riot," explain Seth Cagin and Philip Dray, "angered Congress, prompting it to pass additional legislation aimed at containing the Klan and protecting black freedmen. But local opposition to Republican Reconstruction continued, the Meridian insurrection a rallying point, and in the mid-1870s, the mood in the North began to shift to one of sympathy for the southern white" (201). With the increasing support of Klan activity, power in the state shortly returned to the white Democratic Party, and by the time of the 1954 Supreme Court desegregation decision, Mississippi had long solidified its white police state so well detailed in James Silver's 1963 book, *Mississippi: The Closed Society.*

In 1964, Meridian was the site of the community center operated for the Congress of Racial Equality (CORE) by Mickey and Rita Schwerner. That summer they were assisting the Mississippi Summer Project, a concentrated effort by Northern and Southern civil rights organizations "to bring up to a thousand northern college students, mostly white, into Mississippi to teach disenfranchised blacks at 'freedom schools' about their constitutional rights and to staff a massive voter registration drive" (Cagin and Dray, 29). On June 21 they were joined by a new volunteer, Andrew Goodman, a New York college student. Mickey Schwerner, Goodman, and a black member of the community center staff, James Chaney, all disappeared the next day. Their disappearance attracted national attention and drew a hoard of federal investigators to the state who, in August, discovered their murdered bodies in nearby Philadelphia, Mississippi. The subsequent investigation and 1967 trial in Meridian resulted in "the first successful jury conviction of white officials and Klansmen in the history of Mississippi for crimes against black people or civil rights workers" (Cagin and Dray, 451).

In the novel, these events centering on the Meridian Klansmen and civil rights workers drew Truman and Lynne back to the South: "Truman had had enough of the movement and of the South. But not Lynne. Mississippi— after the disappearance of the three Civil Rights workers in 1964—began to beckon her. For two years she thought of nothing else: If Mississippi is the worst place in America for black people, it stood to reason, she thought, that the Art that was their lives would flourish best there. . . . And so a little over two years after the bodies—battered beyond recognition, except for the colors: two white, one black—of Chaney, Goodman and Schwerner were found hidden in a backwoods Neshoba County, Mississippi, dam, Lynne and Truman arrived" (130). When the (fictional) bombing in April of 1960 becomes visible in the field of Meridian Hill's life, its status as an *event* in her life makes possible her eventual entrance into the history of the civil rights movement. Similarly, the events surrounding Meridian (Mississippi) become a narrative of historical significance within Lynne's construction of her autobiography. The mixture in Lynne's consciousness of a historical event and an autobiographical mandate, moreover, takes place under the rubric of "art." In this way, it becomes another version of Anne-Marion's handwriting on the wall, just as Meridian (Mississippi) represented the handwriting on the wall for the civil rights struggle and, ultimately, for those who violently opposed it.

The context for the art, as Meridian makes clear, cannot be ignored. As Patricia Williams explains in delineating her relation to the Critical Legal Studies movement, "while the goals of CLS and of the direct victims of racism may be much the same, what is so often missing is acknowledgment that our experiences of the same circumstances may be very different; the same symbol may mean different things to each of us" (*Alchemy* 149). In an explanation that can cogently gloss the relationship of *Meridian,* and much African American literature, to postmodernism, Williams states: "For blacks, then, the battle is not deconstructing rights, in a world of no rights; nor of constructing statements of need, in a world of abundantly apparent need. Rather the goal is to find a political mechanism that can confront the *denial* of need. The argument that rights are disutile, even harmful, trivializes this aspect of black experience specifically, as well as that of any person or group whose vulnerability has been truly protected by rights" (*Alchemy* 152). The idea of the "centered subject" around the transparency of which the subject, as Bruner describes it, "accrues" a "Self," has never been transparent for African Americans when contextualized in the issue of rights. "Another way of describing the dissonance between blacks and CLS," according to Williams, "is in terms of the degree of moral utopianism with which blacks regard rights. For blacks, the prospect of attaining full rights under the law has been a fiercely motivational, almost religious source of hope ever since arrival on these shores" (154). Under specific historical conditions, in other words, the idea of the centered subject, of the Self, is not a form of nostalgia. "Where one's experience is rooted not just in a sense of illegitimacy," Williams explains, "but in *being* illegitimate, in being raped, and in the fear of being murdered, then the black adherence to a scheme of both positive and negative rights—to the self, to the sanctity of one's own personal boundaries—makes sense" (154).

In some ways, making sense of the sanctity of one's own personal boundaries always means returning to the meridians—the longitudinal axes that modify the earth's daily rotation with temporal signs, or the place names that memorialize sacrifice and change. Thus *Meridian*—the city, the novel, the character, the word—is defined not only with an array of meanings but in two basic contexts: as a noun, that is, as something defined in and of itself, and as an adjective, that is, as something that modifies another subject. The merging of the modifier and the noun in Meridian's name thus signifies the reconstituting of a self both personal and political. It is the matrix where cultural and national history meet, and it is the name for that body in which the magic of maternity is one with the patriarchal authority of communal faith.

CODA

Democracy

10. FAILED CULTURAL NARRATIVES

America in the Postwar Era and the

Story of *Democracy*

A discussion of Joan Didion's *Democracy* (1984) provides a useful coda for this book for several reasons. The first is that its time frame surveys the period that I have been analyzing throughout, drawing, as it does so, on the motifs of the national narrative that have loomed so large in my argument. The survey recognizes, moreover, in ways that will become apparent, the role of these motifs as performatives, or perhaps more precisely as *failed* performatives. In *Democracy*'s metafictional merging of historical documents and fictional characters, a "real" Joan Didion and a "fictional" one, a self-conscious narrator and a historical reporter, the written novel and its unwritten Other, moreover, the novel assaults the power of fictional containment. The novel's constant undermining of the historical narrative by the personal and the personal by the historical, in other words, makes it impossible to keep the story of "democracy" straight.

Didion begins *Democracy* by describing the novel she had started to write but that no longer seems tenable. As she develops her notes out of the "jettisoned cargo" (a recurrent image in the book) of her unfinished narrative, we learn that the story she intended to write focused on the family and affairs of an Inez Christian, who grew up on Hawaii just after World War II, where her family, "in which the colonial impulse had marked every member" (26), had become prosperous, involved primarily in real estate and construction. In 1955, Inez married Harry Victor, a sort of Kennedy Democrat, who became a U.S. senator and then a failed presidential hopeful toward the end of the Vietnam era. This marriage uniting the Christians and the Victors, with their interests in the Pacific perimeter, has allegorical potential, underscored by the fact that, prior to her marriage, Inez had an affair with Jack Lovett, a CIA operative also specializing in Pacific operations, and during the course of her marriage kept in distant contact with him. The crucial event anchoring these fictions is the murder of Inez's sister, Janet Ziegler, and her sister's apparent lover, Wendell Omura (a Hawaiian congressman), by Inez's father, Paul Christian. Although Paul Christian's motive is never made clear, it may have something to do with his siding with Janet's husband, Dick Ziegler, "who made a modest fortune in Hong Kong housing and lost it in the development of windward Oahu" (25), against Paul's brother, Dwight Christian, who had "construction contracts in Long Binh and Cam Ranh Bay," and who "used Wendell Omura to squeeze Dick Ziegler out of windward Oahu and coincidentally out of the container business" (26). This family catastrophe coincides with the collapse of the American-backed government in Vietnam and is followed, shortly thereafter, by the death of Jack Lovett and Inez's estrangement from her husband.

Didion makes clear the symbolic potential of her unwritten—or at least unorganized—narrative in passages like the following: "in that prosperous and self-absorbed colony the Christians were sufficiently good-looking and sufficiently confident and, at least at the time Inez was growing up, sufficiently innocent . . ." (27); or "The Christians, like many island families, had surrounded themselves with the mementos of their accomplishments, with water colors and painted tea cups and evidence of languages mastered and instruments played, framed recital programs and letters of commendation and souvenirs of wedding trips and horse shows and trips to China . . ." (53–54). In the symbolic subtext, Inez Victor represents Americans facing the dissolution of their patriarchal, hegemonic conception of themselves. Their protocol, manners, status, and Christian morality have been reduced to a series of photo opportunities, euphemisms, and captions—a collage of images that mask a history of infidelity. Their father figure is, it has become clear, insane—obsessed with taking sides and settling issues through homicidal violence. Faced with this hypocrisy, the American (Inez) remains a Victor in name only—as she and her father had been Christians in name only—refusing any of the other associations connected with her husband or nation.

But this allegorical reading explains the novel Didion was unable to write; it glosses not the narrative that *Democracy* contains but the one that it was supposed to contain. In this way, Didion's book is not about the allegories we use to define our position in the world but about the erosion of our ability to believe in our personal and national allegories.

Throughout the post–World War II era, *democracy* has been the name we have given to a narrative of American global politics. Performed as it was on the pages of *Time* and *Newsweek* and on national television networks, the narrative called *democracy* placed Americans in the roles of reader and viewer of a series of adventures in which the heroes and villains were clear, the desirable outcomes known, and the undesirable outcomes contextualized as episodes in a larger narrative that promised a happy ending, one to be effected, I have argued extensively, through the vigilant performance of containment.

In the context of Didion's novel, the containment policy developed, almost exactly during the span of Jack Lovett's professional career, into a narrative of expansion, of "spreading democracy." The policy of containment thus suggested that the narrative democracy contained would also "contain" the spread of communism. Although containment was the name of the policy that was supposed to effect that narrative, the narrative's expansive quality could no longer contain all of its disparate elements without becoming democracy in name only.

Like the novel *Democracy*, the term *democracy* has thus become the name of the narrative it does not contain or, as Didion's narrative strategies suggest, the narrative it intended to contain but never did, overburdened by "facts" that cannot be legitimized within the governing fiction and fictions that cannot be legitimized by the facts. In this sense, the novel is profoundly elegiac, marking as it does not the story of *democracy* but its loss—lost either in its inability to be contained by Kennan's fictions or reconstructed by Didion's history—lost, in other words, in its own narrativity.

The "author," albeit with ambivalence, is also elegized, in that Didion's narrative reveals a rejection not only of authorial authority but also of its political implications. If narrative, de Certeau has suggested, is always an attempt to colonize the Other,[1] then constructing the narrative of *Democracy* will unavoidably implicate its author in the colonialist activity it attempts to expose. For a narrative's authority always relies on a referent outside the narrative, the part that always remains different from the narrative itself, the part that is not the same as the language that refers to it. That difference, de Certeau has shown, legitimizes a narrative, as I noted at length in chapter 2, because without that difference it would only claim to be referring to itself. At the same time, however, that difference means a narrative never captures its referent, it only devises conventions and strategies to disguise its inadequate authority. These conventions and strategies define the hegemonic activity, an activity, as Wlad Godzich points out, whose paradigm can be found in the chivalric quest romance, the goal of which is to reduce the Other "to (more of) the same" (xiii). Didion's *Democracy* not only exposes the personal and national cost of propagating America's colonialist narrative but also investigates both the author's and the reader's complicity in the narrative by attacking the conventional boundaries between reader and text, fact and fiction.

The complex relationship between fact and fiction is suggested by the book's first sentence, a disembodied assertion that may or may not be factual. The sentence contains an image of America's ascent to atomic power: "The light at dawn during those Pacific tests was something to see" (11). Actually, it contains Jack Lovett's assessment of those tests, or even more accurately Joan Didion's account of a conversation with her protagonist, Inez Victor. In the conversation, Inez recounted her conversation with Jack in which he described the tests. The tests take place in 1952 and 1953; the conversation between Jack and Inez takes place in the spring of 1975; the conversation between Didion and Inez six months later. The sentence, furthermore, is presented without quotation marks. We don't know, therefore, who the speaker and/or the audience is, and we don't know the context, or in this case contexts. Learning the contexts, moreover, makes the speaker and audience of this unquoted assertion even more ambiguous. We simply have an ostensive statement of fact: The light at dawn during those Pacific tests was something to see. But what is the claim being made? Is it a claim about the light, given to us on the authority of Jack Lovett, or a claim about Jack's response to the light, given to us on the authority of Inez Victor, or a claim about Inez's conversation, given to us on the authority of Joan Didion, a character who narrates the story of *Democracy?* This Joan Didion is a professional novelist who had made several notes, invented several settings, and made several plans for telling the story named *Democracy*. She is also a professional journalist, one who had taken several notes, conducted several interviews, clipped several magazine articles, and saved several photos, also in the interest of telling the story of *Democracy*. Yet, as we discover, all her research and invention, all her method and technique, have made it harder to tell the story, not easier.

The status of the first sentence thus typifies the problem presented by the book and repeatedly foregrounded by its narrator: that the methods for writing "truthfully," in fiction, journalism, or history, are not techniques for establishing adequate authority but rather techniques for masking the absence of that authority.

As it will later, with the "interview," for example, firsthand knowledge in the book's opening pages proves itself to be inadequate. But if our knowledge of the event—the shot—cannot be acquired from the senses, what does it take to behold Jack Lovett's vision? This question is the quintessential question of authorial authority. By what means do we acquire the reality of a story? Was the light at dawn something to behold? Is Didion presenting this as a fact established on the authority of Jack Lovett's observation, or is she presenting it merely as the fact that it was Jack Lovett's observation?

And, moreover, who is Jack Lovett? To know that would be to know more than the novel will allow—it would be to know, among other things, and most important, what values inform his observation. As Didion implies, authors have the power to tell us these things, that is, to define characters, which is exactly the power that differentiates novelists from journalists. In foregrounding herself in the roles of both journalist and novelist, however, Didion also foregrounds the conflict between the two roles: whereas the journalist depends on received information, the novelist depends on invented information. At the same time, however, Didion knows that invented information depends as greatly on powers of observation as received information does on the ability to invent connections between bits of information. The problem of this symbiosis becomes further complicated because information never arrives in a pure form, but rather it comes framed by a series of inventions and imaginings. Other people's accounts, deceptions, and self-deceptions, their censorship and self-censorship, their selective observations and more selective memories render reportage as much the filter of fictions as fiction is the invention of reportage; the journalist is always already one more fictional frame. But the professional journalist creates a particularly problematic frame, Didion suggests, because she is a person who has trained herself to appropriate experience in the interest of writing about it. Her attempts, in this light, to gather and organize her material become foregrounded as *Democracy*'s plot. The story of the novel's authorship, in other words, becomes one more fiction, in many ways indistinguishable from the fictions it frames.

The second chapter of *Democracy* thus introduces that crisis in authorial authority, beginning with the one-sentence paragraph: "Call me the author" (16). This play on Melville points to the dissolution of authorial authority. When Melville says "*Call* me Ishmael," he acknowledges that his authority to name is stipulative, not essential, by calling attention to its arbitrary nature. Didion, on the other hand, by retaining the authority but dispensing with the name, reveals that the names in all narratives have only one source and that the author in pretending to be someone else is employing a technique to disguise the source, even if that source is to be accepted solely on a stipulative basis. Whereas both Melville's and Didion's versions foreground the arbitrary nature of authorial authority, Melville's version does so by exercising the authority in a stipulative fashion and Didion's by replacing the authority with a tautology that reduces that authority to pure stipulation. By alluding to Melville's biblical allusion, "Ishmael," moreover, Didion's version of authority becomes a version of another author's version of authority, and thus it does not so much claim authority as it does refer to an infinite regress in versions of that claim.

This regress of versions is further underscored by Didion's rejection of her already qualified claim. The opening sentence becomes one she cannot employ. Nor can she assert her authorial presence in the third person—"*Let the reader be introduced to Joan Didion, upon whose character and doings much will depend on whatever interest these pages may have, as she sits at her writing table, in her own room in her own house on Welbeck Street*" (16)—as she tells us "Trollope might begin this novel" (16). She lacks the authority to start the novel in either the first or third person. "I have no unequivocal way of beginning it," she states, "although I do have certain things in mind" (16). But even this assertion is qualified by the fact that "Call me the author" unequivocally begins the second chapter, just as "The light at dawn during those Pacific tests was something to see" unequivocally begins the first, no matter how many recontextualizations follow either sentence. Neither sentence equivocates; what Didion equivocates is her willingness to give a statement representative status.

Didion acknowledges this problem in an observation that merges her roles as journalist and novelist: "My point is this: I can remember a moment in which Harry Victor seemed to present himself precisely as he was and I can remember a moment when Dwight Christian seemed to present himself precisely as he was and I can remember such moments about most people I have known, so ingrained by now is the impulse to define the personality, show the character, but I have no memory of any one moment in which either Inez Victor or Jack Lovett seemed to spring out, defined" (81). The "events" Didion as journalist discusses in this passage are not amalgamations of sensory data but moments when her imagination converted data into a presentation. Clearly, the people were not presenting themselves *to* Didion nor did they necessarily know that their behavior comprised a presentation. The moments when people *seemed* to present themselves, in other words, were the moments when Didion defined them by virtue of imagining a semblance between specific acts and definitive qualities. This semblance, of course, exists not in nature, but rather under the rubric of an author, who of necessity must pretend that acts define characters and, as well, that these acts emanate from the actors rather than the author (just as a reporter must pretend that the interviewee is the source of the information). Didion implies that she knows this is the author's pretense, moreover, when she tells us that these moments are the function not of the way people behave but rather of her ingrained impulse—the impulse of a fiction writer, without which a journalist would be dysfunctional, because without that impulse, a journalist could not render a coherent version of events. Without the context of a coherent version, events cannot acquire meaning, and if events do not acquire meaning, then journalists cannot acquire events. Nor can readers or novelists or any other form of colonizer.

And yet Didion focuses exactly on the failure of that impulse, in regard to her novel's central characters. Inez and Jack are hard to read and hence hard to write about, in other words, hard to acquire, incorporate in a narrative, contain. Their actions, rather than representing Didion's acquisition of characters, represent the failure of Didion's impulse, her loss of authority, her inability to turn events into narrative.

To put the question of authority another way, we could ask of the character Joan Didion what she asks of her characters: At what moment does Didion seem to present herself precisely as she is? How does the author "define" herself? Like Inez and Jack, she seems to evade definition by virtue of existing beyond the limits of her own capacity for observation and definition.

We can posit that the moment when an author speaks to us is the moment when, *by definition,* she appears precisely as she is. Regardless of what we call her, regardless of what she calls herself, regardless of whether we refer to her (or she refers to herself) in the first or the third person, the text always already defines her as "author." But the author of *Democracy,* as we have noted, uses the text both to foreground and to reject those definitions. She goes on to reject the details, characters, and plans for the novel she was planning to write, and finally the possibility of narrative itself, in an unsettling tally sheet of possession and lack:

> I began thinking about Inez Victor and Jack Lovett at a point in my life when I *lacked* certainty, *lacked* even that minimum level of ego which all writers recognize as essential to the writing of novels, *lacked* conviction, *lacked* patience with the past and interest in memory; *lacked* faith even in my own technique.
>
> Cards on the table.
>
> I *have:* "colors, moisture, heat, enough blue in the air," Inez Victor's full explanation of why she stayed on in Kuala Lampur. Consider that too. I *have* those pink dawns of which Jack Lovett spoke. I *have* the dream, recurrent, in which my entire field of vision fills with rainbow, in which I open the door onto a growth of tropical green . . . and watch the spectrum separate into pure color. Consider any of these things long enough and you will see that they tend to deny the relevance not only of personality but of narrative, which makes them less than ideal images with which to begin a novel, but we go with what we *have.* (17; emphasis added)

What Didion *has* tends to deny the relevance of narrative, and what she *lacks* is the authority nonetheless to assert that relevance.

Didion is thus raising the question of what it means to be the author of *Democracy.* What does the narrative of *Democracy* contain, and what kind of authority is necessary to tell it? How is it relevant to its audience and to its author? By raising these questions, Didion destabilizes the authority not only for her own text but the authority, as well, for the text of American hegemony authored globally since World War II under the name *democracy.*

For the word *democracy,* as we have noted, names not a unified narrative but a rubric under which a compendium of fictions is performed. So does the novel *Democracy. Democracy's* fictions include the stories Didion's characters invent to cope with the political necessities of their lives, their personal deceits and self-deceits. About her husband's chronic absence from their home in Hawaii, Inez's mother, Carol Christian, for example, advised her daughters, " 'When a man stays away from a woman it means he wants to keep their love alive' " (24), and when Carol abandoned her family in

Hawaii, Janet and Inez's grandmother characterized Carol's departure as "a sudden but compelling opportunity to make the first postwar crossing on the reconditioned *Lurline*" (22). And, after twenty years of marriage to a public figure, Inez "had come to view most occasions as photo opportunities" (48). When Inez's teenage daughter, Jessie, is found using heroin, each therapist she visits produces another fiction. The first implies that the problem lies in Inez's "substance habituation" (viz., cigarettes). The second "believed that the answer lay in a closer examination of the sibling gestalt. The third employed a technique incorporating elements of aversion therapy" (61).

Democracy also includes the fictions characters invent for public or political reasons. Jack Lovett's first wife described his profession as "army officer," and his second wife described it as "aircraft executive." His visa application identified him as a "businessman" and his business cards as a "consultant in international development." Janet similarly invents incidents in her sister's childhood for a *CBS Reports* interview, and in the interest of her husband's nomination bid Inez has to develop what Harry's aid, Billy Dillon, calls a "special interest": "she insisted, unexpectedly and with some vehemence, that she wanted to work with refugees, but it was decided that refugees were an often controversial and therefore inappropriate special interest" (54). Inez's interests, in other words, do not determine her "special interest," which is special by virtue of being a fiction especially constructed in the interest of a campaign policy. It is a performance out of which a history of her life can be constructed, one aimed at giving that life's events historical status as representations of her personal narrative, but the personal narrative being represented by its special interest is a fiction.

In prepping Inez for an AP interview, Dillon thus provides her a catalogue of convenient fictions:

> The major cost of public life is privacy, Inez, that's an easy shot. The hardest part about Washington life is finding a sitter for the Gridiron Dinner. The fun part about Washington life is taking friends from home to the Senate cafeteria for navy-bean soup. You've tried the recipe at home but it never tastes the same. Yes, you do collect recipes. Yes, you do worry about the rising cost of feeding a family. Ninety-nine per cent of the people you know in Washington are basically concerned with the rising cost of feeding a family. Schools. Mortgages. Programs. You've always viewed victory as a mandate not for

a man but for his programs. Now: you view defeat with mixed emotions. Why: because you've learned to treasure private moments. (50)

Dillon prefaces these fictions, furthermore, with yet another fictional frame: that the fictitious statements do not comprise the material of an interview any more than they do the material of the life to which they ostensibly refer. Rather, they are volleys in a game of tennis.

Nor has Inez the power not to play the game by trying to make a "non-fictitious" statement—that the major cost of public life is "Memory, mainly" (48)—any more than she can by trying to expose the fictional contexts which frame the interview:

> "Here's an example. . . . You looked up the clips on me before you came here."
>
> "I did a little homework, yes." The woman's finger hovered over the stop button on her tape recorder. . . .
>
> "That's my point."
>
> "I'm afraid I don't quite—"
>
> "Things that might or might not be true get repeated in the clips until you can't tell the difference."
>
> "But that's why I'm here. I'm not writing a piece from the clips. I'm writing a piece based on what you tell me."
>
> "You might as well write from the clips," Inez said. Her voice was reasonable. "Because I've lost track. Which is what I said in the first place."

Inez, in other words, has played this figurative game of tennis about her life frequently, as evidenced by the existence of many clips. Having served up numerous fictions about herself, Inez, by the nature of the game, has rendered herself the least reliable witness to her own life and hence the person least qualified to correct or contradict the clips.

The reporter at least *acts* as though she misses that point, for her role as reporter depends on privileging "firsthand" information. If Inez can add nothing to the clips, then not just the interview but the reporter herself is perfunctory. For Inez, playing inside the lines means repeating the fictions already in the clips, as if they referred to an external truth; for the reporter, it means reporting the fictions as if they were not repetitions. Since the reporter's ultimate function, moreover, is to generate yet another clip, the validity of the clips themselves must be preserved at the same time that they must be seen as lacking, as needing some form of supplementation. The clips thus are always already present at interviews, as both the necessary authority and the necessary lack. When Inez tries to indicate the way in which they empower the game, she threatens the game itself, as evidenced by the reporter's verging on turning off the recorder and thus converting Inez's statements into silence.

The reporter's role, of course, is not to convert Inez's speech into silence but into a news clip. The story thus goes out "INEZ VICTOR CLAIMS SHE IS OFTEN MISQUOTED" (51), creating a clip that effectively reverses the implications of Inez's assertion. For the term "misquote" implies the possibility of an "accurate" quote, and more importantly implies that Inez can distinguish between the actual statement and its deformed version, in other words, between the events of her life and those news clips that distort them. Inez refuses, however, to make such a distinction because she sees news clips as comprising the historical narrative that fashions her life. Since those media representations (news clips, photos, and captions) comprise, moreover, the genre known as current events, the fictions include all the sources of contemporary history. As Didion portrays it, then, the sources of historical evidence are not events or facts but an endless chain of recontextualizations, wherein events are always performances generated by fictional frames as well as decoded by them.

This relationship is particularly well exemplified in the book's description of Harry Victor's 1969 visit to Jakarta, on which he was accompanied by his family, by Inez's sister, Janet, by Billy Dillon, and by a special aide, Frances Landau. They are met at the Jakarta airport by Jack Lovett. A personal and/or public fiction frames each character's presence, in a life so infused with official fictions that Inez cannot correlate the specific performance to the specific occasion:

> One of many occasions on which Harry Victor descended on one tropic capital or another and set about obtaining official assurance that human rights remained inviolate in the developing (USAID Recipient) nation at hand.
>
> One of several occasions during those years . . . in which Inez got off a plane and was met by Jack Lovett.
>
> Temporarily attached to the embassy.
>
> On special assignment to the military.

Performing an advisory function to the private sector. . . .

Inez did not remember exactly why Janet had been along (some domestic crisis, a ragged season with Dick Ziegler or a pique at Dwight Christian, a barrage of urgent telephone calls and a pro forma invitation), nor did she remember exactly under what pretext Frances Landau had been along (legislative assistant, official photographer, drafter of one preliminary report or another . . .) (90–91)

With the as yet unwritten news clip framing their discourse, Victor and Dillon articulate the fictions that define the visit:

"Let's get it clear at the outset, I don't want this visit tainted," Harry Victor had said.

"No embassy orchestration," Billy Dillon said.

"No debriefing," Harry Victor said.

"No reporting," Billy Dillon said.

"I want it understood," Harry Victor said, "I'm promising unconditional confidentiality."

"Harry wants it understood," Billy Dillon said, "he's not representing the embassy." (91)

The stipulation "no reporting," like all the other stipulations, of course, actually specifies how the visit is to be reported: as an unofficial, unorchestrated, unreported visit. For all the stipulations articulated here are meaningful only if the visit is reported, a point underscored by Harry's holding a press conference during the visit and Dillon's negotiating with reporters to move it out "in time for Friday deadlines at the New York *Times* and the Washington *Post*" (95). Without the clips, the visit doesn't exist, because the visit is a performance with the clips themselves as the initial audience. As Jack Lovett says to Harry and Dillon, " 'You don't actually see what's happening in front of you. You don't see it unless you read it. You have to read it in the New York *Times*, then you start talking about it. Give a speech. Call for an investigation. Maybe you can come down here in a year or two, investigate what's happening tonight' " (96–97). Because it identifies the initial event as the report and not the incident that the report alleges to describe, Lovett's assertion glosses the structure of *Democracy* as a network of recontextualized performances. The news report becomes a historical narrative making possible other historical narratives that recontextualize the initial report and mandate further recontextualizations.

Democracy's structure is also glossed by Harry's press conference in which he asserts that "the rioting in Surabaya reflected the normal turbulence of nascent democracy" (95). Just as Lovett's did, Harry's assertion reveals the gap between event and reportage. For Harry's statement defines the event—rioting, a grenade lobbed into the embassy commissary—as normal democratic activity. In order to do so, he constructs an implicit narrative—the story of "democracy"—with distinctly normal stages from nascence to maturity. Only by knowing the whole story, by knowing that Jakarta will become a mature democracy, can one define the current riots. The riots thus evidence not democracy's failure but democracy's beginning, at least according to the wire service clips, filed in time to be picked up by the *Post* and the *Times*. The story of *democracy* thus becomes one constructed by the media, and Lovett accordingly captions Harry " 'a congressman. . . . Which means he's a radio actor . . .'" (99).

Harry seemed, indeed, to view his own life as part of an abstract political narrative. Announcing over cocktails, at a London dinner party filled with European dignitaries, that he had slept the preceding night on a carrier in the Indian Ocean, for example, Harry "seemed to perceive the Indian Ocean, the carrier, and even himself as abstract, incorporeal extensions of policy" (81). This proclivity to imply narratives that blur the distinction between the historical and the personal can be seen as well in Harry's public statement after the murder of Congressman Omura (by Harry's father-in-law), "expressing not only his sympathy and deep concern but his conviction that this occasion of sadness for all Americans could be an occasion of resolve as well . . . resolve to overcome the divisions and differences tragically brought to mind today by this incident in the distant Pacific" (149). Even in context, it is difficult to tell what divisions and differences Harry intends, or exactly how this "incident" reflects them. As all evocation of abstractions tends to, Harry's statement attempts simultaneously to extend distance and to diminish it by making the incident close enough to affect "all Americans" but located in that abstract place, the "distant Pacific." For those in the immediate vicinity of the incident—including a member of Harry's immediate family—the site is neither distant nor pacific. But their immediate response is to turn the incident into a distant abstraction so that it will have the kind of immediacy for them that Harry implies it does for "all Americans": the immediacy of a good novel, or today's newspaper, or *People* magazine.

In this way, Inez and Dillon and Dick Ziegler and the Christians each works at converting the incident, for themselves as well as for everyone else, into a good read. These attempts represent personal policies of containment. As Ziegler (who was being driven out of the container business, replaced by Wendell Omura's brother) says to Dillon, "there's considerable feeling we can contain this to an accident" (114). Dillon, realizing that Ziegler's strategy of containment would not work, attempts his own, one that starts with a visit to Omura's cousin by marriage, Frank Tawagata, to ask for "a reading": "A reading on where the markers are, what plays to expect" (141). Dillon wants to get a reading so that he may generate one, one that conforms to the reading implied in Harry's statement, one that would contain Paul's fate in the category of "treatment" rather than "punishment," and one especially that would isolate the murderous behavior from the political and financial circumstances surrounding it: "it had been agreed, above all, that no purpose would be served by further discussion of why Wendell Omura had introduced legislation hindering the development of Dick Ziegler's Sea Meadow, of how that legislation might have worked to benefit Dwight Christian, or what interest Wendell Omura's brother might recently have gained in the Chriscorp Container Division" (143).

Paul Christian, too, constructed his identity as something to be read for public consumption. On his return to Hawaii, Paul presented himself as destitute, taking a room at the YMCA. "He had never to anyone's knowledge spent an actual night there, but he frequently mentioned it. 'Back to my single room at the Y,' he would say as he left the dinner table . . . and at least one or two of the other guests would rise, predictably, with urgent offers. . . . By way of assent Paul Christian would shrug and turn up his palms. 'I'm afraid everyone knows my position,' he would murmur, yielding" (125). At one point Dwight Christian realized that his brother "was no longer presenting himself as a victim of his family's self-absorption" but as "the deliberate victim of the family's malice" (128). Paul was neither, of course, or he was both, depending on how one defines victimization.

Both roles, moreover, are seen here as functions of presentation and self-presentation, that is, of performance. Paul's activities, like Harry's, in other words, form kinds of foreign policies, historical performances that make one's position known through a composite of assertions, actions, gestures, and references. Paul and Harry are representing themselves metonymically, that is, using the techniques of a writer to create their identities. Their failure of narrative authority thus becomes synonymous with the failure to perform, in other words, synonymous with the inability to author a coherent foreign policy, a failure replicated in several ways throughout the novel: Paul's "policy," culminating in the physical and emotional destruction of his entire family, is completely disastrous. Harry's self-presentation becomes both a failed political policy and a failed personal policy. So does Lovett's, as does the policy of the government for which Lovett worked, all policies of containment.

The boundaries between narratives of personal policy and national policy are in fact hard to maintain, because if our history contains both the "free world" and the communist world, it also contains the readers who consumed this narrative, making them participants in the historical performance by virtue merely of the fact that they had consumed it. At the same time, it also protects them by containing them within that narrative in the privileged position of readers, implicated only vicariously in the narratives with which they identified. The narrative of "democracy" thus affected their personal lives only to the extent to which they chose to identify with the text, that is, made consumer decisions. By participating in this narrative named *democracy*, Americans were able to decide on an individual basis how much they each wanted to become involved.

But the characters in *Democracy* can no longer achieve the appropriate distance, nor can they erect the appropriate borders between their personal lives and their national narratives, and Didion similarly cannot exercise the author's choice to divorce her characters' failures from her own. Instead, throughout the book, she exposes directly both her techniques and her shortcomings as author.

Early in the novel, for instance, she presents a list of details she has "abandoned," "scuttled," "jettisoned"—details that comprise what is commonly called the background, details that, as Didion makes clear, are not so much facts as they are prior stories: "those very stories with which most people I know in those islands confirm their place in the larger scheme" (19). These are the stories an author, like a society, normally needs to situate the present. They are the stories, in other words, that the present usurps to colonize the past. But the past is reduced for Didion to headlines, captions, and photos, "the shards of the novel I am no longer writing. . . . I lost patience with it. I lost nerve" (29). Patience and nerve are the two traits necessary to assert connections between those shards, that is, convert them into narrative. First looks, she tells us later, must also be privileged "not only by novelists but by survivors of accidents and by witnesses to murders . . . anyone . . . forced to resort to the narrative method" (31). Again Didion calls attention to a technique for creating emphasis, showing that it is a fictional device upon which truthful reportage depends. Like so many of the other fictional devices Didion can, and unavoidably does, employ, this one is presented in such a way as to call into question the authority it normally asserts.

Didion has it function as a form of reader alert, a warning to all readers that they can be manipulated by techniques, techniques to which they willingly consent in what they believe are special circumstances, but which they also demand without realizing it in their general reading of reality. Later she articulates this "narrative alert" (155) more fully:

> As a reader you are ahead of the narrative here.
> As a reader you already know that Inez Victor and Jack Lovett left Honolulu together that spring. One reason you know it is because I told you so, early on. Had I not said so you would have known it anyway: you would have guessed it, most readers being rather quicker than most narratives, or perhaps you would have even remembered it, from the stories . . . in the newspapers and on television. . . . (152)

This passage not only makes the reader a partner in the creation of stories (in novels, or in newspapers, or on television) but also subtly implies the fictional status of the reader as the person who reads, believes, and by narrative convention helps author fictional events. By convention, by accord, by treaty, author and reader maintain the borders and accept the myths necessary to privilege the fictional state. This is a code that Didion knows well: "I know the conventions and how to observe them, how to fill in the canvas I have already stretched; know how to tell you what he said and what she said and know above all, since the heart of narrative is a certain calculated ellipsis, a tacit contract between writer and reader to surprise and be surprised, how not to tell you what you do not want to know" (154).

Knowledge, in other words, serves the interest of narrative. What the reader will know, by tacit contract, will be determined by the story the reader wants, which, also by tacit contract, will be the story the author provides. This set of allegiances and contracts, wherein the author decides what the reader wants to know and the reader agrees to let her, prevails for the novel Didion intended to write, the narrative intended for *Democracy*, the one for which she has lost patience and nerve. The version of *Democracy* before us, however, will not contain those conventions; its author "no longer [has] time for the playing out" (155).

She also will not accept the responsibility for doing so. In the spring of 1975, at the same time that the Victors and the Christians tried to contain their personal catastrophes and the American policy of containment collapsed in Vietnam, Didion was teaching a seminar at Berkeley on "the idea of democracy in the work of certain post-industrialist writers" (68) as reflected in the author's style "(the hypothesis being that the way a writer constructed a sentence reflected the way that writer thought)" (68). She tells her class to consider "the political implications of both the reliance on and distrust of abstract words, consider the social organization implicit in the use of the autobiographical third person" (69). Then, quoting a textbook assignment on her own writing, cited at the beginning of the novel, she tells the reader (or herself): "*Consider, too, Didion's own involvement in the setting: an atmosphere results. How?*" (69). This request casts the readers in the same role as the class, that of people trying to understand the political implications of the ways narratives are constructed.

At the same time, however, it casts Didion in two roles. The first is as director of the scrutiny, the second as the scrutinized object. In both cases, in other words, as author. For the author directs and controls the scope of observation, the boundaries, the outcome. In so doing, however, the author also reifies a process. The narrative that appears—by contractual agreement—to be unfolding achieves this appearance by virtue of having been fixed and hence insulated from the vicissitudes of change, from the possibilities of intervention, from the effects of criticism and scrutiny. The author's involvement is thus everywhere and nowhere, functioning with absolute power and absolute impunity, the two conditions that militate against democratic activity. To assert the traditional power of the author thus means denying the requisite conditions of democracy—limited power and complete culpability. The responsibility for constructing the narrative of *Democracy* necessarily entails violating the conditions of democracy. As Didion's shifts in perspective make clear, furthermore, the reader shares responsibility for these violations by implicitly participating in a hierarchical relationship, wherein the referents of a text are subordinate to its narrative, the narrative subordinate to the author's control, and the author's control subordinate to the reader's scrutiny. The conditions that surround the text and the author and the reader remain safely out of bounds.

If Didion questions her own willingness to produce the traditional narrative for the traditional reasons, her refusals, she makes clear, result not from a lack of skill but from reluctance to employ her skill without accepting responsibility for the consequences. This can be seen in how extensively her statements about authoring *Democracy* apply, as well, to authoring American foreign policy: "Let me establish Inez Victor" (42), she says, locating her heroine in "the Territory of Hawaii" as part of the Christian family marked by "the colonial impulse." Inez herself thus becomes the establishment of one more Christian colony, one more territorial claim, serving the special interest of *Democracy*.

Maintaining that colony and expanding from it require unimpeded senses of direction and goal, strong powers of concentration and confidence, without which it becomes impossible to sustain the delicate balance that narrative demands in order to institute the illusion of truth. As Didion notes:

> Aerialists know that to look down is to fall.
> Writers know it too.
> Look down, and that prolonged spell of suspended judgment in which a novel is written snaps, and recovery requires that we practice magic. (103)

"That prolonged spell of suspended judgment" that permitted America to expand its policy of containment can only exist contained within these strictly delimited boundaries, and even then only with vigilant maintenance of offices aimed at propping up the illusion: "We straighten our offices, arrange and rearrange certain objects, talismans, props. Here are a few of the props I have rearranged this morning" (103). One prop is a postcard of the Kuala Lampur International Airport with a banner reading "WELCOME PARTICIPANTS OF THE THIRD WORLD CUP HOCKEY" (104). The wording is replete with irony. The word *world* is distributed in the sentence in such a way as to identify the underdeveloped nations and also an international sporting event. The sign greets participants in that sporting event and also identifies the country as a welcome participant in the "third world." The welcome becomes even more ironic given the fact that Kuala Lampus is where Inez ends up, tending to refugees. From the ironic perspective, the sign couples the citizens of the third world with the international sport of the first world, in a subordinate relationship to which they willingly submit.

That ironic perspective, however, is one of the props of Didion's narrative as much as it is a prop of American foreign policy, and as such it is one Didion can no longer employ. As she makes clear: "The morning I bought this postcard was one of several mornings . . . when I believed I held this novel in my hand" (104), just as the authors of American foreign policy believed, in their increasingly rarer optimistic moments, that they held democracy in their hands and could offer it to the welcome participants of the third world, in a form of global gamesmanship. But the novel, like the foreign policy, has gotten out of hand. The policy that offers democracy has become a narrative that does not contain it, and the failure of containment describes Didion's final view of *Democracy*:

> It has not been the novel I set out to write, nor am I exactly the person who set out to write it. Nor have I experienced the rush of narrative inevitability that usually propels a novel toward its end, the momentum that sets in as events overtake their shadows and the cards fall in on one another and the options decrease to zero.
>
> Perhaps because nothing in this situation encourages the basic narrative assumption, which is that the past is prologue to the present, the options remain open here. (220–21)

The basic narrative assumption creates a sense of inevitability and thus allows a novel to manifest destiny. In rejecting that assumption, Didion makes clear, she is denying the manifest destiny of *Democracy* and of the foreign policy that resembles it. In so doing, she reveals the "facts" of American history to be the function of a dubious narrative convention.

She also does this by mixing several kinds of "facts": the facts of Didion's life; the facts of her attempts to write *Democracy*; the facts of the lives, events, and settings she has jettisoned; the facts of the lives, events, and settings that remain; the facts of American history during the period covered by the narrative; the facts of Didion's meetings with the characters. Didion further erodes the boundary between her life and the narrative she produces by introducing herself as a character in the novel, so that Inez Victor becomes not only Didion's creation but also her acquaintance. "Under different auspices and to different ends" (31), she and Inez worked for *Vogue* magazine in 1960. Through Inez, she first met Jack Lovett, who was a "good contact" for Didion after she left *Vogue* and was working as a reporter. In 1971 and 1973, she had discussions with him about Inez. Didion also recalls "being present one morning in a suite in the hotel Doral in Miami, amid the debris of Harry Victor's 1972 campaign for the nomination" (49), when the AP reporter tried to interview Inez. After reading a newspaper story about Janet's murder, Didion tried to call Inez in New York. She visited Dwight Christian at his home, and was at a dinner party in London with Harry. She corresponded with Inez in Kuala Lumpur in 1975, and in August of 1975 spent several days on Martha's Vineyard talking to Harry and Billy Dillon. Later that year, Didion flew to Kuala Lumpur to see Inez.

From these fictitious experiences and interviews, the character, Joan Didion, constructs her narrative, aided by information she has gleaned from the media. She refers to articles, photos, headlines, or captions from over thirty news publications (the *New York Times* is mentioned ten times), sometimes citing the specific date and edition, to let the reader identify with journalistic and historical accuracy the sources of the fictitious information discovered by the fictitious character, Joan Didion, the author.

By foregrounding her roles as author and as character and mixing the levels of "fact," Didion denies the reader the same distance she has denied herself. If this distance has been the privilege of postwar Americans, Didion's rejected narrative reveals the ways in which that privilege was inscribed in and erased by the name of *democracy* that has failed to contain its story in such a way as to make Americans its eternal authors and consumers. In this way Didion defines the contemporary American culture as framed by our failed narrative, which in turn is framed by our futile efforts to consume it and thus reclaim the roles of reader and author, the privileged position from which "involvement" is a matter of personal choice.

As Didion presents it, "democracy" becomes one more signifier divorced completely from its signified, existing, as Jean Baudrillard has pointed out, simply to the extent that it participates in codes of consumption.[2] As an object of consumption, "democracy" has had extensive currency in post–World War II America, becoming perhaps the most conspicuous of our political and social consumables. We have defined ourselves and created our personal narratives by participating in its codes even more completely than we have by purchasing cars or watching movies. In our consumer-oriented society, "democracy" has been the narrative of consumer preference.

We have come, in other words, to regard our historical narratives as consumer choices. Didion emphasizes this not only by commenting on her understanding of narrative technique and reader expectation—that is, of production and consumption—but also by pointing out that Inez's daughter Jessie regarded her heroin use not as "an act of rebellion, or a way of life, or even a bad habit of particular remark; she considered it a consumer decision" (162). With the sense that she—like all Americans in the narrative of democracy—is a consumer and not a participant, Jessie displays the same imperviousness that Harry did when he visited Jakarta (and elsewhere) in 1969; she goes to Saigon in 1975 because she heard that there are "some pretty cinchy jobs" there (113): "because she believed that whatever went on there was only politics and that politics was for assholes, she would have remained undeflected, that March night in 1975, the same night as it happened that the American evacuation of Da Nang deteriorated into uncontrolled rioting, by anything she might have seen or read in a newspaper" (166).

In this way, the collapse of Da Nang intersects inextricably with the breakdown in the Victors' insularity and impunity. Although Jessie continues to function with the distance of a consumer, or more exactly, because she does, that distance is destroyed and, despite her personal narrative, she becomes converted from consumer to refugee, a member of that group for which Inez had not been allowed to show a special interest.

Inez's inability to show a special interest thus becomes synonymous with her loss of special privilege, a point Inez recognizes in April of 1975 as she listens in an apartment in Vientiane to the shortwave for the encoded announcement of America's final withdrawal—the message "Mother wants you to call home" followed by a recording of "White Christmas":

> Inez thought about Harry in New York and Adlai at school and Jessie at B.J.'s and it occurred to her that for the first time in about twenty years she was not particularly interested in any of them.
>
> Responsible for them in a limited way, yes, but not interested in them.
>
> They were definitely connected to her but she could no longer grasp her own or their uniqueness, her own or their difference, genius, special claim. What difference did it make in the long run what she thought, or Harry thought, or Jessie or Adlai did? What difference did it make in the long run whether any one person got the word, called home, dreamed of a white Christmas? The world that night was full of people flying from place to place and fading in and out and there was no reason why she or Harry or Jessie

or Adlai, or for that matter Jack Lovett or B.J. or the woman in Vientiane on whose balcony the rain now fell, should be exempted from the general movement.

Just because they believed they had a home to call.

Just because they were Americans.

No.

En un mot bye-bye. (197)

The elegiac qualities of this passage and of the whole novel are unmistakable. Like all elegies, the novel marks an unbridgeable gap and then seeks a context that will make the gap seem smaller. The gap marked here, however, is between events and the privileged position from which they can be elegized, the position of the author who can contain inside his or her vision the limits of the gap. The book, in other words, is an elegy for the strategies of elegy, which it thus reveals as another version of the myth of containment.

This book has been about narratives that effected strategies of containment in America during the decades immediately following World War II. Had those strategies of containment worked effectively and continued to do so during the subsequent decades, this book would be illegible. Like the strategies of geopolitical containment, however, or of personal containment (so powerfully interwoven in the thematics of Joan Didion's *Democracy*), efficacy came not from consistency but from redefinition. The container and the contained, each in themselves fluid and not discrete entities, were regularly recounted in varying relation to their own Otherness and Sameness, such that, as Holden Caulfield discovered, nonphony performances of public account or personal testimony (history or autobiography) were impossible.

In their stead, cultural narratives suggested the limits of possibility. These narratives naturalized national policies by drawing on a matrix of tropes that comprehended foreign affairs and domestic security through the media of personal performance as it pertained to the quotidian life of a gendered, mating, religious, consuming subject of prosperous middle-class America at its most economically and politically expansionist moment. These narratives maintained a degree of stability by virtue of their necessarily reciprocal infusion of themes from national and international politics. The rivalry with the Soviets, for example, was figured as a gendered narrative while domestic courtship rituals urged fixed roles and expressed suspicion of deviance that characterized the surveillance state of the cold war. The ambivalence about the use of nuclear weapons was figured as both a duality in the nature of the atom and a duplicity of the Other, at the same time that it was figured as the ordained privilege of an unambiguously monotheistic nation; that nation in turn commodified the dual nature through the figure of the secret agent with the (fictionally) ordained license to kill.

These narratives constructed a pervasive image of a normative American: white, heterosexual, upwardly mobile but always middle class (regardless of income or occupation), generically religious, and uncommonly full of "common sense." In the face of these cultural narratives, personal narrative—like that of Holden Caulfield or the millions of Americans for whom his speech was the surrogate—was marked by its own Otherness, by its internalized sense of aberrance and contradiction. Out of these contradictions, postmodern narratives arose, but, like all discourse and all performance, those with postmodern conventions are necessarily marked by their unarticulated Other.

I want to close, therefore, by raising some, for me, troubling questions about some of the codes that inform postmodern discourse. While the full investigation of these issues will have to wait for another book, I want to make a few speculations. The first is that as a culture, contemporary Americans have acquired an exponentially increased access to the performance of narratives. Multichannel television and radio, extensive print media, telephones and phone solicitations, E-mail, snail mail, junk mail, mass education, public transportation, sports arenas, shopping malls, and virtually all urban settings supplement concert halls, movie theaters, and live stages. Everything to date is the tip of the proverbial hyperspace; the terminal is the beginning not of a ride on the information highway but of something more like a roast in the information microwave oven. In the not-too-distant future, the subject may be defined, at least in parts of its life, as the performer of mediations between two information systems it cannot begin to fathom: a CD library interacting with five-hundred on-line channels. Performing these roles—or even the extent to which one has the opportunity to perform them—may constitute and delimit the subject as producer and product of history.

I make this projection of the "future" for the purpose of emphasis, not analysis, in the hope of suggesting some small points about the world as we more or less know it now, if we are in the class of people who, for whatever reason, would buy books like this one.

My first point is that contemporary technoculture has not only inundated us with narrative performances but also with a special kind of performance—the performance of repetition. Although some understandings of the concept of performance suggest that it is whatever escapes repetition, one could argue that at least in some sense of the term, it is possible to perform a repetition: the automatic redial, the sloganlike refrains that comprise the second half of most rock video numbers, the VCR replay, the photo-replay, the nightly news production, television reruns, and a campaign speech are all examples of performing a repetition. I am not interested in speculating on whether one could, or how one would, distinguish the act of performing a repetition from an act of original performance, or whether performing a repetition is a special case of performance or the definitive process by which all performance becomes legible qua performance. I merely want to emphasize as a historically specific condition the enormous capacity for performing repetitions.

This capacity is important because, as I have argued or implied throughout this book, the authority of history is the product of repetition, as the example of the campaign speech suggests. Repeated, quoted, absorbed in news commentary, made into sound bites, commercials, and print ads, the campaign speech becomes a referential description that, for specific people, serves as a historical narrative.

Contemporary Americans, however, have experienced the repetition of one form of narrative more than any other, and the degree of that exposure, it is probably safe to say, is greater than the degree of exposure by any other people to any form of narrative in recorded history. Initially movies, repeated on television, and more often by VCRs, represent reality by means of a very standardized and easily recognizable set of codes; these codes have also been widely adapted by television narratives, such that for many people—perhaps to some degree for most Americans—the codes define "realistic" representation.

These circumstances may account for what strikes me as an uncanny resemblance between the conventions of cinematic representation and the conventions of American postmodernism: the arbitrariness of the frame, a constructed rather than essential chronology, a privileging of a superficial space, an emphasis on role rather than essence, multiple contexts (created by the juxtaposition of plot, genre, and star). The point I want to suggest here is that if containment constituted the dominant narrative during the height of the cold war, cinematic reality may be the dominant source of narrative during the postmodern period (i.e., during the superannuation of the cold war).

To the extent that this speculation is accurate, the shift is not a renunciation of cold war thematics, rather it is a shift from the dominance of thematic narratives to the dominance of formal ones. The cold war will not have been put behind us by postmodern discourse, but it may be always and readily available as an in-the-wings or on-line performance whose cogency, like that of all other cultural narratives, will depend on its ability to conform to the codes of representation rather than to some historical referent. In such circumstances, nostalgia is passé, because the past is now. Clothed in a variety of costumes alluding in different seasons to different eras and epochs, we may be able to call up our past without psychoanalysis, in that identification with it may be an acquisitory rather than a revelatory process. Taken to its logical limits, personal narration could achieve total identification with the cultural discourse in the way that a message on the monitor is one with the data bank from which it draws.

1. APPEARANCE, CONTAINMENT, AND ATOMIC POWER

1. Declaring that "from Stettin in the Baltic to Trieste in the Adriatic, an iron curtain has descended across the continent," Winston Churchill, speaking in Fulton, Missouri, on March 5, 1946, called for Anglo-American cooperation—"the whole strength of the English-speaking world and all its connections" (18)—to prevent "the indefinite expansion of [Soviet] power and doctrines" (19) and thus avoid another war.

2. Andre Fontaine, for example, in *History of the Cold War*, asserts that Soviet-American rivalry "exploded only after their common enemies, Germany and Japan, were crushed in 1945. But its roots go back to two events of 1917" (11).

3. Gaddis is perhaps the most accomplished scholar on the issue of containment. He argues, in *Strategies of Containment*, that although Kennan was reflecting and summarizing already formulated policy, he also had been a chief architect of that policy, having persuasively used within the administration the same arguments he makes in the essay.

4. One might even argue that the entire history of the cold war and, equally, its entire historiography could be constructed around revised interpretations of Kennan's essay and revised evaluations of the policies and practices mandated by each interpretation. It would take a separate bibliographical essay to delineate the scholarship on this issue. Gaddis provides an extensive bibliography. Early critiques of Kennan came most notably from Lippman in *The Cold War*, and Morganthau, in *In Defense of National Interest*, both of whom contested less the adversarial relationship with the Soviet Union than the appropriate American approach to the problem. In 1959, William A. Williams initiated a "revisionist" approach to containment in *The Tragedy of American Diplomacy*, identifying American policy as expansionism motivated by economic necessity. Throughout the 1960s and early 1970s, revisionist interpretations abounded, locating the origins of the cold war chiefly in American policies rather than Soviet. Some of the most important include Alperovitz, *Atomic Diplo-*

macy; Barnet, *The Roots of War*; Flemming, *The Cold War and Its Origins*; Horowitz, *Containment and Revolution*; Kolko and Kolko, *The Limits of Power*; and Wittner, *Cold War America*. In the 1970s, revisionism came under scrutiny ranging from the vitriolic attacks of Robert James Maddox, in *The New Left and the Origins of the Cold War*, to the more moderate studies: Aron, *The Imperial Republic*; Hamby, *The Imperial Years*; and Ulam, *The Rivals*. Two collections of essays with entries by a number of these scholars provide a good cross-section of the debate at the end of the Vietnam era over the policy of containment: Gati's *Caging the Bear* and Paterson's *The Origins of the Cold War*.

2. HISTORY, SCIENCE, AND HIROSHIMA

1. This theme unites White's books, *Metahistory*, *Tropics of Discourse*, and *Content of Form*. The earliest book, strongly influenced by Frye, emphasizes schematic classification, while the later books concentrate on the implications of the tropic process.

2. I refer to de Certeau's *Heterologies*, *The Practice of Everyday Life*, and *The Writing of History*, and to Ricoeur's three-volume study, *Narrative and Time*.

3. De Certeau discusses at length the connection between these two meanings in the first chapter of *The Writing of History*, "Making History: Problems of Methods and Problems of Meaning," 19–55.

4. At stake here is, among other things, the relationship between events and time.

For Ricoeur, as White points out, "narrative is more than a mode of explanation, more than a code, and much more than a vehicle for conveying information. It is not a discursive strategy or a tactic that the historian may or may not use, according to some pragmatic aim or purpose. It is the means of symbolizing events without which their historicality cannot be indicated" (Content, 53). In this regard, Ricoeur and de Certeau seem to be in accord. They differ, however, in their understanding of the relationship between narrative and its referents. For Ricoeur narrative is the mediation that reveals truth, while for de Certeau it is the discourse that creates it by creating exactly the aporias that Ricoeur sees narrative as bridging. For Ricoeur to imagine the truth that exists outside of narrative but is revealed by it, he must perform on time the rupture that is necessary, de Certeau argues, for historical discourse to occur.

5. Chronicling this would require a review of the history of *Macbeth* criticism; suffice it to say that one would be hard-pressed to discover a critique or analysis of the play that did not reflect the contemporaneous cultural assumptions about, for example, agency, power, the state, science, psychology, courage, or ambition.

6. What I call "activity" Lyotard considers "language games"; I have avoided that terminology not because I disagree but because the use would require digressive explanation.

7. See, for example, his discussion of Rousseau and masturbation in *Of Grammatology* or of the "figurative" role of metaphor in "The White Mythology."

8. See Jencks, *The Language of Postmodern Architecture* and *Post-Modern Classicism;* Venturi, *Learning from Las Vegas;* Klotz, *History of Postmodern Architecture;* and Rose, *The Post-modern and the Post-industrial.*

9. These categories of course, are not necessarily mutually exclusive.

10. See Porush, *The Soft Machine;* Ebert, "The Convergence of Postmodern Innovative Fiction and Science Fiction"; Mathieson, "The Influence of Science Fiction in the Contemporary American Novel"; and Jameson, *Postmodernism.*

11. In addition to Jameson, Postmodernism; Lyotard, *The Postmodern Condition;* McHale, *Postmodernist Fiction;* and Huyssen, *After the Great Divide,* the frequently cited include Hutcheon, *The Poetics of Postmodernism* and *The Poetics of Postmodernism: History, Theory, Fiction;* Foster, *The Anti-Aesthetic;* Hassan, *The Dismemberment of Orpheus* and *The Postmodern Turn;* and Barth, "The Literature of Exhaustion" and "The Literature of Replenishment; Hutcheon's *The Politics of Postmodernism* gives a very useful bibliography, broken into special areas of concern, for example, architecture, film, and television.

12. See Boyer, 203–10.

13. For a full description of the classic Hollywood style, see Bordwell, "The Classical Hollywood Style."

14. The striking similarity between these ineffectual precautions and the American "precautions" against the effects of nuclear attack—for example, "Duck and Cover" public service films, air raid drills, bomb shelters—suggest the power of containment as a national narrative, during the height of the cold war, to suppress the futility of these practices.

3. RHETORIC, SANITY, AND THE COLD WAR:
THE SIGNIFICANCE OF HOLDEN CAULFIELD'S TESTIMONY

1. Hesierman and Miller in "J. D. Salinger" make this connection. Others examining the book's relationship to *Adventures of Huckleberry Finn* include Aldridge, *In Search of Heresy* (129–31); Branch, "Mark Twain and J. D. Salinger"; Fledler, "Come Back to the Raft"; Kaplan, "Holden and Huck"; and Wells, "Huck Finn and Holden Caulfield."

2. The relationship between "reality" and rhetoric has been most fully explored by Auerbach in *Mimesis* and, in some ways, modified and extended by Iser's concept in *The Act of Reading* of the "implied reader" who is led by an author's strategies of omission to complete the text's implied "reality." It is important to note, therefore, that I am *not* using the word *negation* here in the sense that Iser does, but rather to suggest the "blanks" of Lacanian discourse—something akin to the "blindness" of a text which, for de Man, its rhetoric signifies. For Lacan, de Certeau notes, " 'literary'

is that language which makes something else heard than that which it says; conversely psychoanalysis is a literary practice of language. . . . At issue here is rhetoric, and no longer poetics" (*Heterologies,* 53).

3. Grunwald, ("The Invisible Man" 20), and French, (*J. D. Salinger* 26), mention this shorter 1946 version.

4. Miller's ("Catcher In and Out of History") response demonstrates that their reading tends to be reductive and ignores much textual evidence.

5. See Oshinsky's discussion of "The Red Bogey in America, 1917–1950" (85–102). The literature on American history and politics in the seven-year period following World War II is, of course, extensive. Caute provides an excellent bibliography in *The Great Fear* (621–50).

6. Approximately one-third of the book is dialogue rather than narration.

7. See Burke's discussion of "god-terms" and the "Rhetorical Radience of the 'Devine' " in *A Rhetoric of Motives* (294–333).

8. Oldsey discusses the movies in this novel in "The Movies in the Rye."

9. See Caute, *The Great Fear* (403–45).

10. Stern: "Those were years in which a person searching for a community of shared socialist and Christian concerns needed the greatest personal support and fortitude to keep from the bottle, from an ignominious abandonment of all previous social concerns, or from the window ledge. Matthiessen chose to end his life, but others of his contemporaries I have known who shared his ideas at some point gave up lifelong commitments to socialism for goals far less honorable during the period" (30).

11. See Foucault, *Madness and Civilization* (241–78).

12. Although I strongly disagree with the continuities Siebers asserts between the "New Critics" and, for example, French poststructuralists, I think he keenly identifies the ways in which New Criticism is codified as part of the cold war criticism, an important factor given the massive expansion of colleges and universities in that period, which facilitated the privileging of specific texts and authors as representative of modernism. An elaborate and insightful working out of the particular critical manifestations of the cold war can be found in Pease, *Visionary Compacts;* see also Schaub, *American Fiction in the Cold War.* Ross provides an excellent analysis of the "liberal" establishment's rejection of mass culture in *No Respect: Intellectuals and Popular Culture.*

13. Another well-regarded although less widely read book from this period is William Gaddis's massive work, *The Recognitions;* for an extensive discussion of the influence of Eliot on that book, see Fuchs, " 'Il miglior fabbro'."

14. Howell in "Salinger in the Waste Land" provides the most extended discussion of Salinger's use of *The Waste Land* in *Catcher;* see also Heiserman and Miller, "J. D. Salinger." French (*J. D. Salinger,* chapter 5) and Lundquist (*J. D. Salinger,* 84–85) also examine the influence of Eliot on Salinger.

15. For a discussion of Caulfield as Christ figure, surrogate, saint, or savior, see

Baumbach, *The Landscape of Nightmare* (55–67); French, *J. D. Salinger* (115–17); and Rupp, *Celebration in Postwar American Fiction 1945–1967* (114–18).

4. GOD'S LAW AND THE WIDE SCREEN: *THE TEN COMMANDMENTS* AS COLD WAR "EPIC"

1. Carter delineates the legal issues of church and state during the cold war in relation to the political pressures that allowed the modification of the Pledge to be signed into law (on Flag Day) in 1954. In this context he connects such 1950s phenomena as Bishop Fulton J. Sheen's hit television show, the crusade to pull out of the U.N., and President Eisenhower's statement (114–40). Miller and Nowak also discuss in detail the political imperatives for both parties to identify "their cause with God's," both as a domestic response to the peaking American religious affiliation and as part of the bipartisan anticommunist foreign policy (84–105). See also Herberg, *Protestant-Catholic-Jew,* for a sociological analysis of religious demographics in the 1950s; Marty, *The New Shape of American Religion,* for a discussion of the social and philosophical implications of what he calls "the new shape of American Religion" circa 1958; and Blanshard, *God and Man in Washington,* and Miller and Nowak for perspectives on the political implications. These works, as well as the numerous polls and public pronouncements they cite, as James Gilbert succinctly notes in *Another Chance,* suggest the attempt to forge an essential "Americanism" (against which "un-Americanism" could be gauged) that defined the "American" necessarily as having some form of religious conviction (233–41).

2. The technology of CinemaScope, the more popular wide-screen format, was similar. CinemaScope achieved its expansive view by photographing through a wide-angle lens that compressed the sixty-degree perspective onto standard 35mm film and then projected the compressed image through an accessory lens that spread it out again. The effects were essentially the same: theaters with standard 35mm projectors could present wide-screen images. (Todd-AO, a more expensive and less popular format, used 70mm film both to record and project; 35mm alternate versions of Todd-AO, however, were also produced to allow wider distribution.) See Barry Salt, *Film Style and Technology* (315–21), and David Bordwell, "The Classical Hollywood Style, 1917–60" (358–64).

I am indebted to Steven Cohan for pointing out that the VistaVision format used for *The Ten Commandments* emphasizes height more than width. Although this distinction is very important to his excellent, very extensive analysis of the film—part of a study of masculinity in American film, forthcoming from Indiana University Press—for my purposes, I think the ideological implications of technological projection of images with overwhelming breadth and/or width are adequately equivalent.

3. For a comparison of the wide frame images see Carr and Hayes, *Wide Screen Movies.*

4. Leuchtenburg also notes that the sale of electric clothes dryers, first marketed in 1946, totaled 1.2 million in 1955 alone, doubling the annual sales of two years earlier (63).

5. See Polenberg, *One Nation Divisible* (130); Miller and Nowak, "The Paving of America" in *The Fifties,* (127–46); Leuchtenburg, "Affluent America" and "The Consumer Culture" (37–69); and Paul Carter, "'You Auto Buy'" in *Another Part of the Fifties* (27–55).

6. Because the movie industry does not participate in uniform public audits and because studio reports involve various ways of measuring receipts, it is hard to gauge the exact revenue of a film, a problem compounded by international releases, rereleases, sales to television, and more recently, video rentals. My source measures only the "rental fee" (i.e., the fee paid to the distributor by the theater) and acknowledges the figures to be estimates. On those bases, despite ten years of moderate inflation, *The Ten Commandments* exceeds by at least 20 percent the rental income of every American film made until 1964, other than *Gone with the Wind* (1939) (the most successful American movie of all time until *The Sound of Music* [1965], aided by twenty-six years of inflation, narrowly surpassed it) (Steinberg, 3–8, 13–16).

7. This is what Fredric Jameson has called the "political unconscious"; my argument, however, will not necessarily link, as Jameson's does, the "political unconscious" to an economic metanarrative. For lucid and astute discussions of film and ideology, see Nichols, *Ideology and the Image,* (9–68) and Turner, *Film as Social Practice* (128–59).

8. Supplemented by Foucault's analysis, of course, it becomes the dissolution of that power, its inability to consolidate exactly what it represents to represent: "Perhaps there exists, in this painting by Velázquez, the representation, as it were, of Classical representation, and the definition of the space it opens up to us. . . . But there, in the midst of this dispersion which is simultaneously grouping together and spreading out before us, indicated compellingly from every side, is an essential void: the necessary disappearance of that which is its foundation—the person it resembles and the person in whose eyes it is only a resemblence. This very subject—which is the same—has been elided. And representation, freed finally from the relation that was impeding it, can offer itself as representation in its pure form" (*The Order of Things,* 16).

9. Although these historical works often contain domestic romances and melodramas, their global context differentiates them from the primarily isolationist domesticity of most of deMille's earlier films. For a good analysis of his silent films, see May "Politics Dissolved: Cecil B. deMille and the Consumer Ideal, 1918–1929" in *Screening Out the Past* (200–36).

10. De Certeau examines this colonizing practice in an array of manifestations, including "religious," "historical," "scientific," and "Freudian" discourses. In all these cases, a discourse creates a narrative of an Other—a past, a biographical event, a set of physical phenomena—that it normalizes according to the discourse's own rules. Since those rules, however, are exactly what differentiates that discourse from the

Other that it is attempting to describe, what is "other" about the Other is everything that remains outside the description of it, created in its name.

11. Surveying the calls in several magazines and books during that period for a new name for capitalism, Miller and Nowak point out that the new name came into vogue in 1956—shortly before the release of *The Ten Commandments*. The phrase "People's Capitalism" was invented by the Advertising Council and then publicized internationally under the auspices of the United States Information Agency. The phrase linked postwar prosperity to America's benign domination by big business and the capacity for all Americans to own corporate stock. It was, Miller and Nowak demonstrate in their chapter, "People's Capitalism and Other Edsels" (106–23), a myth that hid the fact that in 1955 less than 1 percent of all families owned over 80 percent of all publicly held stocks owned by individuals, and that the broad base of stock ownership had not increased greatly among the wage-earning population.

12. In Fiedler's *Love and Death in the American Novel* and the essay from which it germinated, "Come Back to the Raft Ag'in, Huck, Honey," sexual and racial taboos (for men) combine to represent the exotic escape from patriarchal authority and the fear of domesticity. In his astute analysis of the relationship between white and black music, Andrew Ross discusses "the grounds for suspicion of white intellectuals' projected fantasies of an atavistic Other" (68) as typified by Mailer and Podhoretz (and Jack Kerouac).

13. Gilman has demonstrated in extensive detail the connections in Western discourse (particularly nineteenth- and twentieth-century) between the Jew and the black as the sexual Other. Apropos of my assertions about Fiedler, Mailer, and Podhoretz, Gilman is particularly astute in his demonstration that these connections are in part the product of Jewish self-hatred or self-denial. They are also appropriated by the dominant culture as a way of suppressing "Jewishness" as a form of Otherness in disguise; this is the same implicit hierarchy that the film will establish as it lays the groundwork for the conversion in the second half of the film of Moses as anachronistic representation of Jew to Moses as prophetic representation of Christian.

14. "Suture" refers to the method of constructing a coherent cinematic vision by stitching together a sequence of shots that juxtaposes the shot of an object with a shot of the position from which that object was viewed, thereby allowing the film viewer a privileged perspective providing virtually 360 degrees' worth of visual information. See Dayan ("The Tutor-Code of Classical Cinema") and Heath (*Questions of Cinema*) for discussion of the relationship of suture to classic cinema; Silverman (*The Subject of Semiotics*, 194–236) and particularly de Lauretis (*Technologies of Gender*) emphasize the implications for gender issues.

15. DeMille himself, vehemently anti-union, quit the American Federation of Radio Artists and thus forfeited a $100,000 per year radio contract with Lux Radio Theater rather than have his dues used to promote political positions. Subsequently he founded the DeMille Foundation for Political Freedom, a nonprofit organization dedicated to promoting right-to-work laws. See *Autobiography*, 384–492.

16. *Fortune, U.S.A.: The Permanent Revolution* (New York, 1951), cited in Miller and Nowak, 108.

17. See Mason, *History of Housing in the U.S. 1930–1980* (61–96).

18. Clark was not alone in arguing that the growth of the suburbs and the suburban lifestyle were as much ideological as demographic. Tokening the long-awaited and well-earned middle-class access to leisure time and space, the suburban lifestyle also implied a proscriptive way of life, the one way of life that would ensure happiness and, simultaneously, the only one that probably deserved it. Although rarely articulated as such, the lifestyle was thus a patriotic obligation, a way of demonstrating the ideological superiority of American capitalism and, as well, of strengthening the institutions that would repel communist subversion. Even the nondescript, nine hundred-square-foot, two-bedroom Levittown domiciles signified that small piece of private property that made one part of the capitalist system.

19. This general theme, implicit throughout Whyte's section 7 ("The New Suburbia: The Organization Man at Home") of *The Organization Man* is dealt with explicitly on pages 389–90. Bernard Rudofsky is equally condemnatory (*Behind the Picture Window*, 193–201), but Walter T. Martin in "The Structuring of Social Relationships Engendered by Suburban Residence" (104), looks upon this lack of privacy more positively.

20. Their nearly five hundred-page analysis and agenda quoted at great length without comment would no doubt read today as a savage and unremitting satire. It is necessary to note, therefore, how seriously and influentially it was regarded, and how typical its attitudes were. These attitudes appear in a very wide variety of cold war literature, well surveyed by Miller and Nowak, "The Happy Home Corporation and Baby Factory" in *The Fifties* (177–81), and E. T. May, *Homeward Bound* (92–161).

21. Many connections have been drawn within Christian typology between Moses and Christ. See Glasson, *Moses in the Fourth Gospel*; Davies, *The Setting of the Sermon on the Mount*; Marsh, *The Fullness of Time*; Danielon, *From Shadows to Reality*.

22. I am indebted to Tamar Gordon for assistance on this point and for sharing with me the relevant chapter of her unpublished dissertation.

23. Deuteronomy 8:3; Matthew 4:4.

24. Although in 1950 the officers of the Screen Directors Guild already had to sign loyalty oaths, when s D G President Joseph Mankiewicz opposed deMille's attempt to extend the requirement to the entire membership, deMille launched a campaign to unseat him that included locking Mankiewicz out of the s D G office to block his access to membership mailing lists. In a particularly acrimonious meeting to resolve the issue (at one point William Wyler, accused by deMille of treason, threatened to punch the sixty-nine-year-old director in the nose), deMille's faction was soundly defeated. Four days after his victory, Mankiewicz nevertheless voluntarily urged all s D G members to sign the loyalty oath. See Ceplair and Englund, *The Inquisition in Hollywood* (367–69), and Navasky, *Naming Names* (179–81).

25. DeMille turned over his share of the film's earnings "to an irrevocable trust for charitable, religious and educational purposes" (deMille, 251).

26. See Edwards, *The DeMilles: An American Family,* (13–15).

27. See Neal Gabler's study of this phenomenon (*An Empire of Their Own*). De-Mille's debt is graphically represented by a photograph in his autobiography, in which he sits with Jesse Lasky, Adolph Zukor, Samuel Goldwyn, and Albert Kaufman. The caption says: "Partners hoping to avoid pitfalls in 1915" (between pp. 54 and 55).

28. Olive Deering appears in a significant minor role as Moses' sister.

29. The *average* length of the five films was 171 minutes.

5. LADY AND (OR) THE TRAMP: SEXUAL CONTAINMENT AND THE DOMESTIC PLAYBOY

1. As June Howard has convincingly argued in *Form and History in American Literary Naturalism,* the naturalist genre implies strong classism.

2. By Disney opus, I mean the feature-length animated films produced during Disney's lifetime. The rat at the end of *Lady and the Tramp* is another animal that dies, as does Bambi's mother; the cat thrown from the tower in *Cinderella* is not likely to have survived the fall, but the story neither confirms nor denies that supposition. See Leebron and Gartley, *Walt Disney: A Guide to References and Resources.*

3. *Playboy* refused to accept advertisements during its first year of publication, and afterward rejected three out of four requests to advertise. Despite this selectivity, their advertising base grew rapidly, so that they more than doubled the size of the magazine, increasing the number of features as well as the number of ads, although at the end of the decade they still accepted only half of the requests to advertise.

4. My discussion here is limited to the movie James Bond, not to the character from the Ian Fleming novels upon which he is based. Further, I am limiting my examples to the first four movies: *Dr. No* (1962), *From Russia with Love* (1963), *Goldfinger* (1964), and *Thunderball* (1965). Although it is true that the movies were British products—British producers, director, authors—it is equally true that the immense popularity of the films was very much an American phenomenon. Despite his origins in England, by the mid-1960s James Bond had become a profound icon in American culture with a huge American audience at whom the films were chiefly aimed.

5. An advertisement for *The Playboy Gourmet,* a collection of the magazine's food essays and recipes, identified the book as "*Not* the homemaker's all-purpose encyclopedia of ho-hum cookery. *The Playboy Gourmet* is tastefully attuned to the educated palate of the urban male. It samples plebian and patrician, savors foreign and domestic . . . a 250-page plus paean to the art of gourmandise—but above all, to the sheer sensual pleasure of eating and drinking well."

6. THE INVASION OF POSTMODERNISM: THE CATCH-22
OF THE BAY OF PIGS AND LIBERTY VALANCE

1. See Lasky, *J.F.K.: The Man and the Myth* (331); and Sorenson, *Kennedy* (388).

2. See Wyden, *Bay of Pigs* (38–45, 109–110); Etheredge, *Can Governments Learn?* (9–12); and Collier and Horowitz, *The Kennedys* (293–94).

3. See Gaddis, *Strategies of Containment,* for a detailed analysis of how atomic deterence continued to be reconfigured within various strategies of containment. For a chilling description of the connection of these strategies to authorized, and in some cases nearly implemented, plans for using nuclear weapons or initiating a full-scale nuclear attack on the U.S.S.R., see Kaku and Axelrod, *To Win a Nuclear War.*

4. This anticipates what will emerge over the next decade as one of the strongest arguments for the proponents of the Vietnam War—especially those in the liberal establishment—and one of the most heavily critiqued by its critics.

5. According to Hilsman, "many people in the Department of Foreign Service were convinced that the CIA would win disputes no matter what the merits were," and there were rumors that an ambassador had been removed "because he had taken issue with the CIA station chief in his country" (67–68).

6. See, for example, E. Howard Hunt's description of the argument over which exiles to empower and what to tell the recruits, in his *"Give Us This Day."*

7. "If Stevenson was misled, so was Rusk; so were the leaders of the Cuban Revolutionary Council, the members of the Brigade, the Chairman of the Joint Chiefs of Staff, Congressional leaders . . . and even the President of the United States. The CIA had not even tried to use the talents of Robert Amory, their own deputy director for intelligence. Such was the concern with secrecy as perhaps *the* top priority, but ironically that very precaution became the weak link of the whole project" (Parmet, *JFK,* 166).

7. THE RULES FOR FREE SPEECH: SPEECH ACT THEORY
AND THE FREE SPEECH MOVEMENT

1. The confluence of reportage, student documents, reports and newsletters, faculty documents and reports, administration documents and reports, state documents and reports, trial transcripts, essays, and books make this protest movement one of the most fully documented events in recent campus history. Nevertheless, or perhaps necessarily, even the chronological outlines of this event that precede many reports differ significantly in emphasis, focus, or assertion of fact. See Goines, *The Free Speech Movement,* for a very comprehensive compilation of events from the student perspective, that is with a distinct and cogent awareness of the student participants, including many long interview excerpts, written by one of the student participants. Another succinct summary and excellent analysis of the event can be found in Byrne, *Report on the University of California,* commissioned by the Special Forbes Committee

of the Regents of the University of California. Jerome Byrne, as a special council, produced a strong indictment of the university's administration; the regents at first refused to publish the report and finally did so only in a mimeographed version. Another extensive "chronology" of the event can be found in Lipset and Wolin, *The Berkeley Student Revolt*; the one hundred-page, virtually day-by-day summary, prepared by the editors of the *California Monthly,* the Berkeley alumni magazine, contains valuable documentary material, including the numerous press releases, speeches, public letters, petitions, motions issued or passed by legislators, administrators, faculty, and student groups. Two good analytic histories of the event can be found in Draper, *Berkeley,* and Heirick, *The Spiral of Conflict.* Draper provides lucid, insightful, often firsthand analysis from the perspective of the student protesters; Heirick, who draws on internal administration documents and memos, analyzes the ways in which administration mechanisms break down through misinterpretation, miscommunication, and confused lines of authority. Miller and Gilmore in *Revolution at Berkeley,* attempt to present a balanced debate over the issues; although the conservative or pro-administration positions represented are disproportionate to their actual support in the Berkeley university community, the book identifies well the important positions and arguments, not just about the establishment of recruitment tables or invited speakers, but also about the role of university education and its relation to student and faculty rights.

9. RACE, RIGHTS, GENDER, AND PERSONAL NARRATIVE: THE ARCHAEOLOGY OF "SELF" IN *MERIDIAN*

1. It could be said that *narrative* names for Ricoeur what *the trace* names for Jacques Derrida: that bridge of the aporias that creates the myth of presence. To say that presence is a myth, for Ricoeur, however, is merely to defer to a timeless cosmic order in which human experience constitutes itself a large aporia—the presence of an absence in eternity. The aporias in human time, in this light, can be viewed as the aporias in the grand aporia of human existence, and this double negative reveals the site where the reality (of eternal grace) may be glimpsed. The myth of presence is thus not the flaw in Western metaphysics but its informing myth. It does not hide endless logical deferrals but rather reveals the site of the miraculous transformation—for Ricouer a metaphoric substitution—of human experience into reality. To put it another way, for Derrida, the myth of presence constitutes the West's original sin, while for Ricoeur it constitutes the sacramental site of transubstantiation.

2. In the first chapter of *Invisible Criticism,* I argue that the Civil War for black Americans effected a transfer of surveillance and discipline from the personal master to the impersonal state, thus universalizing it. The result in the South was a set of capricious laws, capriciously enforced in such a way as to impel a practiced "invisibility" akin to that of Foucault's "madman," who may return to society ostensibly free, but at the price of anonymity, always a prisoner of his internalized sense of sur-

veillance, always cognizant of himself as Other and knowing that becoming visible as himself will invoke the powers of the state.

3. In his dual biography, Cone devotes half of his chapter on the men's faults to their sexism. Although he details the ways in which "Martin and Malcolm were sexist men" and asserts that the sexism "hindered greatly their achievement of the freedom for which they fought" (274), he also finds their views "partly understandable, since they lived on the threshhold of the rise of feminism in the 1960s and not during the flowering in the 1970s and 1980s. Sensitive and caring as they were, their views would likely have changed if they had lived to encounter the black women who today are developing what Alice Walker calls a "womanist" perspective (274).

4. See also Bettye Parker-Smith, "Alice Walker's Woman" (479).

5. We should also note, as Barbara Christian points out in *Black Feminist Criticism:* "Alice Walker *also* writes of the unwillingness of many black women to acknowledge or address the problems of sexism that affect them because they feel they must protect black men. She asserts that if black women turn away from the women's movement, they turn away from women moving all over the world, not just in America. They betray their own tradition . . ." (91).

6. Cf. Lévi-Strauss: "The social facts which we study are manifested in societies each of which is a *total entity, concrete and cohesive.* We never lose sight of the fact that existing societies are the result of great transformations occurring in mankind at certain moments in prehistory and at certain places on the globe, and that an uninterrupted chain of real events relates these facts to those which we can observe" (*The Scope of Anthropology,* 24). See also *The Savage Mind* (1–33).

7. Roland Barthes stresses this: "The aim of semiological research is to reconstitute the functioning of the systems of significations other than language in accordance with the process typical of any structuralist activity, which is to build a *simulacrum* of the objects under observation. To undertake this research, it is necessary frankly to accept from the beginning (and especially the beginning) a limiting principle. . . . [I]t is decided to describe the facts which have been gathered *from one point of view only,* and consequently to keep, from the heterogeneous mass of these facts, only the features associated with this point of view, to the exclusion of any others (these features are said to be *relevant*)" (*Mythologies,* 95).

8. Deborah E. McDowell notes that this chapter, "as it explores the tension between Stasis (Tradition) and change (Meridian), sets the stage for the flashback of events which form the story of Meridian's development . . ." ("Self," 266).

9. McDowell identifies this contextualizing as an approach "not only useful but necessary to Black feminist critics" ("New Directions," 192). In this light, we might also note Edward Said's insight that identifying any beginning means identifying a context embedded with intentions, and that the Western practice of constituting the Other (a practice Said calls "orientalism") depends on creating specific contexts by creating specific beginnings.

10. Peter Erickson describes something like this when he talks of Walker's "ruminative style," which creates a "meandering, yet disciplined meditation" through

which Walker "establishes a frame of reference in the present from which she can delve into the past" ("Identity," 91). More than delve into the past, however, Walker uses the past to restructure our reading of the present.

11. Christian in *Black Feminist Criticism* stresses the implicit connection here with the tradition of slave narrative: "[Walker presents] in a succinct way the essence of Afro-American motherhood as it has been passed on. At the center of this construct is a truth that mothers during slavery did not have their natural right to their children and did everything, including giving up their lives, to save them. From this truth, however, a moral dictum has developed, a moral voice that demands that Afro-American mothers, whatever the changed circumstances of their lives, take on the sole responsibility of the children. One result of this rigid position is the guilt which permeates mother/child relationships" (238–39).

12. The crucial text, in this regard, is Hélène Cixous's "The Laugh of Medusa"; see also Julia Kristeva, *Powers of Horror*, and Luce Irigaray, "When Our Lips Speak Together." Jane Gallop also suggests, in "Writing and Sexual Difference," the close connection between the literal and figurative body, especially as it applies to the reinscription of self and Other through naming, alluding, and referring: that is, to the attempt to contain difference.

13. In showing the ways in which Meridian rebels against tradition, McDowell astutely lists all of these roles: "Like the mummy woman, Meridian is, at various stages in the novel, a daughter, though not obedient; a wife, though not devoted; a mother, though not adoring . . ." (266).

14. Nancy Chodorow, in *The Reproduction of Mothering,* has argued with great influence that the reproduction of mothering is "a central and constituting element in the social organization and reproduction of gender" (7). Meridian's androgyny, in this light, can be viewed as being represented by the body that has both mothered and not-mothered; her body, in other words, has physically replicated her social roles.

15. For a discussion of the ways all texts provide lessons in how they are to be read, see Iser, *The Act of Reading.*

16. See McDowell, "The Self in Bloom" (274–75).

17. Cf. Walker: "As a college student I came to reject the Christianity of my parents, and it took me years to realize that though they had been force-fed the white man's palliative, in the form of religion, they had made it into something at once simple and noble. True, even today, they can never successfully picture a God who is not white, and that is major cruelty, but their lives testify to a greater comprehension of the teachings of Jesus than the lives of people who sincerely believe a God *must* have a color and that there can be such a phenomenon as a 'white' church" ("In Search," 17–18).

18. Cf. Lévi-Strauss: "The painter is always mid-way between design and anecdote, and his genius consists in uniting internal and external knowledge, a 'being' and a 'becoming,' in producing with his brush an object which does not exist as such and which he is nevertheless able to create on his canvas. This is a nicely balanced synthesis of one or more artificial or natural structures and one or more natural or

social events. The aesthetic emotion is the result of this union between the structural order and the order of events, which is brought about within a thing created by man and so also in effect by the observer who discovers the possibility of such a union through the work of art" (*Savage Mind*, 25).

19. Frank Kermode, in *Genesis of Secrecy*, explains this principle clearly and applies it fruitfully to an analysis of the Gospels. Paul de Man also indicates the ways in which the relationship between the grammatical and rhetorical functions in a text can organize a reading. Although I have not looked at the various "languages"—that is, the interplay of grammar and rhetoric—in this text, it is ripe for such a study, both in terms of the juxtapositions of rhetoric within the "Meridian" section and in the differences among the three sections. In viewing the body of Meridian as text, furthermore, we can see that it performs in an analogous manner if we equate its appearance with its rhetoric and its action with its grammar—a fair equation, I think, based on a reasonable extrapolation from the way de Man uses the terms "grammar" and "rhetoric" in chapter 1, "Semiology and Rhetoric," of *Allegories of Reading*.

10. FAILED CULTURAL NARRATIVES: AMERICA IN THE POSTWAR ERA AND THE STORY OF *DEMOCRACY*

1. See *Heterologies*.

2. Baudrillard's work articulates the ways in which the total divorce of the sign from its referent in contemporary consumer society makes "consumption" an activity devoid of gratification rather than a method for meeting needs. The "American" quality of consumerism is implicit, I think, in his discussion and informs his book-length analysis, *America*.

Aldridge, John W. *In Search of Heresy: American Literature in the Age of Conformity.* New York: McGraw Hill, 1956.

Alperovitz, Gar. *Atomic Diplomacy: Hiroshima and Potsdam.* New York: Simon & Schuster, 1965.

" 'Am I A Fraud?' " *Time* 5 June 1950: 65–66.

Aron, Raymond. *The Imperial Republic: The United States and the World 1945–1973.* Trans. Frank Jellinek. Englewood Cliffs: Prentice Hall, 1974.

Auerbach, Eric. *Mimesis: The Representation of Reality in Western Literature.* Trans. Willard R. Trask. Princeton: Princeton University Press, 1953.

Austin, J. L. *How to Do Things with Words.* Cambridge: Harvard University Press, 1975.

Barnet, Richard J. *The Roots of War: The Men and Institutions behind U.S. Foreign Policy.* New York: Antheneum, 1972.

Barth, John. "The Literature of Exhaustion." *Atlantic* 220:2 (1967): 29–34.

———. "The Literature of Replenishment: Postmodern Fiction." *Atlantic* 245:1 (1980): 65–71.

Barthes, Roland. *Mythologies.* Trans. Annette Lavers. New York: Hill & Wang, 1978.

Baudrillard, Jean. *America.* Trans. Chris Turner. New York: Verso, 1989.

———. *Selected Writings of Jean Baudrillard.* Trans. Mark Poster. Stanford, CA: Stanford University Press, 1988.

Baumbach, Jonathan. *The Landscape of Nightmare: Studies in the Contemporary American Novel.* New York: New York University Press, 1965.

Bazin, Andre. *What is Cinema?* Trans. Huch Gray. Berkeley: University of California Press, 1967.

Beschloss, Michael R. *The Crisis Years: Kennedy and Krushcehev, 1960–1963.* New York: HarperCollins, 1991.

Blanshard, Paul. *God and Man in Washington.* Boston: Beacon, 1960.

Booth, Wayne. *The Rhetoric of Fiction.* Chicago: University of Chicago Press, 1961.

Bordwell, David. "The Classical Hollywood Style, 1917–60." *The Classical Hollywood Cinema: Film Style & Mode of Production to 1960.* Ed. David Bordwell, Janet Staiger and Kristin Thompson. New York: Columbia University Press, 1985. 1–84.

Bordwell, David, Janet Staiger, and Kristin Thompson. *The Classical Hollywood Cinema: Film Style & Mode of Production to 1960.* New York: Columbia University Press, 1985.

Boyer, Paul. *By the Bomb's Early Light: American Thought and Culture at the Dawn of the Atomic Age.* New York: Pantheon, 1985.

Branch, Edgar. "Mark Twain and J. D. Salinger: A Study in Literary Continuity." *American Quarterly* 9 (1957): 144–58.

Bruner, Jerome. *Acts of Meaning.* Cambridge: Harvard University Press, 1990.

Burke, Kenneth. *A Rhetoric of Motives.* New York: Prentice-Hall, 1950.

Byrne, Jerome C. *Report on the University of California and Recommendations to the Special Committee of the Regents of the University of California.* N.p., 1965.

Cagin, Seth, and Philip Dray. *We Are Not Afraid: The Story of Goodman, Schwerner, and Chaney and the Civil Rights Campaign for Mississippi.* New York: Macmillan, 1988.

Carr, Robert E., and R. M. Hayes. *Wide Screen Movies: History and Filmography of Wide Gauge Filmmaking.* Jefferson, NC: McFarland, 1988.

Carter, Paul. *Another Part of the Fifties.* New York: Columbia University Press, 1983.

Cash, Earl. *John A. Williams: The Evolution of a Black Writer.* New York: Third World Press, 1975.

Caute, David. *The Great Fear: The Anti-Communist Purge under Truman and Eisenhower.* New York: Simon & Schuster, 1978.

Ceplair, Larry, and Steven Englund. *The Inquisition in Hollywood: Politics and the Film Community 1930–1960.* Garden City, NY: Doubleday-Anchor, 1980.

Chaloupka, William. *Knowing Nukes: The Politics and Culture of the Atom.* Minneapolis: University of Minnesota Press, 1993.

Charity, A. C. *Events and Their Afterlife: The Dialectics of Christian Typology in the Bible and Dante.* Cambridge: Harvard University Press, 1966.

Chatman, Seymour. *Story and Discourse: Narrative Structure in Fiction and Film.* Ithaca: Cornell University Press, 1978.

Chodorow, Nancy. *The Reproduction of Mothering: Psychoanalysis and the Sociology of Gender.* Berkeley: University of California Press, 1978.

Christian, Barbara. *Black Feminist Criticism: Perspectives on Black Women Writers.* Elmsford: Pergamon, 1985.

Churchill, Winston. "The Iron Curtain Dropped by Russia." *The Origins of the Cold War.* Ed. Thomas G. Paterson. Lexington, MA: D. C. Heath, 1970. 18–22.

Clark, Clifford E. *The American Family Home, 1800–1960.* Chapel Hill, NC: University of North Carolina Press, 1986.

Cleaver, Eldridge. *Soul on Ice.* New York: McGraw-Hill, 1968.

Collier, Peter, and David Horowitz. *The Kennedys: An American Drama.* New York: Summit Books, 1984.

Cone, James H. *Martin & Malcolm & America: A Dream or a Nightmare.* Maryknoll, NY: Orbis Books, 1991.

Conley, Tom. "Translator's Introduction: For a Literary Historiography." Michel de

Certeau, *The Writing of History*, New York: Columbia University Press, 1988. vii–xxiv.

Corber, Robert. *In the Name of National Security: Hitchcock, Homophobia, and the Political Construction of Gender in Postwar America*. New Americanist Ser. Durham, NC: Duke University Press, 1993.

Culler, Jonathan. *Structuralist Poetics: Structuralism, Linguistics and the Study of Literature*. Ithaca: Cornell University Press, 1974.

Danielou, Jean. *From Shadows to Reality: Studies in the Biblical Typology of the Fathers*. Trans. Wulstan Hibberd. London: Burns, 1960.

Davies, W. D. *The Setting of the Sermon on the Mount*. Cambridge: Cambridge University Press, 1964.

Davis, Ossie. "Malcolm Was a Man." *Black Protest: History, Documents, and Analyses, 1916 to the Present*. Ed. Joanne Grant. New York: St. Martin's Press, 1970. 457–59.

Dayan, Daniel. "The Tutor-Code of Classical Cinema." *Movies and Methods*. Ed. Bill Nichols. Berkeley: University of California Press, 1976. 438–50.

de Certeau, Michel. *Heterologies: Discourse on the Other*. Trans. Brian Massumi. Minneapolis: University of Minnesota Press, 1986.

———. *The Practice of Everyday Life*. Trans. Steven Rendall. Berkeley: University of California Press, 1988.

———. *The Writing of History*. Trans. Tom Conley. New York: Columbia University Press, 1988.

de Lauretis, Teresa. *Technologies of Gender: Essays on Theory, Film, and Fiction*. Bloomington: Indiana University Press, 1987.

de Man, Paul. *Blindness and Insight: Essays in the Rhetoric of Contemporary Criticism*. New York: Oxford University Press, 1971.

de Man, Paul. *Allegories of Reading: Figural Language in Rousseau, Nietzsche, Rilke, and Proust*. New Haven: Yale University Press, 1979.

deMille, Cecil B. *The Autobiography of Cecil B. DeMille*. Ed. Donald Hayne. Englewood Cliffs, NJ: Prentice, 1959.

Derrida, Jacques. *Dissemination*. Trans. Barbara Johnson. Chicago: University of Chicago Press, 1981.

———. *Limited Inc*. Evanston, IL: Northwestern University Press, 1988.

———. *Of Grammatology*. Trans. Gayatri Chakravorty Spivak. Baltimore: Johns Hopkins University Press, 1976.

———. "No Apocalypse, Not Now (full speed ahead, seven missiles, seven missives)." *Diacritics* 14.2 (1984): 20–32.

———. "Plato's Pharmacy." *Dissemination*. Trans. Barbara Johnson. Chicago: University of Chicago Press, 1981. 61–171.

———. "The White Mythology." *Margins of Philosophy*. Trans. Alan Bass. Chicago: University of Chicago Press, 1981. 61–171.

Didion, Joan. *Democracy*. New York: Simon & Schuster/Pocket Books, 1984.

———. *The White Album*. New York: Simon and Schuster/Pocket Books, 1979.

Dowdy, Andrew. *The Films of the Fifties: The American State of Mind.* New York: Morrow, 1975.

Draper, Hal. *Berkeley: The New Student Revolt.* New York: Grove, 1965.

DuBois, W. E. B., *Writings.* Ed. Nathan Huggins. New York: Library of America, 1986.

Ebert, Teresa L. "The Convergence of Postmodern Innovative Fiction and Science Fiction: An Encounter with Samuel R. Delany's Technotopia." *Poetics Today* 1 (1980): 91–104.

Edwards, Anne. *The DeMilles: An American Family.* New York: Abrams, 1988.

Edwards, Duane. "Holden Caulfield 'Don't Ever Tell Anybody Anything.'" *ELH* 44 (1977): 554–65.

Ehrenreich, Barbara. *The Hearts of Men: American Dreams and the Flight from Commitment.* Garden City, NY: Anchor/Doubleday, 1983.

Ellison, Ralph. *Invisible Man.* Thirtieth Anniversary ed. New York: Random House, 1982.

Erickson, Peter. "Identity in the Work of Alice Walker." *CLA Journal* 23 (1979): 71–94.

Erins, Patricia. *The Jew in American Cinema.* Bloomington: Indiana University Press, 1984.

Etheredge, Lloyd S. *Can Governments Learn? American Foreign Policy and Central American Revolutions.* New York: Pergamon Press, 1985.

Farnham, Marynia, and Ferdinand Lundberg. *Modern Woman: The Lost Sex.* New York: Harper, 1947.

Fiedler, Leslie. "Come Back to the Raft Ag'in, Huck Honey." *Partisan Review* 15 (1948): 664–71.

———. "The Eye of Innocence." *Salinger.* Ed. Henry Anatole Grunwald. New York: Harper, 1962. 47–53.

———. *Love and Death in the American Novel.* New York: Dell, 1960.

"The First Loyalty." *Time* 31 March 1947: 20.

Flemming, D. F. *The Cold War and Its Origins, 1917–1960.* New York: Doubleday, 1961.

Fontaine, Andre. *History of the Cold War: From the October Revolution to the Korean War, 1917–1950.* Trans. D. D. Paige. New York: Random House, 1968.

Foster, Francis Smith. *Witnessing Slavery: The Development of Ante-bellum Slave Narratives.* Westport, CT: Greenwood, 1979.

Foster, Hal, ed. *The Anti-Aesthetic: Essays in Postmodern Culture.* Port Townsend, WA: Bay Press, 1983.

Foucault, Michel. *Madness and Civilization: A History of Insanity in the Age of Reason.* Trans. Richard Howard. New York: Random-Vintage, 1973.

———. *The Order of Things: An Archeology of the Human Sciences.* New York: Vintage, 1973.

French, Warren. *J. D. Salinger.* New York: Twayne, 1963.

Friedan, Betty. *The Femine Mystique.* New York: Norton, 1963.

Froula, Christine. "When Eve Reads Milton: Undoing the Canonical Economy." *Critical Inquiry* 10 (1983): 321–47.

Frye, Northrop. *Anatomy of Criticism: Four Essays*. Princeton: Princeton University Press, 1957.

Fuchs, Miriam. "'il miglior fabbro': Gaddis' Debt to T. S. Eliot." In *Recognition of William Gaddis*. Ed. John Kuehl and Steven Moore. Syracuse, NY: Syracuse University Press, 1984. 92–105.

Gabler, Neal. *An Empire of Their Own: How the Jews Invented Hollywood*. New York: Crown, 1988.

Gaddis, John Lewis. *Strategies of Containment: A Critical Appraisal of Postwar American National Security Policy*. New York: Oxford University Press, 1982.

Gaddis, William. *The Recognitions*. New York: Harcourt, Brace, 1955.

Gallop, Jane. "*Writing and Sexual Difference:* The Difference Within." *Writing and Sexual Difference*. Ed. Elizabeth Abel. Chicago: University of Chicago Press, 1982. 283–90.

Gati, Charles. *Caging the Bear: Containment and the Cold War*. New York: Bobbs-Merrill, 1974.

Giglio, James. *The Presidency of John F. Kennedy*. Lawrence, KS: University of Kansas Press, 1991.

Gilbert, James. *Another Chance: Postwar America, 1945–1968*. Philadelphia: Temple University Press, 1981.

Gilman, Sander. *Difference and Pathology: Stereotypes of Sexuality, Race, and Madness*. Ithaca: Cornell University Press, 1985.

Glasson, T. Francis. *Moses in the Fourth Gospel*. Naperville, IL: Allenson, 1963.

Godzich, Wlad. "Foreword: The Further Possibility of Knowledge." *Heterologies*. Minneapolis: University of Minnesota Press, 1986. vii–xxii.

Goines, David Lance. *The Free Speech Movement: Coming of Age in the 1960s*. Berkeley: Ten Speed Press, 1993.

Grunwald, Henry Anatole. "The Invisible Man: A Biographical Collage." *Salinger*. Ed. Henry Anatole Grunwald. New York: Harper, 1962. 15–24.

Hacker, Andrew. *Two Nations*. New York: Charles Scribner's Sons, 1992.

Hamby, Alonzo L. *The Imperial Years: The U.S. since 1939*. New York: Weybright & Talley, 1976.

Harper, Phillip Brian. *Framing the Margins: The Social Logic of Postmodern Culture*. New York: Oxford University Press, 1994.

Hassan, Ihab. *The Dismemberment of Orpheus: Toward a Postmodern Literature*. Madison, WI: University of Wisconsin Press, 1982.

———. *The Postmodern Turn: Essays in Postmodern Theory and Culture*. Columbus: Ohio State University Press, 1987.

Heath, Stephen. *Questions of Cinema*. Bloomington: Indiana University Press, 1981.

Hefner, Hugh. "The Playboy Philosophy." *Playboy* January 1963: 41–52.

Heirick, Max. *The Spiral of Conflict: Berkeley, 1964*. New York: Columbia University Press, 1971.

Heiserman, Arthur, and James E. Miller. "J. D. Salinger: Some Crazy Cliff." *Western Humanities Review* 10 (1956): 129–37.

Heller, Joseph. *Catch-22: A Critical Edition.* Ed. Robert M. Scotto. New York: Dell, 1973.

Herberg, Will. *Protestant-Catholic-Jew: An Essay in American Religious Sociology.* Garden City, NY: Anchor, 1960.

Hersey, John. *Hiroshima.* New York: Bantam, 1946.

Heyns, Roger W. "To the Berkeley Campus." Unpublished administrative notice, 30 September 1965.

Hilsman, Roger. *To Move a Nation: The Politics of Foreign Policy in the Administration of John F. Kennedy.* Garden City, NY: Doubleday, 1967.

hooks, bell. *Ain't I a Woman?: Black Women and Feminism.* Boston: South End Press, 1981.

——. *Black Looks.* Boston: South End Press, 1992.

——. *Talking Back: Thinking Feminist, Thinking Black.* Boston: South End Press, 1989.

Horowitz, David. *Containment and Revolution.* Boston: Beacon, 1967.

Howard, June. *Form and History in American Literary Naturalism.* Chapel Hill: University of North Carolina Press, 1985.

Howell, John M. "Salinger in the Waste Land." *Modern Fiction Studies* 12 (Autumn 1966): 367–75.

Hunt, E. Howard. *"Give Us This Day."* New Rochelle, NY: Arlington House, 1973.

Hutcheon, Linda. *The Poetics of Postmodernism: History, Theory, Fiction.* London: Routledge, 1988.

——. *The Politics of Postmodernism.* London: Routledge, 1989.

Huyssen, Andreas. *After the Great Divide: Modernism, Mass Culture, Postmodernism.* Bloomington: Indiana University Press, 1986.

Irigaray, Luce. "When Our Lips Speak Together." *Signs* 6 (1980): 69–79.

Iser, Wolfgang. *The Act of Reading: A Theory of Aesthetic Response.* Baltimore: Johns Hopkins University Press, 1978.

Jameson, Fredric. *The Political Unconscious: Narrative as a Socially Symbolic Act.* Ithaca: Cornell University Press, 1981.

——. *Postmodernism, or, The Cultural Logic of Late Capitalism.* Durham, NC: Duke University Press, 1990.

Jencks, Charles. *The Language of Postmodern Architecture.* London: Academy, 1977.

——. *Post-Modern Classicism.* London: Academy, 1980.

Jones, Ann Rosiland. "Writing the Body: Toward an Understanding of *l'Ecriture feminine.*" *Feminist Studies* 7 (1981): 247–63.

Kaku, Michio, and Daniel Axelrod. *To Win a Nuclear War: The Pentagon's Secret War Plans.* Boston: South End Press, 1987.

Kaplan, Charles. "Holden and Huck: The Odysseys of Youth." *College English* 18 (1956): 76–80.

Karst, Kenneth. *Belonging to America: Equal Citizenship and the Constitution.* New Haven: Yale University Press, 1989.

Keats, John. *The Crack in the Picture Window.* Boston: Houghton Mifflin, 1957.

Kennan, George. *Memoirs 1925–1950.* New York: Pantheon, 1967.

——. "The Sources of Soviet Conduct." *Foreign Affairs* 25 (1947): 566–82.

Kermode, Frank. *Genesis of Secrecy: On the Interpretation of Narrative*. Cambridge: Harvard University Press, 1979.

Kerr, Clark. *The Uses of the University*. Cambridge: Harvard University Press, 1963.

Klotman, Phyllis R. "The Running Man as Metaphor in Ellison's *Invisible Man*." *CLA Journal* 13 (1970): 277–88.

Klotz, Heinrich. *History of Postmodern Architecture*. Cambridge: Harvard University Press, 1982.

Kolko, Joyce, and Gabriel Kolko. *The Limits of Power: The World and United States Foreign Policy, 1945–1954*. New York: Harper & Row, 1972.

Koury, Philip A. *Yes Mr. DeMille*. New York: Putnam's, 1959.

Kristeva, Julia. *Powers of Horror: An Essay on Abjection*. Trans. Leon S. Roudiez. New York: Columbia University Press, 1982.

Lasky, Victor. *J.F.K.: The Man and the Myth*. New York: Macmillan, 1963.

Leebron, Elizabeth, and Lynn Gartley. *Walt Disney: A Guide to References and Resources*. Boston: G. K. Hall, 1979.

Leuchtenburg, William E. *A Troubled Feast: American Society Since 1945*. Updated ed. Boston: Little Brown, 1983.

Lévi-Strauss, Claude. *The Savage Mind*. Trans. Weidenfeld and Nicolson Ltd. Chicago: University of Chicago Press, 1966.

———. *The Scope of Anthropology*. Trans. Sherry Ortner Paul and Robert A. Paul. London: Jonathan Cape, 1967.

Lippman, Walter. *The Cold War: A Study in U.S. Foreign Policy*. New York: Harper & Row, 1947.

Lipset, Seymour Martin, and Sheldon Wolin. *The Berkeley Student Revolt: Facts and Interpretation*. Garden City, NY: Anchor/Doubleday, 1965.

Lundquist, James. *J.D. Salinger*. New York: Ungar, 1979.

Lyotard, Jean-Francois. *The Postmodern Condition: A Report on Knowledge*. Trans. Geoff Bennington. Minneapolis: University of Minnesota Press, 1984.

Maddox, Robert James. *The New Left and the Origins of the Cold War*. Princeton: Princeton University Press, 1973.

Manchester, William. *The Glory and the Dream: A Narrative History of America, 1932–1972*. Vol. 2. Boston: Little, Brown, 1974.

Marshall, Brenda. *Teaching the Postmodern: Fiction and Theory*. New York: Routledge, 1992.

Marsh, John. *The Fullness of Time*. London: Nisbiet, 1952.

Martin, Walter T. "The Structuring of Social Relationships Engendered by Suburban Residence." *The Suburban Community*. Ed. William Dobriner. New York: Putnam's, 1958. 95–108.

Marty, Martin E. *The New Shape of American Religion*. New York: Harper & Row, 1959.

Mason, Joseph B. *History of Housing in the U.S. 1930–1980*. Houston: Gulf Publishing, 1982.

Mathieson, Kenneth. "The Influence of Science Fiction in the Contemporary American Novel." *Science-Fiction Studies* 12 (1985): 22–31.

May, Elaine Tyler. *Homeward Bound: American Families in the Cold War Era.* New York: Basic, 1988.

May, Lary. *Screening Out the Past: The Birth of Mass Culture and the Motion Picture Industry.* Chicago: University of Chicago Press, 1983.

McCanles, Michael. "Machiavelli and the Paradoxes of Deterrence." *Diacritics* 14.2 (1984): 12–19.

McClure, John. *Late Imperial Romance.* New York: Verso, 1994.

McDowell, Deborah E. "New Directions for Black Feminist Criticism." Rpt. in *The New Feminist Criticism: Essays on Women, Literature and Theory.* Ed. Elaine Showalter. New York: Pantheon, 1985. 186–99.

————. "The Self in Bloom: Alice Walker's *Meridian.*" *CLA Journal* 24 (1981): 262–75.

McHale, Brian. *Postmodernist Fiction.* New York: Methuen, 1987.

McWilliams, Carey. "The Graylist." *The Nation* 19 Oct. 1949: 491.

Meese, Elizabeth A. *Crossing the Double-Cross: The Practice of Feminist Criticism.* Chapel Hill: University of North Carolina Press, 1986.

Melville, Stephen W. *Philosophy Beside Itself: On Deconstruction and Modernism.* Minneapolis: University of Minnesota Press, 1986.

"Mike Wallace Interviews Playboy." *Playboy* December 1957: 60–61, 82–84.

Miller, Douglas T., and Marion Nowak. *The Fifties: The Way We Really Were.* New York: Doubleday, 1977.

Miller, James E. "*Catcher* In and Out of History." *Critical Inquiry* 3 (Spring 1977): 599–603.

Miller, Michael V., and Susan Gilmore, eds. *Revolution at Berkeley.* New York: Dial, 1965.

Modleski, Tania. *The Women Who Knew Too Much: Hitchcock and Feminist Theory.* New York: Routledge, 1988.

Morganthau, Hans. *In Defense of National Interest.* New York: Knopf, 1951.

Muller, Gilbert H. *John A. Williams.* Boston: G. K. Hall, 1984.

Mulvey, Laura. "Visual Pleasure and Narrative Cinema." *Screen* 16.3 (1975): 6–18.

Nadel, Alan. *Invisible Criticism: Ralph Ellison and the American Canon.* Iowa City: University of Iowa Press, 1988.

Navasky, Victor. *Naming Names.* New York: Viking, 1980.

"Newsletter." *Playboy* November 1961: 33.

"Newsletter." *Playboy* January 1962: 33.

"Newsletter." *Playboy* February 1963: 37.

New Yorker. 31 August 1946: 15.

Nichols, Bill. *Ideology and the Image: Social Representation in the Cinema and Other Media.* Bloomington: Indiana University Press, 1981.

Noerdlinger, Henry S. *Moses and Egypt: The Documentation to the Motion Picture "The Ten Commandments."* Los Angeles: University of Southern California Press, 1956.

"Nudity and the Foreign Film." *Playboy* October 1954: 44–45.

Ohmann, Carol, and Richard Ohmann. "Reviewers, Critics, and *The Catcher in the Rye.*" *Critical Inquiry* 3 (1976): 64–75.

Oldsey, Bernard S. "The Movies in the Rye." *College English* 23 (1961): 209–15.

Olster, Stacy. *Reminiscence and Re-Creation in Contemporary American Fiction.* New York: Cambridge University Press, 1989.

O'Neill, William L. *A Better World: Stalinism and the American Intellectuals.* New York: Simon & Schuster, 1982.

Oshinsky, David M. *A Conspiracy So Immense: The World of Joseph McCarthy.* New York: Macmillan-Free Press, 1983.

Oudart, Jean-Pierre. "Cinema and Suture." *Screen* 18.4 (1977–78): 35–47.

Parker-Smith, Bettye J. "Alice Walker's Women: In Search of Some Peace of Mind." *Black Women Writers (1950–1980): A Critical Evaluation.* Ed. Mari Evans. Garden City: Anchor, 1984. 478–93.

Parmet, Herbert S. *JFK: The Presidency of John F. Kennedy.* New York: Dial, 1983.

Paterson, Thomas G. *The Origins of the Cold War.* Lexington, MA: D. C. Heath, 1970.

Pease, Donald. *Visionary Compacts: American Renaissance Writings in Cultural Context.* Madison, WI: University of Wisconsin Press, 1987.

"Playbill." *Playboy* June 1957: 2.

Polenberg, Richard. *One Nation Divisible: Class, Race, and Ethnicity in the United States Since 1938.* New York: Viking, 1980.

Porush, David. *The Soft Machine: Cybernetic Fiction.* New York: Methuen, 1985.

Pynchon, Thomas. "A Journey into the Mind of Watts." *New York Times Magazine* 12 June 1966: 146–58.

Raskin, A. H. "The Berkeley Affair: Mr. Kerr vs. Mr Savio & Co." *Revolution at Berkeley.* Ed. Michael V. Miller and Susan Gilmore. New York: Dial, 1965. 78–91.

Richards, I. A., "Am I a Fraud?" *Time* 5 June 1950: 65–66.

Ricoeur, Paul. *Time and Narrative* (3 vols.). Trans. Kathleen McLaughlin and David Pellaver. Chicago: University of Chicago Press, 1984–1988.

Rose, Margaret A. *The Post-Modern and the Post-Industrial: A Critical Analysis.* Cambridge: Cambridge University Press, 1991.

Ross, Andrew. *No Respect: Intellectuals and Popular Culture.* London: Routledge, 1989.

Rudofsky, Bernard. *Behind the Picture Window.* New York: Oxford University Press, 1955.

Rupp, Richard H. *Celebration in Postwar American Fiction 1945–1967.* Coral Gables, FL: University of Miami Press, 1970.

Said, Edward. *Beginnings: Intention and Method.* Baltimore: Johns Hopkins University Press, 1975.

———. *Orientalism.* New York: Pantheon, 1978.

Salt, Barry. *Film Style and Technology: History and Analysis.* London: Starwood, 1983.

"Sassy Newcomer." *Time* 24 September 1956: 71.

Schaub, Thomas. *American Fiction in the Cold War.* Madison: University of Wisconsin Press, 1991.

Schwarz, Ted. *Arnold Friberg: The Passion of a Modern Master.* Flagstaff: Northland Press, 1985.

Schwenger, Peter. *Letter Bomb: Nuclear Holocaust and the Exploding Word.* Baltimore: Johns Hopkins University Press, 1993.

Searle, John. *Speech Acts: An Essay in the Philosophy of Language.* Cambridge: Cambridge University Press, 1969.

Sedgwick, Eve Kosofsky. *Epistemology of the Closet.* Berkeley: University of California Press, 1990.

Siebers, Tobin. *Cold War Criticism and the Politics of Skepticism.* New York: Oxford University Press, 1993.

Silver, James W. *Mississippi: The Closed Society.* New York: Harcourt, Brace & World, 1963.

Silverman, Kaja. *The Subject of Semiotics.* New York: Oxford University Press, 1983.

Sorensen, Theodore. *Kennedy.* New York: Harper & Row, 1965.

Steinberg, Cobbett S. *Film Facts.* New York: Facts on File, 1980.

Stern, Frederick C. *F. O. Matthiessen: Christian Socialist as Critic.* Chapel Hill: University of North Carolina Press, 1981.

Stern, Jane, and Michael Stern. *Sixties People.* New York: Alfred A. Knopf, 1990.

Stewart, Susan. *On Longing: Narratives of the Miniature, the Gigantic, the Souvenir, and the Collection.* Baltimore: Johns Hopkins University Press, 1984.

"Trials—Some People Can Taste It." *Time* 23 January 1950: 14.

"Trials—The Reckoning." *Time* 30 January 1950: 11–12.

Truman, Harry. "Address to the Joint Session of Congress, March 12, 1947." *Caging the Bear: Containment and the Cold War.* Ed. Charles Gati. New York: Bobbs-Merrill, 1974. 3–8.

Turner, Graeme. *Film as Social Practice.* London: Routledge, 1988.

Ulam, Adam B. *The Rivals: America and Russia since World War II.* New York: Viking, 1971.

United States Dept. of State. *The International Control of Atomic Energy: Growth of a Policy.* Washington: Government Printing Office, 1946.

———. *Policy at the Crossroads. General Foreign Policy Series 3.* Washington: Government Printing Office, 1948.

Venturi, Robert. *Learning from Las Vegas.* Cambridge: MIT Press, 1972.

Wallace, Michele. *Invisibility Blues: From Pop to Theory.* New York: Verso, 1990.

Walker, Alice. *In Search of Our Mothers' Gardens.* New York, Harcourt, 1984.

———. *Meridian.* New York: Washington Square, 1976.

———. *The Third Life of Grange Copeland.* New York: Harcourt, 1970.

Wells, Arvin R. "Huck Finn and Holden Caulfield: The Situation of the Hero." *Ohio University Review* 2 (1960): 31–42.

"When the Time is Ripe." *Time* 14 August 1950: 11.

White, Hayden. *Metahistory: The Historical Imagination in Nineteenth-Century Europe.* Baltimore: Johns Hopkins University Press, 1973.

———. *The Content of Form: Narrative Discourse and Historical Representation.* Baltimore: Johns Hopkins University Press, 1987.

———. *The Tropics of Discourse: Essays in Cultural Criticism.* Baltimore: Johns Hopkins University Press, 1978.

John A. Williams. *Africa, Her History, Lands and People.* New York: Cooper Square, 1963.

———. *Captain Blackman.* New York: Doubleday, 1972.

———. *!Clicksong.* Boston: Houghton Mifflin, 1982.

———. *The Man Who Cried I Am.* Boston: Little Brown, 1967.

———. *Mothersill and the Foxes.* New York: Doubleday, 1975.

———. *This Is My Country Too.* New York: Signet, 1966.

———. *Sissie.* New York: Farrar, Strauss, Cudahy, 1963.

Williams, Patricia J. *The Alchemy of Race and Rights: Diary of a Law Professor.* Cambridge: Harvard University Press, 1991.

Williams, William A. *The Tragedy of American Diplomacy.* New York: World Publishing, 1959.

Wills, Gary. *The Second Civil War: Arming for Armageddon.* New York: New American Library, 1968.

Wittner, Lawrence S. *Cold War America: From Hiroshima to Watergate.* New York: Praeger, 1974.

Wolfe, Charles. "Cecil B. De Mille." *American Directors.* Ed. Jean-Pierre Coursodon, with Pierre Sauvage. Vol. 1. New York, McGraw, 1983. 91–99.

Wood, Michael. *America at the Movies, or: "Santa Maria, It Had Slipped My Mind."* New York: Basic Books, 1975.

Wyden, Peter. *Bay of Pigs: The Untold Story.* New York: Simon and Schuster, 1979.

Wylie, Philip. "Deliverance or Doom." *Collier's* 29 Sept. 1945: 18+.

FILMS

Bananas. Dir. Woody Allen. United Artists, 1971.

Dr. No. Dir. Terence Young. United Artists, 1962.

From Russia with Love. Dir. Terence Young. United Artists, 1963.

Goldfinger. Dir. Guy Hamilton. United Artists, 1964.

Interiors. Dir. Woody Allen. United Artists, 1978.

Lady and the Tramp. Dirs. Hamilton Luske, Clyde Geronimi, Wildred Jackson. Disney, 1955.

Love and Death. Dir. Woody Allen. United Artists, 1975.

The Man Who Shot Liberty Valance. Dir. John Ford. Paramount, 1962.

Pillow Talk. Dir. Michael Gordon. Universal, 1959.

The Ten Commandments. Dir. Cecil B. deMille. Paramount, 1956.

Thunderball. Dir. Terence Young. United Artists, 1965.

What's New, Pussycat? Dir. Clive Donner. United Artists, 1965.

What's Up, Tiger Lily? Dirs. Woody Allen and Senkichi Taniguchi. United Artists, 1966.

Alan Nadel is Associate Professor

of Literature at Rensselaer

Polytechnic Institute.

Figures 11, 12, 13, 14 and 15 courtesy The Museum of Modern Art/Film Stills Archive; figure 10 courtesy of Photofest.

Library of Congress Cataloging-in-Publication Data

Nadel, Alan.
Containment culture : American narrative, postmodernism, and the atomic age / Alan Nadel.
p.   cm. — (New Americanists)
Includes bibliographical references and index.
ISBN 0-8223-1701-x (cl : alk. paper). — ISBN 0-8223-1699-4 (pbk. : alk. paper)
1. United States—Civilization—1945–   2. Postmodernism—United States.   3. Arts, Modern—20th century—United States.
4. Arts, American.   I. Title.   II. Series.
E169.12.N324   1995
973.9—dc20   95-16631   CIP